Colt and Its Collectors

Colt and Its Collectors

**Exhibition catalog for *Colt: The Legacy of a Legend*
Buffalo Bill Historical Center
Cody, Wyoming**

by
Maryanne S. Andrus
Paul Fees, Ph.D.
S.P. Fjestad
Herbert G. Houze
Warren Newman
K.T. Roes
Juti A. Winchester, Ph.D

K.T. Roes, Editor
Herbert G. Houze, Cataloger and Contributing Editor
Paul Fees Ph.D., Contributing Editor
Photographs by Paul Goodwin

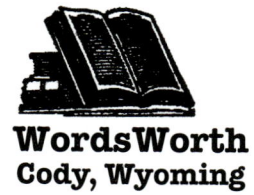

WordsWorth
Cody, Wyoming

for the
Colt Collectors Association

Colt Collectors Association
© 2003 by The Colt Collectors Association

All rights reserved. No part of this publication may be reproduced in any form or by any means without the prior permission of the Colt Collectors Association.

Printed in Canada.

COLT (Stylized "C"), GOVERNMENT MODEL, PEACEMAKER, RAMPANT COLT (Design), SAMUEL COLT, and all other trademarks listed on Colt's Manufacturing Company website (www.colt.com) are registered or common law trademarks of Colt's or New Colt Holding Corp., its parent company and are used under license in this publication. All rights reserved.

ISBN 0-9652942-9-3

Book design for WordsWorth by K.T. Roes and Pat Honstain. Photography by Paul Goodwin unless otherwise indicated.

WordsWorth Publishing
1285 Sheridan Avenue, No. 275
Cody, Wyoming, USA 82414

Dedicated with respect and appreciation
to the members of the Colt Collectors Association
who graciously loaned parts of their collections to this exhibition

And to the volunteers who unselfishly donated countless hours
of time and energy to make this exhibition and catalog possible.

ETIAMSI IMPEDIMENTA SUCCESSUS

Contents

Preface and Acknowledgements — xi-xii
    Les Quick, Past President, Colt Collectors Association

Welcome — xiii
    Robert Shimp, Ph.D., Director, Buffalo Bill Historical Center

A Colt in the Hand: Observations on Guns and Myth — 15
    Paul Fees, Ph.D.

The Colt Legend: Yesterday, Today and Tomorrow — 20
    S.P. Fjestad

Colt and Winchester: Uneasy Rivals — 32
    Herbert G. Houze

John M. Browning — 35
    Herbert G. Houze

Why were so many Colt pistols shipped to the Winchester Company? — 38
    Herbert G. Houze

Samuel Colt's Revolutionary Industrial Workplace — 48
    Maryanne S. Andrus

Behind the Legends of the Gun and the Gunman — 53
    Warren Newman

Ingenuity and Enterprise: The Lives of William F. Cody and Samuel Colt — 57
    Juti A. Winchester, Ph.D.

The Object of Our Affection: Colt and Its Collectors — 63
    K.T. Roes

Paterson Percussion Revolving Pistols, Rifles and Shotguns — 70
    William V. Sisney

Percussion Pistols — 80
    Kathryn Blickhan

Early Colt Cartridge Pistols: — 100
Conversions, New Line, Clover Leaf and Deringer Pistols
    John Blickhan

Model 1877 and 1878 Double Action — 128
    Kurt House

Swing-out Cylinder Double Action Revolvers — 144
    Lynn Kvam

Berdan, Burgess and Lightning Rifles, Double Barrel Rifles and 1883 Shotguns Richard R. Atkinson	178
Post War Rifles and Shotguns Mike McHugh	188
Automatic Pistols Model 1900 to Series 90 Lowell Pauli	196
Woodsman Automatic Pistols Bob Rayburn	254
Machine Guns Tracie Hill	264
Prewar Model 1873, Single Actions and Bisleys Bob Hartman	276
Second and Third Generation Single Action Army, New Frontier and Scouts Gurney Brown	306
Second Generation Percussion Pistols Thomas A. Conroy	336
Colt Commemoratives Kevin Cherry	350
Current Production Models Kathleen J. Hoyt	368
Colt Memorabilia Karen Green	378
Bibliography	393
Index	396

Preface

The Colt Collectors Association, Inc. was founded in December 1980. It is incorporated as a non-profit organization and is affiliated with the National Rifle Association. From an initial membership of 42 collectors, the Colt Collectors Association has grown into an international organization with approximately 2,300 members as of this writing. The Association is dedicated to the preservation of Colt firearms and other Colt related items, along with the study of the history relating to their development and use. Membership allows individuals to participate in one of the most exciting areas of arms collecting.

A quality publication, *The Rampant Colt*, is published quarterly featuring detailed articles in all areas of Colt collecting. The magazine has received several national awards for outstanding reference quality.

An annual All Colt Show is held the first weekend in October at locations around the country. This show offers members the opportunity to meet in a relaxed atmosphere to buy, sell or trade. The Association is staffed by elected officers and directors who receive no salary.

From the time Samuel Colt whittled his first wooden revolver in the 1830s, Colt firearms have evolved into an icon of American ingenuity. From an uncertain beginning in 1836, Colt built a giant arms manufacturing company. His leadership created a company that has produced high quality firearms for more than 160 years and is the oldest manufacturer of revolvers in existence.

This exhibit attempts to present an example of each and every model produced from the company's inception to the present.

Our objective has been to involve as many lenders as possible, rather than limiting the exhibit to a select few. We hope this will be the finest assemblage of Colt Firearms and related material ever assembled at one time for the viewing public to enjoy.

This project is sponsored by the Colt Collectors Association, Inc., with the cooperation of the Buffalo Bill Historical Center. We hope the exhibit *Colt: The Legacy of a Legend* will promote the collecting of Colt firearms and arms in general to help preserve the history of America.

Acknowledgements

No project as complex as this could have been accomplished without the efforts and cooperation of many. The following are to be acknowledged for their spirited gift of time, energy and knowledge.

When this project was conceived several years ago, two members of the Colt Collectors Association's (CCA) immediately stepped forward to enthusiastically embrace the idea. Lowell Pauli and Don Wilkerson possessed the perfect ingredients to manage this project. Lowell, with his background in research and project management and extensive knowledge in Colt firearms as a collector, seemed to be our logical project manager. Don, had an extensive list of Colt publications to his credit, was a skilled researcher in the Colt Archives and, in the opinion of many, was a human dictionary of Colt Firearms information. Don was to be our book project manager. A few months into the project, Don was diagnosed with terminal cancer. Needless to say, this diagnosis altered the allocation of his time. Don left us in May, 2001. Without reservation, Lowell stepped forward and assured the CCA that we had never failed in a project and this would be no exception. Lowell, with the help of many, has made this project a success.

K.T. Roes and Wordsworth Publishing deserve special recognition for shouldering the responsibility of managing the book project. She developed the book concept and structure, compiled and edited the written information, and designed the book layout.

Paul Goodwin's superb color photographs helped make this book a success and his deep knowledge was invaluable to the publisher.

Other public and private institutions who furnished items and assistance for the exhibition and catalog are: Connecticut State Library Museum, Hartford, Connecticut; Lindon Q. Skidmore Charitable Foundation, Kansas City, Missouri; Wadsworth Atheneum, Hartford, Connecticut. To these institutions and their staff, our sincere thanks.

This entire project and resulting book would not have been possible without the cooperation of the Buffalo Bill Historical Center and the Cody Firearms Museum. Our thanks go to the following former and current staff members: Maryanne Andrus, Frances Clymer, Paul Fees, Herb Houze, Lynn Houze, Howard Madaus, Warren Newman, Robert Pickering, Byron Price, Wally Reber, Simeon Stoddard, Juti Winchester and especially Bob White.

To the Colt Manufacturing Company, whose enthusiastic support of this project provided an unending source of information and encouragement. We are especially indebted to the following: Joe Canali, Kathleen Hoyt, General William Keys, Mike Reissig and Beverly Rhoades.

Many other individuals have helped this project in a variety of ways. To each of the following is extended our sincere appreciation for items supporting photography: Mike Patrick and New West, Marshall Dominick, Tracie Hill, Lynn Kvam, and Steve and Linda Evans of S.E.L.L. Antiques,

Sincerely,
Les Quick
Past President
Colt Collectors Association, Inc.

Welcome

The Buffalo Bill Historical Center is proud to host *Colt: The Legacy of a Legend*, the finest exhibit of Colt firearms held in half a century. The Historical Center is at the same time delighted to help present this magnificent catalog.

The Colt company has been an icon of American industry for over 150 years and has contributed firearms to every major military conflict in which the United States has been engaged, from the Mexican War (1846-1848) to the recent Gulf War. The Colt name is legendary, first for the quality and reliability of its products, and in more recent years, as the choice of Hollywood heroes and a cornerstone of a significant genre of Western fiction.

The Cody Firearms Museum of the Historical Center is a logical venue for *Colt: The Legacy of a Legend* since it houses one of the largest collections of American firearms in the world. Opened in 1991, the Cody Firearms Museum houses representative collections of all of the great American firearms manufacturers as well as examples of firearms from the 16th century to the present. It recognizes the importance of sporting and military firearms and demonstrates the role of the firearm in the development of the American frontier.

The firearms industry was one of the first beneficiaries of the innovations of the American Industrial Revolution. Firearms makers were early proponents of the concept of interchangeable parts, and thus helped the United States grow into an industrial world power. The industry also focused on embellishment of the firearm and many beautifully decorated examples are part of the exhibition.

The Colt legacy is represented in this exhibition by over 600 firearms. Each item reflects the company's commitment to quality, and exquisite attention to detail from engineering design to manufacture. The same attention to detail has gone into this catalog, and I believe it will be a valuable reference for Colt collectors and students of the American firearms industry for years to come. It is important to note that this monumental enterprise is a collaborative effort of the BBHC and the Colt Collectors Association.

Congratulations go out to Warren Newman, Interim Curator of the Cody Firearms Museum, and Bob White, Curatorial Assistant, for their commitment to bringing this exhibit to life.

Thanks to the many Colt collectors who made this exhibit possible by loaning the best of their collections to the BBHC. In particular, I would like to acknowledge Lowell E. Pauli and Les and Jan Quick for their diligence, flexibility, enthusiasm and hard work. Thanks also to General William M. Keys, President and CEO of the Colt Manufacturing Company, and Kathleen Hoyt, Historian, Colt Manufacturing Company, for their advice and support.

Many thanks to editor K. T. Roes and book designer Pat Honstain of WordsWorth Publishing who took on the monumental task of editing and publishing this magnificent catalog, a permanent record of this fine exhibition. Congratulations and thanks to Paul Goodwin for the excellent photography that makes this volume so appealing. Many thanks also to Dr. Juti Winchester, Ernest Goppert Curator of the Buffalo Bill Museum, Maryanne Andrus, Curator of Education, and of course, to Warren Newman, Interim Curator of the Cody Firearms Museum for their fine contributions to this catalog.

Our thanks to the Wadsworth Atheneum in Hartford and the Connecticut State Library for lending some very important items for this exhibit. Finally, thanks also go out to Wally Reber, Associate Director of the Buffalo Bill Historical Center for design of the exhibition and to Dr. Robert Pickering, the Collier-Reed Deputy Director for Collections and Education for shepherding the exhibition from original concept to the opening on May 16, 2003.

Robert Shimp, Ph.D.
Director, Buffalo Bill Historical Center

A Colt in the Hand:
Observations on Guns and Myth

Paul Fees, Ph.D.

"Ridin' the range once more
Totin' my old .44"
— Gene Autry, "Back in the Saddle Again"

I am holding a revolver, a Colt's Frontier Six-Shooter in .44-40 caliber, serial number 96,664. Originally blued, the barrel, frame, and cylinder show the patina of age and use, a soft, uneven — gunmetal — gray. The grips are of ivory, yellowed and fissured. The barrel is about 4-1/2 inches long, and there is no front sight. It was shipped with 49 other Colts from the factory on August 15, 1883, to Simmons Hardware, St. Louis, and was then sold in Lampasas, Texas, to E.N. Wolf, chief deputy to his older brother, Sheriff George C. Wolf.

Elvis Newman Wolf (no wonder he called himself "Ell" or "E.N") was my great-grandfather. He spent his life enforcing the law in Lampasas County as deputy sheriff, sometimes elected sheriff in his own right, and in retirement superintended the county jail. My grandfather, Paul D. Wolf, remembered his father celebrating his election as sheriff in 1893 by sawing three inches off the barrel, right to the end of the ejection rod, and replacing the factory walnut grips with ivory.

As I turn it in my hands, as I pull the hammer back and hear the cylinder rotate — click, click, click — the revolver's shape and feel are so aesthetically pleasing that it is almost possible to think of it simply as a museum piece, a marvel of industrial design, a relic of both manufactured and vernacular art. There is also something animate about it. It suggests a promise of adventure and perhaps a threat of danger. In fact, the Hill Country of Texas was not free from frontier justice during the last two decades of the 19th century. E.N.'s and George's brother John, sheriff of neighboring Burnet County, was murdered from ambush in 1892 while attempting an arrest. E.N. engaged in at least two gunfights with this revolver in the line of duty. His son, my grandfather, carried his grandfather's .44 in 1916 as part of a posse that pursued (briefly) Pancho Villa after Villa's raid on Columbus, New Mexico. Not long afterward, Paul Wolf, armed with the same revolver, served a stint as deputy sheriff of Lampasas County.

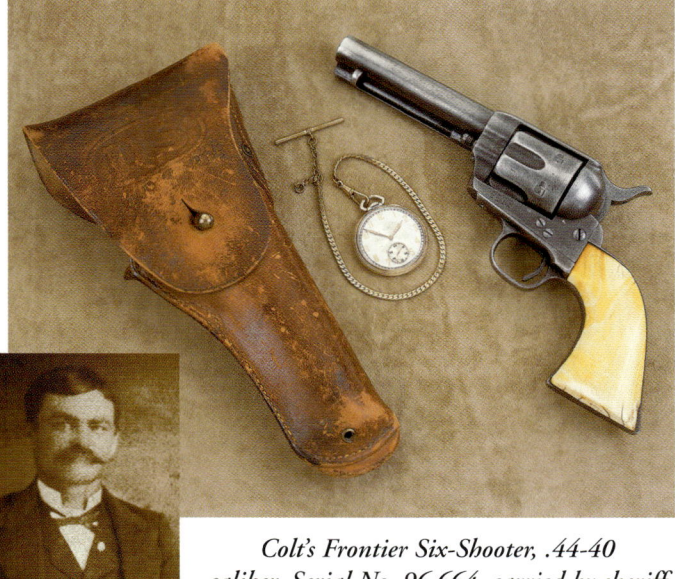

Colt's Frontier Six-Shooter, .44-40 caliber, Serial No. 96,664, carried by sheriff E.N. Wolf. Well-worn holster and pocket watch owned by his son, deputy Paul D. Wolf. Collection of the author.

It should be obvious that to me this is as storied a gun as any museum exhibit. The tales my grandfather told me about it are part of my personal myth, and this Colt revolver connects me vividly to my family's western past.

If I step back from the personal, though, the gun still has a power of suggestion. Like the stagecoach, the tipi, the miner's pick, or the homesteader wife's sunbonnet, the six-gun is an object that cannot help but evoke images of what has been called "the winning of the West." In the imagination, these artifacts are not inert. They tell stories. They are links for the imagination. In other words, they are symbols of America's creation myth, the myth of the West.

A myth, as historians and anthropologists understand it, is a narrative, a complex of stories, that helps us define what kind of people we are. The narrative may be true, or at least based on fact. The life stories of George Washington and Abraham Lincoln, for example, are part of American myth. Most of what we think we know about Washington and Lincoln is true, but their lives are important components of myth nonetheless because they illustrate for us our ideals of American leadership. Washington, of course, fought in and surveyed the wilderness, while Lincoln was himself a child of the frontier.

All of America was frontier at one time. Even to the indigenous peoples, those we came to know as Indians, the land beyond their horizon was frontier. They told their own stories about the places they lived and hunted, and they evolved myths that helped them explain their beginnings and their relationship to the world around them.

Before they crossed the Appalachians, Americans shared a European myth of the frontier. The wilderness was a place of dread for many, but it was also full of possibilities, a place of innocence, of "noble savages," and of undiscovered Edens. It was a new world where Europeans could at least imagine starting over without the corruptions and impediments of civilization. In the first decades of the 19th century, the myth became for Americans, though, a true origin myth. It was in the West where they saw their culture and character take shape, where, whatever their background, they would become "more American" and the nation would no longer be just an extension of the colonies.

In Advice on the Prairie *by W.T. Ranney, the plainsman with his ever-present rifle is warning the emigrants of the dangers ahead. Buffalo Bill Historical Center, Cody, WY. Gift of Mrs. J. Maxwell Moran. 10.91.*

As the American people moved west, many of their tools — Washington's surveyor's transit, Lincoln's ax — became symbolic of the need to measure and clear the land. But no tool became more important and powerful a symbol of the westerner than the gun. Firearms were everywhere present in early America. Modern studies suggest that even in settled areas of the eastern seaboard, half or more of the householders owned guns. In the frontier counties of the eastern states, gun ownership was even higher.[1]

European travelers in the first half of the 19th century remarked with astonishing frequency on the presence of guns. Connecticut observer Timothy Dwight, no friend to the westerner or the westward movement, noted that even in opening unsettled areas of New England, the pioneer "sets out for his farm with axe, gun, blanket and provision."[2]

It was taken for granted that firearms were necessary — perhaps, for some, a necessary evil — for hunting and self-defense.

After the Revolution, the new nation began expanding its frontiers. Settlers followed Daniel Boone through the Cumberland Gap into Kentucky and Tennessee. In the Old Northwest, General Anthony Wayne secured American hegemony in the Ohio River Valley with his victory over the Miami Indian allies of the British at the Battle of Fallen Timbers in 1794. Then in 1803, the United States purchased the largely unmapped Louisiana Territory from France. Its vastness inspired a fearful vision for many Americans of the nation "rushing like a comet into infinite space."[3]

The wilderness hunter began to emerge as a new kind of cultural hero, one who would lead Americans to a different understanding of the skills and character necessary to make the West part of the United States. Boone was the model, and the rifle was his tool.

Born in 1734 to a pioneering Pennsylvania family, reared in the wilds of western North Carolina, Boone first tasted wilderness warfare in 1755 with George Washington as part of General Edward Braddock's ill-fated campaign near present-day Pittsburgh during the French and Indian War. In 1769 he followed ancient trails over the mountains into "Kentucke" and determined to settle in the game-rich country. Indian opposition was fierce, but he persevered and became admired for his skills and daring even among his Shawnee enemies. The cost was high. "My footsteps have often been marked by blood," he later lamented. "Two darling sons and a brother have I lost by savage hands."[4]

Boone was already a legend in the westward saga by the time he died in Missouri in 1820. As the saga became myth, Boone was its first heroic symbol. In 1889 Theodore Roosevelt published the opening volume of his *The Winning of the West*, the epic series whose title would give a name to what Americans saw as their great national endeavor. In it he defined Boone as the ideal hunter hero, vanguard of the strong and defender of the weak, a man who "never blustered or bullied," a model for all Americans because of "his self-command and patience, his daring, restless love of adventure, and, in time of danger, his absolute trust in his own powers and resources."[5]

Boone represented all of the qualities necessary to conquest. He was hunter, explorer, fighter, and leader. He had learned the ways and acquired the skills of the Shawnee, but he remained an "agent of civilization." Above all, he became celebrated as the first of "the mighty hunters of the West, who excel in the use of rifle and pistol, and to which, time and time again, they and those around them have owed their lives."[6] He led the settlement of territories where he and his followers established their own order, safety, and rule of law.

Daniel Boone and his fellow hunters carried Pennsylvania-made flintlock long rifles of small bore but deadly accuracy. Graceful and thin with sharply angled hardwood stocks, the rifles were not just tools. In paintings and illustrations, and in folklore, they became extensions of their owners. At about the time Boone died, a popular song commemorating the 1815 victory of Andrew Jackson and American arms over the British at New Orleans swept the nation. It was called "The Hunters of Kentucky," and it celebrated the rise of the rifleman in its refrain, "We are a hardy, free-born race." No matter where it was made, the "Kentucky" rifle became the indelible symbol of the frontiersman and his conquest of the wilderness.

The rise of the West in the popular consciousness was accompanied by the triumph of the West in politics. Following Andrew Jackson from Tennessee to Washington was a young frontiersman named David Crockett. His rising reputation as a straight-shooting congressman inspired the Young Whigs Club of Philadelphia to present him with the symbol of his fame, a Pennsylvania-made rifle that he dubbed "Pretty Betsy." True to his motto, "Be sure you are right, then go ahead," Crockett engaged in legislative "last stands " — against the forced removal of the Five Civilized Tribes to Oklahoma; for the rights of settlers against land speculators — and proved himself a better hunter than politician. Defeated in another bid for Congress in 1836, he told his constituents, "You may all go to hell, and I will go to Texas." There he found immortality with gun in hand in a last stand at San Antonio de Bexar. Appointed colonel of volunteers, he led the Alamo defenders both in good cheer and in marksmanship. For Americans who came of age after the Second World War, the very image of sacrifice for freedom was Disney's Crockett, Fess Parker, swinging his rifle as a club in defiance of the odds.

The frontiersmen of Kentucky and Tennessee were succeeded by trappers and plainsmen who followed the big game and fur-bearing animals of the Rockies and Great Plains. Their horizons were longer, and their game was bigger. They carried shorter more powerful adaptations of the Kentucky rifle, the best of which were made by the Hawken Brothers of St. Louis and which became known as "plains" rifles. On their heels were gold-diggers, merchants, and pioneer families determined to settle and make over the wilderness and prosper. Of course, much of what they considered wilderness was already used and occupied by Indian people and, in the Southwest, by communities of Mexicans whom they pushed aside as they established their own claims to the land. With victory in the Mexican-American War in 1848, and with treaties and purchases establishing the borders with Canada and Mexico, the United States had by 1853 proclaimed ownership of all the territory that would become the lower 48 states. Those Indian people the westering Americans had pushed aside began to push back, but open conflicts were few.

The U.S. military presence in the West was small, federal representation was spotty, and in most places settlement preceded the flag. Government became increasingly preoccupied with the issues that would split the nation into Civil War. Despite the fact that most migrants along the Oregon Trail and other pathways west encountered few Indians and almost no hostility, the folklore of the trail suggested that only a show of arms would assure safe passage and ultimate title to the Promised Land.[7]

Buffalo and Sitting Bull in Montreal in 1885.
Photograph by William Notman.
Buffalo Bill Historical Center, Cody, WY. P.69.2125.

In the mining and trading camps of the intermountain West, and along the borderlands of Kansas and the central plains, order often enough was enforced at the point of a gun that the need for firearms became an article of faith.

By the end of the Civil War in 1865, more than one in five men and boys of North and South had taken up arms in conflict. In the aftermath, during the highly contentious era of Reconstruction, the nation again looked west. Pushing the railroad across the continent to the California coast became an epic labor for the nation. Settlement increased, and by 1867 ten states had been formed west of the Mississippi. Cowboys drove herds of cattle north from Texas, so recently a Confederate state, to meet the railroads. At the same time, Indian resistance intensified. The United States owned all of what is now the continental nation but exercised power in comparatively little of it. Still, the western territories were common ground for all Americans, and the stories of their "taming" filled the newspapers and magazines of the day.

One young hunter and guide fulfilled all of the expectations of a sensation-hungry public. Armed with a .50 caliber Springfield rifle that he called "Lucretia Borgia" and a brace of Colt's model 1860 Army revolvers, William F. Cody earned a nickname for his marksmanship and hunting prowess. As "Buffalo Bill" he guided and fought alongside the U.S. Cavalry in 19 engagements with Indians and was awarded the Medal of Honor for gallantry. When the Indian fighter turned into a showman, he carried an unusual message of healing to the nation. His first partner on the stage was an ex-Confederate cavalryman, John B. "Texas Jack" Omohundro. The press made much out of the friendship in the West of the former enemies, Yankee and Rebel. When Cody put his great Wild West show into the arena, he hired hundreds of American Indians to play themselves. There they were paid and treated as equal members of the Wild West "family," and to the public they were presented not only as magnificent mounted warriors but as "The Americans," original owners of the continent and creators of unique and durable cultures. Sitting Bull and Buffalo Bill were pictured together in publicity pictures as "Foes in '76, Friends in '85." Soldiers, scouts, and settlers squared off against Indians and outlaws with Colts and Winchesters, and the show program featured an essay on "The Rifle as an Aid to Civilization." But the program also included essays on the values and validity of Indian life, and the show ended with a reconciliation, a coming together in peace — cowboys, cowgirls, cavalry, northerners and southerners, and Indian men, women, and children — in the grand finale.

Matching the flamboyance of the frontier scout in the popular imagination, the cowboy became a new kind of hero of western expansion, but his first public notice was anything but heroic. Rather, he was a symbol of violence. Newspapers and illustrated weeklies depicted the end of cattle drives at the Kansas railheads of the 1860s as free-for-alls among hard-drinking, hard-spending cowboys, all armed. Leaders of the growing cowtowns such as Abilene and Dodge City acted quickly to establish law and order, often hiring men with reputations as gunfighters to counter the rowdy cowboys. And in fact it worked. The incidence of violence in most of the famous trail towns was no worse than in the slums of eastern cities.[8]

Gradually the cowboy took on a new aura as artists such as Frederic Remington and writers such as Theodore Roosevelt romanticized the skills, the dangers, and the rough code of ethics that seemed to govern life on the open range. Beginning in 1883, Buffalo Bill's Wild West presented the cowboy — still so unformed a concept to the public that the program spelled it "cow-boy" — as nothing less than a knight on horseback. By the time Buffalo Bill dubbed the big Texas cowboy Buck Taylor "King of the Cowboys" in 1885, the pulp press was already spinning out tales of chivalric cowboys rescuing damsels in distress, fighting Indians and outlaws, and bringing justice to the frontier.

Annie Oakley, as Nance Barry in the stage play **The Western Girl**, *gets the drop on the villainous LaFonde as she makes the West safe for decent folks.*
Photograph by White. New York, 1903.
Buffalo Bill Historical Center. Cody, WY. P.69.71.

The interesting thing is that as cowboys more and more adopted the trappings of chivalry as a uniform — broad-brimmed hats, chaps and cuffs, brightly-colored scarves and vests, tall boots and spurs, and, almost universally, a Colt sidearm — they began to conform to that Code of the West that Roosevelt and Owen Wister observed and admired. Within the Code, vigilante justice acquired a veneer of civilization as it led to the punishment of wrongdoers seemingly untouched by law, especially when the machinery of civil law was so slow to be established. Self-defense to justify killing was vindicated by state courts that overturned the old common-law expectations that a man should flee from danger.[9]

Wister's Virginian showed that honor lay not in backing down, but in facing evil with courage and a six-gun. "When you call me that, smile," he told Trampas early in the novel, but the climactic duel in the street was the inevitable and honorable showdown between right and wrong.

During the last three decades of the 19th century, guns were as ubiquitous as horses in American life, especially but not exclusively in the West. In fact, shooting exhibitions and competitions were second only to horse-racing in their popularity as spectator sports. The skillful and proper use of firearms was as universally admired as good horsemanship. When she began her crusade to encourage women to own and use firearms, the "American Diana," Annie Oakley, emphasized not only self-defense or the benefits of outdoor exercise, she evoked the historical lineage of American hunters, warriors, and tamers who already were the symbols of America's myth of the West.

The myth was and is, first of all, a myth of conquest — a conquest of weather and wilderness landscape, of hardship, of fear, and, of course, of Indians. Without sacrifice and heroic resistance, conquest would not have been a noble enterprise. It next is a myth of accomplishment. In just a few generations, Americans spanned the continent with railroads, established farms and ranches, built cities and dams, and everywhere introduced law and the Constitution. It is, third, a myth of unity. In the dark days after the Civil War, the western territories — and the great enterprise of bringing them as partners into the Union — belonged to all the states of North and South together. And as Buffalo Bill's Wild West showed, there was a place in the new West for all who called themselves Americans.

Finally, and most important, the myth of the West is a myth of *process*. The United States is always in a state of change, of progress, of growth — of becoming a place that matches our ideals for it. It is a myth of righting wrongs. A hero of Canadian myth is the Mountie, the agent of law. But in Canada, government was established before settlement. In the American West people encountered and overcame extremes of human behavior in the process of establishing self-government. Where there was no law, some stepped forward to secure order. Where sacrifice was necessary, many made the sacrifice. Where some on the frontier called for extermination or expulsion of the native peoples, there were other voices, equally strong, that demanded fair play. Self-examination is part of the myth and plays into our evolving reconsiderations of environmental, social, and political justice.

The seeds of redress were planted as part of the process. And this is where my grandfather's Colt bears such a burden as a symbol. It is an emblem of violence, of course, but also of peace. It stands for those who were first into the fray, representing order and law; it is a symbol for courage and self-defense; it is an admonition that there are still wrongs to be righted; it stands, in fact, for, the whole complex of stories of conquest, accomplishment, and unity that make up the myth of the West. But most of all, perhaps, while it stirs my imagination with the continuing pageant of nation-building, it reminds me that I can still hold the past in my hands.

About the Author

Paul Fees is an independent historian and former curator and a principal in the Cody historical investigations firm of Fees, Spade & Archer.

Notes

1. Michael Bellesiles' sensational book, *Disarming America* (New York: Alfred Knopf, 2001) claimed just the opposite. Bellesiles' work has been thoroughly discredited by scholars such as James Lindgren and Justin Lee Heather in "Counting Guns in Early America," *William and Mary Law Quarterly* 43(5), 2002; and Judith McGaw whose edited volume *Early American Technology* (Chapel Hill: University of North Carolina Press, 1994) had suggested results different from those claimed in *Disarming America*. The controversy over Bellesiles' work has led to renewed research which is likely to show even higher rates of gun ownership than those cited.

2. Timothy Dwight, *Travels in New England and New York*, 4 vols. (New Haven, 1821-1822), II, p.464

3. Fisher Ames, quoted in Russell Blaine Nye, *The Cultural Life of the New Nation, 1776-1830* (New York: Harper and Row, 1960), p.120. See also, Reginald Horsman, *The Frontier in the Formative Years, 1783-1815* (New York: Holt, Rinehart and Winston, 1970)

4. John Filson, *The Discovery, Settlement and Present State of Kentucke: ... To which is added, an Appendix, Containing I. The Adventures of Col. Daniel Boon, One of the First Settlers ...* (Wilmington, Delaware, 1784), pp. 80-81. For a fuller development of the hunter in the myth of the West, see Paul Fees, "The Hunter Hero in America," in Paul A. Hutton, ed., *Sunrise in His Pocket: The Life, Legend, and Legacy of Davy Crockett* (Norman: University of Oklahoma Press, 2003). The literature on Boone, Crockett, and other legendary frontiersmen is large and growing. They and the related myth are discussed at length in Richard Slotkin, *Regeneration Through Violence: The Mythology of the American Frontier, 1600-1860* (Middletown, Conn.: Wesleyan University Press, 1973). Good starting points for Boone and Crockett are Michael Lofaro, *The Life and Adventures of Daniel Boone* (Lexington: University Press of Kentucky, 1986), and David Crockett, *A Narrative of the Life of David Crockett of the State of Tennessee*, with annotations and introduction by James A. Shackford and Stanley J. Folmsbee (Knoxville: University of Tennessee Press, 1973). For Buffalo Bill Cody, the best biography is still Don Russell, *The Lives and Legends of Buffalo Bill* (Norman: University of Oklahoma Press, 1960). For a discussion of Buffalo Bill and the myth of the West, see Paul Fees, "In Defense of Buffalo Bill: A Look at Cody in and of his Times," in Chris Bruce, ed., *The Myth of the West* (Seattle: University of Washington Press, 1990).

5. Theodore Roosevelt, *Episodes from "The Winning of the West*, (New York: G.P. Putnam's Sons, 1900), p.19

6. From "The Rifle as an Aid to Civilization," program, Buffalo Bill's Wild West, 1885, p.23

7. See, for example, the chapter on "Overland Trail Narratives" in Bruce Rosenberg, *Code of the West* (Bloomington: Indiana University Press, 1982)

8. The question of cowtown violence is discussed in Robert R. Dykstra's groundbreaking study, *The Cattle Towns* (New York: Alfred Knopf, 1968)

9. Violence in the West has a wide literature. The best place to start is W. Eugene Hollon, *Frontier Violence: Another Look* (New York: Oxford University Press, 1974). The best discussion of the roots and myth of violence is Richard Maxwell Brown, *No Duty to Retreat: Violence and Values in American History and Society* (New York: Oxford University Press, 1991). Every consideration of the cowboy, honor, and violence in American myth should begin with a reading (or re-reading) of Owen Wister's *The Virginian*, first published in 1902 and still in print in many editions, including a recent centennial edition, with illustrations by Thom Ross, published in 2002 by the Buffalo Bill Historical Center.

The Colt Legend
Yesterday, Today and Tomorrow

S.P. Fjestad

Certainly, the golden age of American firearms manufacturing was the last five decades of the 19th century. The demand for America's state-of-the-art handguns, rifles, and shotguns was enhanced significantly by the California Gold Rush beginning in 1849, when thousands migrated to California in search of fortune. Just as important for this new demand was the American Civil War, which tore the country in half between 1861 and 1865. The third demand spike occurred once the 1,800-mile transcontinental railroad was completed in 1869, and a new flood of settlers began heading west of the Mississippi in search of a new way of life. For many of these new pioneers, firearms were among their most important tools, since they were used for survival and protection.

During the last half of the 1800s, fortunes were made by firearms companies that offered innovative designs coupled with mass production capabilities, taking advantage of ever-more-powerful ammunition. The short list of early American firearms magnates includes Samuel Colt (1814-1862), Oliver Winchester (1810-1880), John Browning (designer, 1855-1926), Eliphalet Remington (1793-1861), and Charles Parker (1809-1902).

While all these men and others, such as John Marlin, Horace Smith and Daniel Wesson (Smith & Wesson), and J. Stevens, also made major, individual achievements within the firearms industry, it can certainly be argued that Samuel Colt and Oliver Winchester were the two largest and most prominent trees in this manufacturing forest. Both men and their companies were pioneers in arms making, and were immortalized for their role in the development of the American West.

Of the two, Colt certainly had the most interesting personality – he was a mixture of skilled inventor and tinkerer, unflappable promoter, mass production genius, salesman extraordinaire, industrialist, circus act pitchman, wild frontiersman, uneducated yet savvy street scavenger, iconoclast and last, but certainly not least, a fun loving rogue.

*The Rampant Colt,
emblem of the Colt company.*
Colt's Manufacturing Company, Inc.

Colt presented a sharp contrast to Oliver Winchester, who had been educated at Yale University and had already become a successful and wealthy businessman before venturing into the gun business. Having already developed one of America's first dress shirt manufacturing companies, Winchester was much more of a stuffed-shirt socialite than the flamboyant and controversial Samuel Colt.

It is important to remember that Samuel Colt died before any of the other major firearms industry heavyweights, except for Remington, who was 21 years older. Colt was only 47 when he died in 1862, just at the beginning of the Civil War. Everything that he accomplished financially had happened in only 16 years, during his third business attempt.

Samuel Colt's story is certainly longer and more action-packed than those of most American industrialists of the time, and few could claim such colorful experiences, always seasoned with financial difficulties and even near-ruin. Above all, Samuel Colt was a talented entrepreneur and gifted promoter – skills that served him well during his lifetime. Another person could not have accomplished what he did. Colt was an original, and realizing this, he never changed, and eventually, made the most of it.

While Colt's international travels are well documented, their tremendous impact on Samuel Colt's developing business acumen cannot be underestimated. Certainly Colt was one of the most talented and aggressive 19th century U.S. industrialists, but few people realize Colt was one of America's first businessmen to travel extensively throughout Europe and England. Traveling as quickly as he could on steamers, sailboats, trains, carriages, and horses, Colt always had an agenda while traveling for business. His list of carefully selected VIPs included kings, presidents, czars, rulers, and only the top military officers of many foreign countries. Colt's friend and patron Governor Thomas Seymour of Connecticut obligingly appointed him aide-de-camp, with the rank of colonel. Thereafter, anticipating large future international sales, he marked the barrel address on top of all of his early guns with "Address Col. Colt," with the "Hartford, CT. U.S.A.," "New-York, U.S.A.," or "London" address. Colt wanted to make sure everyone knew exactly how to find him. Indeed, these were his most important "business cards."

When traveling overseas after 1856, Colt was usually accompanied by his wife Elizabeth. The couple traveled in style, availing themselves of the highest standards of luxury afforded at the time. If Colt were alive today, he'd be a platinum preferred member with many airlines, and would probably watch his timepiece carefully as the plane took off, definitely not quoting scripture if the flight was late.

A hallmark of Colt's lengthy overseas journeys was his customary practice of giving away many of the Armory's finest makings. Colt deeply believed in his products, and always maintained that if someone had confidence in Colt's guns, he would also believe in Colt. He never hesitated to give something away if he thought that it might come back to him in the form of a large commercial order or military contract. In fact, some of the finest Colt firearms ever manufactured were given away by the Colonel himself. Most of these presentation guns were highly decorated and cased pistols with personalized inscriptions. They remain at the top as the most desirable items available to Colt collectors today, and represent the pinnacle of Colt collecting and investing. Perhaps the most famous of all his giveaways are the three highly engraved and decorated revolvers he presented to Czar Nicholas I of Russia during the winter of 1854-1855. The 3rd Model Dragoon, Model 1849, and 1851 Navy, all elaborately engraved and delicately gold inlaid by Gustaf Young, one of the best U.S. engravers at the time, are now priceless, and still reside at the Hermitage in St. Petersburg. No doubt, they represent some of the greatest pieces of Americana of all time.

The Life and Times of Samuel Colt

Samuel Colt was born on July 19, 1814, in a farmhouse on Lord's Hill, close to the town of Hartford, Connecticut. He was the third son of Christopher and Sarah Colt. His siblings included sister Sarah Ann (born 1808), brother John Caldwell (born 1810), Christopher Jr. (born 1812), and James Benjamin (born 1816). Christopher Colt Sr. was a descendant of John Colt, Jr., who was born in Hartford in 1658. John Colt Sr. and his wife Mary Fitch had originally emigrated from Manchester, England, and arrived in Boston's harbor on September 4, 1633. Sarah Colt was the daughter of Major John Caldwell, a banker, merchant, and at the time, the richest man in Hartford. Christopher Colt was living on Hartford charity when he met Sarah. When Major Caldwell learned that his daughter and Christopher Colt were thinking of marriage, he was quick to help Christopher get started in a professional trade. Dubbed the "West Indies" trade, or "Triangle" trade, this risky but lucrative shipping trade transported three main items – molasses, rum, and slaves.

By the end of the War of 1812, Christopher Colt had built a paper fortune in the ocean shipping of these highly desirable commodities. During this heady time, Sarah Caldwell Colt could spoil her children relentlessly, and the Colt children initially grew up getting what they wanted. But a combination of circumstances – the end of the legal importation of slaves in 1808; British harassment of American shipping; the United States embargo and non-importation acts curtailing trade with Europe; and the War of 1812 – led to a near-stoppage of commercial shipping. The business quickly went into a financial tailspin, and by 1820, the company declared bankruptcy.

Christopher Colt gave the following advice to Samuel circa 1833:

"Begin life with the least show and the least expense possible; you may at pleasure increase both, but you cannot easily diminish them. Do not think your estate your own while any man can call upon you for money and you cannot pay. Be in no man's debt. Resolve not to be poor. Whatever you have, spend less. Poverty is a great enemy to human happiness; it destroys Liberty and makes some virtues extremely difficult."

Always aware of new trends, Christopher Colt started raising silkworms on tender Connecticut Valley mulberry leaves, and at Ware, Massachusetts, he started one of the first silk mills in the United States.

The delicate Sarah Colt, probably exposed to more ups and downs than she could handle and now worried about her children, died of tuberculosis on June 16, 1821. For Samuel Colt, the loss was devastating. Aunt Price, widowed sister of Christopher Colt, moved in to help the fledging family. On March 12, 1823, Christopher Colt married Olivia Sargent, daughter of a prosperous Hartford mechanic. The first thing she did was to cut down on household expenses. Sarah Ann was sent to live with relatives, John was turned over to an uncle, and Samuel ended up with a farmer in Glastonbury, Connecticut, with the understanding that he would help out with farm chores and attend the Glastonbury school. When he left home, Samuel took along his gun, an old horseman's military pistol, supposedly inherited from Grandfather Caldwell, that he already had experience repairing. Even at this early age, Colt was keenly interested in experimenting in firearms design and practicality.

Living in an oppressive Puritan environment, Samuel Colt, after one year, decided he had had enough. He packed his little bundle of clothes and moved north to Ware, Massachusetts to help his father in his newly established silk business. In this radically different environment, young Samuel was fascinated with the machinery of silk making. For the first time, he experienced firsthand a true division of labor, in which, in a factory setting, different tasks in the manufacturing process were performed in sequence by specialized workers.

William T. Smith was the chemist in charge of the laboratory on the premises, and he quickly took a personal liking to Samuel. Smith taught Colt how to correctly incorporate the right ingredients of black powder, how to inhale laughing gas, and other chemistry tricks that made a firm impression. Samuel put in three years at the silk plant in Ware, before enrolling in the Amherst Academy. Not exactly known for his academic achievements (including his unique approach to spelling), on more than one occasion he was disciplined by the rigidly stern Reverend Royal Washburn, president of Amherst. There was no room to hide Samuel Colt's emerging personality among the student body of only 33, and it soon became clear that he didn't accept the rigorous and boring school routine.

The Young Prankster

In July, 1829, the young prankster distributed handwritten posters with barely legible letters proclaiming that "Samuel'l Colt will blow a raft sky high on Ware Pond July 4, 1829." A nice group of spectators had gathered around the millpond, observing in quiet amusement the small wooden raft floating distantly. Without warning, the drifting raft with a heavy load of too-much gunpowder was detonated, soaking most of the openmouthed, prominent citizens with an unexpected rain of water and mud. Angry, many of them circled and cornered Samuel, swearing vengeance. It was a grim situation, until the strong arms of Elisha King Root intervened to protect Samuel from the near-mob. Root had worked as a bobbin boy in a mill in Ware and later had moved to Connecticut Valley to learn the gun trade. As both of them wiped off the muddy water from their faces and clothing, Root emerged a hero in Colt's mind for gently getting Samuel out of the jam. Interestingly, Root was much more interested in how Samuel had made such an explosion with his limited knowledge, than in trying to clean his clothes off.

The two quickly became friends, and Samuel informed Root of his ideas for making a mechanism for a repeating gun. Root showed him the rudiments of technical sketching, so that the design could be better realized on paper. In those days, factories were not using blueprints, and mass-produced parts were not interchangeable. Colt never forgot this meeting, and learned many things from the experienced Root, as history has shown.

Meanwhile, mother Olivia (written name – Mother O. S. Colt) kept the disciplinary pressure on the family. During the spring of 1829, Sarah Ann, regulated to a maid-like existence with little hope, and having just turned 21, committed suicide by taking arsenic. Shortly thereafter, the family in ruins, both John and Samuel Colt decided they had had enough.

A Boy Becomes a Man on the High Seas

Samuel quit school, went to Boston, and contacted Lawrence & Stone, a shipping company. Samuel wished to enlist with as a midshipman in training. John, meanwhile, went to Norfolk, Virginia in a similar attempt to try to get on the USS *Constellation*. Even though Samuel's parents had encouraged him to go back to Amherst, they outfitted the impatient lad with $90 worth of sailing gear, including a $1 jackknife. On the morning of August 2, 1830, apprentice seaman Samuel Colt was seen at the top of the rigging in a checkered shirt and trousers, loosing the topsail. His ship, the brig *Corvo*, sailed quietly out of Boston Harbor and after four months on the high seas, Samuel, now an experienced sailor, arrived in Calcutta. The *Corvo* carried a cargo of Yankee cotton and a few passengers, including a couple of missionaries.

On the long voyage back, Colt spent his leisure time doing what many sailors preferred – whittling. Envisioning his revolving cylinder and rotating and locking mechanism, perhaps inspired by the ship's windlass and pawl assembly, Colt began to carefully carve the key components, including the six-shot cylinder, the hammer, and retaining pin. The ratcheting mechanism needed for the gun to fire was significantly different from previous designs, and by the time the *Corvo* dropped anchor again in Boston Harbor early in 1831, Colt had a working idea of how this new mechanism was going to operate.

Samuel Colt as a young sailor, whittling his revolutionary invention.
Colt's Manufacturing Company, Inc.

In a short time, these crude wood patterns would go from design to production and would quickly change the evolution of firearms. Eventually, they would achieve worldwide success. Colt's father and mother Olivia did not recognize the gangly, six-foot, curly golden haired young man with a considerable beard waving to them as the *Corvo* docked. He may have appeared to be in his mid-twenties, but he was only 17.

Samuel lost no time in convincing his father, still in the silk business, that he should underwrite the making of a prototype by a local gunsmith. The person selected was Anson Chase. On Dec. 30, 1831, Samuel paid Chase $15 on account for work performed on both a pistol and rifle. However, more payments were falling due, and Samuel received an offer for another stint as a sailor. This time, the trip would require 26 to 30 months.

The Celebrated Dr. Coult

Samuel was in a pinch – he needed money, and Christopher no longer wanted to fund his prototype project. His next move was pure Colt – totally unpredictable and slightly irrational. He decided to become a traveling lecturer, giving demonstrations up and down the East Coast. Self-described as the "Celebrated Dr. Coult of New York, London, and Calcutta," Coult coined the name from an earlier family English spelling. In his shows, he introduced laughing gas to his willing audience participants, all of whom paid small pocket change to get inside. He also lectured on natural philosophy, chemistry, and other points of interest.

After a lecture tour, he returned to Hartford, picked up his rifle and pistol prototypes from Chase, and proceeded to go to Washington, where he already had a letter of introduction to Henry Ellsworth, of the famous Hartford Ellsworths, and a close friend of his father. Ellsworth was the commissioner of patents, and he would prove over the years to be an important contributor to Colt's future empire, both granting and extending Colt's exclusive patent on his revolving cylinder action. The patent commissioner persuaded Colt not to get a patent yet, as the guns needed some additional time and money to smooth out the rough edges. "Dr. Coult's" traveling shows continued to gain popularity, making him some money for what he really wanted to do - manufacture guns.

While at home in Hartford for Christmas in 1833, Colt picked up another pistol made by Anson Chase. The price was approximately $26. In February 1834, Samuel Colt had an appointment with John Pearson, a fledgling Baltimore gunsmith. By the end of May, over $400 had been paid to Pearson for several pistols, including one brass, and two rifles. These initial prototypes would go on to demonstrate Colt's idea for the design later patented by him in 1836.

Even though Colt continued his laughing gas tour, he was still over a month behind in payments to John Pearson, who was working diligently on Colt's designs and ideas. On April 11, 1835, Samuel moved to Baltimore, and rented a room. He and Pearson began diligent work on improving Samuel's ideas through the preparation of patent models. A new shop was readied, and an assistant by the name of Fred Brash was hired to help Pearson. In June, Samuel visited New York to see his cousin Dudley Selden, a son of a well-to-do lawyer. Dudley advised Samuel to go back south and have some patent drawings created. Now that Colt was off the show circuit, money was getting tight (a reoccurring central theme in Samuel Colt's early history), and Colt had to sell his music box, which he had used during his many "Dr. Coult" appearances. During this time, Colt borrowed $300 from an uncle, Roswell Colt of Paterson, New Jersey, to help make overdue payments to Pearson.

New Design Patented Domestically and Internationally

Colt pawned a Pearson pistol for train fare to Washington, where he submitted patent illustrations by J.W. Post, a patent draftsman. These plates, carefully drawn on 15fi x 20-inch sheets of parchment, were done in India ink. While color patent drawings were standard at the time, Colt declined color due to the increased cost, and instead paid $16 for these services. Henry Ellsworth assured Colt that he would be receiving a patent shortly, and Colt went back to Hartford to borrow $1,000 from his father.

Meanwhile, he secured several other notes, and on August 24, 1835, Colt sailed from New York to London to obtain international patent rights. After a stormy three-week trip, he arrived in London in search of an English patent agent. The well-known and expensive firm of Lemuel W. Serrell was retained and after $600 in gold coins had been exchanged, an English patent was issued for Colt's design.

Next on his list was Scotland, where he went to Edinburgh to inquire about Scottish patents. Some scribes suggest it was here that Colt fell in love with Carolyn Henshaw, a good looking, blonde haired, German 16-year-old orphan stranded in Scotland, hardly able to speak English. Colt was now 21 years old. There is somewhat of a literary dispute as to whether they were married in Scotland, but regardless, they set out for Paris together, where Colt also had his revolver design patented.

The Young Samuel Colt, framed drawing, circa 1832. Dr. George Priestel Collection.

The Patent Arms Manufacturing Company

In early January 1836, Samuel and Carolyn returned to the U.S. with their cash nearly depleted. Thereafter, Samuel commuted regularly between their residence in Hartford to Baltimore, Washington, and New York. On February 25, 1836, Samuel received patent # 9,430 for his revolving firearms design. (It was later reissued as Patent # 138 after a destructive Patent Office fire). Finally, Colt had a patent. Now all he needed was a company to produce his new firearms design.

With the help of many of his cousin Dudley Selden's friends and business acquaintances, venture capital started to come in, and a charter of incorporation was filed on March 5, 1836, for The Patent Arms Manufacturing Company, to operate on the Passaic River in Paterson, New Jersey. While self-elected officers were busy attending to the finances of this new company, Samuel Colt went to Baltimore to see Pearson again. Upon arriving, Colt was delighted to find that Pearson and Fred Brash had further simplified his idea. Colt was still in arrears in payment, angering Pearson. Even so, Pearson diligently kept working, stifling his frustration, and shipped the finished rifle to Colt in New York in April 1836. Colt was now $1,000 behind in Pearson's payments, but even though Colt had the money to pay Pearson regularly, he did not. Pearson could no longer work on speculation, and had become tired of Colt's unfulfilled payment promises. After all, it wasn't his dream, and he wasn't going to get rich.

On May 16, 1836, Pliny Lawton, a friend of Christopher

Colt's, arrived in Paterson, New Jersey to set up the new shop for Patent Arms Manufacturing Company. Even though Pearson's prototypes were available to work from, it was soon discovered that while patented, they were not practical to shoot, operate, or manufacture. Meanwhile, Samuel went to Washington in an effort to get a government contract. At the time, there was controversy within the military about the best weapons to suit them at the time. While Samuel was canvassing anyone in Washington who would listen to him regarding his new revolver design, the Paterson plant was busy trying to set up for mass production, no easy task. The military selected John H. Hall's improved rifle design, and Colt returned to Paterson having accomplished little, except to rack up more unwanted expenses with nothing to show for it.

Colt, not wanting to face the wrath of Selden, to whom he now owed quite a sizable sum and an unpaid balance of 100 stock shares, intentionally left for New York to avoid him.

During these challenging early days, the first arms produced at Paterson were the ring lever rifles that used the single shot breech loading rifle design from the 1835-36 patents. The rifle configuration was an eight-shot with a 29-32 inch barrel, with the bore in the .454 - .458 in. range. Later, the company purchased a rifling machine. There were three frame sizes for the revolving pistols made in Paterson, New Jersey. No. 1 was the smallest (Pocket Model in .28 cal, 5 shot), No. 2 and 3 were medium sized (Belt Model in .31 or .34 cal., 5 shot), and No. 5 was the largest (Holster Model in .36 cal., 5 shot).

In addition to this new line of firearms, Colt and Lawton devised an interesting line of accessories to be used with their new gun, including a bullet mold, nipple wrench, and a unique combination powder and ball flask. A few guns were selling, and during Christmas of 1837, an ad ran in the Paterson *Evening Star*, declaring that Colt's rifles "are now offered for sale for the first time." Colt realized that the only way he could ever get rich within this new industry was through a sophisticated mass production operation, which had yet to be invented. He also needed larger orders to keep this machinery profitable, and the fastest way to do that was through a large government purchase.

The Florida Fiasco

An opportunity for the company presented itself in early 1838. One of the more progressive officers of the small Army of the United States was Colonel William S. Harney, Commanding Officer of the Second Regiment of U.S. Dragoons. The misadventure started with a potential military contract for Colonel Harney's troops stationed in Florida's Everglades. The seemingly insignificant 65-year-old war with the Seminole Indians had become annoying, and more than 2,500 regular Army troops were stationed in the Everglades (half the U.S. Army at the time) under Harney's new command. He wanted only the best for his troops. His goal was simple – he wanted to fight the Seminole Indians using his new tactics and weapons, and finally provide the United States a victory after this long conflict.

On January 17, 1838, Samuel Colt received the following letter from Col. Harney:

Mr. Colt:
I have barely time to tell you that I have been greatly disappointed in not having received the guns yet. I mentioned what I had done to Genl Jesup who approved of *everything*. If you have not started them yet lose no time in doing so for I wish them very much. I am still *more confident* that they are the only things that will finish the *infernal war*. If you can bring one hundred Genl Jesup will take them all. Try also to bring some pistols.
   Very Respectfully,
   W.S. Harney

During this difficult time, the Patent Arms Manufacturing Company was in dire straits financially, and Colt was continually in the hot seat with the company's board of directors. However, the company agreed to send Colt to Florida on a bonded expedition by steamer. His purpose – to secure the delivery and payment for an important U.S. military 100-rifle order. Leaving Paterson in early 1838 with 10 cases of repeating rifles, Colt finally arrived in Camp Jupiter, Florida almost a month later. General Thomas Jessup, Harney's commanding officer, had ordered only 30 rifles, but the number was finally increased to 50. In March 1838, Colt caught a steamer back to New York with a government draft for $6,250 for the rifles and an additional $25 for 25,000 percussion caps.

On the way back, the always-impatient Colt thought the journey was going too slowly, and he and several others, plus a crew of four, boarded a smaller vessel. While trying to land on an Atlantic beach in northern Florida, the ship capsized. After spending four hours in the cold, turbulent coastal waters, the shipmates finally made it to shore. Unfortunately, they lost all their belongings. Especially difficult for Colt was the all-important $6,250 payment, lost as he went overboard. On April 11, 1838, he left St. Augustine for New York again, but not before he had returned to the scene of the shipwreck, looking in vain for his belongings and government payment.

Returning to Paterson in May of 1838, Colt had to face an unsympathetic board. He was without payment for the 50 rifles he had personally delivered and a promise that the remaining 50, which had been shipped separately, could be sold shortly. Unfortunately, it all hinged on the speed at which the U.S. government could reissue another draft for payment. Finally, on July 25, Colt cashed the second $6,250 check, then paid the balance he owed to the Patent Arms Manufacturing Company. Thus, the long and fateful Florida business trip reached its overdue ending.

Still not happy with Colt's performance, especially his penchant for racking up sizeable expenditures while living lavishly on the road, the company changed his status. On October 24, 1838, Colt signed an agreement that provided a royalty fee for every firearm made and sold by the company. He would receive $4 for every arm "fired from the shoulder" and $1.50 for pistols.

Samuel the Salesman and Entrepreneur

During the fall of the same year, Colt attended the Mechanics Institute of New York annual fair, a large public exhibitions focusing on advancements in science, the arts, and new inventions. Gold medals were issued for excellence in product or design and the fair attracted investors willing to capitalize new products and inventions. During the show, a Mighill Nutting of Portland, Maine, exhibited a rifle with a revolving cylinder. The similar design made Colt uncomfortable, and he immediately wanted the Patent Arms Manufacturing Company to initiate a lawsuit against a possible patent infringement, although no legal action was taken at the time.

With a Washington military contract never far from his mind, Colt returned, and sold some guns to various companies in small quantities. Colt managed to survive the winter in Washington, while in New Jersey, Pliny Lawton finished one of the first three models of the new carbine. Colt and Selden's relationship continued to deteriorate, and Selden wrote Colt that if he didn't pay back the $2,000 owed to the company and to him personally, he might throw Colt in jail.

Although a small quantity of revolvers continued to sell, the company struggled, and Samuel, worried about the directors throwing him in jail, had only enough money for a ticket to Maine, to make an attempt to shut down Nutting's new invention. Even though a 100-gun order was received from Colonel George Bomford in the summer of 1840, it was not good enough to keep the doors open. In September 1842, the Patent Arms Manufacturing Company officially closed, after manufacturing approximately 2,700 guns, mostly in .34 or .36 caliber.

Colt wound up in debt, and there was an ongoing controversy with his former employers, who suspected him of some type of financial foul play.

Family Tragedy, Allegations, and Complications

To make matters worse, Colt's normally civil brother John, who had been writing a textbook on bookkeeping in New York City, had killed a printer with a hatchet after a dispute involving a $20 disparity over a printing bill. Afterwards, he stuffed the body in a packing case and had it delivered with other freight bound for New Orleans. Unusually warm weather aided someone smelling the rapidly decomposing body on the docks, which led to John's arrest and subsequent trial, during which he was convicted of first-degree murder and sentenced to be hanged on November 18, 1842.

Earlier that year, Carolyn Henshaw had given birth to a son, Samuel Caldwell Colt, and during the murder trial, told the court that she had met John Colt in Philadelphia in 1840, but did not live with him until she came to New York the following January. The story goes that John, out of pity, had made Carolyn his common law wife. The constantly gallivanting Samuel Colt was probably not saddened with this family development, as her low social status as his partner might impede his career ambitions, always at the forefront in Samuel's bent-for-success mind, regardless of cost.

On the day of the scheduled hanging, Samuel Colt was the first to see John in his cell, and at 11 am, Dr. Henry Anthon, rector of St. Mark's Church, announced that after John and Samuel had conferred, it had been decided that John would make Carolyn his lawful wife. John then handed the minister $500 to be used for Carolyn's welfare, which he had received from Samuel, a substantial contribution from a man whose factory had closed less than a month earlier. After the marriage in jail, the couple remained in the cell for an hour, after which Carolyn departed with Samuel. A few hours later, the sheriff and Dr. Anthon returned to escort John to the hanging scaffold, but the prisoner was already dead in his bed. A knife with a broken handle was found lodged in his heart, and while there was much speculation about how the knife got into the cell, nothing was ever proved.

In the days that followed, Colt secretly arranged for Carolyn and her young son to go to Germany. He justified this to brother James by stating, "She speaks and understands German and can best be cared for in the German countries. I have made all the necessary arrangements, and will somehow provide the needful." At his insistence, she changed her name to Miss Julia Leisester, but the boy grew up as Samuel Caldwell Colt. Carolyn and her son remained abroad, supported by Samuel. Eventually, she became attracted to a young Prussian officer, Baron Fredrick Von Oppen. His father questioned her background and suspected that money, not love, was Carolyn's motive. But Colt used his influence to ensure a quiet marriage and afterward did everything possible to make the couple and young Samuel Caldwell Colt happy.

Samuel the Inventor

In the years that followed the family scandal, Samuel worked on several other projects that involved a new waterproof cartridge made from a special tin foil. During 1843, he received a military order for 50,000 rifle cartridges and 50,000 carbine cartridges. Once the powder arrived from the New York Ordnance Depot, the foil maker Mr. Müeller and Samuel worked all summer rolling out the tin for the cartridges. On December 9, this large cartridge inventory was finally shipped out of a rented Paterson shop. Samuel had intentionally given orders that this warehouse not be heated, as he was concerned about the risk of fire. The cartridge business and Samuel's interest in an underwater mine for protecting harbors against enemy ships led him to an acquaintance with Samuel F. B. Morse and his electromagnetic telegraph. The Navy granted Colt $6,000 for a test of the mine. Colt supplied Morse with batteries and wire, and won a contract for laying 50 miles of underwater wire from Washington to Baltimore.

In May of 1846, the same month in which war was declared in Mexico, the New York and Offing Magnetic Telegraph Association was incorporated by Colt, and a new set of investors was established with the rights to construct a telegraph line from New York City to Long Island and New Jersey. Again, mismanagement, partly due to Colt's negligence, resulted in the downfall of this operation, and at 32 years of age, Colt once again found himself despondent and destitute.

Texas, The Paterson, and The Walker

There was some good news on the horizon for Colt, however. In Texas, a rapidly escalating conflict with Mexico was developing, and the large No. 5 Paterson; dubbed "Texas Paterson" was earning a good reputation in the field fighting Comanche Indians. Colonel Samuel Hamilton Walker, originally from Maryland, and now captain of the Texas Rangers, wrote Colt the following letter on Nov. 30, 1846:

"The pistols which you made for the Texas Navy have been in use by the Rangers for three years, and I can say with confidence that it is the only good improvement I have seen. The Texans who have learned their value by practical experience, their confidence in them is unbounded, so much so that they are willing to engage four times their number. In the summer of 1844, Col. J.C. Hays with 15 men fought about 80 Comanche Indians, boldly attacking them on their own ground, killing & wounding about half their number…the result of this engagement was such as to intimidate them and enable us to treat with them."

General Zachary Taylor, commander of the United States troops in Texas, wanted 1,000 Colts within three months. Furthermore, Colonel Walker thought it would be a good idea to redesign the Paterson with a larger .44 caliber with heavier frame (4 lbs., 9 oz), an exposed, fixed trigger with guard, and a simpler, more reliable revolver mechanism which would fire six shots. Between Colt and Walker, the Walker revolver was designed. It was the original .44 cal. Magnum, and even though Hollywood's "Dirty Harry" now takes a lot of credit for the caliber's reputation, it was nevertheless invented by Samuel Colt 125 years earlier.

Shooting Buffaloes with Colt's Revolving Pistol. After George Catlin. Buffalo Bill Historical Center. 6.83.

Even though Colt had a $25,000 order for 1,000 guns, he had no way to manufacture them. Samuel persuaded Eli Whitney Jr., a Connecticut contractor for army muskets, to manufacture 1,000 revolvers. Six months later, they were ready, and a pair of guns for Walker, who had continuously written Colt about the length of delays, was finally delivered four days before he was killed in action. Shortly thereafter, Colt obtained another order for 1,000 revolvers. This time he borrowed approximately $5,000 from Elisha Colt, his banker cousin, and other Hartford businessmen. He leased a factory on Pearl Street in Hartford and a work force was quickly trained.

By December of 1847, Colt had started his own factory, Colt Patent Fire-Arms Manufacturing Company (hereafter referred to as Colt's), and promised to turn out 5,000 guns annually. Especially vital to this new company was Elisha Root, his old contact, whom he had first met at Ware during the raft explosion. Root was working for the Collins Axe Factory until Colt offered him the unheard-of salary of $5,000. As head superintendent, it was Root who designed and constructed the incomparable Colt factory and installed its new equipment. While Root managed the factory, Colt became the president and primary salesman.

Finally, a third order for 1,000 revolvers was received, even though there had been problems with the first two contracts due to the long arbors and overloaded cylinders. By the end of 1850, Colt had produced 3,000 Walker revolvers, first in a small factory on Pearl Street, and then on Grove Lane in the center of Hartford.

Following the success of the Walker, Colt's followed up with the Dragoon models. They were an evolutionary design of the Walker, and manufactured with design improvements in both Whitneyville (c. 1847) and in Hartford. Approximately 8,390 Dragoons were purchased by the United States government between 1847 and 1860 and the success of this modified and improved revolver spread quickly throughout the world.

During 1848, Colonel Samuel Houston of Texas wrote Colt in Hartford, hoping to purchase a smaller caliber revolver, using the Dragoons as the pattern. The resulting gun, or the Baby Dragoon (Model 1848), was a .31 caliber, 5-shot, available in various barrel lengths. A year later, during Colt's first profitable year in business, the Model 1849 Pocket revolver was introduced. It was offered with either five or six shots and the new smaller design guaranteed the practicality many Americans now wanted in a personal defense handgun. This new configuration was an instant success and sales topped almost 330,000 in 24 years. Once this model was established, Colt never looked back.

1849 – The California Gold Rush and the Start of the Colt Empire

In 1849, the California Gold Rush was underway. In two years, the population of California had swollen from 20,000 to 2 million, and when the rush was over two years later, at least $70 million in gold had been discovered. The demand for the new reliable, smaller Dragoon in .31 caliber, now commonly referred to as the Model 1849, was considerable, and both orders and production continued to increase. During the same year, Colt made a second trip to Europe, traveling as far east as Turkey. Patents were obtained in several more European countries, and when he returned, the plant was moved into a large, vacant building on Grove Street.

Measured in sales, the Model 1849 pocket revolver would be the most successful percussion revolver in history. By the end of production in 1873, over 300,000 had left the Hartford factory. But Samuel Colt saw a need for a handgun that would fill the gap between the heavy Dragoon models and the lightweight pocket model. In 1850 Colt introduced another revolver, similar to the Model 1849, that would have an even more dramatic impact on his fortunes. Generally known as the Model 1851 Navy (the cylinder was roll-stamped with a scene depicting the Texas and Mexican Navies in combat) the .36 caliber revolver with its 7 fi-inch barrel fit comfortably in a belt holster and proved to be an accurate and effective weapon. Its weight, its aesthetic lines, its reliability and ease of handling, and particularly its low cost of manufacturing (Colt was able to sell the Model 1851 for $21) would create an international sensation. It was one of the favorite cavalry sidearms of the Civil War.

As important as anything else during 1851 was the obtaining and renewal of key patents. Colt's patent attorney, Edward N. Dickerson (Colt called him Ned), was one of the gunmaker's most valuable associates. With Colt's help, Dickerson became the leading patent attorney of the period, and anyone who infringed on Colt's patents met swift resistance. It was Dickerson who successfully prosecuted the Massachusetts Arms Company lawsuit, giving Colt a virtual monopoly in revolving cylinder manufacture in the United States, until his patent expired in 1857. Because of his continual involvement with patent rights, Colt himself became an expert on patent law, and if time had permitted, he could have served as his own attorney in the complex and challenging field. Between Colt and Dickerson, very few American companies dared to come up with a Colt copy (most copies were European). It was a sure way to end up in court.

The Colt Armory

1851 was a busy year for Colt. He purchased a large tract of land in the South Meadows, which fronted the Connecticut River. Even though it was swampy lowland, and prone to spring flooding, Colt eventually acquired 250 acres at the cost of $60,000 for his new factory location. To make sure the entire new location wouldn't be subject to flooding, he built a large dike nearly two miles long around it, and planted French willows on top to prevent erosion. The project, Hartford's first redevelopment, took two years and $125,000 to complete.

As sales continued to grow, the facility on Grove Street was hopelessly inadequate for the volume of orders. The new Armory, made of Portland brownstone, was finally ready in August of 1855. More responsible than anyone else for this state-of-the-art firearm manufacturing facility was Elisha Root, who was unrivaled at the time for both designing and implementing much of the machinery that gave this new facility its large, mass production capacity. When it opened, the *Hartford Times* called it "the greatest individual enterprise ever attempted in this country." It was 500 feet long, steam heated, and gas lighted.

But as important as anything else was its most visible feature, the elaborate onion shaped blue dome with gold stars

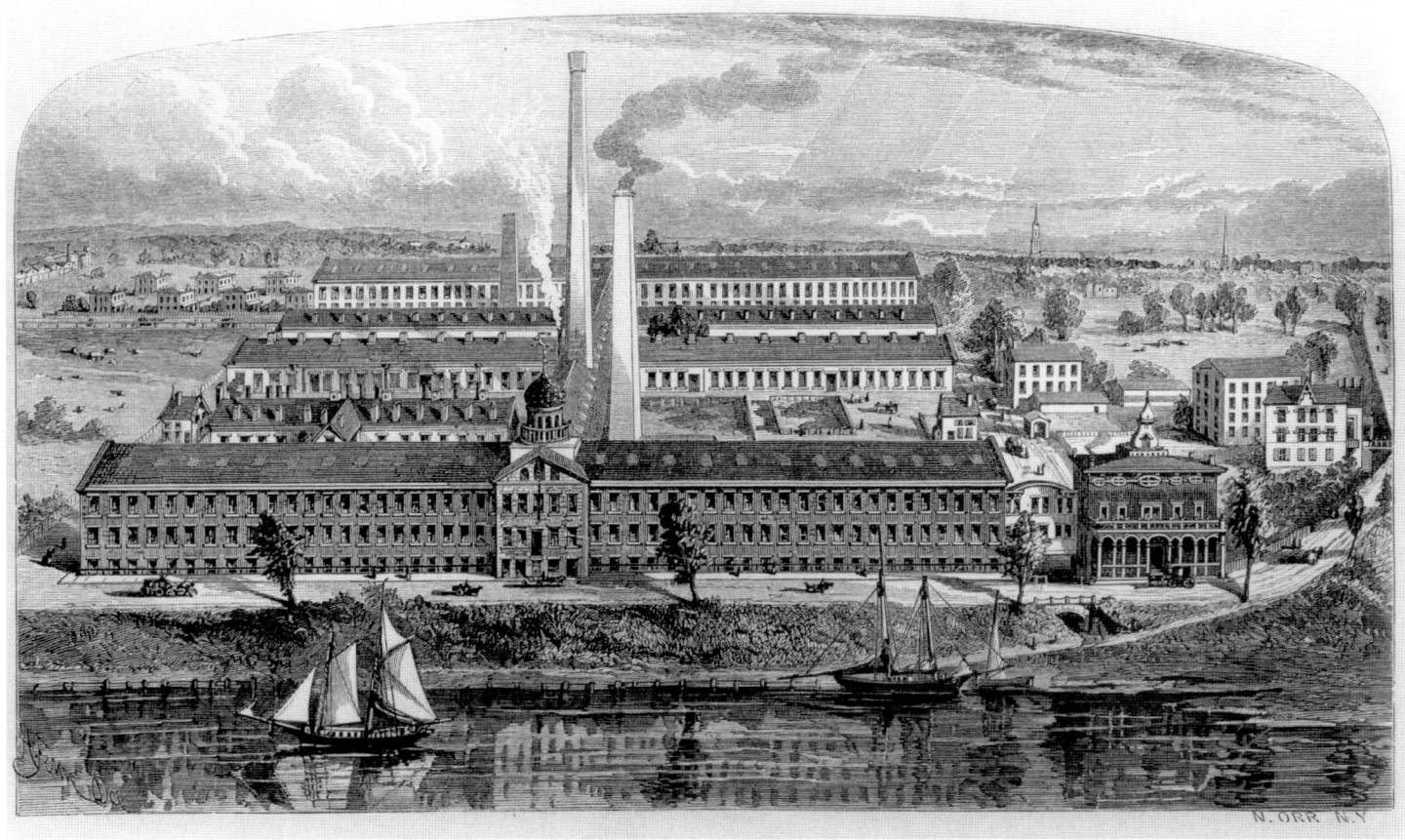

The Colt's Patent Fire-Arms Manufacturing Company factory, completed in 1861. Colt's home "Armsmear" is visible to the right of the two smokestacks. Herbert Houze Collection.

measuring 60 feet in diameter, supported by columns and crowned by a golden sphere on which perched a four-foot statue of a rampant colt, holding a broken spear. The unusual shape of the blue dome was no doubt influenced by Colt's earlier trips to Turkey and Russia, where this type of dome architecture was common. The new blue dome, with the rampant colt, dominated the Hartford skyline, and was viewed by the citizenry as a symbol as flamboyant as Samuel Colt himself.

The rampant colt symbol was adopted from the original coat of arms for the ancestral Colte family, first appearing in Waltham Abbey, Essex, England, in 1559. Samuel Colt investigated his British ancestors during his trip in 1851, and adopted the English Colte family coat of arms, changing the original "full speed" colt to a rampant colt, rearing with front legs elevated. The broken spear represented knightly service and valor in the battlefield. Colt's rampant colt first appeared on an engraved Navy revolver given to patent attorney Edward Dickerson in 1851. The rampant colt has gone on to become Colt's easily recognized trademark worldwide, appearing on millions of firearms, company brochures, catalogs, and related accessories. No other American firearms manufacturer has developed such a unique and fitting trademark.

By 1857, the Colt's Arms Manufacturing Company was turning out nearly 150 finished guns a day, at a price of $24 each. Colt paid his workers well, but insisted on maximum effort in return. In one of Colt's directives at the time, he stated, "Every man employed in or about my armoury whether by piece wirk or by days wirk is expected to wirk ten hours during the runing of the engine, & no one who does not cheerfully concent to du this need expect to be employed by me." Colt considered tardiness a cardinal sin and any hourly Colt employee not inside the Armory by the clanging of the steam gong at 7 a.m. would find himself locked out until noon.

Colt and His Family

Well on his way to fame and fortune, Samuel Colt needed two more things: a wife and a house. In 1853, he had met the two daughters of Reverend William Jarvis of Middletown, Connecticut. Samuel chose Elizabeth as his bride, even though at 30 she was 12 years younger than he was. The extravagant June 5, 1856 wedding rocked Hartford's conservative social registers, and easily ranked at the top of the list of East Coast high society functions. Following an all-night bachelor party, Samuel and his friends traveled to the wedding in Middletown aboard a chartered steamboat, the *Washington Irving*. With the Colt band playing at its liveliest, the musicians joined the groom's party on board, in front of a flag-draped Armory, cheered on by an immense crowd of spectators as the ship left dock.

The wedding itself was spectacular. The bride's dress and jewelry were rumored to have cost nearly $8,000, and the wedding cake was six feet tall, trimmed with sugar pistols and rifles and a small statue of young Colt on top. Elizabeth and her family met her groom's party at the Jarvis family mansion for the ceremony, and they were married in the parlor by Connecticut's Episcopal bishop. After the ceremony and a brief reception, the entire wedding party, including the Colt band, took the evening express train to New York City, where a large reception was held at the St. Nicholas Hotel, which had been rented in its entirety for the celebration.

Elizabeth Jarvis Colt.
Gerald S. Hayward, on ivory,
Courtesy Wadsworth Atheneum,
Hartford, Connecticut
Bequest of Elizabeth Hart Jarvis Colt.
1905.65

The next morning, the Colonel, his bride, her brother Richard, and sister Hetty, and a multilingual translator sailed on the *Baltic* for a six-month trip to Europe. When they returned, Samuel began to build his palatial Armsear mansion on the western edge of his property. By the end of 1858, Samuel, Elizabeth, and new infant Caldwell Colt had comfortably settled into Armsmear, and everything seemed peaceful, if only for a little while.

The London Armory

By 1851, Colt had obtained national fame and had released a new cap and ball model, the 1851 Navy in .36 caliber. It was an immediate success domestically, but overseas, Colt was still relatively unknown. The first World's Fair, the Great Exhibition of 1851, was to be held in London, Feeling the necessity to display, Colt brought an array of some 450 revolving firearms of Pocket, Navy, Dragoon, and rifle types, and set up in the American section. The display became an overnight sensation, and thousands of people visited this popular exhibit area. Colt was a featured speaker during the exhibition, on the topic of the "application of machinery to the manufacture of rotating chambered breech firearms." The distinguished audience was composed of members and guests of the highly respected Institute of Civil Engineers, of which Colt was ultimately elected a member.

The trip must have had an indelible impact on the young Colt, who was very much an anglophile. He now concentrated on getting a new plant established in London. While E.K. Root, Colt's Hartford production genius and the other capable workers kept the plant running full tilt, Colt busied himself with acquiring a suitable building for a new plant in London. It was his first attempt at organizing a production facility overseas, and not everything went as smoothly as it had in Hartford. The new London Armory was easily the most technologically advanced firearms factory in England and Europe at the time, but it was not well received by the staid English gunmakers, who regarded Colt as an arrogant young upstart. Production finally began in 1853, and during the four years of operation, the London Armory produced approximately 48,000 revolvers.

Charles Dickens took a tour of Colt's new factory, and approved, especially of the way the workers were treated. The plant's steam engine however he classified as "indefatigably toiling" and loud.

Problems soon beset the operation, mostly stemming from a lack of sales. The European firearms marketplace was more sophisticated than America's, and as a result, Colt faced stiff competition from London gunmakers, especially the London Armoury Company.

Samuel and his bride Elizabeth also visited the London Armory in the summer of 1856, and Colt must have been in a different mood. The Armory had been limping along for five years, facing intense competition from British manufacturers, and soon would be closed for good. During this difficult time in London, Colt's brother James sued Samuel over his alleged share of the London Armory's profits, claiming they amounted to over $400,000. The end result of the suit required James to pay Colt's damages of $10,184, and Samuel was ordered to pay James $5,897.50. James was the overall loser, but more important, the feud between the brothers was never successfully resolved. Finally, in November 1856, Samuel realized that he could no longer keep the London plant open without sizeable military contracts, and his London dream became a memory.

Hartford's Charter Oak Tree

No look at the story of Colt's can be complete without mentioning Hartford's most venerable piece of history – the Charter Oak tree. The historic tree was believed to have been the resting-place of the original copy of the Fundamental Orders of Connecticut of 1639, one of the first written constitutions in the New World. Legend tells of a Captain Joseph Wadsworth, who hid the document from the British in the hollow of the great oak in 1687. Generations of Hartford citizens and residents had cherished the tree and its history.

On August 21, 1856, at 12:50 a.m., a violent windstorm knocked over the great oak after almost 800 years of life. Many Hartford citizens, including Samuel Colt, were saddened by the loss of the tree. Samuel's friend, I.W. Stuart, owned the land that the Charter Oak had stood upon, and Samuel decided to use the wood of the tree. He commissioned a delicately carved cradle from local cabinetmaker John Most. In a community still dominated by Congregationalists of the old puritan stripe, this was the most egregious and self-aggrandizing display of ego that had ever graced the threshold of this once insular and proper New England town. The cradle, with its eight colt heads, two rampant colt finials, and carved Colt family coat of arms, swung from gnarled oak posts and was shaped like a canoe. Additionally, Samuel had pistol grips carved from the wood, and revolvers with Charter Oak grips were given away to many of Hartford's most reticent citizens. Some of the revolvers had "CHARTER OAK STOCK" engraved on the straps.

The Hartford city council commissioned John Most to create a chair for the president of the council from the Charter Oak. Most carved a beautiful, ornate piece, with vines and leafy twinings that made the chair appear to have grown into its final shape. A sensation was created when the council decided that the price was too high, and refused to buy it. Samuel Colt, disgusted, declared the chair "a bargain at any price." He gave Most a handsome premium over his asking price, just to own the chair the city council had scorned. Colt felt it was the symbol of the hypocrisy of the Old Guard citizens, and kept the chair on prominent display in his library.

As a fitting gesture in memory of the Charter Oak, Colt decided to call a recreation parlor he had set aside in a new office building "Charter Oak Hall." It was to be for the cultural enjoyment of his employees.

Prelude to a Civil War

With the election of Abraham Lincoln in 1860 rumblings of secession and even civil war were common. If war broke out, however, few Americans expected it to last more than a few months. Colt's Armory continued to produce the Models 1849, 1851 Navy, and the Root-designed 1855 side hammer in ever-larger quantities. The factory's gross revenues averaged $237,000 annually until the outbreak of the Civil War, when they soared to over $1 million. During the tense pre-war era, Colt shipped guns to all sides in the potential conflict. His last shipment of 500 guns to the new Confederacy left for Richmond, Virginia three days after the attack on Fort Sumter, packed in boxes marked "hardware."

With America now embroiled in the Civil War, domestic arms production reached new, unprecedented heights. Colt, a staunch status quo Democrat, supported the Union and the Constitution. He opposed the Republican anti-slavery platform and hoped that war would be averted. However, always pragmatic, he had quietly prepared the Armory in advance for a major five-year conflict requiring maximum production capacity.

During a vacation in Cuba in early 1861, Colt wrote to his key employees, Elisha Root and Horace Lord (former superintendent at Eli Whitney) exhorting them to "run the Armory night and day with a double set of hands – make hay while the sun shines."

Surviving without the Colonel

At the peak of activity, Colt became ill over Christmas, 1861, catching a cold and becoming delirious. Colt's staggering business responsibilities were finally beginning to wear

Colonel Samuel Colt, 1856
Gerald S. Hayward, on ivory,
Courtesy Wadsworth Atheneum,
Hartford, Connecticut
Bequest of Elizabeth Hart Jarvis Colt.
1905.67

down his seemingly inexhaustible energy. It was also no secret that he had suffered for some time from gout, inflammatory rheumatism, as well as rheumatic fever, and had fully indulged in the pleasures of life, in addition to laboring from dawn to dusk.

At the end, he ruled his domain from a roll top desk at the Armory, smoking cigars and writing his own misspelled letters in his left-handed scrawl. Colt was worn out, and no doubt depressed by the premature deaths of four children within five years. With his father at his side during his final days, Samuel became delirious. Christopher Colt later commented, "…last Sunday, he talked incessantly all afternoon – and until 2 o'clock Monday morning, making poetry and singing to airs that he was familiar with…his brain has been overworked, till its functions have given out. It is in fact too active for his physical powers of endurance…"

Samuel Colt died January 10, 1862 due to a combination of his health complications, his power of speech the last to go. Of his children, only young Caldwell Colt, age three, had survived infancy, only to witness his father's funeral at an early age.

The spectacular funeral that followed four days later was one of the most extravagant in 19th century American history. Colt himself had planned it, like the last act of a grand opera. Some 1,500 of Colt's workmen filed in pairs past the metallic casket in the parlor of Armsmear. A half-mile away, the Armory was quiet, its hundreds of machines idle, and the test ranges silent. After a simple Episcopal service, the workers formed two lines, through which the phalanx solidly marched, drums muffled, colors draped, and arms reversed. Behind them, eight pallbearers bore the coffin to the private graveyard near the lake. At the time, Colonel Samuel Colt was America's best known and wealthiest inventor, a controversial figure who had dared to dream his ambitious dream, and had made it come true.

However, no one had been ready for Samuel Colt to die, especially just at the beginning of the Civil War. Things had to be accomplished. Without Colt's charismatic leadership, what would happen to the company?

Shortly before he died, Colt handed the family reins over to his brother-in-law, Richard Jarvis. He simply told him, "You and your family must do for me now, as I have no one else to call upon. You are the pendulum that must keep the works in motion." Two of his own brothers were dead, and the other, James, a hot tempered and petty politician, had proven to be a miserable failure as Colt's manager in the short-lived London plant.

Colt's entire estate, which was controlled by Elizabeth Colt and their only son Caldwell, was valued at $3.2 million, giving Elizabeth an income of $200,000 a year for life. Included in the estate were hundreds of trees and plants from his expansive greenhouse, over 500 gallons of distilled spirits, 14 carriages, 9,996 shares of Colt's stock valued at $2 million, 346 cases of wine and champagne, and 5,400 cigars. Besides Elizabeth and Caldwell, Colt's major beneficiary was Master Samuel Caldwell Colt, "son of (his) late brother John Colt," whom even Mrs. Colt regarded favorably.

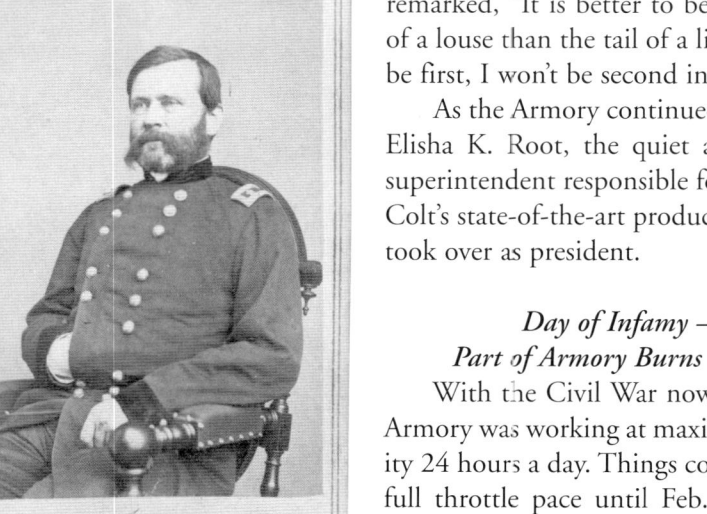

General William B. Franklin presided over the rebuilding of the Colt Armory.
Herbert Houze Collection.

While living, Colt had adapted the motto, "Vincit qui patitur," or "he conquers who is patient." He also once remarked, "It is better to be at the head of a louse than the tail of a lion. If I can't be first, I won't be second in anything."

As the Armory continued to prosper, Elisha K. Root, the quiet and brilliant superintendent responsible for setting up Colt's state-of-the-art production facility, took over as president.

Day of Infamy – Part of Armory Burns Down

With the Civil War now raging, the Armory was working at maximum capacity 24 hours a day. Things continued at a full throttle pace until Feb. 4, 1864, a day of infamy in Hartford. Just after 8 a.m., the deep tones of the Colt steam gong emergency alarm were heard. Smoke was discovered pouring from one of the wings of the main brownstone building over the polishing room. The fire seemed centered in the attic near the main driving pulley for the machines. Men carried a hose to the location to put out the fire, but there was no water. Within minutes, all the upper stories were ablaze, and the top floor, heavy with wooden patterns, collapsed. The workmen below, who according to plant custom were locked into their departments during shifts, grew panicky but were soon released.

Everyone tried to get out as fast as they could, and a few workers escaped by the windows with their hair ablaze. The fire created a black pall of smoke, and thousands rushed to the scene. Unable to put out the fire due to inadequate equipment, Elizabeth Colt, accompanied by her father, watched as the beautiful Colt dome teetered, then descended into the flames at 9 a.m. As it fell, she burst into tears, no doubt reminded of her husband's funeral. It was one of the worst calamities to strike any Hartford industry, leaving 900 men out of work when their labor was needed the most. The damage exceeded $1,250,000, and only about a third of it was covered by insurance purchased by Elizabeth, something that Samuel Colt had always considered trivial and had not carried in his lifetime. Miraculously, only one employee had perished in the blaze that destroyed both the office and the oldest half of the Armory, which contained most of Root's machinery, as well as all of the company drawings and models.

Rebuilding the Blue Dome

Following the fire, many questioned the future of the famous Colt Armory. Elizabeth Colt provided the answer within a day. She ordered it rebuilt exactly as her husband had left it, regardless of the cost. Also of major consequence was the September 1865 death of president Elisha Root. Elizabeth Colt's brother, Richard Jarvis, now headed the company. A new executive, William B. Franklin, who had graduated from West Point in the same class as General Ulysses S. Grant, wasted no time carrying out the widow's wishes. In April, the foundations were laid, and the new Armory work was finished in early 1867, topped with a new dome.

Elizabeth Colt took a risk rebuilding the old Armory to its previous capacity, especially since the Civil War was over, and there was no longer a demand for pistols and rifles from either military or commercial buyers. Colt's output during the war had exceeded 378,000 revolvers and 114,000 muskets. When the Civil War officially ended in April 1865, after almost four years, Colt's Armory had averaged an output of approximately 335 completed guns every day, seven days a week. Colt's was the only armory in the world that could have produced that volume of firearms at the time.

During the welcome peacetime that followed the Civil War, the demand for firearms declined sharply. As a result, Colt's leased portions of its factory to other manufacturers in an effort to keep as much revenue coming in as possible. Approximately 600 men remained in the main building, and in addition to producing rifles and pistols, they also manufactured Baxter steam engines, sewing machines, and printing presses.

In 1867, Colt's manufactured the first machine gun designed by Richard Gordon Gatling, patented during 1862. The Gatling Gun, a multi-barrel rifle that operated by turning a crank, was capable of firing more than 200 shots per minute. Mark Twain, Hartford's most prominent literary resident, remarked after firing the new Gatling Gun:

"It is a cluster of six to ten savage tubes that carry great conical pellets of lead, with unerring accuracy, a distance of two and one-half miles. It feeds itself with cartridges, and you work it with a crank like a hand organ, and you can fire it faster than four men can count. When fired rapidly, the reports blend together like a watchman's rattle…I like it very much, and went on grinding it as long as they could afford cartridges for the amusement – which was not very long."

Elizabeth Colt, her hair with trademark top knot having turned gray, then snowy white, reigned over Hartford's society – an idealized church woman, colonial dame, and benefactress. She kept a firm watch on Armsear and the Armory, and funded a new Episcopal Church of the Good Shepherd. Its unique architecture startled every churchgoer in the city. The arches of the doorway and the sacred mottos in stone were adorned with various parts of Colt guns, and the machines that made them. She also insisted on previewing the sermons before they were delivered on Sunday.

When a new decade began in 1870, the evolution of Colt's firearms continued with the introduction of the 1871-72 Open Top.

The Colt Single Action Army

In the early 1870s, William Mason had been diligently working on a new revolver, using a solid frame and the top strap of an early Root model. This was desperately needed, since Colt's was now considerably behind developing a revolver for the new metallic cartridge, which had been patented in 1853, and popularized by Smith & Wesson's military contract during the Civil War. The new design featured a barrel screwed into the frame, and the unique loading allowed the cylinder to be inserted from the rear through a gate in the frame, utilizing the new metallic cartridges.

In 1872, the new six-shot revolver in .45 caliber was introduced, and it quickly became known as the "Peacemaker." Fame came fast, and the new Colt Single Action Army (SAA) did so well during the military trials that the Army ordered 14,400 within two years. In 1878, the new .44-40 caliber that Winchester had introduced five years earlier with its now famous Model 1873 rifle was added. It was immediately popular with many new settlers who could now use the same cartridge for both their rifles and revolvers.

The demand for this new revolver aided greatly in the company's sales. A new wave of post- Civil War settlers was heading west of the Mississippi in record numbers, always thinking about protection from Indian hostilities and outlaws. Colt's revolvers quickly gained a reputation as deadly and reliable. While competitor Winchester's lever action rifle was known as "The Gun That Won the West," the legendary Colt testimonial became "God created all men, Sam Colt made them equal."

After the Civil War, the regular army declined rapidly in size. By 1868 General Philip Sheridan complained that there were only 2,600 troops available for service on the Great Plains. As total army strength declined to just 19,000 officers and enlisted men, their numbers were spread thin on Reconstruction duty in the South, garrisoning coastal and border defenses, and protecting railroad workers and emigrants on the transcontinental trails. Widely separated commands in the West required new tactics to try to confront Indian foes: small, highly mobile units armed with new breechloading Springfield carbines and rifles and with repeating revolvers. In the most celebrated confrontation, on June 25, 1876, the highly decorated Civil War general George A. Custer, now a Lieutenant Colonel, and 271 men of the Seventh Regiment of Cavalry, all armed with Colt's Single Action Army revolver, were killed at the Little Bighorn by combined Sioux, Cheyenne and Arapahoe forces. The devastating news from far-off Montana reached the East on the eve of America's Centennial celebration in Philadelphia.

New Designs and Offerings

During 1877, Colt's introduced the new double action Lightning Model revolver, originally conceived by Samuel Colt in 1842. This new double action design, allowing the

Colt & Winchester: Uneasy Rivals

The origins of the Colt-Winchester trade war of the 1880s can be traced to the mid-1870s when Winchester began offering a wide variety of English shotguns at its New York City Depot.

Offering prices considerably lower than American-made shotguns, Winchester quickly became a dominant player in the marketplace. The firm's ability to undercut the competition was due to the method by which it acquired these arms. Writing to the Colt company's management on March 27, 1875, the firm's London agent, Baron Fredrich von Oppen outlined Winchester's arrangements with their English suppliers.

"The Winchester sporting rifle is making head way though rather slowly, in this market. Birmingham importers sell them with scarcely any profit, taking them in exchange for double barrel guns sent over to America."

Winchester's control of the lucrative New York shotgun trade was not seriously challenged until 1878, when the Colt company began production of its own double barrel shotgun. Heavily promoted by the firm's New York "Allies" as an American-made product superior to "inferior imported shotguns," it gradually began to make inroads into Winchester's market.

In retaliation, the Winchester company not only began increasing its imports of double barrel shotguns for its New York Depot, but also began offering P. Webley double action revolvers there. As these competed directly with Colt's new .38 and .41 caliber Lightning series of revolvers, the Hartford concern was not amused.

By 1882 the trade war had escalated to the point that Colt recognized that its markets would continue to be eroded unless something was done. The solution that was decided upon was to compete directly with Winchester in the highly profitable lever action rifle business. To that end, Colt's entered into an agreement with Andrew Burgess to begin manufacturing a .44 caliber rifle based upon patents he held. Recognizing that sales of this model through Colt's "Allies" would seriously reduce the income generated by their Model 1873, Winchester began planning its next move.

Aware that the Colt company had also begun work on developing a slide action rifle, Winchester had its new chief designer, William Mason, a former Colt employee, do the same. At the same time, he was also asked to design a single action revolver similar to that made Colt. By late March of 1884 working samples for both designs had been completed and the Winchester company began implementing its counter-moves.

In mid-May of 1884, the firm flooded the New York market with shotguns by selling its existing inventory at a loss to one of Colt's "Allies," J. P. Moore & Son. Having hit Colt in the pocket book, Winchester's president, Thomas G. Bennett, made arrangements to meet with Colt's general manager, Major General William Buell Franklin, on June 1, 1884 to discuss Winchester's plans to begin production of Mason's single action revolver and slide action rifle.

While no transcript of that meeting has survived, Bennett made the following entry in his diary under the date June 1, 1884.

"In Hartford. Lunched with Gen Franklin. Agreed not to interfere in each other's Markets. Ret'd 4pm"

Subsequent events cast some light on other aspects of this gentlemen's agreement. As production of the Burgess Rifle continued until it was abruptly halted in January 1885, it appears that Franklin asked Bennett for permission to recoup Colt's investment in the model's tooling. However, the ever-cautious Bennett kept his firm's options open by continuing the preparation of tooling drawings for both the Mason carbine and pistol over the same period. Once manufacture of the Burgess ceased, Winchester discontinued any further development of Mason's designs. It also ceased the importation of British revolvers in late 1884.

Though the agreement between Bennett and Franklin was never put into writing, the two firms abided by their decision and did not compete directly until Winchester introduced its slide action .22rf caliber rifle in 1890. By then, existing markets were broad enough to absorb the products of both firms without financial detriment to either.

H.G.H.

gun to be fired from either single action or double action mode, was quickly accepted by both civilians and military, even though the new revolver had some operational shortcomings.

In 1878, Colt's expanded its line to include the Model 1878 hammer double barrel shotgun. It was a quality, American-manufactured side-by-side, built to compete with the better-known Parker. When it was released, it was the highest priced item in the Colt lineup. It was followed by the Model 1883 hammerless double barrel shotgun. Only the best materials and workmanship were utilized, and the price tag reflected this, as in many cases, they were more expensive than most of the better quality side-by-sides from England.

During this period, Colt's also released one of its rarest models, the double rifle. It was based on the Model 1878 shotgun action, and chambered for various .45 calibers, including the popular .45-70. It had been Caldwell Colt's inspiration, probably stemming from an interest in similar British rifles of the time. While scholars are uncertain, it is thought that the total production for the double rifle was fewer than 40.

The Colt-Burgess lever action rifle was introduced in 1883 in .44-40 cal., and named after its inventor, Andrew Burgess. It was Colt's first attempt to take away some of Winchester's lucrative rifle business. It has been claimed, but without proof, that Colt's agreed to cease production of its lever-action Burgess rifle when Winchester likewise ended producing its competitive revolver. In any case, this rifle was not commercially successful, and went out of production in early 1885. It was followed by the more popular Lightning Model rifle, which was chambered in small, medium, and large calibers, and framed accordingly. Although Colt's never achieved Winchester's success in the rifle business, the Lightning Model rifle was in production until 1902, with over 89,000 manufactured.

The evolution of firearms was again changed in 1887, when P. Vieille of France invented smokeless gunpowder. The new powders led to the development of more powerful cartridges, requiring in turn stronger firing mechanisms and metallurgical advances in the steel used in the making of barrels and receivers. Of equal importance, the new smokeless powders were virtually non-fouling compared with the dirty black powders and they cleared the way for the invention of modern rapid-fire repeaters and machine guns.

John Browning Comes to Hartford

John and Matt Browning made a timely first visit to the Armory in early 1881. The Browning brothers had been working on a repeating mechanism that would handle black powder. They brought their new automatic machine gun for a trial, and general manager John Hall had welcomed them warmly. "We smoked up the factory with those .45-70s, and waked echoes clear back to the Colonel himself," John Browning would proclaim later. Meanwhile, Colt officials could not believe their eyes after 200 rounds had been fired without a hitch. This was the unassuming beginning of a cordial and profitable association with the inventor that lasted until his death in 1926. Soon, this machine gun would be known as the Colt 1895 Peacemaker. It was promptly demonstrated to Navy representatives. After three minutes of continuous fire and 1,800 rounds, despite the barrel turning bright red, it never faltered.

During the same year, Browning test fired his .38 cal., recoil operated, semi-automatic pistol. Upon signing a royalty agreement the next year, every future semi-automatic pistol produced by Colt's was based on his designs. With the advent of smokeless powder cartridges, and Browning's adaptation of his recoil-operated action to accommodate them, the era of the modern semi-automatic weapon had arrived.

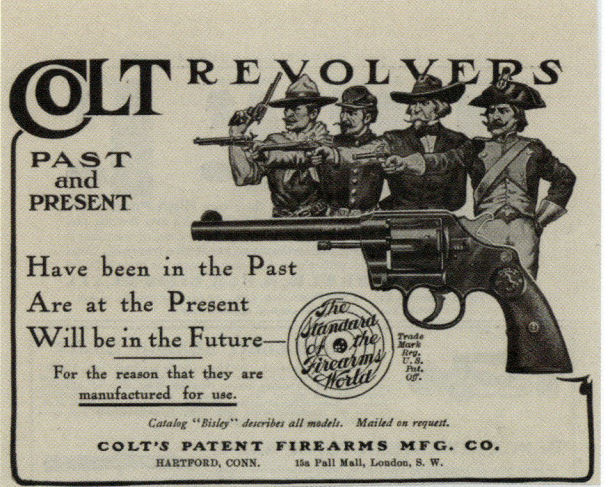

Colt's advertising was effective and frequent. This advertisement appeared in Outdoor Life *in 1908.*
MS 102 Clinton Schafer Collection.
Buffalo Bill Historical Center.

In the factory, John Browning developed a strong friendship with Fred Moore, a young man in the model room. The two worked closely on all of Browning's ideas, and at John's tactful suggestion, Moore was promoted to the head of the machine gun division, and then to production manager for the entire factory.

As the century came to a close, near the mid-point of America's industrial dominance, Connecticut was ranked eleventh among the states in industrial manufacturing, and Colt's future looked extremely bright.

More Family Tragedy
Caldwell Colt Dies Controversially

The Gay Nineties continued to be a prosperous time for Colt's. Undoubtedly the biggest news during the first half of the decade was the untimely death of Caldwell Colt. Affectionately nicknamed "Collie" by his mother, the younger Colt was better known for his sailing escapades and adventures on board his schooner *The Dauntless*, than for designing the double rifle.

Caldwell, 36 years old, died in a hotel in Punta Gorda, Florida, in mid-January 1894. The cause of his death was reported as heart failure after a severe case of tonsillitis, but soon rumors circulated aboard his ship *Oriole*, which he kept in Florida for winter cruising, that he had been shot by a jealous husband who had caught him in bed with his wife. Elizabeth Colt's only surviving son was now gone. Again stricken with grief, the *grande dame* of Armsmear promptly erected an elaborate memorial to her son next door to her church, which would serve as a parish house and recreation hall. When completed, it cost $300,000, and its unusual architecture incorporated portholes instead of windows, with the second floor patterned after a ship's deck.

A New Century

As the party favors were being prepared for the upcoming 20th century, Colt's celebrated with the introduction of its first semi-automatic pistol, the Model 1900. Even though only 4,274 were made, one of the most limited productions of all Colt's pistols, it was a successful prelaunch for later Models 1902 and the .45 ACP cal. Model 1905, both of which resulted in military contracts.

Things looked promising in Hartford in 1901. The Armory had become much busier with the new semi-auto pistol production, even though there was some unrest regarding the new union movement, fighting for a nine-hour workday and overtime pay. By this time, many employees had worked for Colt's all their lives, as had their fathers before them. A strike at Colt's was averted due to their allegiance to the company, even though many other businesses were experiencing labor problems.

Ailing president Richard Jarvis, Colt's chief executive officer for 36 years, was impatiently waiting his retirement, and Elizabeth Colt was worried about her brother's ill health. Soon after completing his tenure, Jarvis became an invalid, and lived in Armsmear during his final days, dying only a year later, on the 19th anniversary of Caldwell's death.

Widow Elizabeth Colt decided the time had come not merely for another change in presidents, but to sell the Armory. Before the labor dispute, she had instructed her managers to find a private buyer. Vice president John Hall and his chief *aide de camp*, William C. Skinner, approached the Boston and New York financial firm of Armstrong & Schirmer. Colt's capital stock amounted to over one million dollars, but Elizabeth Colt received substantially more. In June, the sale of the Armory through this brokerage agreement was consummated, and the 54-year duration of Colt family ownership ended.

Now matronly and somewhat resembling Queen Victoria, Elizabeth Colt still rode about Hartford in her carriage, since not only did she disdain Edison's new invention – electricity – but also would have nothing to do with the latest method of travel – the automobile. In 1905, Elizabeth Colt prepared herself for dying. Many of her dearest possessions were willed to the Wadsworth Athenaeum museum in Hartford, including the Colonel's personal gun collection, snuff boxes, portraits, Dresden china, and many other important historic artifacts. She also left orders that her five horses were to be shot and buried.

On August 21, 1905, Elizabeth Hart Jarvis Colt died suddenly at the summer home of her niece, Elizabeth Hart Beech Robinson, in Newport, Rhode Island. Compared to her husband's spectacular and well-orchestrated funeral, her funeral at the Church of the Good Shepherd was spartan, although the Colt band played a march outside while the mourners emptied from their carriages. Given her strong ties with the Church, she bequeathed $800,000 to maintain the church and parish house.

Colt's new president, John Hall, kept Colt's work force relatively steady with 600-800 workers, now Hartford's fourth largest company. During this time, business opportunities seemed unlimited for newcomers and factories like Colt's depended on the unending stream of immigrants who descended on their city during 1900-1930. Hall lasted only a year as Colt's president before he died and was succeeded by Lewis C. Grover, a past assistant superintendent. By the end of December 1908, Charles L. F. Robinson of Newport, a wealthy yachtsman and husband of Elizabeth Colt's niece, and other investors had in effect taken over financial control of the company. The Boston and New York interest that had bought out Elizabeth Colt in 1901 had formed a holding company, Colt's Arms, in the state of New York, although the Armory retained its identity as Colt's Patent Fire-Arms Manufacturing Company. Grover's ill health forced him to step down in January 1909, and he was followed as president by Colonel William Skinner, who ran the Armory for two years, receiving a salary of $7,500 annually.

A 1925 ad in Hunter, Trader, Trapper *made dramatic claims for the accuracy of the Colt .45. MS 102 Clinton Schafer Collection. Buffalo Bill Historical Center.*

By 1910, nearly 30,000 Russian Jews, Italians, Swedes, and many other nationalities were now calling Hartford home, resulting in a large, capable work force for the city. Demand had once again increased for Colt's firearms, mostly due to Browning's new semi-automatic design, and on Saturday nights, Hartford's bars were full of Irish, German, Russian, Swedes, and other immigrants.

For the past tax-free decade, Colt's had been enormously profitable. Although no sales figures had been published, the

John M. Browning

It would not be an exaggeration to say that the Colt company's financial survival during the 20th century was due in large part to John M. Browning. From his mind came the designs for some of the firm's most popular and profitable models: the early semi-automatic pistols, Government Model of 1911 and Woodsman; the Browning Light Machine Gun of 1917, as well as the .50 caliber Browning Heavy Machine Gun.

Born in 1855, John Moses Browning learned the trade of a gunmaker in his father's shop. Later working with his brother, Matthew, he established his own gunshop in Ogden, Utah. There he developed and patented a lever-actuated, dropping breech block rifle. This design was subsequently purchased by the Winchester Repeating Arms Company of New Haven, Connecticut and manufactured as that firm's Model 1885 Single Shot Rifle. Over the next two decades the Winchester company purchased 40 more of Browning's patents. While many of these designs were not commercially produced, others became the basis for some of Winchester's most popular models, such as the 1886, 1892 and 1894 repeating sporting rifles.

Although Browning's relationship with Winchester was profitable, it was not an exclusive one. Consequently, when Browning developed a design for a machine gun in 1890 he approached the Colt company regarding its manufacture. When this arm was introduced in 1895, it marked the beginning of Browning's long relationship with Colt. In 1896 the inventor licensed his patent for a semi-automatic pistol to Colt. This arrangement ultimately led to the Colt company becoming the leading manufacturer of self-loading pistols in North America.

The association of John M. Browning with the Colt's Patent Fire Arms Manufacturing Company lasted until the inventor's death in 1926.

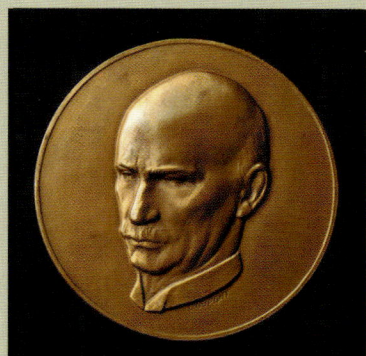 

J.M. Browning. Medal. Buffalo Bill Historical Center. Gift of Olin Corporation, Winchester Arms Collection. 1988.8.1148.1

The most fitting assessment of Browning's contributions to firearms design is that written in 1931 by Captain Paul A. Curtis:

"It is difficult to find words to accurately describe John M. Browning's achievements. To say that he was a great gun designer is inadequate; to say that he was the Edison of the modern firearms industry does not quite cover the case either, for he was greater than that ... Browning was unique. He stood alone, and there never was in his time or before, one whose genius along those lines could remotely compare with his."

To the Colt company, he was a godsend.

H.G.H.

annual stock dividend payments ranged from 13 percent to 35 percent, and averaged 22 percent. The year 1911 was noted as the best in 40 years, and appropriately, a total of 40 percent in dividends was paid. Robinson concentrated on cultivating the foreign marketplace, and he made a landmark trip to Europe, giving Fabrique Nationale of Liege, Belgium an exclusive license to sell Browning's semi-automatic pistols in Europe (except England). Colt's could also boast of its new government contract for the new Model 1911 .45 ACP automatic pistol, and as a result, sales shot up 44 percent in 1912.

In 1914, on the hundredth anniversary of Samuel Colt's birth, employment had risen to 1,200 and the Armory was using all 350,000 square feet strictly for the manufacture of firearms. In 1914, it had earned almost $1 million on sales of only $2, 284,000. In 1915, its earnings had jumped to $2.5 million. By 1917, employment had more than doubled in the last twelve months, now totaling nearly 4,000 employees, while the market value of its stock had risen from $160 to $775 per share.

Prelude to World War I
John Browning Sets Up Shop in Armory

William Skinner, once again Colt's president after Robinson's death in 1916, told the shareholders during the annual meeting that the backlog of worker orders now exceeded $30 million, approximately three years worth. Despite the expenditure of $2.5 million on new equipment and buildings, the plant would soon have to been enlarged again. Colt's net profit had soared 160 percent to $6,346,000. Five days later, on April 6, 1917, Congress declared war against Germany, and the United States joined the struggle to keep the world safe for democracy.

Soon after the American war declaration, a balding, tall, slim, ramrod straight man with sharpshooter eyes returned to Hartford. Quickly finding an apartment for his wife and children, he proceeded immediately to his old desk in an obscure corner of the Armory that had been reserved for him in the past. For the next two years, John Moses Browning stayed close to the work he loved. Now in his sixties, he still dreaded the limelight, and was quite unassuming, although unlike most inventors, had become immensely rich from a lifetime of designing and perfecting the manufacture of firearms. Even though he had also worked for Winchester and Remington, Colt's biggest competitors, his relationship with Colt's lasted nearly 30 years.

The following month, Browning put the final touches on his latest and most powerful weapons: the 37-pound heavy machine gun and the relatively light, rapid firing 15fi-pound automatic rifle, both in .30 caliber. Browning was a hands-on designer, typically seen walking around the factory floor ready to overcome any problem on the spot, swinging a cheap pair of spectacles, and munching from a bag of peanuts that he always carried. If he was having a plant production problem or difficulty with a particular new design or modification, the empty peanut shells were usually flying.

During this hectic time, United States ordnance officials approached Browning with a request that he assign full rights to the government for both weapons, and for his .45 caliber pistol for the duration of the war. In addition, they asked that he also supervise production in every factory. "We know our offer is only a fraction of what you would receive from royalties on orders already booked, and this may not be acceptable," they said. Browning was offered $750,000 for this assignment, less than six percent of what he normally would have been entitled to, or more than $12,000,000. "Major," the inventor replied, "if that suits Uncle Samuel, that's all right with me."

Colt's and World War I

Because of Colt's already heavy backlog orders on the Maxim-Vickers machine guns and Browning-designed pistols, the firm had to rely on other manufacturers to fulfill contracts. By the end of November 1917, Colt's subcontractors had already completed 41,000 machine guns and 43,000 automatic rifles, compared to Colt's 1,000 and 9,000 respectively. By the time the armistice was declared on November 11, 1918 to the jubilant Hartford citizenry, Colt's had delivered to the United States military more than 425,000 automatic pistols, 151,700 revolvers, 13,000 Maxim-Vickers machine guns, and 10,000 new Brownings. At the time of the armistice, Colt's received another contract for one million .45s at $14.50 each. During this period, under the exemplary leadership of President Skinner and production manager Fred Moore, the Armory had gone all out to maintain maximum war production, and towards the end, more than 3,500 men working on handguns alone were producing 2,200 pistols a day.

War is always good business for those firearms companies that are fortunate enough to acquire lucrative military contracts and have the production capacity to manufacture them on time. Nothing could prove this point better than what happened to Colt's during the World War I. Not only had the Armory shipped $66 million worth of armaments and ammunition between 1914 and 1918, it had earned $21.5 million doing so. The company's surplus cash reserve was now an astonishing $6 million. During 1918 alone, sales had skyrocketed to nearly $32 million, and employment peaked at nearly 10,000. Of the total, 2,200 worked in the Meriden, Connecticut plant, acquired for the additional war demand, and now for sale. In his 1920 company report to the smiling shareholders, president Skinner proudly reported that, "The company doesn't owe a dollar to anybody, and the whole plant is now equipped with the latest machinery." If Colt had been alive to hear such a glowing summary, he no doubt would have been proud.

Post World War I Trials and Tribulations

The celebration didn't last long. A year later the cash surplus had shrunk by $800,000, in part due to Skinner's willingness to manufacture the large amount of wartime commercial orders that had accumulated at Colt's pre-war prices, even though materials and labor costs had risen sharply. Additionally, without the large military contracts and commercial sales lagging pre-war numbers, 100,000 square feet of the Armory space was now vacant. Once again, Colt's started renting its surplus space, in addition to diversifying by buying a factory that molded hard plastics. This move was the brainchild of Vice-President Samuel Stone, who wanted to utilize the strength of the Colt trademark to launch a line of "Coltrock" products, including electrical plugs and switches, tobacco humidors, buttons, and other items.

Colonel Skinner, a Colt employee since 1880, decided to finally retire as president in 1921, after another year of erosion of Colt's surplus fund and a drop in employment numbers to a 20th century low. Samuel Stone succeeded Skinner as Colt's ninth president, and during the early 1920s, the company tried to stay profitable with non-gun items, since military contracts were almost nonexistent and commercial sales had dropped substantially.

A notable event during 1921 occurred when Colt's decided to produce the soon-to-be famous Thompson submachine gun for the Auto-Ordnance Company. The gun had been officially nicknamed the "trench broom" and was preferred by many of the gangsters of the late 1920s. Once World War II started however, the revised Model 1928 A1 received international respect from the battlefields of Europe, and 1.75 million were made before the end of the war in 1945.

During 1923, Colt's had established an electrical division by acquiring the Johns-Pratt Company of Hartford for $1,237,000. Moving the electrical manufacturing machinery into the Armory filled up 200,000 additional square feet of the 900,000 foot total, and added more than 500 employees to the Colt work force. Stone proved to be a quiet but effective leader during this difficult post-war transition period, settling a wartime government tax dispute by paying less than 25 percent of the $2 million claimed owing. By 1926, earnings had returned to $662,000. During the 10-year post-World War I period, Colt's had developed several new double action models, including the popular Detective and Banker's Special and the unusual single shot Camp Perry target pistol.

The Great Depression and the Armory

During 1929, forever remembered as the year the Great Depression started, Colt's kept its promise to shareholders and paid its standard $8 annual dividend. The plastics division, now considered to be the best in the country for custom moldings, was enlarged. The Armory's work force, at 1,581 when the stock market crashed, was still at a quite respectable 1,200 when the Depression ended, despite record low revolver sales in 1932. Yet, Colt's refusal to lay off most of its employees had cost its surplus fund $1,000,000 in the first four years of the devastating depression, during which time the United States standing army had been reduced to only 30,000, smaller than the army in Turkey.

Starting in 1933, shipments and earnings began rebounding, and all workers received bonuses. Even though things were looking up, Colt's was about to face a major crisis. Over the decades, management had drawn a firm line between themselves and the regular production workers. Pampering or any type of special treatment of the employees was seen as a sign of managerial weakness, whose "do no wrong" attitude had over time created resentment in the rank and file employees. The weakest and lowest link in the management team was the important but underpaid and insensitive foreman, who in many cases, viewed the workers under his control as another type of machine who could either produce a necessary quota or not. This resulted in a type of caste system that divided the plant, with the hourly workers at the bottom, their immediate supervisors and foreman in the lower middle, and management at the top.

Additionally, Colt's had maintained a company union called the Independent Association for Colt Employees, more of a company social club than a legitimate labor union. Times had changed however, and with the Depression still fresh in most employees' minds, America's work force was much more pro-union than it had ever been. So it came as no surprise that in late 1934, Colt's employees voted 813-153 to disband the staid and unproductive association. Several months later, three craft unions from the recently established American Federation of Labor (A.F. of L.) attempted to bargain with the company. Even though there were frequent meetings with encouraging rhetoric, Colt's management refused to make an agreement or offer a counter-proposal.

For ten months, the standoff continued, but on March 13, 1935, soon after the first shift reported to work, 1,000 men and women walked off their jobs and stationed pickets in front of the office. Even though there was no disorder, the popular employee slogan was, "It's surrender, or strike." Soon, Colt's foremen began visiting the strikers at their homes in an attempt to get them back to work. The visits were unsuccessful, although a few non-strikers continued to cross the ever-increasing picket lines daily. At the start of the fourth week, more than 500 manned the picket line with more than two dozen policemen on hand to protect returning Monday morning non-strikers. Both the bitter strikers and uncompromising management had become entrenched in their positions.

On May 28, President Stone returned from Washington and a meeting with the Secretary of War regarding Germany's instability and Hitler's rise to power. President Stone had just returned home when a striker and several radical labor sympathizers detonated multiple sticks of dynamite on his front porch. Even though all the windows were shattered and the blast was heard for miles, Stone was unhurt. After two months, Stone and Colt's refused a proposed arbitration settlement, stating that more than 800 employees had returned to work, and that more than 500 of them had signed an agreement that they did not want a union to represent them.

Finally on June 3, the 13-week-old strike ended, and all talk of better representation and increased wages was forgotten during a final confrontation. The only matter deliberated was the return to work of the 300 remaining strikers, which Colt's accepted, as long as they were not guilty of any strike violence. While neither party could claim a clear victory, Colt's labor relations had forever changed, and President Stone afterwards commented, "It's a new world. My time is gone. I'm no longer the boss who can walk around the factory and call most everybody by his first name, and the employees no longer look to me as the one to give them a fair deal. We'll have a union, no question."

Mother Nature and the Armory – 1936-1938

With scars just starting to heal after the 1935 strike, work was resumed, but things were different and tension pervaded the Armory until the following March. It had been an especially wet spring, and the Hartford Red Cross had already announced its readiness in case of an emergency. The last time the Connecticut River had flooded was in 1854, and Colt had looked like an entrepreneurial visionary when he had built the two-mile, 30-foot protective dike that had saved the new Armory he was building from a major flood that had turned the rest of the city into an inland sea.

For 80 years, Colt's famous dike had protected the Armory, Armsmear, tenants in Potsdam village, and the South Meadows without fail, come hell or high water. After dark on March 12, 1936, despite sandbagging by hundreds of volunteers that raised the dike by several feet, the raging, muddy waters poured over the top and raced across the meadows towards the Armory. Within minutes, the entire first floor was under water and the second floor was also two feet deep, and rising. Quarter-ton molds were upended, and sheets of steel thrown around like tissue paper. Three hours later, a 20-foot wall of water roared through Hartford's squatter village, smashing the shacks and leaving the screaming inhabitants instantly engulfed in water in the pitch dark. Fortunately, rescue craft had already mobilized to haul these families out of their precarious predicament. The following day, Friday, all of Hartford was without power and utilities. On Saturday the river finally crested at 37.56 feet, well above Colt's 30-foot dike, and six feet higher than the previous record. The first of 25,000 typhoid shots were administered to the refugees and relief workers, and Hartford's East Side was especially devastated. When it was all over, Colt's bill for damaged machinery, equipment, and loss of inventory totaled $747,000. Despite the lost production time, a positive note was sounded when labor and management worked hand-in-hand to clean up the mess, reversing some of the ill will that had lingered from the strike the year before. Still, the company man-

Why were so many Colt pistols shipped to the Winchester Company?

Colt collectors are often surprised to learn from factory letters that pieces they own were originally shipped to the Winchester Repeating Arms Company of New Haven, Connecticut.

Over the years, various theories have been put forth to explain these shipments. It has been said for example, that revolvers and semi-automatic pistols sent to the Winchester company were test pieces, or that they were intended for resale. Others have stated that such Colts were intended to accompany rifle orders that Winchester had received.

There is a measure of truth in all of these explanations. The Colt company did ship revolvers and pistols to Winchester for testing. These arms were sent to that firm's ballistic laboratory to insure that Winchester-manufactured ammunition functioned properly in Colt's products. However, shipments such as these do not account for instances when 50 or more pistols of the same caliber were sent to New Haven. Transfers of that type had an entirely different origin.

Throughout the late 19th and early 20th centuries, the Winchester company maintained a salesroom in New York City. Aside from showcasing its own firearms, Winchester offered a wide variety of other products. Included among these were "REVOLVERS OF ALL KINDS, INCLUDING COLT'S, SMITH & WESSON'S, MERWIN, HULBURT & CO.'S AND REMINGTON'S." Consequently, some Colts shipped to Winchester were for resale.

The largest number, however, were destined for export. Under a series of agreements which the Winchester company had negotiated with various foreign governments, the New Haven firm had secured the exclusive rights to represent the American arms industry in those countries. As a result, if a dealer in China, India or the Straits Settlements (modern day Singapore and Malaysia), wanted an American-made firearm for a customer, he could not order it directly from the manufacturer. Rather, the order had to be processed through Winchester.

Under these exclusivity agreements, Winchester would purchase the arms needed and prepare the bills of lading, acquire the necessary customs documents and arrange shipment, all for a fee charged to the suppliers. In doing so, the Winchester Repeating Arms Company became the largest arms exporter in the United States.

By far, the largest number of arms exported in this manner were shipped to the following firms in the Indian subcontinent:

Army & Navy Co-Operative Society (Bombay, Calcutta, New Delhi and Karachi (Pakistan])
Blackwood & Bryson
Coombes Company Limited
Lancelot Dent & Company
Goolamhoosain & Allibhoy
I. Hollis & Sons
Walter Locke & Company Limited (Calcutta and Lahore)
Lyon & Lyon (Calcutta)
R.B. Rodda & Company (Calcutta)
A. Scott & Company
enkatasubbiah C. R. Chetty
Ward & Herring Company

Smaller quantities were sent to dealers in Britain's African colonies, Korea, Siam and the Straits Settlements, where Winchester also held import rights.

In light of this, it is entirely possible that a Colt listed as having been shipped to Winchester may have seen service in the Indian Hill Country or on the African veldt.

H.G.H.

---

aged to earn more than it had during 1935, and a 10 percent bonus was paid to all employees.

Things progressed normally until 1938, the year Colt's released its conversion kits for the Govt. 45 and .22 Ace. The summer had been unusually wet and muggy, and on September 17, a torrential rain began with flood warnings soon after. The "Big Blow of 1938," now officially classified as a hurricane, caused the Connecticut River to rise dramatically, and winds of more than 100 miles per hour were reported. At 4:10 p.m. on September 18, the clock on top of the old State House stopped, and the entire city of Hartford shut down. Even though Hartford fared much better than the neighboring towns of New Haven and New London during the hurricane, afterwards, the Connecticut River became quite swollen.

With the catastrophe of 1936 still fresh in everyone's minds, volunteers began sandbagging the dike immediately. The army of sandbaggers worked quietly and quickly, with the water rising as fast as they could get sandbags in place. By Friday morning, the dike was only one sandbag in height above the raging river when it crested at 35 feet. This time the workers could declare a victory over the river. The score was now Nature: 1 and Colt's: 2, but Hartford did not want a rematch. A flood commission was established, and $10 million was appropriated to erect a dike 45 feet high.

World War II and the Armory

With conflict raging in Asia and Europe, by 1940 Colt's had begun hiring hundreds of new employees every month in preparation for a potential war, and by April 1941, the work force had doubled, to 5,600. At this time, many of Colt's employees were second and third generation and the old timers were telling the new batch of workers what to expect if war broke out. In the middle of this new wave of war demand, the left wing United Electrical, Radio & Machine Workers of America, CIO, finally unionized Colt's work force. After a week of general unrest and periodic work stoppages, thousands of employees began to walk out of the Armory, many headed for a mass meeting at the Polish National Home. The walkout lasted two days, and on August 7, the Union easily defeated the Independent Arms Craft to became the second largest local in New England.

At the same time, military demands for manpower dramatically reduced the traditional industrial labor pool. Ever-increasing government contracts dictated that Colt's work force had keep pace, and as a result, the newly hired employees included women (4 out of 10 as compared to 1 out of 10 during World War I), the physically handicapped, the deaf, the blind, and the elderly. As Herb Walker from personnel wryly remarked, "If they're warm, we take them." Though there were already a few people of color employed at the Armory, it was at this time that the workforce began to be truly integrated and black employees were for the first time recruited. Gradually, more and more were taken on as laborers and handlers, and several years later, many had already advanced to higher skilled jobs.

Early in 1942, War Production board chairman Donald Nelson proposed that joint labor-management committees be formed to help relieve the now critical labor shortage. During November, all work was stopped briefly so Colt's employees could witness the presentation to president Stone of the "E-Flag" at the state Armory on Broad Street. Colt's was one of the first industries in America to receive the designation, the "E" signaling excellence for outstanding production by both the Army and Navy.

After Pearl Harbor was attacked, the Armory worked three shifts of seven and a half hours each, with every eighth day off. The grueling schedule was bound to result in employee fatigue and excessive absenteeism, as well as substandard quality measured in rejected parts. The schedule was changed to two long shifts on a six-day schedule. During 1940-1942, at the peak of manufacturing supply and demand, Colt's net earnings ranged from $1,368,000 to $2,561,000, despite price reductions and government renegotiations over so-called excess profits. Beginning in July 1943, Colt's was beginning to show a loss every month, which had accumulated to over $3.5 million by late 1944. By January 1944, orders for .50 caliber aircraft machine guns had fallen by 40 percent and in mid-year the electrical division was sold to General Electric. During the beginning of this slowdown, layoffs were inevitable, and in 18 months, Colt's cash surplus had plummeted from $8.3 million to $4.9 million.

While the Armory's machinery had served it well during World War I, by World War II Colt's was behind in technological upgrading, and adopting modern manufacturing techniques. Although nearly $5 million had been invested in the gun division since 1938, the Armory's floors were cluttered with antiquated machinery, some of which dated back to the Colonel and Root. World War II-era government inspectors were astonished to find that in many cases, instead of essential manufacturing data being recorded on blueprints or in operational manuals, the knowledge was only contained in the minds and memories of the aging foremen and craftsmen. Coupled with this was Colt's decades-old practice of inside piecework.

Production levels had never been adjusted upward to reflect the efficiencies of new machinery. Even though some of the machines were fairly new, there had been no increase in productivity due to outdated labor practices.

As a result, Colt's Armory was now inefficient, and paying the price for relatively low output, excessively high costs and continual friction between the work force and management. This condition was illustrated by the fact that while the government had ordered 1,800,000 Govt. .45s from Colt's during World War II, the Armory had been able to deliver only 400,000 pistols, the rest subcontracted to other manufacturers. Furthermore, upstart competitors such as High Standard in New Haven were more than happy to point out Colt's weaknesses to the government. The bottom line is that Colt's had manufactured fewer guns during World War II than it had in the Civil War or World War I, despite a larger work force and more spacious facilities. More important, the United States military had lost confidence in Colt's ability to produce wartime military contracts in a timely manner.

President Stone, now 75, could no longer deal with the Armory's deep-seated problems and the ongoing union controversy. Graham Anthony, a tall, ambitious Southerner who had moved to Connecticut in 1915, agreed to run Colt's for five years, beginning April 6, 1944. Years later, Anthony recalled how he had saved the Armory from disaster.

"They called me there in 1944 – there was a war on, or I wouldn't have gone. I suppose you could say it was in a mess. My first month we did $6 million worth of business and managed to lose $225,000 – something was dreadfully wrong. It's a long story of management and labor relations. I checked and found fantastic payrolls. More than 1,000 men were earning $500 a month or more. I recall one man whose only duty was to swab out machine gun barrels with a greasy rag, once the guns were test fired. He did nothing else. On piecework, in the year 1943, he made $13,600."

Meanwhile, turmoil within the union was increasing, and on his first day of work, President Anthony was confronted by union leaders who insisted that all 16,000 employees would walk out the next day unless Anthony made an immediate decision on various grievances. Anthony's exact words were,

"Tell them to go to hell." The following day, 2,500 workers walked out in protest, despite a no-strike pledge in their contract and without the sanction of union officials. In the following months, many other employees simply left their jobs.

Financially, Colt's had already lost $729,000 for the month, and the total loss was $1,135,000 for the year to date. In dire straits, the company laid off 643 employees and discharged 133 obstructionists on May 20, 1944.

During the week of July 4, as Colt's was prepared to lay off another 10 percent of its greatly reduced work force of 3,000, the Ringling Brothers Barnum & Bailey Circus arrived in Hartford, and set up its large tent on Barbour for an annual spectacular. July 4 had been a warm, summer afternoon, and more than 6,000 spectators were under the Big Top when one of the Flying Walendas spied flames from his high perch above and cried, "The tent's on fire!" The fire, started by a careless cigarette, quickly spread to the oil-soaked canvas, and within minutes, the entire tent was engulfed in flames. In the ten minutes of chaos that ensued, more 139 died, and 225 were seriously burned, many of them Colt's employees.

Obviously, 1944 was not a good year for Colt's, and the Armory was probably especially relieved when peace was declared in May and August 1945. Many of Colt's employees were on vacation during the week of V-J Day, and when they returned to the Armory the following Monday, they discovered that almost everyone had been laid off, since all government contracts had been canceled overnight.

Peacetime and Renewed Poverty

Once again, Colt's was unprepared for peace, and the arms division was completely shut down, with only the dishwasher and plastics divisions operating. A sign of the times and the end of an era occurred in June of 1947 when the original H-shaped West Armory built by the Colonel in 1861, was torn down at an expense of $80,000. During the same year however, Colt's showed its first profit in four years, a modest $149,186, due mostly to the renewed manufacture of its pre-war models, including a redesigned Woodsman .22 caliber target pistol. During the one hundredth anniversary of the Walker pistol, the company name was changed from the century-old "Colt Patent Fire-Arms Manufacturing Company" to "Colt's Manufacturing Company," (hereafter also referred to as Colt's). Meanwhile, Graham Anthony was glad to have reached the end of his five-year agreement, as it seemed fruitless to him to try to revive the ailing Armory. A major change occurred in the board, and the many new stockholders were more interested in turning a quick profit from their investment than in the long-term financial success of the company.

At the annual meeting in April 1949, a return of $100,000 was reported for the previous fiscal year. The board agreed to retire all stock tendered during the month of April 1950 at $52 a share – more than $12 above the market, in exchange for a commitment that the three outside board directors would resign. At this time, there were 195,000 shares outstanding with a total value of $13.4 million, or $68 per share. Of the total, 127,000 shares were tendered, consuming $6.6 million of Colt's surplus. It was a crippling blow, and the timing couldn't have been worse.

The Last Half of the 20th Century

The Korean Conflict, which lasted from 1950-1952, injected some new life into the Armory, but it wasn't enough for a permanent recovery. The government's confidence in Colt's had never fully recovered from the production failures at the end of World War II. Sales for this three-year period totaled $37 million, with profits of $2,278,000. The truce and the resulting cutback in military orders exposed the underlying weaknesses of the Armory. The backlog of defense related work dropped $7 million, and in July 1954, the Ordnance Department terminated almost all of Colt's contracts. Sales fell to $16.7 million, compared to $21.3 million

COLT PRESIDENTS
1855 to present

Samuel Colt	1855-1862
Elisha K. Root	1862-1865
Richard Jarvis	1865-1901
John Hall	1901-1902
Lewis C. Grover	1902-1909
William C. Skinner	1909-1911
Col. Charles L.F. Robinson	1911-1916
William C. Skinner	1916-1921
Samuel M. Stone	1921-1944
Graham H. Anthony	1944-1949
B. Franklin Conner	1949-1955
Chester Bland	1955-1958
Fred A. Roff, Jr.	1958-1962
David C. Scott	1962-1963
Paul A. Benke	1963-1969
William H. Goldbach	1969-1972
David C. Eaton	1972-1976
C. Edward Warner	1976-1981
Gary W. French	1981-1990
Richard F. Gamble	1990-1990
Ronald E. Stilwell	1990-1992
Ronald C. Whitaker	1992-1995
John F. Jastrem	1995-1996
Ronald L. Stewart	1996-1998
Steven M. Sliwa	1998-1999
Lt. Gen. (ret.) William M. Keys	1999-present

the year before, while profits slumped to only $246,670. The work force was cut from 1,864 to 750.

But the most important announcement in 1954 was that the board of directors had decided to forsake the Armory, since it had become too big and expensive for the company's needs, In turn, the board purchased 117 acres of farmland near Hartford's new Bradley International Airport at a cost of $260,000. President Connor's explanation was, "We need a modern, one story building." The only good news was that the new plant layout would retain the old blue dome in a prominent position.

Concurrent with the threat of closing down the Armory, Burton W. Bartlett, treasurer of Bartlett & Brainard, a leading local contracting and construction firm, and Chester Bland, well-known Hartford entrepreneur, had been quietly buying up Colt stock. By August, Bartlett astonished Colt's board by proclaiming that he and Mr. Bland controlled the majority of Colt's stock. Bartlett was immediately elected chairman.

In early 1955, the company once again approached the government for more defense business in order to survive. During this cost-cutting period, chairman Bartlett insisted that he see and approve every company purchase requisition, from tons of steel to tens of paperclips. He had a reputation for calling the company suppliers and continually haggling over prices. Working at Colt's had now become suffocating, and morale dropped to an all-time low, with company stock values dipping to $13 per share with no dividend paid.

Spread over its 16 acres, the Armory's 20 buildings now looked almost deserted, even though nine other firms had rented space. The main office was leased to Pratt & Whitney Aircraft, and for a while, there was no more talk about building a new one-story plant in Windsor Locks. Each new month added to the mounting deficit, and the arrival of a financial savior seemed improbable during this grim time.

An Unwanted Buyout

Out of the doom appeared a Mr. Leopold D. Silberstein, whom newsmagazines had dubbed a "corporate fisherman." Having fled from the Nazis in 1933, first to Holland and then to England, Silberstein arrived in New York after the war, bringing with him about $150,000 for corporate bargain hunting. Within four years, his fast and furious financial transactions had enabled him to acquire a dozen companies worth $50 million for only $1 million in down payments, all incorporated under one holding company called Penn-Texas.

Shortly thereafter, Silberstein sought to control Pratt & Whitney, much bigger than all of Penn-Texas. Resisting the unwanted takeover, Pratt & Whitney put up a valiant fight, but in the end, Silberstein owned 520,000 of Pratt & Whitney's 868,000 available shares. It had cost Silberstein $8 million in hard cash to acquire Hartford's largest industrial concern at the time.

Colt directors saw Silberstein as a potential bridegroom, and if nothing else, he could keep the Armory afloat, now with only $1 million in cash reserves. By the end of September, the Armory joined Pratt & Whitney as a Penn-Texas subsidiary, exactly a hundred years after the incorporation of the company by Samuel Colt. The following month, Silberstein put in a new slate of officers and directors, and Sidney Stewart, the general manager of the lucrative Chandler-Evans division of Pratt & Whitney, succeeded Bland as president. Stewart, saw himself as a transition president and troubleshooter and tried to straighten out the already large mess created by his two immediate predecessors. Production was now in a shambles; semi-finished parts were being moved from floor to floor and building to building, up and down, and back and forth. There was almost no production control, and the sales department had virtually no personnel.

Colt's Manufacturing Company stock certificate. 1955.
Robert B. Hartman Collection.

Even though Colt's name was still alive, the Armory had sold its soul to an outside interest. Perhaps the crowning indignity was when Silberstein decided to give away the entire Colt collection of firearms, going all the way back to 1836. He gave the entire collection to the Connecticut State Library. Some doubted his sincerity and suspected his real motivation was to take advantage of a hefty tax deduction.

Continuing his corporate pillaging, Silberstein's next victim was the Fairbanks-Morse Company of Chicago, manufacturers of diesel engines, pumps, and scales. Even though Silberstein tried to take control twice, he was rebuffed each time. Finally, Morse mounted a counterattack, and with the help of a pugnacious Washington attorney named Alfons Landa, Penn-Texas was turned away and Silberstein had agreed to sell back 300,000 shares and make no further effort to gain control. By the end of the year, the Penn-Texas empire was crumbling, and its leader had to sell off six of its subsidiaries to pay its debts. His stock price had dropped from $22 to $4 per share. Colt's ownership now was in the hands of Fairbanks-Whitney, a holding company that included what was left of Penn-Texas.

The Reintroduced SAA and Factory Commemoratives

While it didn't create a big splash at the time, the original Single Action Army Model, not produced since 1940, was reintroduced during 1956, at a price of $125. By 1960, more than 33,000 had been manufactured, and once again, the world's most recognizable revolver was available. Every outgoing United States president since Ulysses Grant has received a Peacemaker revolver. The SAA has been in production ever since, and is now a field of collecting unto itself, with prices ranging from $600 to over $300,000.

In 1961, Colt's released the first in what was to be a long lineup of commemorative firearms – the 1961 Geneseo, Illinois 125th Anniversary Derringer. This new firearm marketing concept was the brainchild of Robert E. Cherry of Cherry's Sporting Goods in Geneseo, IL. A World War II radio operator/gunner on a B-25 armed with a 75 mm cannon and machine guns, Cherry was now an experienced and savvy firearms dealer. When asked in the mid-1990s if he had thought the commemorative industry would achieve such huge success, Cherry simply replied, "Yes" and smiled. Over the next three decades, Colt's manufactured thousands of factory commemoratives in various configurations, in addition to subcontracting special/limited edition firearms for different organizations, groups, distributors, and events.

Colt's AR-15/M-16 Production and the War in Southeast Asia

In 1960, Americans elected John F. Kennedy over Richard Nixon by less than half of one percent of votes cast. Once again, there was a new blip on the world's major conflict radar screen. In Vietnam, the United States had begun taking steps to impede Communist raids into both South Vietnam and Thailand.

During this time, other companies like the non-gun TRW, were trying to find ways to cut manufacturing costs while chasing the lucrative military contract for the United States-backed M-14 rifle. Colt's had decided to stake its future on another recent design – the new assault rifle AR-15, originally invented by Eugene Stoner for the Armalite division of Fairchild Engine and Airplane Corporation, even though the American military did not appear to be interested. Colt's soon acquired the exclusive manufacturing and patent rights for this new lightweight, low recoil rifle, which would come to be labeled "the world's deadliest weapon."

Combining the light weight of a submachine gun and the accuracy of a sniper's rifle with the firepower of a machine gun, the AR-15 fired over 700 rounds per minute, compared with 500-600 rounds per minute for the Browning Automatic Rifle and 400-500 for the Army's .30 caliber light machine gun. Amazingly, it used only .223 caliber ammunition but its muzzle velocity made up for its size in destructive power. It disproved the old concept that the bigger the bullet, the greater the killing effectiveness. Loaded, it weighed only seven pounds, compared with 19.4 pounds for the long-range BAR, ten pounds for the M-1 and M-14 rifles, and a bit over five pounds for the .30 caliber M-1 Army carbine.

The United States Air Force soon expressed an interest in this new rifle, considering the AR-15 rifle as a possible replacement for the .30 cal. M-1 carbine carried by airborne troops in Vietnam. By the end of 1963, the Air Force placed an order for more than 25,000 rifles, now given the military designation M-16. The Army however, was reluctant to abandon many years of frustrated development and delayed production of the M-14, in addition to thinking the smaller .223 caliber was too small, the accuracy poor, and the mechanism prone to jamming. In 1962, the Army told Congress that it would stick with the M-14. Claiming major modifications in the design, Army Ordnance officers reversed their decision only a year later, stating they were interested in the capacity of the M-16 for air assault and guerilla fighting. It was Colt's first military contract in nine years, company morale was at a post-war high, and everyone was ready to forget about the company's despondent period of the 1950s.

With Army acceptance, the military contracts started rolling in. Large capacity manufacturing was once again the major issue, no different than during the three previous major conflicts – the Civil War, World War I and World War II.

Anticipating an Army contract, employment had been increased in 1963 from 600 to 850, and at the end of the year, Colt's reported a loss of nearly $1 million. In May of 1964, the parent company was reconstituted, and the result was a name change to "Colt Industries." Determined not to fail during this critical time of potential high production, a top new management team consisting of George Strichman and David Margolis, previously from IT&T, were brought in. During this time, Colt's president, Fred A. Roff, Jr. resigned for personal reasons, and David C. Scott, a General Electric executive, became Strichman's choice as the new interim president. Later that year, Scott would select Paul Benke as the new president.

The conflict in Southeast Asia escalated into a full-blown war, completely supported by the United States military and new president Lyndon Johnson, following the assassination of President Kennedy the previous November. The M-16 rifle was already making a reputation for itself in the wet combat conditions of Vietnam. Army contracts were coming in at an almost alarming rate, and a move to the 200,000-square-foot Knudsen building was set for the first quarter of 1965.

A seemingly small and minor international military affair was turning out to be a long, grueling, and unpopular war in the United States. More and more soldiers were drafted and since most of them left the country with an M-16 rifle, production was once again at maximum at Colt's. During 1964, sales totaled $171.7 million, with profits of $3.6 million. In 1965, two years after the first Army contract, General William C. Westmoreland urgently requested that all of his troops in Vietnam be equipped with the M-16 rifle. During June of 1966, the Army ordered 403,905 additional rifles at a price of slightly above $110 each. Employment was now at 1,600, and 700 were working only on the M-16 contracts. At the end of 1967, Colt M-16 orders had totaled almost one million guns.

Reminiscent of the end of World War II, Colt's employees held a five-week strike during the summer of 1967 after a wage dispute, holding up M-16 deliveries. Once again, the military became distrustful of Colt's ability to produce, and was a looking for a scapegoat. Congress now became furious, and ordered a House Armed Service Subcommittee investigation, which quickly criticized the Army's "unbelievable" mismanagement of the M-16 program.

By 1968, bloated with the profits of expedited military contracts, sales had gone to an off the charts high of $663,900,000, with profits of $20.8 million. During this unprecedented time of military manufacture, Bill Goldbach, formerly of TRW and famous for lowering the cost of mass production, was the production czar. During his tenure, Colt's reached a production of 50,000 M-16 rifles per month. Also of note is Colt's purchase of 24 acres in Rocky Hill, south of Hartford, and the construction a one-story plant totaling 89,000 square feet. Colt's also leased 40,000 additional square feet in the West Hartford complex, where all M-16 rifles were assembled. Somewhere, once again, Samuel Colt was smiling, and probably smoking a big cigar.

Even though Colt's extraordinary recovery between 1963 and 1969 seemed almost a miracle, not everything had gone perfectly. In the jungles of Southeast Asia, where more than 500,000 American troops were stationed, complaints abounded of the M-16 rifle jamming. These performance complaints were actually due to poor field maintenance, humid jungle conditions, and some ammunition problems. The Army finally concluded that no fault could be found with the gun's basic design or quality, and "the principle cause of the difficulty in Vietnam was inadequate maintenance." After the problems had been resolved, Colt's responded by chrome plating the barrels and beefing up the buffer assemblies.

As the war ground on, Colt's once again came under attack in the fall of 1971. Based on the affidavits of several Colt's employees, The Connecticut Citizens Action Group accused the company of cheating on government quality control tests by hiding malfunctions and performing illegal repairs. Additionally, it had been proven that between 1967 and 1971, that over 60 M-16 rifles had been stolen, and Colt's export manager was indicted for selling more than 2,000 M-16 rifles to a South African arms dealer between 1972 and 1975. As the war began winding down in 1972, Goldbach left Colt's.

Since the military M-16 contracts had almost come to an end, Colt's again had too much overhead and too few orders. David Eaton became the new president, and immediately, a plant-wide retooling was undertaken to diversify into more sporting arms. It was a needed maneuver, since during Vietnam, the company had concentrated most of its efforts and manufacturing capability on the military M-16 contracts. Since the disastrous 1950s, Colt's handguns had lost market share to Smith & Wesson, now the dominant supplier in law enforcement equipment. Only the venerable Colt Government Model was still popular, now improved and renamed the Mark IV. As had happened many times over the past century, Colt's was once again scrambling for profits after another amazing recovery.

COLT HISTORIANS

1957 to 1972 - Ron Wagner

1972 to 1993 - Marty Huber

1993 to present - Kathleen Hoyt

The Bicentennial and New Custom Shop

During 1971, due to increasing demand created by historical interest and reenactment groups and organizations preparing for America's upcoming bicentennial, Colt's began producing its "Authentic Blackpowder Series" of replicas and reproductions, including replicas of those revolvers manufactured between 1847 and 1873. All cap and ball guns were made using the older designs and specifications, but with improved metallurgy and modern production techniques.

In 1976, Colt's officially launched its Custom Shop in response to consumer requests for special orders, custom features, engraving and ornamentation, and individual personalization, mostly for the re-released SAA revolver. As a result, almost any combination of finishes, engraving patterns and options, grip choices, and barrel lengths could be custom ordered. This new division immediately became popular, and since, the Custom Shop has turned out thousands of specially created firearms, many of which have become quite collectible. Supervised by Al DeJohn, a Colt veteran of over 40 years, the Custom Shop craftsman were soon back-ordered. By 1978, the Tiffany Single Action revolver was created, gold inlaid with gold and silver Tiffany-style grips and elaborate gold and silver vermeil case by Tiffany & Company. The 150th Anniversary of the Patent Firearms Manufacturing Company occurred in 1986, and for the occasion, a single revolver was made. This Special 150th Anniversary Exhibition Revolver from the Custom Shop was sold for $150,000 at a Las Vegas auction.

Colt's and The New Military Handgun Contract

Colt's was hurt by management shortsightedness during the early 1980s when the United States Department of Defense ordered the first tests for a new service pistol. It would be in 9mm caliber (originally designed by the German military in 1908), the official NATO handgun cartridge. Dr. Ugo Beretta, Beretta's Italian president, and Bob Bonaventure originally approached Colt's in early 1984, with the idea of pooling their resources – Beretta's proven design, Colt's name, and a subcontract for American manufacture. However, Colt's believed that since the Model 1911/1911A1 had been the Army's official sidearm for more than 70 years, Colt's could circumvent the upcoming military trials for a new military sidearm in 9mm caliber by refitting all existing .45s, altering them into 9mm pistols. The reception at Colt's had been a cool one, and the Beretta delegation left without an agreement, or even a hint of cooperation.

The XM9-Service pistol trials finally began in 1984, and the Army tested the Smith & Wesson M459A, Beretta Model 92SB-F, SIG-Sauer Model P226, Heckler & Koch Model P7, Walther Model P88, Steyr Model GB, and Fabrique Nationale's Browning Model ADA and Colt's Model SSP. After the smoke had settled, Beretta emerged as the

Army's choice, but an official announcement was delayed because of lawsuits brought forward by Smith & Wesson and Heckler & Koch. Both firms claimed they had been unfairly eliminated from the competition, and demanded a new trial.

On September 1, 1988, a competition was once again conducted, and only two other companies besides Beretta decided to compete in the new XM10 Army trial - Smith & Wesson and Sturm, Ruger & Co. Once again, the Beretta 92SB-F was determined to be the clear winner, and the firm was awarded an Army contract in May, 1989, for almost 57,000 M9 pistols (new military designation), worth $9.9 million. Additionally, Beretta USA was awarded other military contracts resulting in over 430,000 M9 pistols being manufactured for all branches of the United States military between 1986 and 1999.

Colt's was unable to bring its own 9mm caliber double action pistol to market. While Colt's finally released its double action Double Eagle Series 90 pistol during 1990, it's design was not well-regarded and it came too late. An Italian-designed pistol succeeded in winning the contract to supply pistols to the United States Armed Forces.

More Union and Financial Woes

By the end of 1977, 300 of Colt's 1,400 employees were laid off due to the cessation of M-16 military contracts, and in the spring of 1978, the Rocky Hill facility was shut down, with most of the employees transferred to West Hartford.

In 1982, the firearms division of Colt Industries occupied only a small portion of the once -great Armory complex, now starting to show its age, and looking worn and unkempt. All manufacturing and offices had been moved to West Hartford, except for the production of the M-16 rifle.

Colt's employee troubles once again flared up in March of 1985, when the union rejected the final proposal for a new contract. Still, employees remained on the job, mostly out of fear that a move outside the city was pending. Even though the city and state offered $1.8 million for the renovation of the Armory, Colt's eventually turned the help down. Rank and file employees had become unhappy, objecting to what they considered harsh discipline, and refused to work overtime. Finally, on January 25, 1986, the UAW walked out, and the longest, most bitter strike in Connecticut's industrial history had begun. Picket lines surrounded the entrances to both plants, demonstrations and police altercations were frequent, and several strikers were arrested. While management accused the strikers of setting fires, sabotaging machinery and other acts of violence, the company remained open by hiring hundreds of untrained replacements. The situation worsened until early 1987, when the union urged Connecticut's legislators and congressional delegation to demand an end to Colt's military contracts.

Even though Colt's had been the only supplier of M-16 rifles since 1963, the Army had been down this road before with Colt's labor problems during World War II. No doubt more than a little concerned, the Army announced in October, 1988, that a Fabrique Nationale subsidiary, located in Columbia, South Carolina, would be awarded the $112 million contract for the M-16A2 rifles. The Army insisted that its decision had not been influenced by Colt's strike or its product quality, but rather was based solely on price - $420 per rifle, compared to Colt's $477.50.

By April of 1989, Colt Industries had had enough, and put the Firearms Division up for sale despite its profitability, reported to be $20-$50 million annually. The decision to sell quickly sparked the formation of a coalition of private investors, whose goal was to keep Colt's in the State of Connecticut. In an agreement signed on March 22, 1990, C.F. Holdings Corp. purchased the assets of the Firearms Division for approximately $75 million. On or around this date, CFPI Inc, a Colt Industries affiliate, transferred ownership to the Colt intellectual property ultimately to CF Intellectual Property Limited. At this time, a new company called Colt's Manufacturing Company, Inc., that was a wholly owned subsidiary of C.F. Holding Corp., became the operating company to run the firearms business. It was a complicated financial arrangement, that involved two foreign banks and $25 million from Connecticut's state pension fund (a 64 percent interest). Also as part of the deal, the company agreed to pay $13 million in back wages to the strikers, because of labor law violations. It was the largest settlement of its time in the history of the National Labor Relations Board.

Almost exactly two years later, the now cash-strapped company filed for bankruptcy, jeopardizing the future of 925 employees and the $25 million state investment. For weeks, potential major lenders and investors had been meeting frequently in an effort to solve the company's financial woes, and finally, the Connecticut Department of Economic Development came through with a $3 million line of credit. Austria's Creditanstalt also cooperated by advancing $7 million. President Ron Stilwell was elated with the new financial breathing room.

Colt products have embedded themselves in the American culture and language, ranging far from their origins. This colorful label adorned a fruit box.
Karen Green Collection.

At about the same time, the state had almost failed in putting together a package of public and private incentives to keep U.S. Repeating Arms, the maker of Winchester rifles and shotguns, from pulling out of New Haven. Smith & Wesson turned to England, where Tompkins LLC agreed to underwrite Smith & Wesson's return to the handgun marketplace.

Spending two years in federal bankruptcy court, Colt's creditors and investors, supported by a legion of attorneys (fees finally totaled $6.4 million) fought over the terms of a settlement that would facilitate recovery. Unsecured creditors were owed $7 million, and Connecticut's $25 million initial investment had melted down to only $10 million.

During 1993, an attempt was made for refinancing by Greenwich multimillionaire William R. Berkley and the state of Connecticut. Berkley backed out, partly due to the difficulty of reacquiring the rights to the Colt name. The collapse of these negotiations resulted in the loss of a $40 million sale of M-16 rifles to the Dutch government. "We're damaged goods," moaned new president Ronald C. Whitaker.

Getting Bailed Out Again

Finally in the spring of 1994, a new group of potential buyers emerged with stronger ties to Connecticut. Merchant bankers Zilkha & Co. had been initially courted by the Connecticut Development Authority. On September 28, 1994, an agreement had been signed which provided senior secured debt from $17.5 million, $10 million for the unrestricted use of the Colt name, and unsecured creditor claims of $3.6 million. Whitaker wasted no time in making cuts where needed, and stated, "Mismanagement, not the union, was killing us." Within 75 days, he had removed 25 percent of the salaried workforce.

During this most recent financial transition period, the new Colt .22 target pistol was released, and an $11 million U.S. contract for 24,000 of the new M-4A1 carbines was secured. During mid-year, the last of the gun operations ended in the original Armory after 147 years of production, not to mention blood, sweat, and tears. Somewhere, Samuel Colt was sadly shaking his head.

Colt's Ushers in the New Millennium

In the five years leading up to the new millennium, Colt's changed presidents more often than at any time in its history. In addition, the company discontinued many models that were not selling well. Its product lineup during the last half of the century was the slimmest it had ever been. In late 1999, Colt's discontinued many of its consumer handguns, and during October, the announcement was made to discontinue all double action revolvers, including Custom Shop offerings. Consumer AR-15 rifles production remained, even though the Crime Bill of 1994, with its paramilitary concessions, lowered the demand. The Custom Shop meanwhile, continued to stay busy, its highlight an annual auction at Colt Collectors Association (CCA) show, where an elaborately engraved and inlaid handgun (usually a SAA) is sold.

Its rich and colorful history is part of the legacy of Colt. While the past has certainly revealed Colt's strengths and weaknesses, the company's future will depend on how well it can fit in to today's changing commercial and military marketplaces.

Colt's employees are continuing the legacy of Samuel Colt.

Meanwhile, Colt's Historical Department has been extremely busy providing valuable information to collectors on the original configuration of Colt models going all the way back to 1861. This factory information, including watermarked letters, is provided for a fee, and has become a quality service for Colt aficionados worldwide. Kathleen Hoyt, Colt's current historian since 1993, describes the evolution of the Historical Department:

"When I first came into the department we were kind of tucked away doing the letter thing and some public relations work but not really connected to the main body of Colt. Beginning with the sale of the company in 1990 and continuing with the sale in 1994 an appreciation of the history of Colt and the preservation of the legacy has been a main focus of the new company. In light of this, the potential of the Archive Department to be involved as a main contributor has been realized. So I would have to say that during my tenure as Historian the most significant change in the job would be the evolution of the department into an integral part of the mainstream business of Colt."

Colt's is one of America's oldest and best-known industrial concerns. Its survival and success in the coming decades will depend upon how accurately the company assesses the constantly changing firearms marketplace, develops products for consumer demand, and how well it can meet the military's changing needs with new designs and configurations. Members of the Colt Collectors Association hope that the collection of Colt's firearms pictured in this text and represented during this special exhibition at the Cody Firearms Museum will be augmented with new designs and models in the future.

Somewhere, the flamboyant Colonel Samuel Colt is smiling on this commemoration.

In late 2002, Colt's transferred its military rifle business to Colt Defense LLC, while Colt's continues with its handgun business. The current President and CEO of both companies, LTGEN Wm. M. Keys, USMC (ret.), has made the following statement regarding the future and longevity of the Colt companies.

Introduction to the New Millennium by LTGEN Wm. M. Keys, USMC (ret.)

"Colt has entered the new millennium bringing with it our heritage of quality craftsmanship and service to all our customers. While the emphasis of our businesses have shifted more towards providing the U.S. Armed Forces and our allies with the M4 carbine and M16 rifle, we still have not forgotten about the handgun side of our business that started the process of "Colt" becoming one of the best known trademarks in the world today. Since September 11, Colt's sales to military and law enforcement organizations have been our top priority. Colt's relationship with the U.S. Government goes back to Colonel Samuel Walker and the Mexican American war where Samuel Colt first introduced the Walker blackpowder revolver. It grew stronger over the years with the introduction of Browning family of automatic weapons and 1911 frame pistol. Both of which still exist today."

"Even with this heavy military emphasis, our handgun business continues to manufacture the handguns that have become the standard of which all other handguns are measured. Python, Gold Cup, Government Model and Single Action Army are still being produced today, as well as reproductions of the M1911A1 and Series 70 product line. Colt recently teamed with Gunsite Training Academy to design and produce a handgun that is truly a "shooter's" firearm that brings to market another contribution to Colt's legacy of producing superior 1911 frame pistols. Our objective has been to produce our product lines to the same exacting quality standards as in the past, using the most advanced technological systems available today. Starting in 1836, no other firearm manufacturer has earned greater fame or recognition than Colt. In design as well as performance, the Colt's companies each strive to give to the customer a firearm that is known to be the finest in the world."

About the Author

S.P. Fjestad is the author & publisher of the *Blue Book of Gun Values*, now in its 24th Edition, with over one million copies in print worldwide. He is also the publisher of the 2nd Edition *The Book of Colt Firearms* by R.L. Wilson, and *Colt Blackpowder Reproductions & Replicas* by Dennis Adler. Additionally, Mr. Fjestad has written many articles that have been published in *American Rifleman, Outdoor Life, Guns & Ammo, Sports Afield, Shooting Sportsman*, and many other magazines and publications. Mr. Fjestad is a longtime Colt Collectors Association member, and has acquired more than a few Colts in his collection.

Sources and Additional Reading

Adler, Dennis, *Blue Book of Modern Black Powder Values*, Minneapolis, MN: Blue Book Publications, Inc., 2002.

Adler, Dennis, *Colt Blackpowder Reproductions & Replicas*, Minneapolis, MN: Blue Book Publications, Inc., 1998.

Armsmear – The Samuel Colt Biography. Palm Springs, CA: Beinfeld Publishing, 1976.

Boorman, Dean K., *The History of Colt Firearms*. New York, NY: Lyons Press, 2001.

Cary, Lucian, *The Colt Gun Book*. New York, NY: Arco Publishing Company, Inc., 1961.

Edwards, William B., *The Story of Colt's Revolver*. New York, NY: Castle Books, 1957.

Fjestad, S.P., *Blue Book of Gun Values*, 23rd Edition. Minneapolis, MN: Blue Book Publications, Inc., 2002.

Grant, Ellsworth S., *The Colt Legacy – The Colt Armory in Hartford, 1855-1980*. Providence, RI: Mowbray Company, 1982 (usage includes multiple quotations, paraphrasing, and historical information/facts.)

Grant, Ellsworth S., *The Colt Armory – A History of Colt's Manufacturing Company, Inc.,* Lincoln, RI: Mowbray Company, 1995 (usage includes multiple quotations, paraphrasing, and historical information/facts.)

Haven, Charles T. and Frank Belden, *A History of the Colt Revolver*. Fairfax, VA: National Rifle Association, 1997.

Hosley, William, *Colt – The Making of an American Legend*. Amherst, MA: University of Massachusetts Press, 1996.

Kirkland, K.D., *America's Premier Gunmakers – Colt*. New York, NY: Exeter Books, 1988.

Millennium Year by Year, London, England, DK Publishing: 1999.

Mitchell, James L., *Colt – The Man, the Arms, the Company*. Harrisburg, PA: The Telegraph Press, 1959.

Rohan, Jack, *Yankee Arms Maker – The Story of Samuel Colt and his Six-shot Peacemaker*, revised edition. New York, NY: Harper & Brothers, 1948.

Rosa, Joseph G., *Colonel Colt London – The History of Colt's London Firearms, 1851-1857*. Stoney Creek, Ontario: Fortress Publications, Inc., 1976.

Wilson, R.L., 2nd Ed. *The Book of Colt Firearms*. Minneapolis, MN: Blue Book Publications, Inc., 1993 (usage includes an upgraded chapter of the Historical Outline of the Colt Firearms Company, multiple quotations, paraphrasing, and historical information/facts.)

Wilson, R.L., *The Colt Engraving Book, Volume One*. New York, NY: Bannerman's, 2000.

Wilson, R.L., *The Colt Engraving Book, Volume Two*. New York, NY: Bannerman's, 2001.

Wilson, R.L., *The Colt Heritage*. New York, NY: Simon and Schuster, 1979.

Wilson, R.L., *The Rampant Colt – The Story of a Trademark*. Spencer, IN: Thomas Haas, 1969.

Wilson, R.L., *Samuel Colt Presents*. Hartford, CT: Wadsworth Athenaeum, 1962.

Wilson, R.L., *The World of Beretta – An International Legend*. New York, NY: Random House, Inc., 2000.

Samuel Colt's Revolutionary Industrial Workplace

Maryanne S. Andrus

Samuel Colt's name is indelibly linked with the revolver that bears his name. He is less remembered for the contributions he made to America's Industrial Revolution, yet Colt was a pioneer in employee relations and in what became known worldwide as the American system of manufactures.

Upon independence from England, the economy of the United States was overwhelmingly agricultural. There was little capital available for investment. Roads were largely unimproved, and transportation was difficult and mostly local. Nearly all of the commerce among the states occurred along the long Atlantic seacoast, and the port cities from Boston in the north to Savannah in the south handled more trade with European than with American markets. Most manufactured goods were imported, and the production of even such basic needs as cloth was limited to farm homes and small urban workshops. But a second American Revolution was on the horizon, and it would transform the United States in only a few generations into an industrial and commercial rival of England and Europe.

Woodcut engraving by Nathaniel Orr. Herbert Houze Collection

The spur to America's industrial revolution was the manufacturing partnership established on the banks of the Blackstone River at Pawtucket, Rhode Island, in 1790. With the backing of commercial giant Moses Brown, a recently arrived English immigrant knowledgeable in the intricacies of spinning machinery, Samuel Slater, built the first water-powered textile mill in America. Within a year, George Washington's Secretary of the Treasury, Alexander Hamilton, issued his Report on Manufactures, a survey of American industry with recommendations for protective tariffs and other federal encouragement of manufacturing. Though Hamilton would not see his entire agenda adopted, his efforts to organize a national banking system bore fruit, and American capital became available for investment in technology, in manufacturing, and in the building of canals, steamboats, railroads, and other improvements in transportation. Through immigration and a high birth rate, the nation's population more than tripled by 1830 to 12,866,000, adding not only to the available workforce but also creating markets for manufactured goods.

England unwittingly contributed to the early development of American manufacturing. Beginning in 1805, during the Napoleonic Wars, its interference with American shipping provoked Congress and President Thomas Jefferson to retaliate with the Non-Importation (1805) and Embargo (1807) Acts. While merchants in the northern states and exporters in the southern states suffered from the interruption in trade, a scarcity of British and French manufactured goods gave impetus to home-grown industry.

Meanwhile, with no entrenched commercial or labor opposition to innovation, the United States became fertile ground for invention both in technology and in the implementation of new means of production. In 1790 inventor Oliver Evans built a grist mill in Delaware in which each step in the flour-making process was performed by machines, in sequence. The system was later adapted to other factories and other goods resulting eventually in assembly-line mass production. Eli Whitney in 1793 invented the cotton gin allowing for the rapid removal of seeds from short-staple cotton. In 1792 the South had exported only 150,000 pounds of cotton. By 1800 exports of cotton had boomed to 17,000,000 pounds. In 1798, a government contract to build muskets led Whitney to adapt European experiments in precision tooling to the manufacture of interchangeable parts for gun locks. Precision and interchangeability were concepts readily seized upon by other American manufacturers, especially in the development of the machine industry itself, another innovation in which factories produced tools, dies, and production machinery for other industrial applications.

Other inventions similarly revolutionized other industries. In 1834 Cyrus McCormick patented the first practical grain reaper. In 1837 John Deere invented a plow with steel plowshare and moldboard. Elias Howe in 1846 patented the sewing machine. In 1844 Samuel F. B. Morse transmitted the famous phrase, "What hath God wrought" by Morse Code on a telegraph wire between Baltimore and Washington, D.C.

The organization of factories underwent a similar revolution in ingenuity. In Massachusetts in 1814, Francis Cabot Lowell, who had perfected a power loom, built a factory integrating all the steps necessary to turn raw cotton into cloth.

Lowell and his successors created a virtual company town to house the factory workers, mostly girls and young women from the rural countryside, in a paternalistic boarding-house system that governed virtually all aspects of their work and leisure time. Elsewhere in New England and the northeast, factories began to produce clocks, shoes, tools, and other goods that once had been the province of craftsmen.

One of the last production innovations that would come to define the American system of manufactures was an extension of Eli Whitney's efforts in large-scale gun-making. At United States armories in Springfield, Massachusetts, and Harper's Ferry, Virginia, assembly line demands led to the specialization of labor. At Harper's Ferry in 1807, for instance, workers were each assigned one of the twenty-one separate procedures in the making of a musket lock.

By 1851, when Queen Victoria and Prince Albert opened their Great Exhibition at the Crystal Palace in London and invited the world to display its industrial wares, the United States was ready. American inventions caught the attention of Europeans, but it was American methods that inspired the most admiration, especially the means of mass production: mechanization, organization of materials and production, quality control, and division of labor. Nothing impressed the British more than Samuel Colt's Navy Revolver, notable not only for its quality but also for its having been mass-produced for sale at just $21. Colt helped show that the United States had come of age as an industrial power only 75 years after proclaiming its independence. His triumph was such that Colt was induced to build a factory in England.

Within two years the British government had sent a delegation to its former colonies to study the American system of production. At Hartford they would find a plant where Samuel Colt was still making changes to improve the means of production as well as the climate of productivity. Colt was building his third Hartford factory, one in which not only the technology and the organization of the manufacturing process would place it among the most advanced in the world, but one in which the organization of the work force would assume the dimensions of a social experiment.

Building upon the technological innovations and industrial techniques of others, Samuel Colt had shrewdly incorporated every proven feature of modernization to ensure the successful manufacture of his gem - the repeating firearm. For instance, Colt had witnessed the use of the dangerous and cumbersome revolving flintlock firearm in use, but he improved the cylinder and adapted it to the newly perfected percussion cap ignition system, patenting the new revolver in the U.S. and abroad in 1835 and 1836.[1] Then, never content to leave the operation and production of these arms to chance or another man's vision, Colt sought to undertake every aspect of manufacturing. In the early, tenuous years of production, he was fund raiser, inventor, salesman, and production manager. Once ensconced in his long-dreamed-of Hartford factory, Colt broke with the "status quo" of 19th century employment conditions and added his own unique and dynamic form of management to the factory system.

Against the backdrop of American manufacturing, it is clear that in some ways Samuel Colt set out to build a company that mirrored his own personality and values. He embedded his unique philosophies and discipline into his employees' work life. In other ways, his dictates for "acceptable" work habits mirrored his Yankee upbringing. Hartford's past had not traditionally centered on industrialism but instead wore an aura of gentility associated with its position as state capital. Hartford's old guard was characterized by a strong resistance to change.[2] In sharp contrast, Samuel Colt was not conforming; consequently, the establishment of Hartford disliked him as "a rowdy, pushing youngster."[3] Samuel had the final word in the ongoing clash: his factory was permanent, a noted landmark of Hartford.

In this setting of traditional "blue blood" gentility, Colt and a few of his competitors sought to create work environments that were modern and efficient, dispelling the quaint ways of the past. In his unique innovations for employee comfort - and ultimately for the most efficient work force-Samuel outdistanced all of his competitors. He was a man driven to achieve, who personified the Yankee penchant for hard work. His father-in-law described his conformity to this most recognizable "Yankee" trait. Rev. Jarvis said, "Samuel Colt is without exception the hardest working man that I know of. He works from 5 or 6 o'clock in the morning until 7 or 8 o'clock in the evening and it seems that the more he has to do, the more he enjoys himself."[4] This was a lifelong pattern that he followed through temporary failures and monumental success.

Samuel Colt did not live to see his beloved factory destroyed by fire in 1864. His widow rebuilt it on the same site.
Colt's Manufacturing Company, Inc.

As he pushed himself, so he pushed his workers. Colt was fair, yet very demanding of his employees. He hired the most qualified experts he could find, largely respected his employees and was generally liked in return. He strictly laid out his standards for successful employment and then stuck by his ideas tenaciously. One announcement read: "Every man employed in or about my armoury whether by piecewirk or by days wirk is expected to wirk ten hours during the runing of the engine & no one who dose not chearfully concent to du this need expect to be employed by me. [sic] Samuel Colt. Hartford, March 12, 1856."[5] The employee who was late to his workstation at the Colt factory learned the dour, stubborn side of Samuel Colt very quickly. "Tardiness he looked upon as a cardinal sin. Any laggard not inside within a minute of the clanging of the steam gong at seven o'clock in the morning found himself locked out until noon."[6] The hard-driven work ethic that typified the 19th century New England Northeast was clearly forged and polished in factories like Colt's.

Samuel Colt was an uncompromising individual, as stubborn and unflagging in pursuit of his vision as any son of the Yankee North. Except for his inclination for continuous work, he broke with almost every conforming social more that New Englanders held dear. "To many, his brash nature and new-fangled ideas made him seem an outsider - a wild frontiersman rather than a sensible Yankee."[7] His life is an illustrative study of unconventional vision and ruthless ambition pitted against the restraints of a culturally conservative community. One side of his stubborn individualism is seen in his driving ascent to the heights of capitalism. In apparent defiance of Hartford's Puritan distaste for ostentation, Colt installed on top of his factory an

> "elaborate, onion-shaped blue dome, supported by columns and crowned by a golden sphere on which perched a rampant colt holding a broken spear. Colt was inspired by the Byzantine churches he saw in Russia…and wanted the Armory seen and admired by everyone. What better way to shake up the stagnant traditions, which he felt stultified the city and at the same time to attract the attention and wonderment of steamboat passengers on the Connecticut River." [8]

Historian Jack Rohan agreed, stating: "He wanted to be able to feast his eyes on the creation of his brain and hands whenever the mood was on him; to point out to his guests the industrial dukedom of which he was the overlord."[9] The trappings of wealth were, for Samuel Colt, a testament to his vision and hard work and a repudiation of the ill will that some city fathers held for him.

From 1851-1855, the building of the Armory itself, on swampy meadowland along the Connecticut River, defied the city fathers' pessimistic view that his buildings would wash away with the spring floods. Inspired by the Dutch system of dikes, Colt's nephew, architect H.A.G. Pomeroy, designed and built two miles of embankment that defended over 200 acres from the river waters. French osier willows planted along the top of the earthen dam capped the two-year reclamation project. The mature root system of the willows held the edifice fast.[10] Within the shelter of the dike, Samuel built his long-envisioned empire, described in 1856 as "second to none in the extent and success of its operations. Now, the estimated value of buildings and machinery forming his establishment is about $1,000,000 with nearly 500 men employed." [11]

In fact, Colt had built nothing less than the largest armory in the world.

During its long history, the Colt company has made forays into manufacturing items with no connection to firearms. The so-called "Colt Rock" line of hard plastics included electrical plugs and switches and tobacco-related items.

As he built his complex of factory and the mansion he grandly named "Armsmear," Colt went to great lengths to ensure that his employees were working in the most efficient and comfortably effective environment that he could create. "There are about fifty dwellings, mostly occupied by workmen. The whole are erected on a tract of land embracing 150 acres, formerly inundated by the Connecticut River."[12] He wanted employees to live close to their work site, in well built, convenient housing; consequently, he built a group of four-family houses near the factory grounds. Because he "held the view that workmen were more cheerful and efficient, enjoyed their leisure more, when they could go home from their work washed clean of factory grime," Colt installed washstands with soap, towels and hot or cold water.[13] Rohan concluded that when Samuel Colt established the washbasins, they were a concession to the comfort of employees that was close to revolutionary for the times.

Also seen as drastic were his ideas on working hours. Where 12 or 13 hours were customary for a normal workday, Colt felt that men could not achieve consistent, high quality work when pushed for such lengths of time. He shortened the workday for all employees to ten hours per day, including one hour for the noon meal break. When employees sought to shorten this dinner break to one-half hour in order to leave earlier in the afternoon, he vigorously rejected the idea, stating: "Only fools and slaves would gulp their midday meal in half an hour. I want neither in my employ."[14] Colt rooted out unfair production standards that benefited general contractors but placed the common laborer at disadvantage. Instead, he implemented a minimum scale of pay per piece, and no contractor was permitted to pay his men less than the prescribed price.

To address the needs of workers for social interaction and relaxation, Colt built "what probably was the first social center erected by an employer in the United States - Charter Oak Hall." The recreation compound was in a new office building, which he outfitted with an assembly room and theater, a meeting hall, recreation rooms with games, and reading rooms with books and periodicals. Recalling the rejuvenation he had witnessed in the faces of audiences he had performed for, during his traveling days as "Dr. Coult," he realized the benefits that occasionally company-produced art exhibits, fairs, musicales, and theatricals would provide to entertain the staff. At Charter Hall employees and their families could socialize on their own time, relaxing in a pleasant environment and becoming "family" members of the factory. Samuel Colt encouraged debating among the employees, holding that "the salvation of the nation rested on the ability of its people to think intelligently."[15] Colt was a social engineer with the ways and mean—the influence—to organize cultural improvement; this he undertook to ensure a dynasty of highly efficient, successful manufacturers.

A great admirer of music, Colt purchased brass musical instruments, uniforms, and instruction for a company band and worked diligently to have factory workers and craftsmen trained as musicians. After prolonged and unsuccessful efforts at making musicians from gunsmiths and craftsmen, Colt struck upon a radical solution to provide himself and his employees with a quality band while also undertaking a new manufacturing endeavor with willow furniture. Herein is a shining example of Colt's exceptional ability to mold men and material to his will, resolving two unrelated situations with one brilliant, but costly solution.

As the trees on the dike matured, Colt was brought to the realization that the willow could be manufactured into furniture, and he was sure that he could make a profit at this sideline venture. As skilled willow workers were impossible to find in America, Colt asked his German agent, C. F. Wappenhans, to locate and recruit willow workers. These furniture specialists were living in communes around Germany and Holland and all refused to leave their families, friends, and neighbors. Colt's remarkable response was to write Wappenhans for lengthy descriptions of the habits, customs, homes, and community buildings of one of these communes, a village called Potsdam. Their folkways, craftsmanship, and the fact that all willow workers were highly skilled brass musicians were all described for Colt in great detail. Colt next directed that the entire village of Potsdam be moved, "bag, baggage, dogs, and livestock, to America."[16] By the time the immigrants arrived in Hartford, Colt had built a reproduction of their original Swiss town, complete with Swiss-style architecture, a beer garden, a bandstand, brass instruments, and sheet music. The workers produced willow furniture that Colt was able to sell less expensively than his American competitors and the reputation for great music from the Colt Company band equaled that of his firearms across the state of Connecticut for decades.[17] More important, the measure of the leader who spared no expense or detail in building an environment of comfort and familiarity for his laborers—thereby achieving his own goal—is forcefully etched. When asked for his opinion on Colt's armory following his visit there, J. Nasmith, the inventor of the steam hammer answered:

"It produced a very impressive effect, such as I shall never forget. The first impression was to humble me very considerably. I was in a manner introduced to such a skillful extension of what I knew to be correct principles, but extended in so masterly and wholesale a manner, as made me feel that we were very far behind in carrying out what we know to be good principles. What struck me at Colonel Colt's was that the acquaintance with correct principles had been carried out in a bold, ingenious way, and they had been pushed to their full extent; and the result was the attainment of perfection and economy such as I had never met with before."[18]

The power of Colt's personal drive, his beliefs and personality all helped mold the culture within the factory. The business was his creation, run at his will and sometimes at his whim. One of the darker sides to his demanding leadership is seen in his efforts to coerce his employees to vote for the Democratic Party in the tumultuous pre-Civil War era. Eschewing political activism, Colt was a pragmatist who believed, with many of Connecticut's industrialists, that civil war would ruin the prosperity of the manufacturing North. He therefore sided with the conservative Democrats who stressed the solvency of the Union and the Constitution and sought to suppress ideological and crusading impulses among his employees. At the height of tensions during the 1860 political campaigns, Colt fired 66 men, the majority of them professed Republicans. The Republican workers bitterly accused him of coercive labor practices, a charge that Colt denied. However, a few months earlier he had suggested that "he pen a resolution urging us [manufacturers] all to discharge from our imploymen [sic] every Black Republican…until the question of slavery is for ever set to rest and the rights of the South secured permanently to them." Clearly, some of Colt's dictates, for allegiance and loyalty, far exceeded lawful or reasonable limits. But Samuel Colt was undaunted in his demands upon workers. To the end of his life, Colt maintained, "'It is better to be at the head of a louse than at the tail of a lyon!'…If I cant be first I wont be second in anything."[19] Stemming from this kind of highhanded control over workers' lives, the machine economy led America to its first distinctive classes and divisions of power. Manufacturers, specialized inventors, industrial bankers, capitalists, corporate lawyers and industrial mangers were significant power wielders.[20] Colt filled at least two of these substantive roles. On the other end of the economic scale, a sobering feature of the Industrial Revolution was the growth of a class of workers entirely dependent upon wages for subsistence and prey to the fluctuation of the market for their employment. The new, typical industrial workplace submerged personal associations between boss and employee. In many industries, the factory system of mass production had in large part replaced the dependence upon skilled workers and tradesmen with a new reliance upon

One of a set of buttons, with rampant colt, commissioned by Samuel Colt.
Herbert Houze Collection.

unskilled labor. Immigration and growing urban populations created a vast labor pool, and management began treating labor as a commodity and the unskilled laborer as expendable. Many children toiled long hours alongside adults. Workers were discouraged, sometimes brutally, from organizing to improve wages, hours, and oppressive working conditions.

Samuel Colt's paternalistic system alleviated many of these abuses, and he thereby earned the loyalty of most of his workers through his usual reliance on fair play. Rather than distance himself from his employees, Colt made himself accessible to them. For instance, when encouraging a debate in the social center, Colt never dictated the topics that men could discuss, even if the arguments ran counter to Colt's own ideas. Also, if a worker was dismissed for poor performance, that employee could appeal the dismissal directly to Colt, provided he was in Hartford at the time of the conflict.[21] He was visionary in creating a work environment that enhanced productivity and personal loyalty in most craftsmen and laborers. While other industrialists clung to a "workhorse" mentality about driving employees as hard as possible, Colt managed his employees with a firm hand and humane working conditions that put him far ahead of his competitors.

Samuel Colt personified the essence of a largely self-made man who became a formative force in American capitalist dominance. In the right place at the right time, fortified by an age of optimism and invention, and springing from a seedbed New England's industrial development, Samuel Colt's own ingenuity, business acumen, and legendary work habits allowed him to flourish as an inventor and industrial giant. "He would become a legend in his own time, and at his death, one of the wealthiest men in the country-as much a symbol of manifest destiny in the industrial world as westward expansion was in the political world."[22] The hungry ambition of America's laborers was the perfect match for his meteoric rise as an industrial giant of the 19th century. He set the traditional means of managing laborers at naught, forged into uncharted waters of workplace etiquette, and created a new work culture built for the most part on loyalty, respect, and discipline. This heritage of "running a good company" has extended well past Colt's actual oversight of the factory. Having weathered the storms of strikes and decreasing sales in the 20th century, employees are still noted for their longevity and loyalty to the Colt company.

About the Author

Maryanne S. Andrus, Curator of Education at the Buffalo Bill Historical Center, has studied and interpreted American folklore and social history in the western and southern regions of the country for seventeen years. Material culture of the 19th century has been one of her continuing interests.

Notes

1. Boddington, Craig, ed. *America: The Men and Their Guns That Made Her Great.* (Los Angeles: Peterson Publishing Co., 1981), page 33
2. Edwards, William B. *The Story of Colt's Revolver.* (Harrisburg, Pennsylvania: Stackpole Company, 1953)
3. Edwards, *The Story of Colt's Revolver,* page 317
4. Wilson, R. L. *The Colt Heritage, the Official History of Colt Firearms from 1836 to the Present.* (New York, New York: Simon & Schuster, 1989.) page 111
5. Edwards, *The Story of Colt's Revolver,* page 318
6. Grant, Ellsworth L. *The Colt Legacy.* (Providence, RI: Mowbray Company, 1982.) page 10
7. Grant, *The Colt Legacy,* page 2
8. Grant, *The Colt Legacy,* page 11
9. Rohan, Jack. *Yankee Arms Maker: the Incredible Career of Samuel Colt.* (New York: Harper & Brothers Publishers, 1935.)
10. Edwards, *The Story of Colt's Revolver,* page 316
11. Edwards, *The Story of Colt's Revolver,* page 316. Grant, *The Colt Legacy,* page 10
12. Edwards, *The Story of Colt's Revolver,* page 316
13. Rohan, *Yankee Arms Maker: the Incredible Career of Samuel Colt,* page 188
14. Edwards, *The Story of Colt's Revolver,* page 315

15. Rohan, *Yankee Arms Maker: the Incredible Career of Samuel Colt,* page 189
16. Rohan, *Yankee Arms Maker: the Incredible Career of Samuel Colt,* page 191
17. Rohan, *Yankee Arms Maker: the Incredible Career of Samuel Colt,* pages 190-194
18. Howe, *Adventures and achievements of Americans: a series of narratives illustrating their heroism, self-reliance, genius and enterprise.* (New York: G.F. Tuttle,1859).
19. Grant, *The Colt Legacy,* pages 13 and 14
20. Bailey, Thomas A. & David M. Kennedy. *The American Pageant: A History of the Republic.* (Massachusetts & Toronto: D.C. Heath & Co., 1987), page 299
21. Rohan, *Yankee Arms Maker: the Incredible Career of Samuel Colt,* page 189
22. Boddington, Craig, ed. *America: The Men and Their Guns That Made Her Great,* page 39

Additional sources

Beard, Charles A. & Mary R. Beard. *New Basic History of the United States.* Garden City, New York: Doubleday & Co., Inc, 1960.

Fischer, David Hackett. *Albion's Seed: Four British Folkways in America.* New York: Oxford University Press, 1989.

Hindle, Brooke, and Steven Lubar. *Engines of Change: The American Industrial Revolution,1790-1830.* Washington, D.C.: Smithsonian Institution Press, 1986

McGaw, Judith, ed. *Early American Technology.* Chapel Hill: University of North Carolina Press, 1994

Slotkin, Richard. *The Fatal Environment, The Myth of the Frontier in the Age of Industrialization, 1800-1890.* New York: Atheneum, 1985.

Behind the Legends of the Gun and the Gunman

Warren Newman

The mountain men of the fur trade era carried a "possibles bag," so called because it was possible to find in it almost anything. The West of legend is a possibles bag of the imagination. Yet within the tales of miraculous exploits and sudden death, and in an examination of the technology of conflict and conquest, it is also possible to discover the real face of danger and true feats of skill and daring, enough to give substance to the tales.

In our vivid imagining of the untamed American West, one of the most compelling stories of violence has two parts. One part is the man; the other is the gun. There is a man who might be a ruthless, indiscriminate killer; there is another, his nemesis, a lawman – a sheriff or a marshal. In the myth they are frequently destined to meet in mortal conflict, often beneath a blazing sun, on the dusty main street of a flimsy little frontier town. The street seems deserted, but upon closer scrutiny it becomes apparent that there are people nearby; people hiding, in the wood frame stores, and in the bank, and in the saloon; hiding, and waiting, and watching, for the men to appear and play out their deadly roles in a drama of life and death. There is in these nervous watchers both hostility and homage: hostility toward the killer, born of the pain and fear he has imposed upon them; homage for the lawman, born of admiration and hope. Suddenly, as if from nowhere, the outlaw killer and the courageous lawman appear in the street. For a breathless minute they stand motionless, watching each other. Then with resolute strides they begin to close the distance separating them, the measured cadence of their boots becoming strangely symbolic of their intense determination.

Gradually the other part of the story, the gun, becomes apparent, and of urgent importance. The hands of the men hover near the burnished handles of their holstered pistols, glistening in the glaring sunlight. As if on some silent cue, their hands move with practiced quickness; the deafening roar of gunshots displaces all other sound; and, after a lingering moment of strained apprehension, the realization emerges — the lawman stands; his antagonist is fallen, obviously dying in the dust. The gun in the myth, and in the hand of the victor, is a Colt, a Model 1873 Single Action Army Revolver, known to him and to us, without conscious irony, as the Peacemaker. The man and his gun have, for a time, brought a sense of relief and a measure of peace back into the lives of the watchers, who cautiously emerge from the frame buildings to affirm in gratitude the victory of good over evil, the triumph of hope over fear.

Jesse James at 16.
Buffalo Bill Historical Center,
Cody, Wyoming.
Vincent Mercaldo Collection. P.71.2167

The storied West of adventure and violence has many facets and many faces. It would grow to include cowboys, Indians, rustlers, wagon trains, settlers, uniformed cavalry, Pony Express riders, Wells Fargo stagecoaches, gamblers, dance hall girls, proper ladies, farmers, miners and cattle barons, men and women of all races and a dozen nationalities, as well as hundreds of stories of honor and dishonor, of courage and cowardice, of hope and fear. It would ultimately include many types of men and many makes of guns. And the legends created around them would become an integral and substantial part of the fiber and the fabric of our nation. How do the legends of the Old West stack up against our scientific skepticism?

The stories often were based on real events, however rare. Though there were others less notable, just three shootouts supplied all of the grist necessary to satisfy the creators of sensational pulps and screenplays. First was the prototype for all stand-up gun duels between evenly matched opponents. On July 21, 1865, James Butler "Wild Bill" Hickok faced his sometime friend, Davis Tutt, on Public Square, Springfield, Missouri. They apparently had exchanged hard words over a purported gambling debt. Tutt took Hickok's watch from the table and left. Later, Hickok saw Tutt emerge from the courthouse 75 yards away and shouted, "Dave, don't cross that square with my watch." Tutt and Hickok drew and fired almost simultaneously. Tutt was shot in the chest and died. Hickok was arrested and tried, but a jury deliberated only ten minutes before deciding Hickok had acted in self-defense. Few such confrontations are recorded in western history, but none more would be needed to establish the legend of the showdown.

A second classic and cinematic showdown took place near the O.K. Corral, Tombstone, Arizona Territory, on October 26, 1881. Three Earp brothers — lawmen Virgil, Wyatt, and Morgan — and Wyatt's friend John "Doc" Holliday, faced cowboy badmen Ike and Billy Clanton and Frank and Tom McLaury at point blank range. Virgil told his opponents that he was there to arrest them and ordered them to disarm. Thirty seconds and eighteen shots later, both McLaurys and Billy Clanton lay dead or dying. Virgil, Morgan, and Holliday were wounded. The Earps and Holliday were tried and exonerated.

Equally sustaining of the legend of the intrepid gunman was Billy the Kid's escape from custody at Lincoln, New Mexico, on April 28, 1881. Though shackled, he overpowered and killed his guard, then turned on the arresting deputy who had time before the fatal blast to shout, "He's killed me!"

There were showdowns of a different kind that gave life to the legends of western violence in the popular press. On September 7, 1876, aroused citizens of Northfield, Minnesota, fired on the James and Younger gang during an attempted robbery of the First National Bank. The cashier and an innocent bystander were killed along with two of the gang members. Though Frank and Jesse James escaped, both Cole and Bob Younger were wounded, captured, and sent to prison. Almost a generation later, on October 5, 1892, the Dalton gang met a similar fate at Coffeyville, Kansas. The only survivor of the gang, Emmett Dalton, though severely wounded, would live to serve his prison time and migrate to Hollywood where he helped advise filmmakers about the romance of the outlaw days. Finally, in April, 1892, the Johnson County War pitted the hired guns of big business against the cowboys and homesteaders of northeast Wyoming. Heroic cowboy Nate Champion stood off the hired posse for almost a day before being killed, long enough for the enraged citizens of Buffalo, led by the local sheriff, to surround the "invaders" at the TA Ranch and force their rescue by the U.S. Cavalry.

Similar stories and the genuine adventures and exploits of characters such as James Butler "Wild Bill" Hickok began to reach eastern drawing rooms shortly after the Civil War. In February 1867 Harper's New Monthly Magazine featured an article by George Ward Nichols about Wild Bill that embarrassed even Hickok with its exaggerations of his deadly prowess. However, it inspired a generation of journalists to seek the wild in the western borderlands. The images created by the wild West were reinforced in the popular culture of the day — in bloodthirsty stage plays known as "border dramas" and in arena shows such as Buffalo Bill's Wild West. They were augmented by pulp fiction paperback productions such as "Street and Smith's New York Weekly" and the novels of "Beadle's Dime Library," by the prolific efforts of hack writers such as Prentiss Ingraham and Ned Buntline, by the works of mainstream novelists such as Owen Wister (The Virginian, 1902) and Emerson Hough (The Covered Wagon, 1922), and through the striking sketches and powerful paintings of Frederic Remington and Charles Russell. All of them would be superseded shortly after the turn of the century by action-packed Saturday afternoon "cowboy movies" and serials as well as periodic high-end western epics and classic screen productions. It is noteworthy that the first motion picture produced as a story rather than as simply a novelty was Edwin S. Porter's western "The Great Train Robbery" in 1903.

Wild Bill Hickok, wearing Colt 1851 Navy revolvers.
Buffalo Bill Historical Center, Cody, Wyoming.
Vincent Mercaldo Collection. P.71.1632.1

Confusing the issue was the active cooperation of authentic participants in the western saga in the creation of their own legends. Buffalo Bill Cody, of course, is usually known less for the Medal of Honor he was awarded for gallantry in the Indian Wars than for his dime novels, stage plays, and the great Buffalo Bill's Wild West which carried a narrative of the winning of the West across two continents. Lincoln County, New Mexico, Sheriff Pat Garrett capitalized on the most significant act of his career by telling (with ghostwriter Ash Upton) The Authentic Life of Billy the Kid (1882), published less than a year after his controversial killing of the Kid. Texas cowhand William Levi "Buck" Taylor, introduced to Wild West show audiences in 1884 as the first "king of the cowboys," had by 1907 begun playing cowboy for Pennsylvania moviemaker William Selig. He was not the first, nor would he be the last in the stampede of real cowboys to the screen. Frank James and Cole Younger, once ruthless killers and members of the James-Younger gang that terrorized the post-Civil War Midwest, briefly operated a Wild West show. Before he died in Los Angeles in 1929, Wyatt Earp had told his own version of the story of the O.K. Corral through the sympathetic author Stuart Lake and had even been paid as an expert advisor for western films.

Not surprisingly, the filters of camera lens and selective memory led to an emphasis on romantic hardship, heroic action, and matchless gunmanship. Not surprisingly as well, questions began to be raised about the legends, the realities, the probabilities and the improbabilities conveyed in the burgeoning 20th-century popular culture of the West. Some of the same questions raised about the actors in the real drama of the West need to be asked about the guns. Were they really as accurate, as deadly, and as influential as they have been portrayed?

Sometimes the guns of the outlaws and lawmen, of the cowboys and Indians, and of the hunters and mountain men are made to seem almost to have lives of their own. Occasionally in such films as "Winchester '73" and "Colt .45" they have been the titles and subjects of their own stories and motion pictures. Their legendary representations are such that many contemporary marksmen consider them overrated and deride the depictions of both the shooters and the guns of the frontier era. It is contended that the skills of the gunmen were exaggerated for effect and that the guns themselves could not have performed at the levels demanded by the stories. Even Buffalo Bill, in a 1917 deathbed interview seemed to have acknowledged the fact. "No, we could not shoot as good as you do today. We did not have as accurate guns, either in rifles or revolvers, or loads. And we could not afford the ammunition with which to practice," he said. "But we did the work, all the same. We had to."

As the noted scholar of the gunfighter era, Joseph Rosa, has noted, the witnesses to western shooting exploits were not necessarily trained observers. However, there is a body of observational and experimental evidence that tests the claims of accuracy, range, and reliability of the guns of the frontier. And beginning early in the 20th century, modern shooters began attempting to reproduce the purported exploits of legendary gunmen. Could buffalo hunter Billy Dixon at the Battle of Adobe Walls really have shot a Comanche warrior from his horse from more than half a mile away? Was killer John Wesley Hardin truly fast enough to draw his Colt Lightning revolver and shoot a man who already had the drop on him? Wild Bill Hickok, dubbed "the Prince of Pistoleers" in the popular press, was credited with such feats of marksmanship as drawing his Colt Model 1851 Navy revolver in the blink of an eye and placing five shots within a six-inch circle at fifty yards. One of the great exhibition shooters of the late 19th century, Walter Winans, pointed out that marksmanship alone was not the key to survival, and indeed it was Hickok's coolness and readiness to kill that made his skills so deadly. But the capabilities of both the men and their weapons have been sustained.

In 1876 the U.S. Army conducted a series of tests at long range on the comparative accuracy of different makes of handguns fired from a fixed rest. At 50 yards the mean absolute deviation of shots on target for the .45 caliber Colt Single Action Army revolver was 3.11 inches; for the Smith & Wesson No. 3 American revolver, 4.33 inches; and for the Model 1875 Remington revolver, 4.1 inches. This means that five shots from any of these handguns could be placed in a circle of 18 inches or less. Army trials of a .45 caliber Colt Peacemaker in 1898 showed that at 100 yards a five-shot grouping could be placed within a three-foot circle. These are noteworthy indicators of accuracy for these firearms, particularly at such a distance, since a revolver is designed primarily for short-range shooting. Such results make it apparent that while the guns and cartridges of the frontier West might seem clumsy by current standards, their technological sophistication made them capable of remarkable feats of accuracy.

Near-impossible feats of cowboy shooting are a standard of American popular culture. Kid Colt comic book. Karen Green Collection.

More recent tests of frontier firearms have also provided a measure of substantiation of their effectiveness. It has been demonstrated that six shots can be put in a two-foot circles at 100 yards with a vintage cap-and-ball revolver, that tin cans thrown into the air can be hit consistently with them, and that it is possible to drive a can along the ground without letting it rest. Each of these feats has been attributed to the better shots of the frontier. In informal but controlled tests of classic frontier revolvers conducted by modern experts, three Colt revolvers proved remarkably accurate. The first of the three was the Model 1851 Navy .36 caliber percussion revolver so cherished by Wild Bill Hickok. Fired from a hand rest, it was capable of putting three bullets in a 3-inch group at 25 yards. In a close second place was a .45 caliber Model 1873 Single Action Army cartridge revolver. It put three rounds in a 3 1/2 inch group. Third was a .44 caliber Model 1860 Army percussion revolver that shot a 5-inch group. These results are very impressive, particularly in view of the age of the guns. They compare favorably with contemporary production guns and lend credence to the marksmanship claims made during the age of the gunfighters. Not surprisingly, these three Colt models were among the most popular and admired weapons of the day.

The range asserted for the Sharps rifle by buffalo hunters such as Billy Dixon has long been considered suspect. Their claims of kills at distances of up to a mile have often been regarded as exaggeration or imagination, but in 1992 at an invitational test shoot it was demonstrated that a .50 caliber 650 grain bullet with a 35-degree muzzle angle could travel downrange for over 3,245 yards (1.8 miles), and that a 650 grain projectile of the same caliber with a muzzle angle of 45 degrees could cover a range in excess of 3,600 yards (2+ miles). On the same occasion relatively inexperienced shooters were able after limited practice to score consistent hits at 956 yards, just over half a mile, on a steel buffalo target.

Speed with the early revolvers is also a much-debated matter, but in January 1934, expert gun-handler Ed McGivern proved that some of the stories about the capabilities of the old Colt Single Action Army were not entirely fanciful. In one demonstration he drew the revolver and fired five shots into a human-sized target at ten feet in 1.6 seconds. In another show of speed he drew and fired one shot into the target in one-fourth of a second. In yet another test of both the man and the gun he was able by drawing and fanning the hammer to put five shots into the target in 1.2 seconds. In the last instance all five shots were close enough together to be covered by the palm of the hand. Almost all of his previous shooting had been done with modern double-action revolvers. He obviously made the transition to the aging single-action revolver quite handily.

In similar demonstrations aimed at confirming the skills and cunning of shooters such as Hardin and Hickok, modern gun-handlers have shown that Hardin, for example, could pretend to surrender his guns, butts forward, then spin and fire them in a motion almost too rapid for the eye to follow. The plausibility of Hickok's legendary dexterity in drawing, cocking, and firing a pair of revolvers that he kept tucked into his waistband has been established beyond question.

And as for "old West" marksmanship, then, as now, most guns can shoot better than the person doing the shooting can. But modern marksmen have repeatedly showed that while the feats of the noted gunmen may be legend, the legend is founded on substance. The aura of legendary violence surrounding the gunman has its own foundation in fact as well. No matter their skills, their coldbloodedness, and the superiority of their chosen weapons, many of the storied shooters — Jesse James, Pat Garrett, Wild Bill Hickok, and John Wesley Hardin among them — were murdered by men willing to shoot from concealment or from behind, at close quarters, taking no chances of matching their victims' purported speed and marksmanship.

The stories and tall tales of the wild West still stir the modern imagination and are revealed not just in popular entertainment. In Vietnam, American GIs spoke of precarious locales as "Dodge City" — "getting out of Dodge" meant abandoning a dangerous position. To "saddle up" was to move out against "the bad guys" in "Indian country," beyond the defensive perimeter. In the European press, the United States is often compared to a "lone gunslinger" in its single-handed pursuit of foreign policy objectives. And as if to prove that it could have happened just the way the stories have it, reenactors, Cowboy Shooters, and the enthusiasts of the Single Action Shooting Society continue to lend credibility to the claims of legend.

About the Author

Warren Newman is a retired senior U. S. Navy officer now serving as Interim Curator of the Cody Firearms Museum at the Buffalo Bill Historical Center in Cody, Wyoming. He is a lifelong student of firearms technology and history, a certified firearms and personal defense instructor, a specialist in cross-cultural communications and organizational development, and a veteran of the Vietnam War.

Sources and Additional Reading

Boorman, Dean K. *The History of Colt Firearms.* New York, 2001

Cunningham, Eugene. *Triggernometry: a Gallery of Gunfighters.* Norman, Oklahoma, 1996

Greener, W. W. *The Gun and its Development.* London, 1910

Marohn, Richard C. *The Last Gunfighter.* College Station, Texas, 1995

McCarty, Lea F. *The Gunfighters.* Oakland, California, 1991

McGivern, Ed. *Fast and Fancy Revolver Shooting.* Chicago, 1975

Rosa, Joseph G. *Age of the Gunfighter.* London, 1993
Wild Bill Hickok, Gunfighter. College Station, Texas, 2001

Thomas, Chauncey. "Buffalo Bill's Last Interview," Outdoor Life 39(5), May, 1917

Venturino, Mike. "How Far will a Sharps Shoot?" in Robert W. Hunnicut, ed., Shotgun News Treasury, 1997-2000. Peoria, Illinois, 2001

Walter, John. *The Guns that Won the West.* London, England, and Mechanicsburg, Pennsylvania, 1999

Wilson, R. L. *The Peacemakers: Arms and Adventure in the American West.* New York, 1992

Ingenuity and Enterprise:
The Lives of William F. Cody and Samuel Colt

Juti A. Winchester, Ph.D.

Two of the best-known names in American history are those of Samuel Colt and William F. "Buffalo Bill" Cody. While it is true that each was a self-made man and both made their worldwide reputations with a firearm, a thoughtful examination of their lives reveals that they had much more than these obvious things in common though they belonged to separate generations and had vastly different personalities and destinies. This essay is not intended as a complete biography of either Cody or Colt but instead serves to highlight some points of similarity and contrast between the two men whose names stand like bookends on the American experience in the West.

Loss of a parent early in life proved to have a profound effect on both Cody and Colt. Born near Hartford, Connecticut on July 19, 1814, Samuel was the third child born to Sarah and Christopher Colt. Christopher had received his start in the West Indies maritime trade from his father-in-law, Major John Caldwell. As a result, the young Colt family experienced the fluctuations in fortune connected with sea trade before and after the War of 1812, at first reaping its benefits. As the daughter of the richest man in Hartford, Sarah had not known anything but a life of luxury, and the Colt children grew up firmly accustomed to their wealthy mother's unwavering indulgence, despite the family's uncertain economic condition. In 1820 the ups and downs of the business resulted in bankruptcy for Major Caldwell as well as Christopher Colt. Soon after, Sarah Colt became sick and died, some say from the shock of becoming impoverished.[1]

The remaining Colt family faced a future of difficult choices. At first, Christopher brought his widowed sister into his home to care for the children. Aunt Price was as indulgent as Sarah had been, and adding to the rising domestic chaos was her inability to control the headstrong and energetic Colt children. Not quite two years after his wife's death, however, Christopher Colt found a woman who he hoped would bring order to his unsettled home and work life, and bring a much needed dowry with her. He married Olivia Sargent, the practical daughter of a successful mechanic in Hartford. The new Mrs. Colt aimed to set the household finances in order and cut back expenses, to the dismay of her newly acquired brood. All but two of the Colt children were spread among relatives, with eight-year-old Samuel sent to an uncle to attend school and help with the farm. After a year, Samuel returned to work in his father's silk mill, but finding nothing compelling in that business to hold him in Hartford, after a few more years eventually decided to seek his fortune in a different trade from his father's. It was while trying a life at sea that Colt received his inspiration for the revolver, and his life's course was set for good. For the young man, his natural mother's death changed the course of his life and set Samuel on the road to his later achievements.

Death created disruption and, later, opportunity in Cody's life as well. William Frederick Cody was born on February 26, 1846 near LeClaire, Iowa, to a family of a little more than modest means. His father, Isaac, was a successful farmer with an adventurous streak who aspired to leading communities of emigrants to settle in the West. A former schoolteacher with somewhat delicate health, Mary Laycock Cody raised her four children with the help of at least one domestic servant. After the death of the Cody's eldest son, Samuel, Isaac moved his family west and became one of the first settlers in the newly opened territory of Kansas in 1854. Young Will attended school and spent his boyhood hours riding, learning to hunt, and helping around the farm as the family settled in the Salt Creek Valley, just north of Fort Leavenworth.[2]

The 1850s were marked with political strife, and the Codys' new homeland was earning the epithet "Bleeding Kansas" as settlements near the Missouri state line became caught up in the escalating Border War that was a prelude to the Civil War. Not long after coming to the Salt Creek Valley

William F. Cody
Buffalo Bill Historical Center.
Cody, WY. 1.69.6017

Samuel Colt
Colt's Manufacturing Co. Inc.
Hartford, Connecticut

Isaac became caught up in the fray, and when induced to make a free-soil speech in town, he was stabbed by a partisan. He initially recovered from his wound, but his health was compromised. Cody continued to work, recruiting emigrants to come to Kansas and settle. In 1857, while helping some new arrivals during a rainstorm, Isaac Cody became sick and died from a chill. At the age of eleven, Will took it upon himself to grow up in a hurry and start earning money to support his mother, sisters, and younger brother.

The Russell and Majors freighting firm gave young Will Cody a job and in doing so set him on the road to acquiring a lasting reputation. As a teamster's helper, he made several trips across the plains from Leavenworth to points west. At one point he almost surely served as a rider for the now legendary Pony Express, though some historians doubt the veracity of this and others of the adventures Cody claimed in his autobiography. In any case, it was on the death of his father that he turned away from the role of a farmer and took up his improbable but exciting destiny as a frontiersman.

Both Cody and Colt worked at diverse and sometimes unlikely occupations in order to gain the necessary capital to allow them to pursue other interests. Samuel Colt returned from his year working at sea on board the brig *Corvo*, excited about his idea for a revolver. He brought a wooden model to his father, hoping that he could get support for a prototype of what he believed would be the next great step in firearms technology. Christopher Colt put up the money and engaged a mechanic to make two working models of Samuel's design, but the trials produced unsatisfactory results. His father wanted nothing more to do with the project for the time but Samuel was driven to continue and hit on a scheme to make money to support his dream. Styling himself as "Dr. Coult of New York, London, and Calcutta," he put together an ostensibly scientific demonstration of the effects of nitrous oxide (laughing gas) and took the show on the road in 1832, filling auditoriums with paying customers. Until June of 1835, Colt traveled with his demonstration while conducting his firearms work via correspondence, sending money and trying to direct the manufacture of pistol prototypes so that he could obtain patents on his designs. When he achieved this goal, Colt left his "scientific" demonstration career behind him and never looked back. As he became more successful, Colt continued to depend on the mails, relying on both family members and trustworthy managers to keep things going while he personally exerted his energy and wielded his growing influence to promote his rapidly developing business. Historians can trace the progress of his ideas and success and at the same time gain a glimpse of Colt's personality through his surviving correspondence.

Long-distance business dealings also characterized many of Cody's financial activities because of his extensive travels as he pursued a stage career and later as he toured with his Wild West. Always a man of many interests, Cody juggled the myriad day-to-day tasks associated with his traveling shows while trying to maintain his role as absentee landlord, manager, or active business partner in a kaleidoscope of projects. From 1872 to 1886 he acted out his daring prairie exploits in the nation's theaters, but as he did so, Cody knew that stage fame would be short-lived. He purchased a ranch in Nebraska with hopes of becoming a cattle baron and then attempted to run the ranch *in absentia* through letters to the foreman. As Cody became more successful and took to the road with the Wild West, his other interests increased exponentially, and he spent practically all of his spare time trying to stay current with his correspondence and in touch with his outside business affairs. Like Colt, Cody relied on family members and trustworthy managers to keep things going in his absence, but his goal was to become successful enough in his investments and projects that he could one day retire from show business and remain at home to enjoy the fruits of his labor. Interestingly, Samuel Colt quit the stage when he approached fulfillment of his primary objective. This allowed him to take a direct hand in developing his business, subsequently achieving success and finally building a home that he was actually able to occupy. In contrast, Cody divided his capital and his energy between his show and his other investments while at the same time providing financial support to his extended family. Even after his interest in maintaining a traveling show must have waned, Cody's debts forced him to remain on the road.

The elaborate volume Armsmear *was commissioned by Elizabeth Colt after her husband's death.*
BBHC Photo. Dennis Russell Collection.

In the 19th century, the gamble of mine investment tantalized men who had money and imagination, and this was true of both Colt and Cody. In 1857, Samuel Colt became one of several directors of the Sonora Exploring and Mining Company which was prospecting for precious metals in southern Arizona at a time when the territory was barely formed and its mineral wealth could only be surmised.[3] Through this company, Colt's name became linked with the Cerro Colorado or Heintzelman Mine located in the Santa Rita mountains near present-day Aravaca.[4] Little is known about how much Colt benefited from this investment, but today the town of Aravaca remembers that Colt sent a shipment of books to the mine in 1858, thus creating the first library in the territory.[5]

Barely 50 years later, William Cody bought several mines near Oracle, another mining town in southern Arizona only a hundred miles from Cerro Colorado. Buoyed by the promises of his mine superintendent, Cody poured hundreds of thousands of early 20th-century dollars into the operation hoping to find a rich vein of gold. But his faith in his managers was misplaced, and he gained almost nothing from his investments. He did see some modest earnings from a scheelite (tungsten ore) strike, but not enough to break even. Buffalo Bill's presence in Arizona did not go unnoticed, however. Influential men in 1911 proposed to nominate Cody to represent Arizona in the United States Senate when Arizona finally was to take its place in 1912 as the forty-eighth state in the republic. Buffalo Bill made some statements to the national newspapers, mostly in regard to woman's suffrage (which he wholeheartedly supported) but that is the known extent of the "campaign" for Senator Cody, and his nomination never went any further than an amused discussion of his ability as a straightshooter to quell unruly debates.[6] In the end, Buffalo Bill lost almost his entire investment in his Arizona mines. Ironically, after his death in 1917, World War I production of military materiel heightened the demand for the steel-hardening properties of tungsten, and the mine became a paying concern for subsequent owners. It does not seem that either Colt or Cody reaped the hoped-for piles of money from their Arizona interests, but each man left his mark on the Arizona Territory nonetheless.

Samuel Colt and William F. Cody share a significant date in common: both men died on January 10, Colt in 1862 and Cody 55 years later in 1917. Each was laid to rest on January 14, and both occasions were marked with magnificent and memorable funerals, so very appropriate for the men who had left such a large and lasting imprint on American culture. In the case of these men, however, the end of their lives did not signal the end of their influence on American culture and society. Tellingly, the families that Cody and Colt left behind spent the rest of their own lives dealing with the heavy legacies left them.

In the 19th century there were few roads available to women for professional success. Many women who were married to prominent men, however, became important contributors to the success and reputations of their husbands while carving out economic security for themselves. Jessie Benton Frémont promoted the military and political careers of her husband, John Charles Frémont, by editing, perhaps even writing, the published accounts of his exploits and his memoirs. Though he made and lost several fortunes as explorer, U.S. Senator from California, and the Republican Party's first candidate for president in 1856, it was her writing that provided the family's income during lean times, especially after his death in 1890. Elizabeth Bacon Custer not only enhanced the public's appreciation of her late husband's "martyrdom" in 1876, she created an aura of dedicated widowhood that deflected much of the criticism of General Custer until after her death in 1933.[7]

Both Elizabeth Colt and Louisa Cody had worked to promote their husbands' reputations and to ensure their families' financial stability while their husbands flourished. Elizabeth had taken a direct hand in developing the culture of the Colt company, and she helped manage its fortunes after Samuel's death. Louisa had protected herself and her children from Buffalo Bill's financial adventures by putting much of their property in her name and managing it for the family. Additionally, in the end, both of them would find themselves as widows managing the memories and reputations of their late husbands.

Mary Jester Allen and daughter Helen, who as an adult helped her mother in the management of the Buffalo Bill Museum, walking in Seattle, 1906.
Buffalo Bill Historical Center. Cody, WY. P.41.1

Mrs. Colt preceded both Mrs. Frémont and Mrs. Custer in fostering her own reputation by guarding that of her husband. Four years after Samuel Colt's untimely death in 1861, Elizabeth Colt commissioned a biography of her husband and his legacy. The volume was aptly titled *Armsmear*, which was the name of the Colts' home, and author Henry Barnard used the book's pages to describe the grounds, the factory, and the house in great detail. The book is a model of mid-19th century literary convention, but it does not contribute much that would be of use to future scholars in its treatment of Colt himself. Barnard frames his vignettes concerning Colt with quotations in Latin, French, Greek and German. He makes references to biblical and classical themes, invoking Herculaneum and other "vanished" civilizations while describing the manufacture and sale of contemporary weapons. Barnard adds occasional snatches of poetry and includes affecting descriptions of the cemetery where some of Colt's children were buried, a sentimental theme prevalent in Civil War-era American popular culture. There is more information about the life and death of Hartford's Charter Oak tree than of Samuel Colt in Barnard's biography. Interestingly, most later works about Colt continue to be almost invariably centered on his property and the mechanics of the revolver while relegating information about his life to the margins of the narrative.

What did Colt's widow have to hide about her husband? His business dealings were solid, and he left his estate in splendid order for his descendants, but he also left behind a child from a previous and seemingly secret marriage. Colt had married Caroline Henshaw in England in 1835 when he was but 21 years of age, and later came to regret his youthful indulgence. While the record of their marriage surfaced after Colt's death during the probate period, no divorce decree has ever been found, although Caroline later publicly married Samuel's brother John, practically on the gallows. After his brother's execution, Colt sent Caroline to Germany and had her name changed to Julia Leicester, and there she married into minor German nobility. While Colt regretted his early first marriage, it must have been difficult for him to put the resulting child aside when all but one of his own children died in infancy. To his credit, the firearms magnate left a considerable inheritance to his "nephew" Samuel Caldwell Colt who dropped out of sight soon thereafter.[8] In addition to Colt's indiscretion concerning Caroline/Julia, there had been periods of contentiousness within the Colt family, and the matter of brother John being hanged for murder had the potential to cast a lurid shadow over the rest of the clan. However, contemporary American gossip seemed to leave Colt's family alone, although there must have been some general knowledge of the man's life circumstances. The author of an essay appearing in *The Art Journal for 1876* directly compared Colt to the biblical Joseph, writing of him that

> "...the man who had been sold into slavery, who had been betrayed by his brethren, who had conquered evil fortune, and who had risen to power and wealth, and had then turned with lavish generosity toward his old father and brothers, was no unfitting prototype of the boy and man who went through the hard rebuffs, the tremendous disappointments, and the subsequent successes of Colonel Colt."[9]

The 19th century's apparent custom of respect for the dead protected public widows like Elizabeth Custer and Elizabeth Colt. For the family of William F. Cody this respectful period of mourning no longer held true. Buffalo Bill lived longer and died much later than Colt or Custer. The World War had crushed the complacent acceptance of old-fashioned gentility and brought with it a disillusionment with traditional heroes. The pundits of the Jazz Age would come to seem more interested in creating and debunking celebrities. Immediately after her husband's death in 1917, Louisa Cody was hounded by a variety of individuals, including reporters and writers, her husband's former creditors, and citizens of three states who jockeyed for position in their bids for the old scout's burial place.

Twenty months after the Colonel's death, the Codys' last living daughter and her husband became victims of the Spanish Influenza outbreak of 1918 and died suddenly, leaving three young children in their grandmother's care. By the end of 1921, Mrs. Cody had died as well, leaving almost none of the immediate family in place to keep the name unsullied and the debunkers at bay. It was not long, however, before a niece of Buffalo Bill, Mary Jester Allen, assumed the role of protector of her famous uncle's reputation. As a young single woman, "Mayme" Jester had toured with Buffalo Bill's Wild West as a salaried publicist. Now Mrs. Allen had a multitude of concerns on her agenda, among them her uncle's reputation as it reflected on herself as "public kin," and she would incidentally make a living from his memory.

Mary Jester Allen wanted the public to think of Cody as a refined yet natural gentleman of taste. In 1927 she opened the Buffalo Bill Museum in Cody, Wyoming, filling it with Western artifacts, American Indian cultural objects, mounted game animals, and his personal memorabilia including items given to him by European nobility. She housed this collection in a building designed to recall the house at Buffalo Bill's TE Ranch.[10] The stage was set for a complete and thoroughly controlled interpretation of William F. Cody's life and distinguished career, except for one nagging incident: Cody's 1876 "duel" with the Cheyenne leader Yellow Hair. Only weeks after Custer's decisive defeat at the Little Bighorn, Cody and the Fifth Cavalry encountered some Cheyennes at Warbonnet Creek in northwestern Nebraska, and a fight ensued. Buffalo Bill engaged in a single-handed fight with Yellow Hair and

Mary Jester Allen hired artist Robert Lindneux to paint a heroic portrait of her uncle in his most famous deed as a warrior.
First Scalp for Custer. 1928. 168.5 x 72", oil on canvas, Buffalo Bill Historical Center, Cody, WY. Gift of the Coe Foundation. 121.67

killed him, taking his scalp in the heat of the moment. For years afterward, Cody occasionally recounted this incident as part of his stage plays and his Wild West. The fight with Yellow Hair had been a defining moment in Cody's career and helped cement his reputation in a United States anxious to quell what was seen as "the Indian problem."

Mrs. Allen could not reconcile the image of her uncle cold-bloodedly taking the scalp with the image of "Nature's Nobleman" that she was busy enshrining in her museum. She required a clear statement to persuade the public that the Yellow Hair scalping was fiction, so she hired western artist Robert Lindneux to create an image to suit her purpose. The resulting painting showed Cody on the battlefield, triumphantly holding aloft Yellow Hair's warbonnet. When the painting was unveiled in 1928, Lindneux further showed himself to be an ally to his patroness by giving numerous interviews to the press in which he cited his exhaustive research into the matter as his justification for changing the story. Lindneux claimed to have interviewed participants, including even the Fifth Cavalry's adjutant, General Charles King, and thus invoking the authority of witnesses and of blood kin (represented by Mary Jester Allen) he refuted the story as Cody himself had told it during his lifetime, instead claiming that the scalping was the invention of dime novelist Ned Buntline.

The "new" scalping story found some adherents, but some Americans chose to publicly and vocally disagree with Mrs. Allen's assertion of historical authority and authenticity. Surviving members of the Fifth Cavalry who had been at the Warbonnet Creek fight gave statements to the press contradicting the artist and his painting, including General King who bitterly denounced Lindneux's inaccuracies, and the "Legion of Defenders of the Achievements of William F. Cody (Buffalo Bill)" was established in Denver. While the debunkers had been at work on Cody's reputation without making much headway, it was this seeming defection by the Cody family that spurred the formation of this group. There is scant evidence that they did anything beyond making their own statements to the press. In the end, the painting remained on display at the Buffalo Bill Museum, and until her death in 1960, Mrs. Allen vigorously protected her famous uncle's memory while remaining the sole interpreter of the Buffalo Bill Museum's collections. The American public seemed to indulge her this error of interpretation.

Bit designed and patented by William F. Cody. Buffalo Bill Historical Center. Cody, WY. 1.29.3

Samuel Colt's storied career coincided with the beginning of the opening of the West, and his development of the revolver and other weapons contributed measurably to the progression of events that followed. Affordable and effective, Colt's weapons played a role in white-Indian conflicts and were carried by forty-niners in the California gold rush at the century's midpoint. When Arizona became a territory of the United States and President Abraham Lincoln sent the Territorial Governor to the region to set up the local government in 1864, members of the official party carried Colt revolvers.[11] Colt's personal involvement with western expansion ended with his death, only a few years before William F. Cody's involvement in it began. Cody made a living and a reputation from the "wildness" of the West, and his Wild West depended on imagery created by events both real and imagined, including daring exploits, exciting rescues and gunplay. By the end of the 19th century, "Colt's revolvers," like hats and buffaloes, had become a symbol of things western, and many cast members of the Wild West carried Colts as part of their cowboy gear when they rode onto the world's stages. In 1916, Buffalo Bill himself patented a decorative horse bit modeled to resemble a Colt revolver, drawing on the power of this symbol.[12] In the end, both men as well as the weapon that links them have become symbols of 19th-century American expansion.

About the Author

Juti A. Winchester, Ph.D. is Curator of the Buffalo Bill Museum and Western History at the Buffalo Bill Historical Center in Cody, Wyoming.

Notes

1. Good biographical information regarding Samuel Colt must be mined from a variety of sources. Most works concerned with Colt interweave information about the man with detailed accounts of his work with firearms technology; the delight of the gun collector is the bane of the scholar. One biography principally devoted to Colt's life is Jack Rohan, *Yankee Arms Maker: The Incredible Career of Samuel Colt* (New York: Harper & Brothers, 1935). Other works that contain biographical information include R. L. Wilson, *The Colt Heritage: The Official History of Colt Firearms from 1836 to the Present* (New York: Simon & Schuster, n.d.) and William B. Edwards, *The Story of Colt's Revolver: A Biography of Samuel Colt* (Harrisburg, PA: The Stackpole Company, 1953). Wilson's treatment of Colt is tucked among technological explanations and rich illustrations, and as the "official" history of Colt firearms is necessarily laudatory in nature. Edwards' work is similarly structured to Wilson's, but he indulges in a "tell-all" examination of Colt's life and work. Surprisingly, the most pointed-to "primary" source for information about Colt is the least useful for biographical purposes. In 1866, Elizabeth Jarvis Colt commissioned a "biography" that elucidated details about the Colt home, the grounds, the various firearms and their development and workings, and the Colt factory, but told little of substance about the man. See [Henry Barnard], *Armsmear: The Home, the Arm, and the Armory of Samuel Colt. A Memorial* (privately published, 1866; reprint, foreword by Arnold Marcus Chernoff, introduction by R. L. Wilson, Beinfield Publishing Inc., 1976).

2. Much has been written about the life and career of William F. Cody. The two most useful works are Don Russell, *The Lives and Legends of Buffalo Bill* (Norman, OK: University of Oklahoma Press, 1960) and Nellie Snyder Yost, *Buffalo Bill: His Family, Friends, Fame, Failures and Fortunes* (Chicago: Sage Books, 1979). Several of Cody's woman relatives ventured to "set the record straight" with their own versions of his life story. See Helen Cody Wetmore, *Last of the Great Scouts: The Life Story of Col. William F. Cody "Buffalo Bill"* (Duluth: Duluth Press Publishing Co., 1899; reprint, Lincoln: University of Nebraska Press, 1965); Elizabeth Jane Leonard and Julia Cody Goodman, *Buffalo Bill: King of the Old West*, ed. James Williams Hoffman (New York: Library Publishers, 1955); Louisa Frederici Cody and Courtney Riley Cooper, *Memories of Buffalo Bill* (New York: Appleton, 1919). Journalists and other authors have also added to the literature regarding Buffalo Bill, but most of the time these accounts more closely resemble the Cody character of dime novel fame, rather than the complex and interesting man of reality.

3. Thomas Edwin Farish, *History of Arizona*, Vol. I (Phoenix: State of Arizona, 1915), 279-280.

4. Will C. Barnes, *Arizona Place Names*, introduction by Bernard L. Fontana (Tucson: University of Arizona Press, 1988), s.v. "Heintzelman Mines" and "Cerro Colorado."

5. Fred Noon, "Arivaca History," *Arivaca Visitors Guide* (Arivaca, AZ: *The Connection* Newspaper, 2002).

6. "Buffalo Bill For Woman Suffrage: Possible Future U. S. Senator Also Defends Taft's Use of Troops," *New York Journal*, March 23, 1911. Cody told the reporter, "I ain't running for Senator. I simply feel very proud that some of the good citizens of Arizona look upon me as a fitting candidate." A reporter for the *New York Telegraph* invoked the image of a Colt revolver while he mused that Cody would make an effective sergeant-at-arms for the Senate, declaring that "if there is anybody in public life rash enough to match his mouth against the Cody six-shooter, trot him out." "'Buffalo Bill' Belongs in Senate," *New York Telegraph*, March 28, 1911.

7. Catherine Coffin Phillips, *Jessie Benton Frémont: A Woman Who Made History*, with an introduction by Christine Bold (San Francisco: J. H. Nash, 1935; Lincoln: University of Nebraska Press, Bison Books, 1995); Shirley Leckie, *Elizabeth Bacon Custer and the Making of an American Myth* (Norman: University of Oklahoma Press, 1993).

8. Edwards, *Colt's Revolver*, 42-43 and chapters 23, 40, and 44 passim. Edwards also finds that John C. Colt had a marriage previous to his union with Caroline Henshaw (61). Although he was putting both his former wife and their child aside, Samuel Colt might have found it conscionable to provide for the child even after Caroline's German marriage, because Von Oppen's father first objected to the marriage and later cut them all out of his estate. He was deeply suspicious of the woman's background and young Samuel's origin.

9. M. E. W. S., "Armsmear," in *The Art Journal for 1876*, vol. 2, New Series (New York: D. Appleton & Co., 1876), 324. The author made this comment in reference to the stained-glass window of Joseph in the chapel at Armsmear. "M. E. W. S." must have held some sympathy for Colt as well as personal knowledge of the disappointments in the firearms magnate's life.

10. The Buffalo Bill Museum building was supposed to be an exact reproduction of Colonel Cody's beloved old log ranch house, but a comparison of photographs of the TE Ranch buildings and the structure in Cody shows that Mrs. Allen constructed an idealized log cabin much larger than the original.

11. "We always sleep with two of Colt's revolvers on a stand by our bedside" wrote Margaret McCormick to a friend. Mrs. McCormick was the wife of Richard McCormick, Secretary of the Territory. Secretary McCormick was a member of the original Governor's Party and later became the second governor of the territory. Letter from Margaret McCormick to Emma Denike, February 18, 1866. Margaret McCormick-Emma Denike Correspondence, Archives and Library, Sharlot Hall Museum, Prescott, Arizona.

12. United States Patent No. D 49,949, November 28, 1916.

The object of our affection: Colt and Its Collectors

K.T. Roes

It's a rare person who doesn't collect something.

From a humble assemblage of matchbook covers to the immensely varied accumulations of monarchs, collecting is a universal human endeavor.

The urge to collect has many roots, some darkly psychological and others purely utilitarian. It also has many results, ranging from obsession to joy. In addition, the human desire to accumulate lies at the heart of every museum on the planet.

Entering the word "collecting" in an Internet search engine produces 4,560,000 results. Entering "gun collecting" narrows the focus some, but still offers 238,000 options for further examination. Entering "Colt gun collecting" produces 6,650 results.

That avid interest is best represented by the Colt Collectors Association (CCA), a 2,500-member group with an international membership list. The CCA is a relatively young organization, formed 20 years ago by Colt aficionados who were members of the Texas Gun Collectors Association.

Since the CCA membership focuses on every aspect of Colt collecting, it was logical that the club would want to share its vast accumulation of objects and knowledge. The Cody Firearms Museum at the Buffalo Bill Historical Center quickly emerged as the ideal venue.

Colt collectors are nearly as varied as the guns they prize. The acquisitive impulses that drive them form a long list as well. Some collectors are searching for beauty, others value history. Some are seeking the rare and almost unobtainable. Others are fascinated by engineering skill, technology or metallurgy. Most admire Samuel Colt as an innovator and a salesman.

Interestingly, Colt collecting started with Samuel Colt. It's not surprising that the inventive self-promoter who built a firearms empire would also have been the first Colt collector. Samuel Colt was self-aware enough to assemble a substantial collection during his short life. After his death, his personal collection became the core of the firearms collections at the Connecticut State Library and the Wadsworth Atheneum, both in Hartford.

Colt collecting can strike at any age. Many collectors can track the origin of their interest to early childhood but others have come to it in later years, when affluence has aided accumulations.

Dave Grunberg of Vernon, Connecticut is a collector whose path began as child, although he did not acquire his first Colt until many years later.

Growing up in Buenos Aires, Argentina, Grunberg engaged in the usual activities of children the world over. One day, while playing outside, he found what appeared to be an expensive fountain pen lying on the ground. The police officer who was asked to help return the pen to its owner rewarded the young Grunberg by offering to let him hold his Colt .45 caliber semiautomatic pistol. The Spanish-speaking young boy had trouble deciphering the inscription on the top of the gun but he never forgot the heft of the heavy weapon.

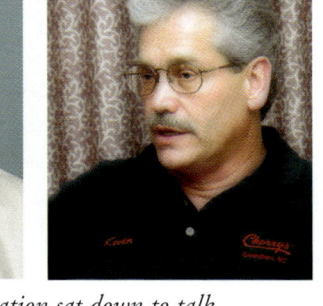

Three members of the Colt Collectors Association sat down to talk about their passion during a recent All-Colt Show in Austin, Texas. Left to right: Kitten Blickhan, John Blickhan and Kevin Cherry. Pat Honstain Photos.

Years later, after his family had emigrated to the United States, Grunberg served in the United States Army.

"They issued me a Colt .45. It was like *déja vu*, here I am. So I carried this thing for about four years and upon my discharge, I read in a flyer about a Colt for sale," he recalled. After buying the inexpensive gun, Grunberg learned that it had been made in Italy and was not a bona fide Colt at all.

"Then I started getting serious about owning some real Colt firearms," he said. "My affinity was always towards the single actions or cowboy guns. I watched the black and white serials every weekend and you always wanted to emulate them, whether it was Roy Rogers or Hopalong Cassidy. My hero was Randolph Scott."

Living near Hartford, Connecticut, the long-time center of Colt manufacturing, Grunberg found it easy to meet collectors and Colt factory employees who guided him as he refined his interest in second and third generation engraved firearms, his passion today.

At first, Grunberg was satisfied with purchasing embellished guns created by others but soon, he had the idea of creating something that would be what he calls "historically important." In 1999, with the millennium celebration approaching, Grunberg commissioned an engraved gun to mark the occasion. To begin the process, he persuaded the Colt factory in Hartford, Connecticut to open on a Sunday, the first day of the millennium, when the factory was shut for the weekend. Computers were started up and a bill of sale generated that would show Grunberg's purchase on January 1, 2000.

Grunberg believes the engraved guns should be protected by an equally attractive case. He has commissioned fine leather cases which also bear engraving, reasoning that a gun without a case "is like seeing the Mona Lisa unframed."

Collectors Lowell Pauli (left) and Tor Karstensen enjoy the friendships they've made as members of the CCA. Pat Honstain Photos.

Growing up in Norway, Tor Karstensen had different early influences.

"I got my first gun from my father, at the age of 5, in 1945," he recalled. "It was a small .22 revolver. I couldn't use it for serious use, of course, but I played with it. Right after the war there were a lot of guns available in Norway, so we young people got interested and started gun clubs."

"There were 350,000 German soldiers in Norway when the war ended and they left all their guns there. Norway was flooded with guns. A lot of them were taken to the sea and dumped but a lot of them remained among the people of Norway. We have always been a country where a lot of guns existed," Karstensen explained.

By the time Karstensen was 20, he was a full-fledged gun collector. His first "American" gun was a 1911 Colt .45, although it had been made in Norway. As Karstensen's gun collecting interest matured, he completed his collection of M1911 pistols. Now, he has a complete collection of Kongsberg Colts, manufactured in Norway under a 1915 licensing agreement.

Karstensen is always on the lookout for what he calls "sleepers." He is hopeful that someday he will find "a rare gun in an attic" which has great value.

An engineer, first for Boeing and then as director of maintenance activities for Scandinavian Airlines, Karstensen has an affinity for mechanical things. He describes the Colt Peacemaker (Single Action Army) as a gun with "a nice aesthetic design ... a really neat, thoughtful gun."

Illinois collector John Blickhan agrees. He chose to focus on Colt collecting in part because they "have prettier lines than any other gun. They just look right and feel right."

John Blickhan had always liked old guns. At one time he had collected "almost the full realm of Winchesters and Civil War carbines." After concluding that his interest was too broad, he chose Colt as his focus. Because the earliest of collectible Colts, the Patersons, were expensive and rare, Blickhan decided to "start with the Walker and end with the Single Action Army." What he had not realized at first was " there are a lot of guns and variations in between."

Blickhan's wife Kitten is the second half of a collecting team. Women are relatively rare among Colt collectors, she acknowledged.

The Colt Collectors Association was founded in 1980 by a group of avid collectors of Colt firearms and memorabilia. The CCA was established for the purpose of promoting the collecting of all types of Colt firearms and memorabilia and to provide a means of exchanging knowledge among Colt collectors and to offer an annual show and meeting for members and guests with an emphasis on a convenient and quality location.

The organization is now over 2,200 strong with members in all 50 states and many foreign countries. There is an annual three-day show which travels around the country for convenience and to promote attendance. Members keep in touch by reading *The Rampant Colt*, the official magazine of the Colt Collectors Association, published quarterly.

The Colt Collectors Association, Inc. is a nonprofit organization incorporated in the State of Texas, and is affiliated with the National Rifle Association. The association is staffed by elected officers and directors who receive no salary or travel expense compensation.

A membership application may be obtained from the CCA Secretary, P.O. Box 2241, Los Gatos, CA 95031-2241.

"I'm an anomaly as a woman. I don't think there are very many women who take an active collecting role. They may support their husbands, and man a table at a show but they don't actively shop for guns. It's a rare thing to have a woman take such an intense interest in it."

"We decided early on that it was a hobby we could share as a couple," she explained. "Now, we have both become a collecting monster," each with a different set of collecting goals.

Blickhan relies on his wife to spot alterations in firearms, an unfortunate but all-too-frequent happening in the collecting world. "She has a keen eye," he explained, and a calm approach to purchases. "I fall in love with every gun," he laughed.

"We don't watch television. We tinker with guns. I like to research and find out information. In the winter time, we're down there (gun room) almost every night," he said.

Kitten Blickhan is on the CCA board along with California collector Karen Green, the club's secretary. Although she started her interest in Colt because her husband is a collector, Karen Green soon developed a fascination with Derringers and in Samuel Colt, Colt family and company memorabilia. Now, members of the CCA laughingly refer to her as "Karen Colt."

After a 19-year CCA membership and a nine-year stint as secretary, Green is aware of the benefits of collecting and the friendships that grow over time.

"Collecting has encouraged us to travel more. We've had some very enjoyable experiences. I just wish we had more time to devote to it. There's so much to know and so much to learn. And there are so many wonderful people who share this collecting interest," she explained.

Nearly every Colt collector agrees. The collecting fraternity is filled with fast friendships, despite the distances separating members. As CCA historian Lowell Pauli put it, "My best friends don't live in Oregon where I live. They are members of the CCA. I may not see them as often as I would like to but they are still my best friends."

Colt collectors are found all over the world. Volker Gremler, Germany, frequently travels to the United States to Colt shows and events. He is fascinated by the history of Colt and brings a European perspective to the spirited political discussions that are a staple of Colt get-togethers.

"I'm a gun nut. Yes, of course. The bug has bitten me almost 50 years ago. I have a virus inside me," he says. "But it is something more than just having old rusty guns in your basement. Collecting guns gives you pleasure."

Firearms collections represent sizeable investments. As Dave Grunberg explained, "It almost becomes like a 401K. It's like fine art. It appreciates through the years and it's almost inflation proof."

However, Grunberg put his finger on a common thread, when he said, "For some people, what I do is sheer lunacy. But for me, it's enjoyment."

Most collectors understand that the enjoyment is transitory. They know they are in a temporary custodial role.

Case in point. Ice Crusher Collection.
"I got one. Then I found another and now one of my friends claims I have cornered all the ice crushers in the Rocky Mountain West," says Cody Enterprise newspaper publisher Bruce McCormack. He collects Iceomat and Dazey ice crushers of the 1940s and 50s. A recent addition to his house allowed for the permanent display of his collection. Pat Honstain Photo.

"We are just caretakers," explained Kevin Cherry, current CCA president. "We are caretakers of these guns until the next generation comes. When we die, or our children inherit them, or they are sold at auction, then the next generation of caretakers comes along. They will take care of those guns until it's time for them to pass them along to somebody else."

When the caretaking is formal and institutional, an object may become inaccessible to private owners, Cherry noted. If guns are given to a museum, they are lost, perhaps forever, to collectors. Some of the most significant and valuable presentation Colts are in St. Petersburg, Russia, in the State Hermitage Museum. Few American collectors have had the opportunity to see for themselves the fabulous gold-mounted revolvers.

Museums and collectors often have different goals, according to Buffalo Bill Historical Center deputy director Dr. Robert Pickering.

"We collect for the public good and for the long term," he explained. "Museums are interested in education in its broadest sense."

Pickering said it's not always the case that a firearm donated to a museum will remain there forever. Some donors attach stipulations that a gift can never be sold, so strict that "they are not just strings; they are heavy steel cables."

But other donors will give a gift which is unrestricted in nature, allowing the museum to sell it for the purposes of upgrading, using much the same set of criteria as individual collectors do: age and condition.

Collectors often fear that their gifts will not be on permanent display. But even guns that aren't on display are still of value to museum visitors, Pickering explained.

"There are study collections and there are exhibit collections," he noted, explaining that many collectors and scholars use the study collections at the Cody Firearms Museum, even though they are not part of the main exhibition.

"Just because it's not on display doesn't mean it's not useful," he added.

Museums function to "save and protect" items for future generations, Pickering said. In that arena, museums and collectors have the same goals.

Indeed, if not for collectors, museums would not exist. Religious objects assembled by the collectors of the early Church were viewed by the faithful and preserved for future wonderment. Later, *Wunderkammer* (Cabinets of Curiosities) allowed European nobility a means of showing off their elevated status and affluence. The famed British Museum came grudgingly into being in 1753, when collector Sir Hans Sloane died and left some 80,000 objects to King George II.

Some Colt collectors have made plans to give their collections to museums. Others hope their children will continue the family tradition.

The thrill of the chase – finding a gun that's older, more rare or in better condition than the one before – propels collectors ever forward. Collectors used words like "joy," "thrills," "excitement" and "happiness" to describe their favorite activity. Finding the right gun even has medicinal purposes.

"It's dynamite when you get bit by bug," Pauli said. "I can be down in the dumps and then I find something great and suddenly, I'm euphoric."

Colt collectors are fascinated by a long list of variables: condition, age, historical significance, barrel lengths and markings, serial numbers, proof marks, barrel addresses, styles of engraving, trigger guard markings and sizes, finishes, sights and grips.

Some, like Lowell Pauli, hope to find every variation of a particular model. As he explains it, "If they made it, you have to have one." In his case, Colt automatic pistols are the focus. He follows a plan and is ruled by a budget, so is constantly upgrading his collection, finding slightly better models, "just a tick better," and selling others.

The quest is nearly endless. Pauli laughs, "I'll quit when I have them all."

About the Author

K.T. Roes is a former journalist residing in Cody, Wyoming. Her publishing firm, WordsWorth, focuses on regional memoirs and western history.

Notes

1. Pauli, Lowell. Interview by K.T. Roes, video tape recording, Austin, Texas, October 5, 2002.

2. Green, Karen. Interview by K.T. Roes, video tape recording, Austin, Texas, October 5, 2002.

3. Grunberg, David. Interview by K.T. Roes, video tape recording, Austin, Texas, October 5, 2002.

4. Karstensen, Tor. Interview by K.T. Roes, video tape recording, Austin, Texas, October 5, 2002.

5. Cherry, Kevin. Interview by K.T. Roes, video tape recording, Austin, Texas, October 5, 2002.

6. Blickhan, John. Interview by K.T. Roes, video tape recording, Austin, Texas, October 5, 2002.

7. Blickhan, Kitten. Interview by K.T. Roes, video tape recording, Austin, Texas, October 5, 2002.

8. Gremler, Volker. Interview by K.T. Roes, video tape recording, Austin, Texas, October 5, 2002.

Cummings, Neil and Lewandowska, Marysia. *The Value of Things* (Birkhäuser, Basel, Boston, Berlin, 2000)

Muensterberger, Werner. *Collecting: An Unruly Passion: Psychological Perspectives* (Princeton University Press, Princeton, New Jersey, 1994)

R.L. Wilson, *The Colt Heritage*, (Simon & Schuster, New York. 1979)

The Collections

In many respects this illustration represents the dreams of many Colt collectors. Pictured here are the three primary Colt revolvers produced by the Patent Arms Manufacturing Company of Paterson, New Jersey (in descending order, the Number 5 Holster Pistol [s.n. 448], the Number 3 Belt Pistol [s.n. 95] and the Number 2 Pocket Pistol [s.n. 417], as well as the Improved Model 1844/1845 Pocket Pistol marketed by John Ehlers of New York City.

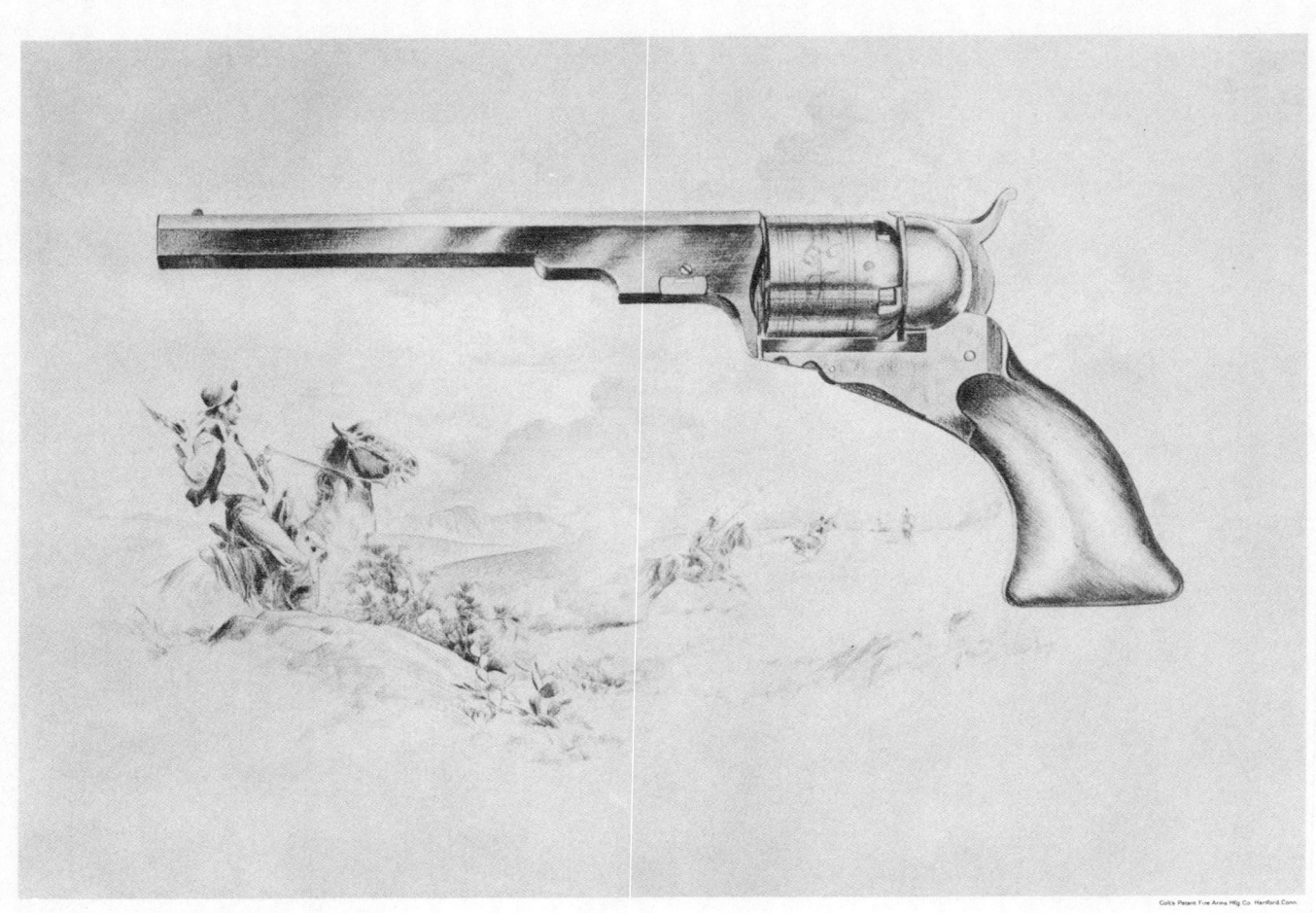

Colt Texas Paterson .40 cal-1836

In 1943 the Colt company issued a series of prints illustrating six of its more famous revolvers. Fittingly, the Paterson era was represented by the Number 5 Pistol, commonly known as the Texas Paterson due to its adoption for service by the Republic of Texas in 1839.

Paterson Percussion Revolving Pistols, Rifles and Shotguns

By William V. Sisney

Although the Patent Arms Manufacturing Company in Paterson, New Jersey, eventually failed, the cause of its demise was not due to any deficiency of Samuel Colt's revolver designs but rather his financial inexperience.

During its relatively short life, slightly over 4,200 revolvers, rifles and shotguns were produced at Colt's Paterson factory. While technical problems were encountered with some of the early models (such as the ring lever rifles), the arms incorporating exposed hammers were well received. As a result, sales of the Number 1, 3 and 5 Pistols, together with the improved carbines and shotguns introduced in 1839, far outstripped those for the internal hammer rifles.

Potential purchasers of these new arms were probably attracted to them in equal parts by their novelty and their association with events taking place elsewhere in North America. Realizing that public sentiments strongly supported the newly-formed Republic of Texas, Samuel Colt shrewdly trumpeted the fact that 180 of his Number 5 Pistols had been purchased for that state's Navy. Likewise, the purchase of another one hundred Number 5 revolvers for the U.S. Pacific Fleet also was prominently mentioned in the firm's advertisements.

Despite the published testimonials regarding their reliability and worth, Paterson era arms were not technically perfect. The Ring Lever series of rifles were

Cased Patent Arms Manufacturing Company Number 3 Belt Pistol, .34 caliber, 5½" barrel, serial number 95. Manufactured in 1838 or 1839, this revolver has a square-back cylinder typical of early production examples. It is also fitted with flared grips which afforded a better grip than the straight ones used on the smaller caliber Number 1 and 2 Pistols. With the exception of the cap dispenser, all of the accessories are original. Also included in the case is a spare cylinder bearing the same serial number as the revolver.

Robert W. Pershing Collection.

mechanically complex and prone to the breakage of internal parts. More perplexing to the inventor was the problem of chain fire or the discharge of all the cylinder's chambers at once. This startling occurrence was caused when combustion gases ignited adjacent chambers. Though Colt was eventually able to reduce the probability of that happening, his corrective design was not completed until after the Paterson enterprise had failed.

While exact production figures for the Patent Arms Manufacturing Company are unknown, the table at right represents the best estimates now available.

Following the closure of the Paterson factory, John Ehlers assembled a number of revolvers using components he had purchased at the firm's bankruptcy auction. It is estimated approximately 500 Improved Number 1 Pocket Pistols and Number 2 Belt Pistols having loading levers were made by Ehlers.

Number 1 Pocket Pistol	500
Number 2 (1837-1840) and Number 3 (1838-1839) Belt Pistols	850
Number 5 Holster Pistol (1838-1840)	1000
Number 1 Rifle (1837-1838)	200
Number 2 Rifle (1838-1841)	500
Improved Carbine (1838/9-1841)	950
Improved Carbine (1839-1841)	225

Cased Patent Arms Manufacturing Company Number 2 Belt Pistol, .31 caliber, 4.5" barrel, serial number 417. Manufactured in 1838 or 1839, this revolver is accompanied by a full set of accessories including: a spare cylinder serial number 417; single cavity bullet mold; combination screwdriver-nipple wrench-pricker- bullet press; cleaning rod; percussion cap dispenser, and; combination powder flask-bullet dispenser. The Patent Arms Manufacturing Company's "DIRECTIONS FOR USING COLT'S REPEATING PISTOLS" is pasted onto the interior of the case lid.

Robert W. Pershing Collection.

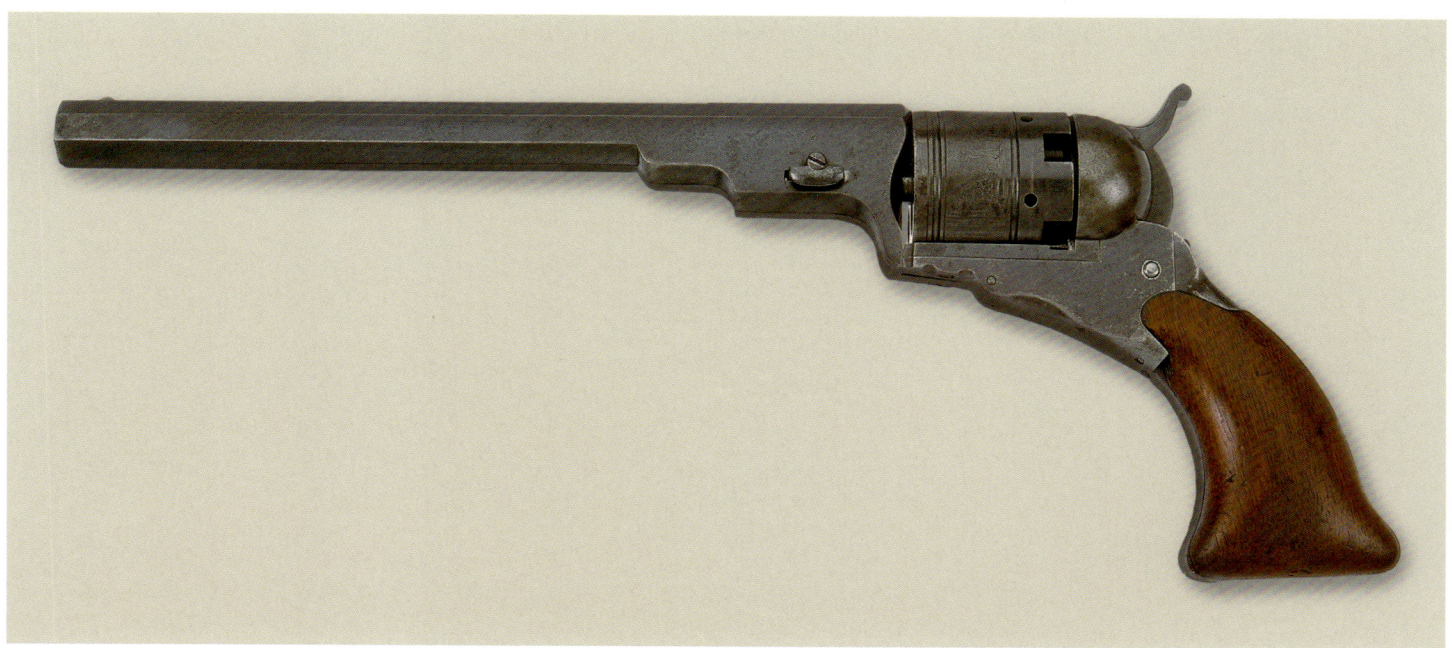

Patent Arms Manufacturing Company Number 5 Holster Pistol, .36 caliber, 9" barrel, serial number 448. Made from approximately 1838 to 1840, the Number 5 Holster Pistol was the most popular of all the Patent Arms Manufacturing Company's revolvers due to its substantial size and comfortable flared grips. Of the approximately 1,000 made, only 12 have survived with 9" barrels.

Robert W. Pershing Collection.

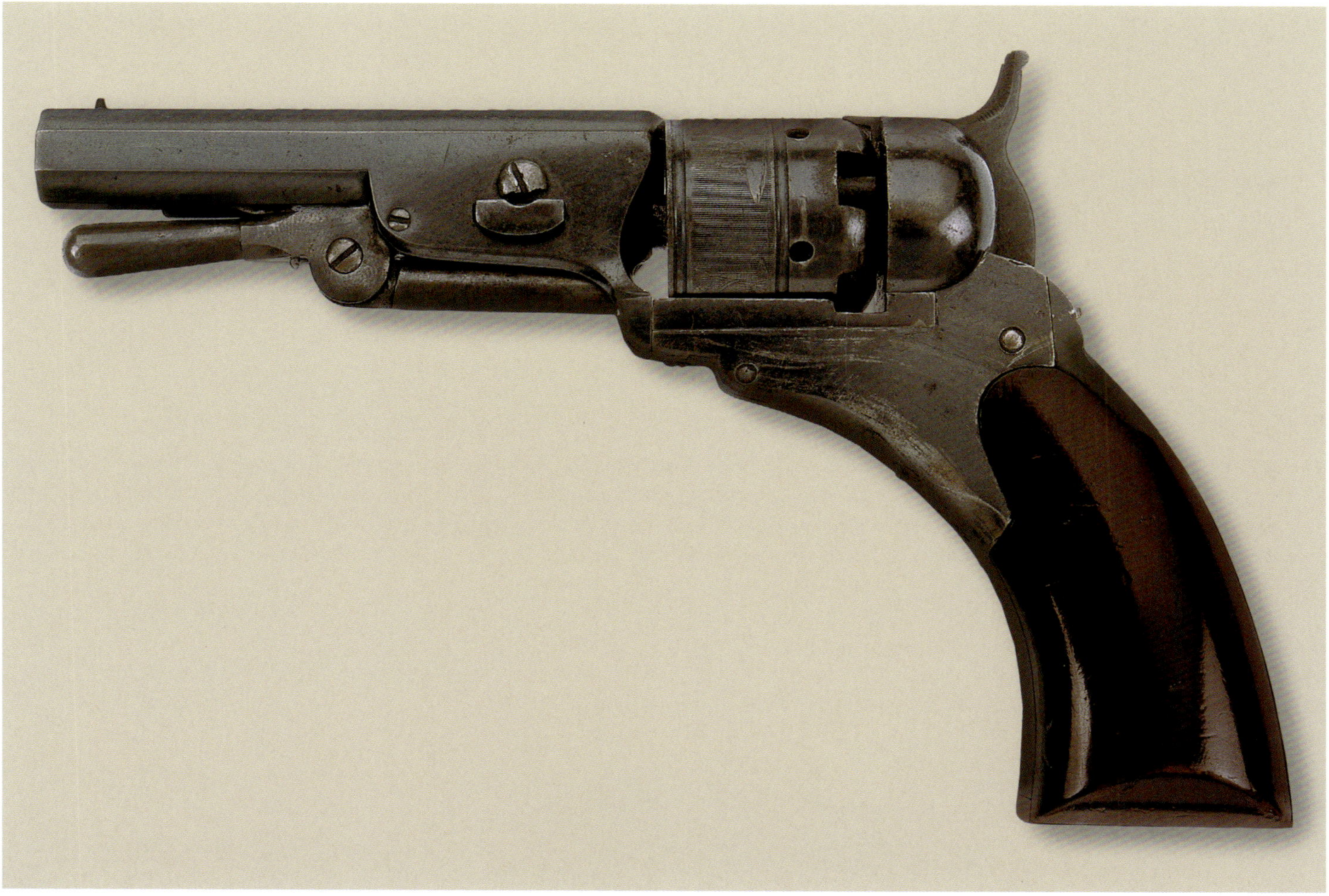

John Ehlers Improved Colt Pocket Pistol of 1844/1845, .28 caliber, 3" barrel, serial number 47. Following the collapse of the Patent Arms Manufacturing Company, its principal assets (including pistol and rifle parts) were sold at auction. John Ehlers, the firm's secretary and treasurer, purchased the majority of these pieces and began production of .28 and .31 caliber pocket pistols. Ehlers' revolvers are identified by the presence of a lever and link loading rod, as well as the barrel inscription "-Patent Arms Paterson N.J.Colt's Pt-" Approximately 500 pocket and belt pistols in both calibers were assembled by Ehlers.

Robert W. Pershing Collection.

Cased Patent Arms Manufacturing Company Number 1 Revolving Rifle, .36 caliber, 32" barrel, serial number 177. Accompanied by its normal accessories and a spare cylinder serial number 177, this set illustrates the case layout used by the Paterson factory. The rotation of this rifle's cylinder and the cocking of its internal hammer were brought about by pulling down the ring-lever located below the cylinder. Approximately 200 rifles of this model were made in 1837 and 1838.

Paul Sorrell Collection.

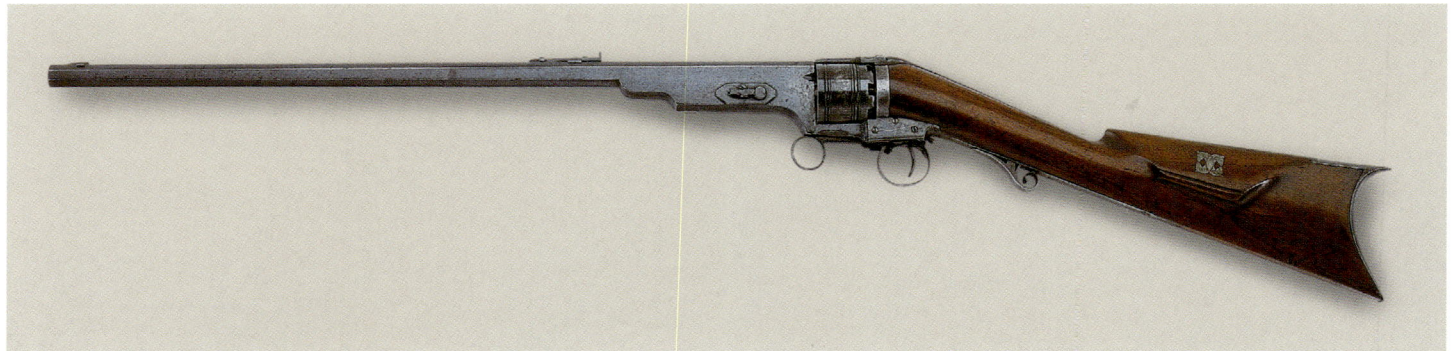

Patent Arms Manufacturing Company Number 1 Revolving Rifle, .36 caliber, 24.75" barrel, serial number 187. Although Samuel Colt was to become famous for his pistols, the first firearms made by the Patent Arms Manufacturing Company were the Number 1 rifles. This example has a pair of German silver back-to-back horse's heads inlaid on the left cheekpiece of the stock. The right recoil shield also has a capping cut-out, a feature rarely encountered on this model. Of the 200 made, 50 were purchased by the U.S. Army for use by the Mounted Dragoons during the Seminole War.

Robert W. Pershing Collection.

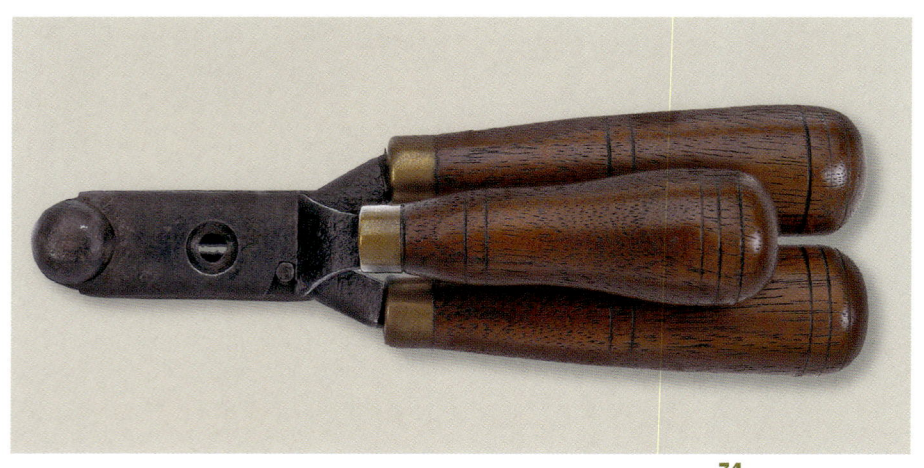

Patent Arms Manufacturing Company .36 caliber Bullet Mold, circa 1839-1840. This style of mold, which casts a single round ball, was furnished with Number 1 Revolving Rifles. The shorter arm located on top with a wood handle moves the sprue cutter which cuts off the waste lead attached to the cast ball, while the lower two arms allow the mold to be opened or shut.

Robert W. Pershing Collection.

Patent Arms Manufacturing Company Number 2 Revolving Rifle, .44 caliber, 28"/32" barrel, serial number 377. Introduced in 1838, approximately 500 Number 2 Rifles were produced before the Paterson works ceased operation in 1841.

Carl Kohlhorst Collection.

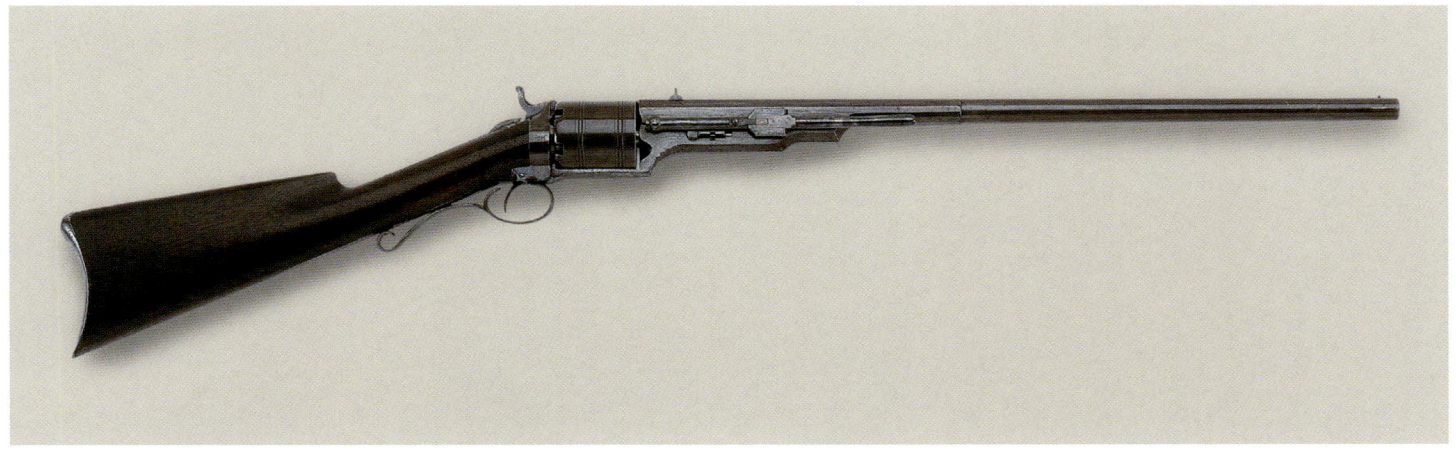

Patent Arms Manufacturing Company Revolving Carbine, .525" caliber, 24" barrel, serial number 796. Now known as the Model 1839 Carbine, this model was the most popular of all the Paterson era longarms. During its production life from late 1838 through 1841, approximately 950 were manufactured. Of that number, 360 were purchased by the U.S. Government and another 300 by the State of Texas. In 1842, 50 were sold to the State of Rhode Island during the suppression of the Dorr Rebellion. The majority of these carbines were purchased for resale by Samuel Colt in 1848.

Carl Kohlhorst Collection.

Patent Arms Manufacturing Company Carbine Bullet Mold. Among the accessories originally supplied to the State of Rhode Island in 1842 were 5 six-cavity bullet molds. It is believed that these molds accompanied the 46 carbines purchased by Colt in late 1847.

Robert W. Pershing Collection.

Patent Arms Manufacturing Company Carbine Powder Flask. Each of the carbines purchased by the State of Rhode Island in 1842 was accompanied by a powder flask which was probably of this pattern (i.e., with an embossed stand of flags motif above crossed revolving rifles and pistols). As with the other accessories originally accompanying those carbines, the flasks are also believed to have been purchased by Colt in late 1847.

Robert W. Pershing Collection.

Patent Arms Manufacturing Company Percussion Cap Dispenser, circa 1840. Constructed of two brass plates hinged below a suspension ring, the lower section is cast with spiral grooves to hold percussion caps. These are fed under spring pressure to the capping aperture at the bottom of the device. The exterior of the lid is cast with the company's names, as well as a prancing horse above two crossed pistols.

Robert W. Pershing Collection.

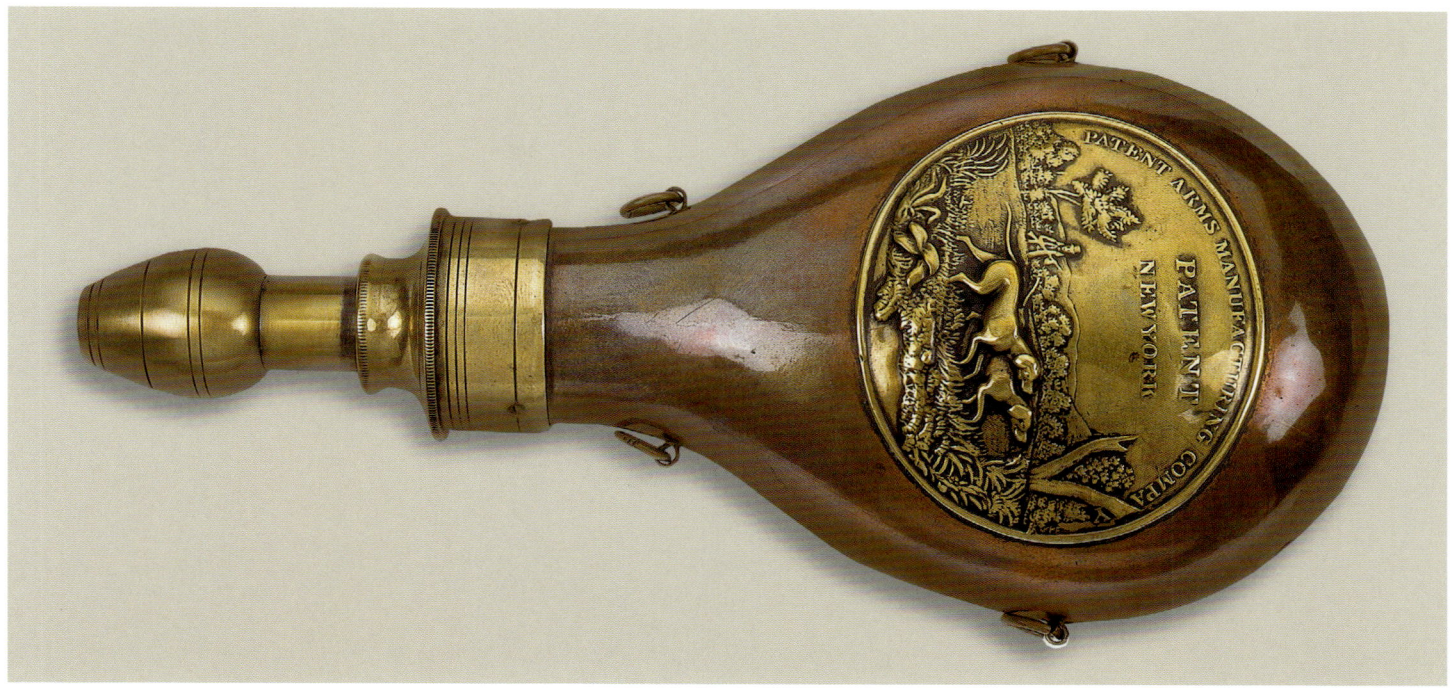

Patent Arms Manufacturing Company Powder Flask, circa 1839. Flasks of this type with a plunger top were used both with late production Number 1 Revolving Rifles, as well as the Model 1839 Carbine. The copper body has an applied circular boss that is cast with the company's name surrounding a hunting scene.

Robert W. Pershing Collection.

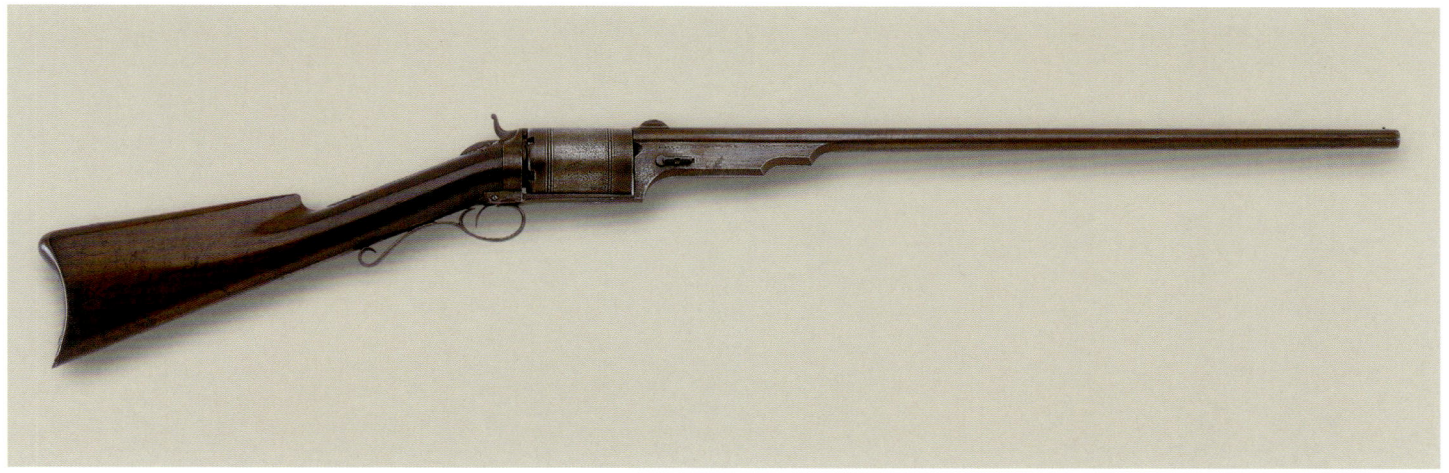

Patent Arms Manufacturing Company Revolving Shotgun, .63 caliber, 27.25" barrel, serial number 216. Approximately 225 shotguns of this type with a conventional exposed hammer were made between 1839 and 1841. Now commonly referred to as the Model 1839 Shotgun, their bore size varied from .60 to .63 caliber. Most of these arms, such as the example illustrated here, had Damascus steel or twist barrels.

Robert W. Pershing Collection.

Patent Arms Manufacturing Company Powder Flask, circa 1840. Flasks of this pattern were made for use with that company's revolving shotgun. The flask's body is constructed of pressed horn, while the combination powder measure and charger is made of brass.

Robert W. Pershing Collection.

During Samuel Colt's lifetime, his Hartford factory produced a wide variety of handguns designed for both civilian and military use. From .28 and .31 caliber pocket pistols to large bore revolvers of .44 caliber, they were regarded as the best of their times.

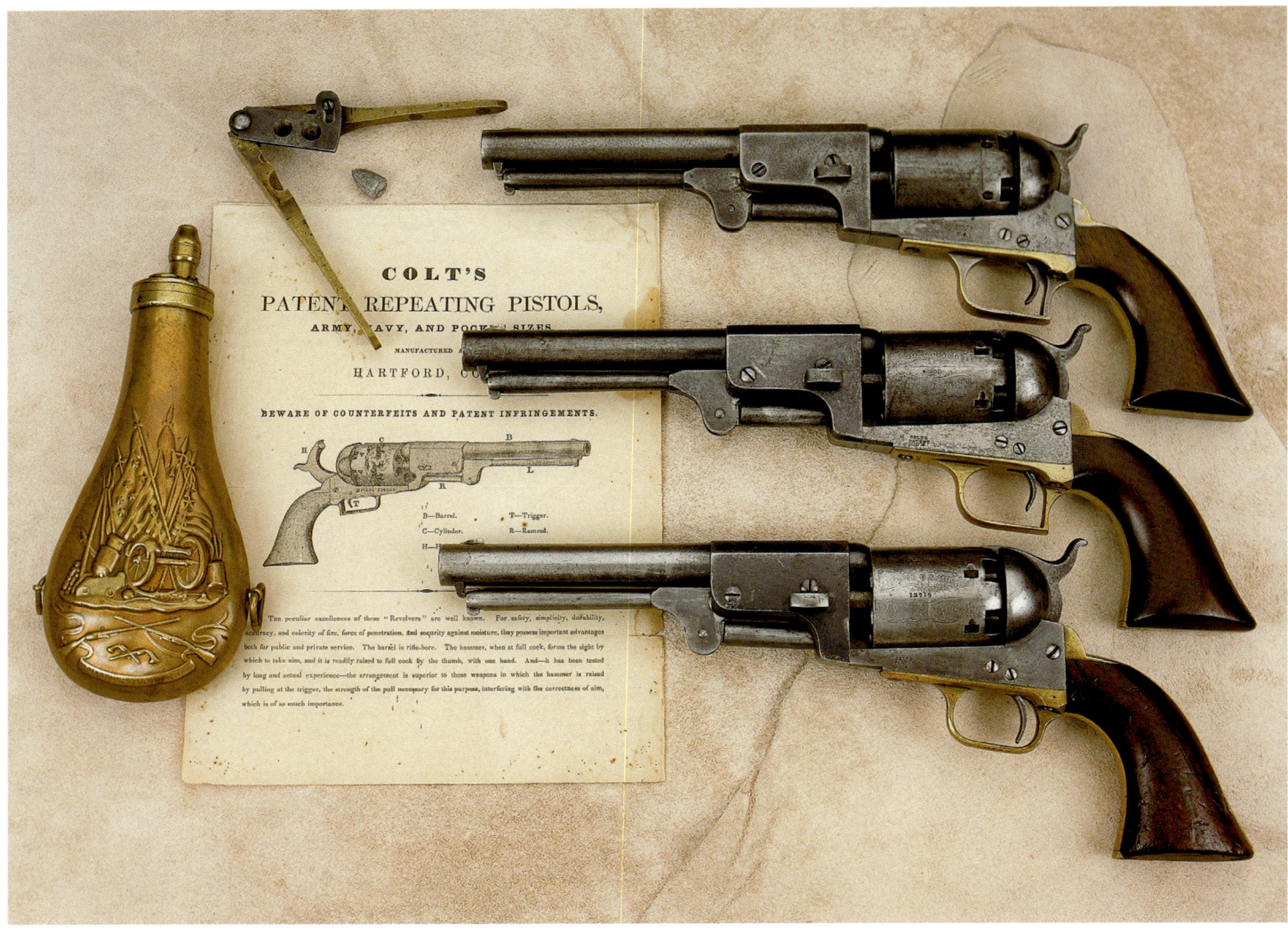

Immediately following the Mexican War, the U.S. Government placed orders with Samuel Colt for .44 caliber Holster Pistols. From 1848 to 1860, these orders were fulfilled with a series of pistols now known as the First, Second and Third Model Dragoons (top to bottom). Sturdy and dependable, these pistols established the Colt revolver's reputation as a formidable side arm.

Percussion Pistols
By Kathryn Blickhan

Following the collapse of the Paterson enterprise, Samuel Colt continued perfecting the design of his revolvers. By incorporating a cylinder having an integral ratchet on its rear surface he was able to dispense with the complicated cylinder turning mechanism that had been used in Paterson era pieces. This change, together with the chamfering of the chamber mouths (to reduce the chance of chain fire) resulted in revolvers which have become synonymous with his name.

The first of the new series were the .44 caliber Holster Pistols that were jointly developed with Captain Samuel Walker for the U.S. Regiment of Mounted Dragoons in 1847. Made at Whitneyville, Connecticut, by Eli Whitney, these pistols were an instant success. Using the profits generated from their sale to the government, Colt established a factory in Hartford in 1847 to manufacture a lighter version.

Over the next two and a half decades this facility was to produce hundreds of thousands of revolvers bearing the Colt name. In the beginning, Colt devoted his attention to .44 caliber Holster Pistols since their sale to the U.S. Government generated needed capital. He then designed a series of smaller caliber pocket pistols for the civilian market. In 1851 he expanded the product line to include a medium caliber (.36) revolver christened the Belt or Navy Model which is now popularly known as the Model 1851 Navy Colt.

In 1855 a new Pocket Pistol was introduced which featured a solid frame and a ratchet or creeping loading lever. The latter design was later used in the series of New Model Pistols first introduced in 1860.

Based upon observed serial numbers and factory records, production estimates for the Hartford factory are listed on the chart on the following page.

Cased and Engraved Colt Pocket Pistol (Second Pattern Model 1849), .31 caliber, 6" barrel, serial number 67506. Most likely made in 1853, this revolver was engraved by Gustave Young with exquisite, flowing scrollwork typical of special presentation arms. In contrast to the vast majority of Colt pistols, it was not boxed in a partition case. Rather, it was supplied with a case having form-fitted recesses for the piece, as well as its accessories, including a spare cylinder. The second pattern or Model 1849 Pocket Pistols had fully rounded trigger guards instead of the previously seen version with a squared back.

Pete Holder Collection.

In addition to pistols, Samuel Colt's Hartford works manufactured a number of percussion longarms. While some of these, such as the New Model series of carbines, rifles and shotguns or, the U.S. Special Rifle Musket, are well known to collectors, others are not. Included in the latter category are the modified Paterson-era carbines produced in 1848, and the percussion rifled muskets sold to Russia, as well as Italy, in 1856 and 1859. Production estimates for these and the other models produced by Colt are as follows.

Transitional Whitneyville-Hartford Holster Pistol (1847)	240
First Model Holster Pistol (1848-1850)	7,000
Second Model Holster Pistol (1850-1851)	2,700
Third Model Holster Pistol (1851-1860)	10,500
New Model Holster Pistol (1860-1873)	200,500
First Model Pocket Pistol without loading lever (1847-1850)	15,000
Second Model Pocket Pistol (1850-1873)	325,000
.28 Caliber New Model Pocket Pistol	28,000
.31 Caliber New Model Pocket Pistol	14,000
First Model Belt/Navy Pistol (1850-1851)	4,200
Second Model Belt/Navy Pistol (1851-1873)	211,000
New Model Navy Pistol (1861-1873)	38,800
New Model Police Pistol (1861-1873)	48,000
New Model Pocket Pistol of Navy Caliber (1865-1873)	22,500

Improved Paterson Carbines (1848)	40
Russian Contract Rifled Muskets (1855-1856)	3,130
New Model Carbines, Rifles, Rifle Muskets (1856-1864/65)	11,580
New Model Shotguns (1860-1863)	1,400
Italian Contract Rifled Muskets (1859)	23,510
Modified U.S. Model 1841 Rifles (1861-1862)	11,368
U.S. Special Rifle Muskets (1862-1865)	109,500

Colt Whitneyville-Walker Holster Pistol, .44 caliber, 9" barrel, serial number C Company 99 (inset). In 1847 Samuel Colt designed a revolver that incorporated a number of features suggested by Captain Samuel Walker of the United States Mounted Rifles. The result was a six-shot, four-pound nine-ounce handgun later to become known as the Colt Walker. Under a contract later approved by the Secretary of War, Colt was authorized by Walker on January 4, 1847 to manufacture a minimum of 1,000 of these revolvers for the United States Government. Of those, 220 were issued to Company C of the Mounted Dragoons which was commanded by Walker. As Colt did not have a manufacturing facility in 1847, these Holster Pistols were made at Eli Whitney's factory in Whitneyville, Connecticut. Fewer than 175 Whitneyville-Walker Holster Pistols have survived to this day.

C. John Blickhan Collection.

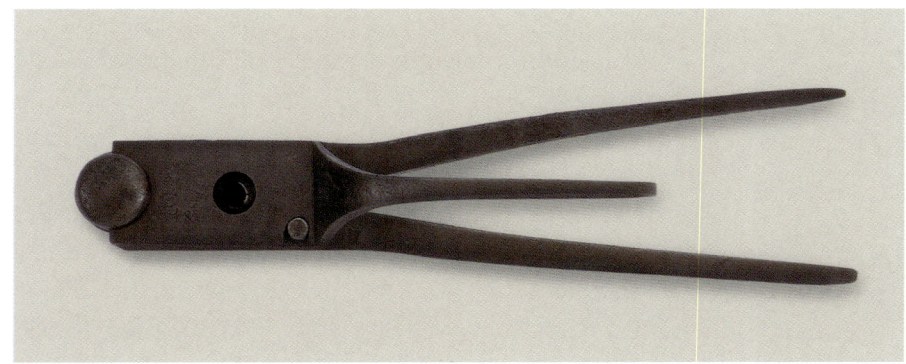

Colt Whitneyville-Walker Holster Pistol Bullet Mold. As part of Colt's contract with Samuel Walker, he was to supply one single cavity bullet mold for every 10 pistols delivered. As most of these arms saw service during the Mexican War, few of the accompanying molds have survived. While following the pattern used for the molds produced during the Patent Arms Manufacturing period, the Walker molds were constructed solely of iron.

Robert W. Pershing Collection.

Colt Whitneyville-Walker Holster Pistol Powder Flask. Embossed with a stand of flags above crossed Colt revolving rifles and pistols, flasks of this type are believed to have been made by John Matthewman of New Haven, Connecticut, using dies cut by a man surnamed Bogshon. Colt's contract with Walker stipulated that one flask was to be supplied with each pair of Holster Pistols.

Robert W. Pershing Collection.

Colt Whitneyville-Hartford Holster Pistol, .44 caliber, 7½" barrel, serial number 1146. During the initial set-up period of Colt's Hartford factory, approximately 240 Holster Pistols were made using frames and other parts left over from Colt's contract with Samuel Walker. Identifiable by the oval grip recesses cut into the rear shoulder of the frame, these pistols had shorter barrels and cylinders. These changes resulted in a pistol that weighed 4 pounds 2 ounces instead of 4 pounds 9 ounces.
Paul Sorrell Collection.

Colt Second Model Holster Pistol (Second Model Dragoon), .44 caliber, 7½" barrel, serial number 10600. Under the 1808 Militia Act, state governments were granted yearly allocations to purchase arms with federal funds. The State of Massachusetts used monies from this source to purchase 50 pairs of Colt Holster Pistols in 1851 or 1852. All of these pistols were marked with the letters "MS" to indicate their ownership by the state.
Paul Sorrell Collection.

Colt First Model Holster Pistol (First Model Dragoon), .44 caliber, 7½" barrel, serial number 1343. Produced for the United States Government under a contract dated November 2, 1847, this revolver was made at Colt's Hartford factory in 1848. Based upon the backstrap inscription(inset), it was originally issued to the "U.S. Revenue Brig C. W. Lawrence," commissioned into the Revenue Service on October 11, 1848. A return of its stores indicates that the vessel was originally equipped with 12 Colt revolvers. While stationed in San Francisco, this ship's captain, Alexander V. Fraser, was granted a leave of absence. At that time (June 13, 1851), he was loaned one of the ship's Colt revolvers "to be returned on his arrival to the U.S."
C. John Blickhan Collection.

Colt Second Model Holster Pistol (Second Model Dragoon), .44 caliber, 7½" barrel, serial number 9207. The inspection marks found on this pistol indicate that it was originally purchased by the U.S. Army. Given its serial number it most likely formed part of the 1,000-revolver order placed with Colt on February 4, 1850.
Herbert A. Lyman Collection

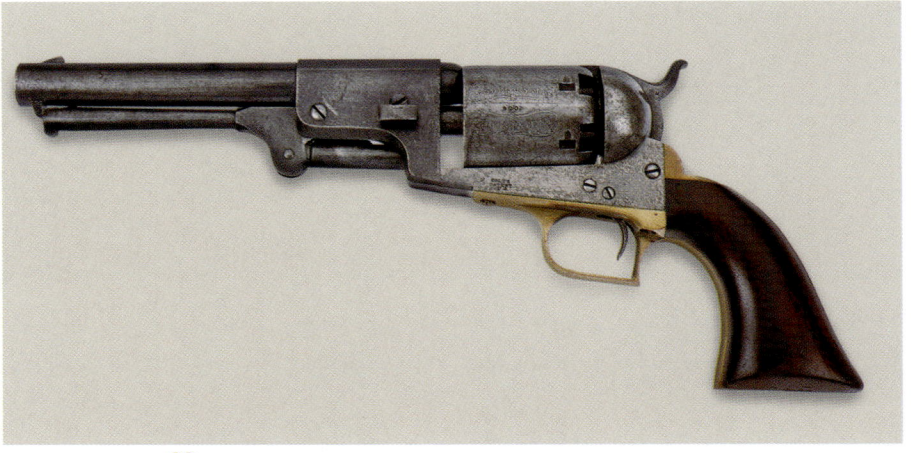

Colt Third Model Shoulder Stocked Holster Pistol (Third Model Dragoon), .44 caliber, 7½" barrel, serial number 17136. This revolver was originally shipped with a matching attachable shoulder stock to the New York City retailers, Cooper & Pond, on February 16, 1861. It is engraved on the left angled flat of the barrel forward of the breech (inset) with the inscription "C. L. Dragoons," indicating that it was originally issued to a member of the Crocheron Light Dragoons. Named in honor of John Crocheron, who supplied the funds needed to equip the unit, the Crocheron Light Dragoons was raised in Alabama in January of 1862 under the command of Captain Robert W. Smith. Six months later after the Battles of Corinth and Shiloh, the unit was reorganized and became part of the 3rd Alabama Cavalry.

C. John Blickhan Collection.

Cased and Engraved Colt London Third Model Holster Pistol (Third Model Dragoon), .44 caliber, 7½" barrel, serial number 13. During the four years it was in operation, Colt's London factory produced approximately 700 Holster Pistols. This finely engraved example can be dated by its serial number to 1853.

Paul Sorrell Collection.

Colt Third Model Holster Pistol (Third Model Dragoon), .44 caliber, 7½" barrel, serial number 17539. A significant number of Colt revolvers were fitted with attachable shoulder stocks serial numbered en suite with the pistols they accompanied. The serial number of the stock fitted to this revolver (17545), while not matching, is relatively close.

Herbert A. Lyman Collection.

Colt Third Model Holster Pistol (Third Model Dragoon), .44 caliber, 7½" barrel, serial number 12719. Produced under contract for the U.S. Army, this revolver bears the "WAT" inspection marks of Captain William A. Thornton, who commanded the Ordnance Depot at New York City. Prior to the American Civil War, the government purchased approximately 4,330 pistols of this pattern. Of that number, 946 were issued as pairs with accompanying attachable shoulder stocks.

Herbert A. Lyman Collection.

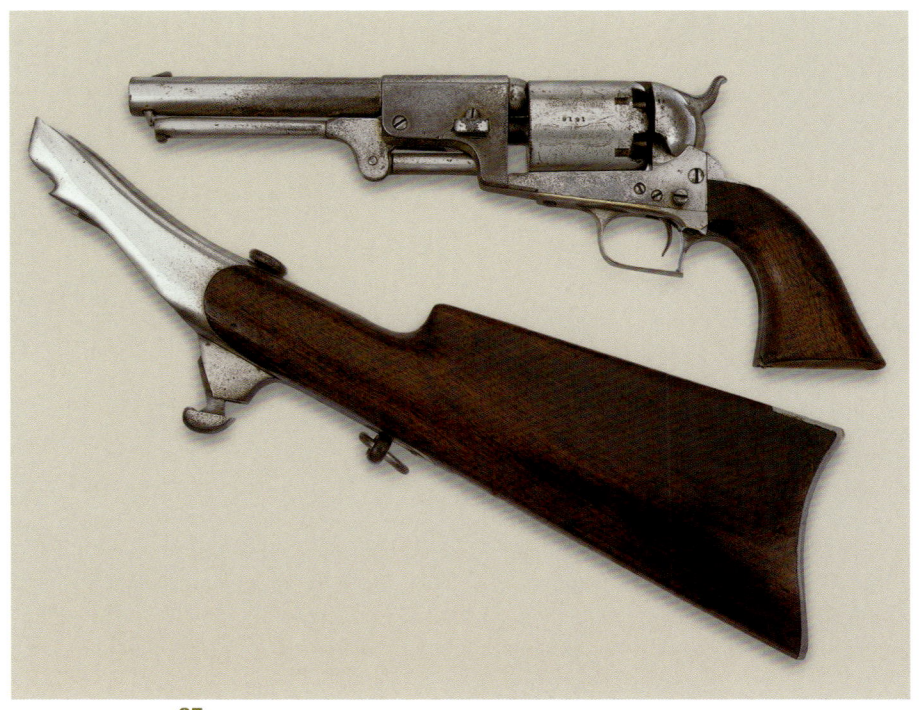

Colt Second Model Shoulder Stocked Holster Pistol (Second Model Dragoon), .44 caliber, 7½" barrel, serial number 9191. The Second Model Holster Pistol can be distinguished from the First Model by its rectangularly shaped cylinder stop slots. Though this revolver was most likely made in 1851, it was later fitted with an attachable shoulder stock of the type patented by Colt in January of 1859. As both the pistol and stock's furniture are tin-plated, the piece was probably used as a sample to demonstrate that finish. During 1858 and 1859, Colt experimented with various types of plating, one of the more unusual of which involved a newly found metal, platinum.

Derek Povah Collection.

Cased and Engraved Colt Shoulder Stocked Navy Pistol (Model 1851 Navy), .36 caliber, 7½" barrel, serial number 68218. This finely engraved revolver is accompanied by its matching third pattern attachable shoulder stock which is engraved en suite. The revolver was originally owned by Major Henry Hill.

C. John Blickhan Collection.

Special Order Colt Third Model Shoulder Stocked Navy Pistol (Model 1851 Navy), .36 caliber, 12" barrel, serial number 63197. This revolver is fitted with a first pattern attachable shoulder stock which has two prongs that lock into slots cut in the backstrap which can then be secured by a knurled set screw. The barrel has a folding rear sight and a standing front sight. Navy Pistols with this length were only made on special order and are extremely rare. Likewise, first pattern attachable shoulder stocks are rarely encountered.

Robert W. Pershing Collection.

Colt First Model Holster Pistol (First Model Dragoon), .44 caliber, 7½" barrel, serial number 2352. Often referred to as the "Fluck Model Dragoon", after John J. Fluck, who theorized that pistols of this type were manufactured using a mixture of Whitneyville-Walker and Hartford-made parts, recent research has demonstrated that they were in fact made to meet the requirements of Colt's second revolver contract with the United States Government dated November 2, 1847. Based upon the serial number of this example, it probably formed part of the second shipment of pistols sent to New York on August 9, 1848. With the exception of two revolvers, all of the arms received under the November 2, 1847 contract were shipped to the St. Louis, Missouri, Arsenal for issuance.
Herbert A. Lyman Collection.

Colt London Third Model Holster Pistol (Third Model Dragoon), .44 caliber, 7½" barrel, serial number 7. This gold-inlaid and engraved revolver is believed to have been used as a promotional piece following Colt's establishment of his London factory in 1853. The style of the engraving, as well as the gold inlaid centaur and lion motifs located on either side of the barrel lug are quite different from those found on Hartford engraved arms. In light of this, it is probable that the revolver was decorated in England.
Derek Povah Collection.

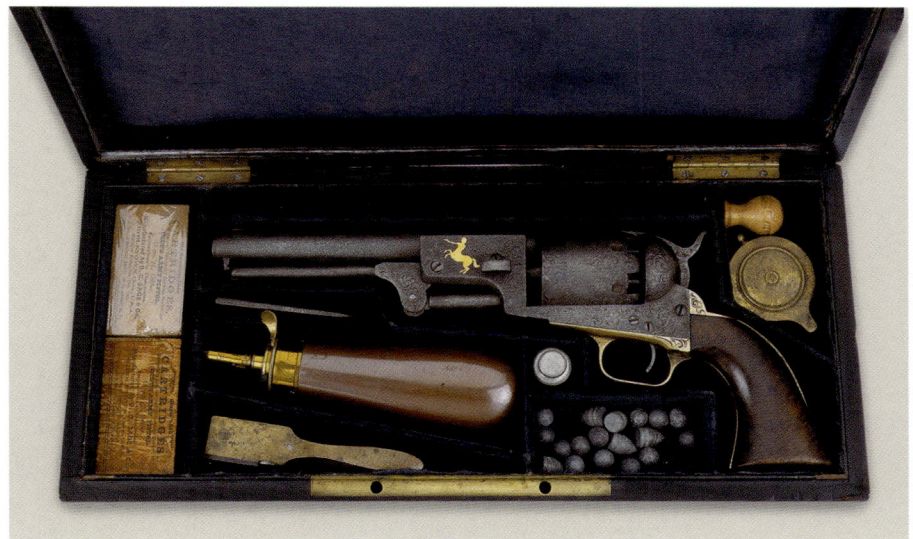

Colt Third Model London Holster Pistol (Third Model London Dragoon), .44 caliber, 7½" barrel, serial number 537. In late 1852, Samuel Colt opened an armory located by the Vauxhall Bridge in London to manufacture revolvers for the British market. During the five years of its operation, it is believed that approximately 700 pistols of this pattern were produced.
Herbert A. Lyman Collection.

Colt Old Model Pocket Pistol (Model 1849 Pocket), .31 caliber, 3" barrel, serial number 57832. Despite the lack of evidence that revolvers of this type were ever used by Wells Fargo Express, pocket pistols having 3" barrels without loading lever assemblies are commonly called "Wells Fargo" models. It is estimated that approximately 6,000 were produced between 1851 and 1860.
Herbert A. Lyman Collection.

Colt Pocket Pistol (Model 1848 Baby Dragoon), .31 caliber; 6" barrel, serial number 12066. Shortly after production of Holster Pistols had begun at Colt's Hartford works, Colt's introduced a reduced scale pocket pistol that incorporated some of the same features (e.g., oval cylinder stop recesses and a square back trigger guard). Made without a loading lever, approximately 15,000 were made before the model was discontinued in 1850.
Dr. Robert M. Sandfort Collection.

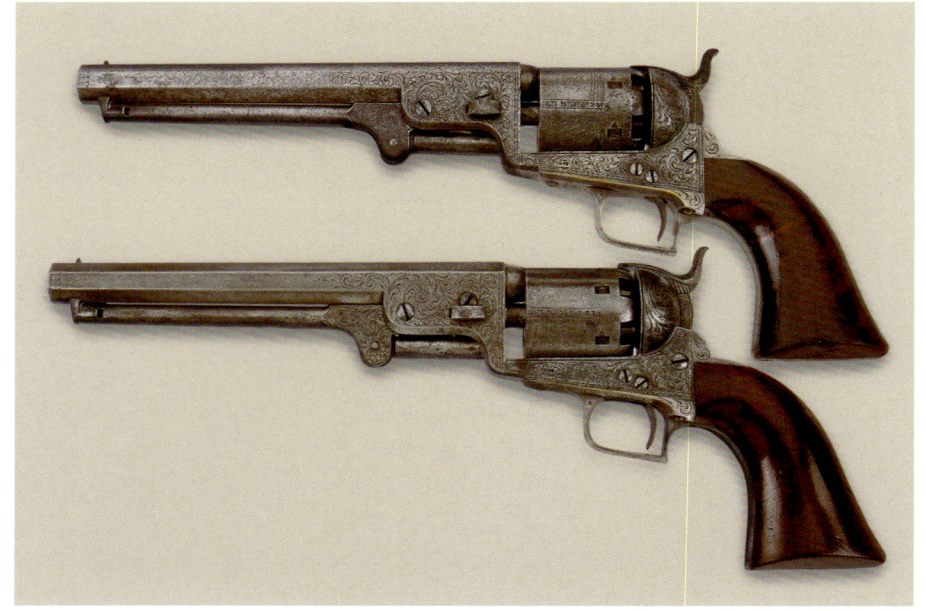

Pair of Engraved First Model Squareback Trigger Guard Belt or Navy Pistols, .36 caliber, 7½" barrels, serial numbers 2872 and 2873. This pair of revolvers was probably manufactured in 1851 and feature the square back trigger guards found on early production pistols of this type. The scrolling vine foliage engraved on these pistols is of the same style as is found on other Hartford Colts of the period.
Derek Povah Collection.

Engraved Colt Pocket Pistol (First Pattern Model 1849), .31 caliber, 4" barrel, serial number 12874. Introduced in 1850, Colt's improved Pocket Pistol was fitted with a loading lever similar to that found on the firm's Holster Pistols. Although made in Hartford, the barrel of this revolver bears the hand-engraved address inscription "COL. COLT / LONDON." This anomaly is explained by the fact that the pistol was made as part of a suite of exhibition pieces sent by Colt to England in 1851. All were engraved with the same patterns of scrollwork (including number 12571 presented by Colt to Queen Victoria's husband, H.R.H. Prince Albert). It is believed that this pistol was displayed by Colt at the Exhibition of Art-Industry held in Dublin, Ireland, in 1853.

Pete Holder Collection.

Colt Model 1851 Belt or Navy Pistol, .36 caliber, 7½" barrel, serial number 52435. This standard production Navy Pistol was made circa 1856. Documentation accompanying the revolver indicates that it was carried during the Civil War by William H. Conway (1835-1864). Conway served as a private in Company H, 11th Texas Infantry (O. M. Robert's Raiders) and was killed in action at Pleasant Hills, Louisiana on April 9, 1864.

Derek Povah Collection.

Sample Colt Second Model Holster Pistol, .44 caliber, 7½" barrel, no serial number. This revolver has a modified frame and barrel based upon the design protected by Samuel Colt's U.S. Patent Number 7,613 issued on September 3, 1850. To increase the structural integrity of his revolvers, Colt reconfigured the frame to include a top strap over the cylinder. To allow the removal of the cylinder, the barrel was hinged to the frame at the bottom of its bolster and held to an extension of the top strap by a wedge. Though a thoroughly practical concept, the design never entered production.

Raymond Baldwin Museum of Connecticut History (Gift of the Colt's Patent Fire Arms Manufacturing Company)

Cased and Engraved Colt Model 1849 Pocket Revolver. .31 caliber, 6" barrel, serial number 79447. The 1849 Pocket was the largest selling Colt in the 19th century.

Derek Povah Collection.

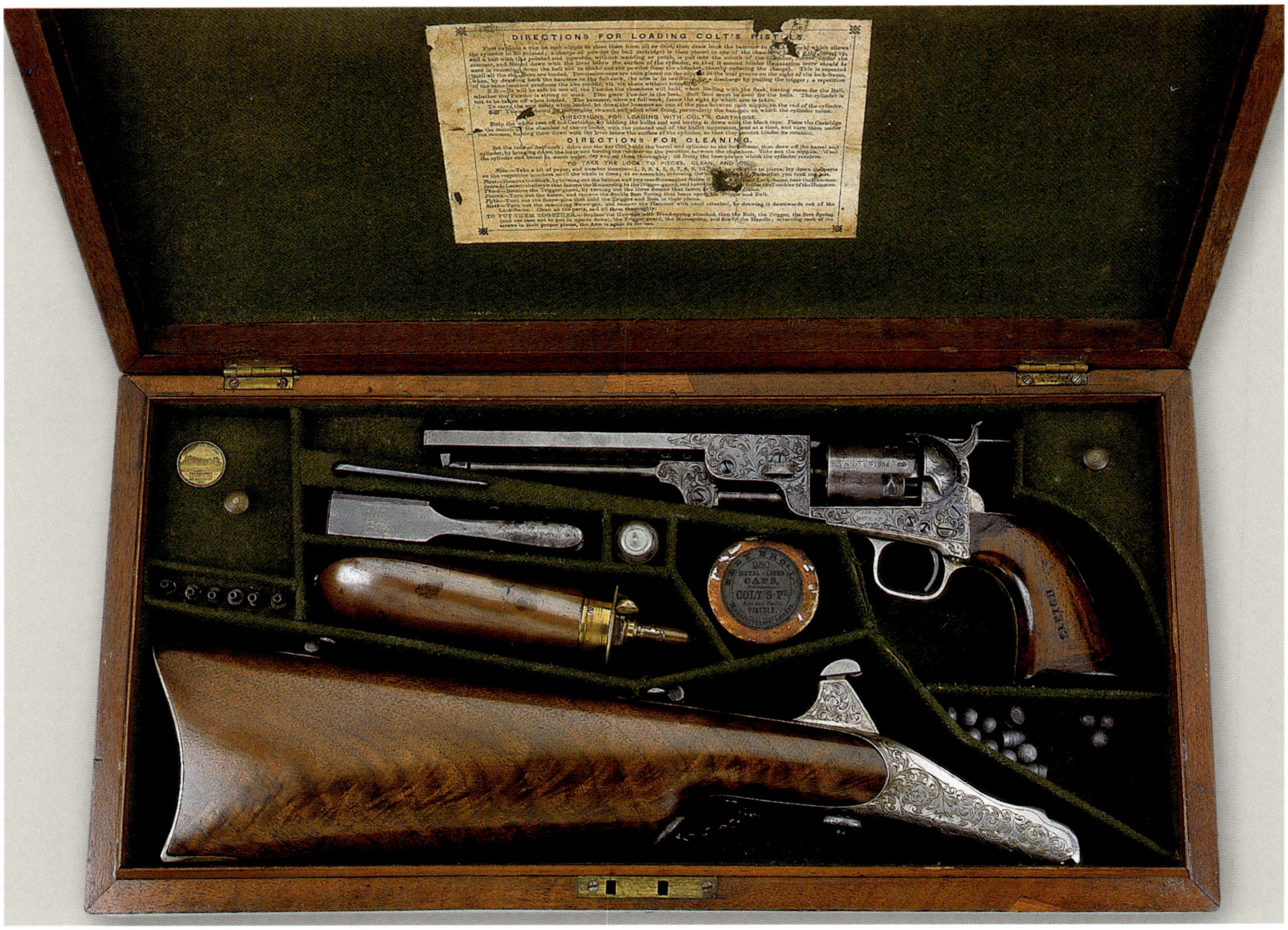

Cased and Engraved Colt Shoulder Stocked Model 1851 Belt or Navy Pistol, .36 caliber, 7½" barrel, serial number 91994. The canteen stock accompanying this pistol was patented by Colt on January 18, 1859 (No. 22, 627). Though made and engraved in the United States, this pistol was sold through the Colt company's London Agency circa 1859-1860. Both the revolver and the attachable shoulder stock are made of well-figured walnut of the type found on Colt presentation arms of the period.

C. John Blickhan Collection.

Cased and engraved Colt Model 1851 Belt or Navy Pistol, .36 caliber, 7½" barrel, serial number 74065. The style of engraved scrollwork found on this ivory-gripped pistol is typical of that cut by Gustave Young, who worked for Colt from 1852 to approximately 1869.

Paul Sorrell Collection.

Cased and Engraved Colt Model 1851 Belt or Navy Pistol, .36 caliber, 7½" barrel, serial number 91995. Numbered consecutive to the preceding revolver, this pistol is also accompanied by a canteen style shoulder stock. The original owner of this pistol carbine was Robert John Hudson (1838-sometime after 1889) of Roundhay near Leeds, England, whose name is inscribed on the backstrap. Hudson served as an officer in the 7th West Riding Rifle Volunteers (Leeds), which was raised in anticipation of a possible invasion by France.

Pete Holder Collection.

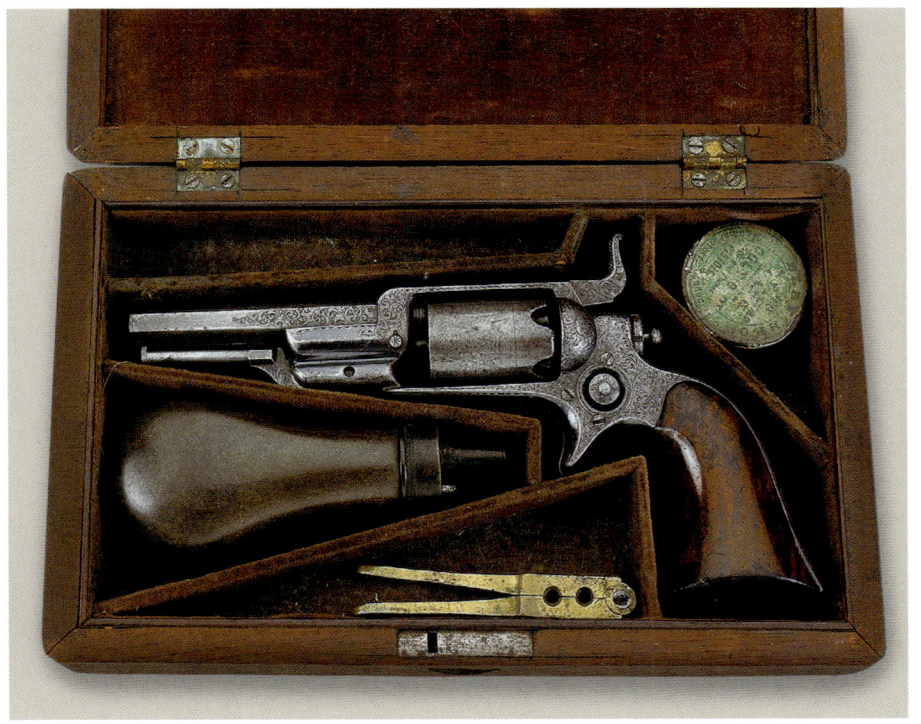

Cased and Engraved Colt New Model (1855) Pocket Pistol, .265 caliber, 3½" barrel, serial number 2615. Made in 1855, this New Model Pocket was engraved with standard pattern scrollwork by Gustave Young.

Logan B. Reed Collection.

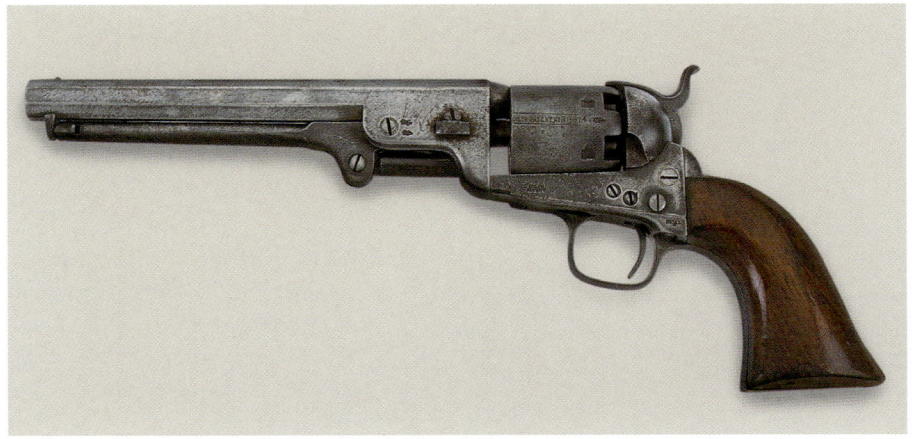

Colt Model 1851 London Belt or Navy Pistol, .36 caliber, 7½" barrel, serial number 39974. In the years between 1853 and 1856, Colt's London factory produced approximately 37,500 Navy Pistols.

Lewis E. Yearout Collection.

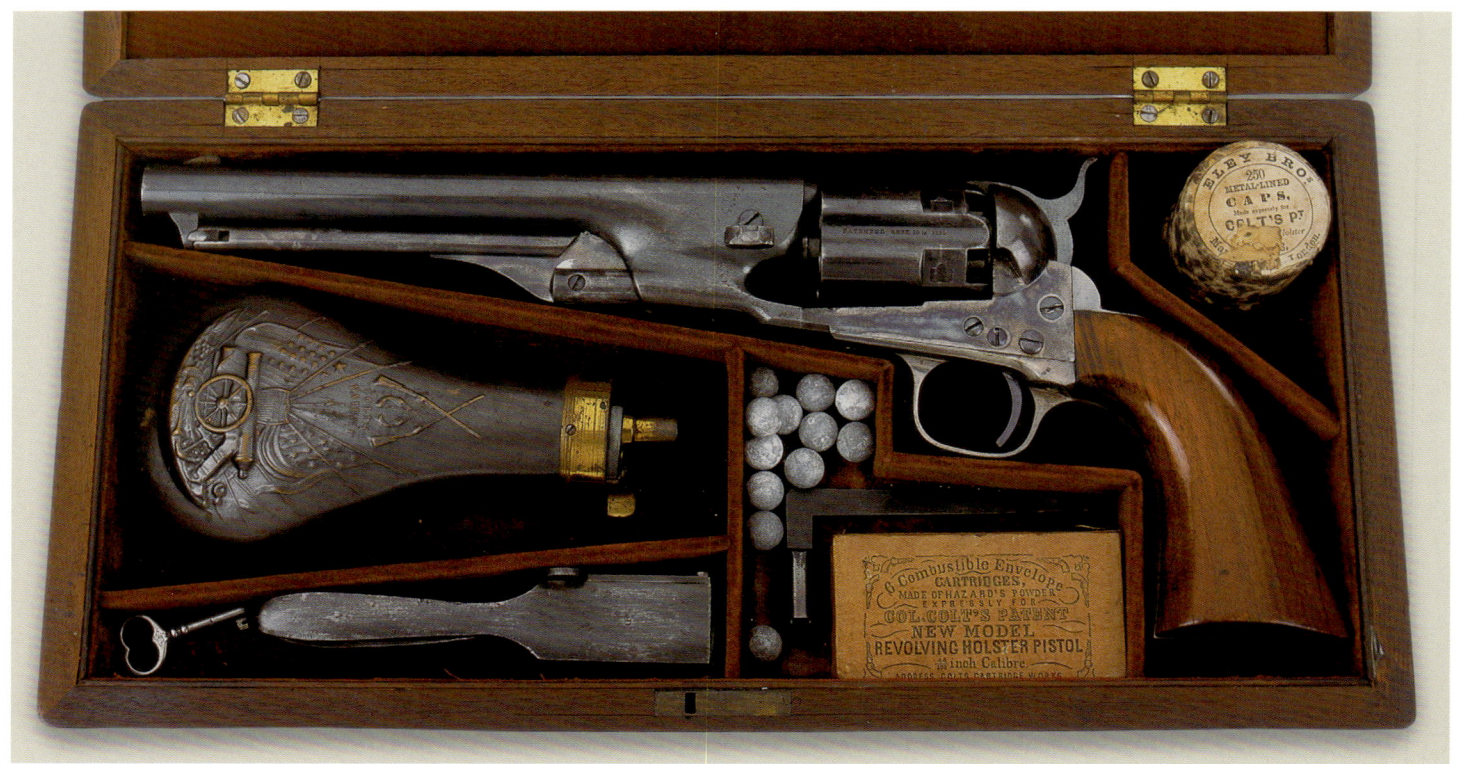

Cased Colt New Model Army Pistol of 1860, .44 caliber, 7½" barrel, serial number 928. When the New Model Army was introduced by Colt in 1860, it featured a fluted or "corrugated" cylinder of the type seen here. The purpose of these flutes was to reduce the net weight of the revolver. However, when it became clear that the company would have to mass-produce the model, the fluted design was discarded due to the amount of machining it involved. During the relatively brief period the fluted cylinder New Model Army Pistol was made, it is estimated that fewer than 4,000 were manufactured.

Carol K. Wilkerson Collection.

Cased and Engraved Colt New Model (1855) Pocket Pistol, .31 caliber, 3½" barrel, serial number 7466P. The .31 caliber New Model Pocket Pistol was introduced in 1860 and manufactured until 1870. During that period, approximately between 14,000 and 15,000 were made. This particular example was presented to H. B. Hayes by Colonel Hazard, owner of the Hazard Powder Company in May of 1863.

C. John Blickhan Collection.

Colt Enlarged Caliber Navy Pistol, .40 caliber, 7½" barrel, serial number 1. Originally part of the Colt's Patent Fire Arms Manufacturing Company's arms collection (1887 Inv. No. 260), this revolver was made in June of 1858, to demonstrate the feasibility of an "enlarged caliber" Navy Pistol. It is believed that fewer than five revolvers of this caliber were made in various forms (i.e., with standard or fluted cylinders) and finishes (blued, platinum plated, etc.) for testing by the U.S. Navy Bureau of Ordnance in July 1858.

Jim Supica Collection

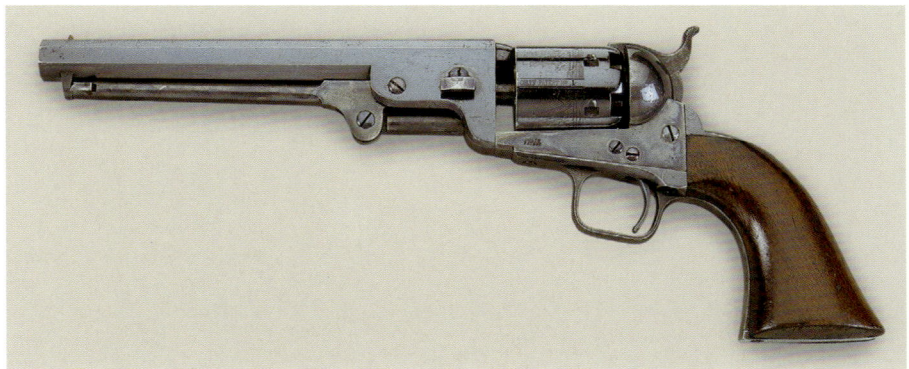

Cased Pair of Engraved New Model (1855) Pocket Pistols, .31 caliber, 3½" barrels, serial numbers 25292 and 25296. Based upon the construction and form of the scrollwork found on these revolvers, they were apparently engraved by Gustave Young. The case lid escutcheon is inscribed: A Token of Esteem / Presented to / Alfred Duffie / G. L. / Indiana Boys / Harris Light Cavalry.

Martin Lane Collection.

Skeletonized Colt New Model Army Pistol of 1860, .44 caliber, 8" barrel, serial number 11474. Skeletonized pistols were used both within the factory as display pieces and by armorers working at government arsenals to demonstrate the mechanical function of Colt revolvers.

Mr. & Mrs. Michael Ward Collection.

Cased Pair of Colt New Model (1862) Police Revolvers, .36 caliber, 6½" barrels, serial numbers 7875 and 8354. This pair of distinctively decorated pistols was probably presented to their original owner, Captain Silas Crispin of the U.S. Army Ordnance Department, by Samuel Colt in November or December of 1861. The ivory grips are carved in high relief with the "Flaming Bomb" symbol of that branch of the army.

C. John Blickhan Collection.

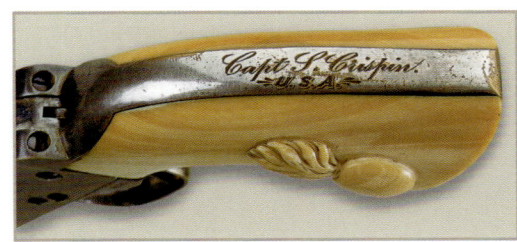

Cased Colt New Model Navy Pistol of 1861, .36 caliber, 7½" barrel, serial number 19568L. Made circa 1864 for sale through the company's London Agency, this revolver was later retailed by William Steele of Manchester, England. In contrast to the vast majority of the approximately 38,000 New Model Navy revolvers made, this example is fitted with an iron trigger guard and backstrap.
C. John Blickhan Collection.

Cased Colt New Model Army Pistol of 1860, .44 caliber, 8" barrel, serial number 161882. Manufactured shortly after the end of the American Civil War, this revolver illustrates the high polish commercial finish used by the Colt company from mid-1865 onward.
Richard & Audry Kravarik Collection.

Cased and Engraved Colt New Model Pocket Pistol of Navy Caliber, .36 caliber, 4½" barrel, serial number 7289. The New Model Pocket Pistol of Navy Caliber was the last percussion revolver to be introduced by the Colt company. Records indicate that production began in early 1865 and that they were serial numbered separately from other Colt models. This example was probably made in late 1865 or early 1866.
C. John Blickhan Collection.

Cased Colt New Model Army Pistol of 1860, .44 caliber, 8" barrel, serial number 154488L. Produced for sale through the Colt company's London Agency circa 1865, this pistol was proved at the London Proof House. As was typical of revolvers destined for the English market, it is fitted with an iron trigger guard and back strap.
C. John Blickhan Collection.

Experimental Colt Revolving Carbine, .44 caliber, 21 1/16" barrel, serial number 8. This carbine incorporates a number of features which indicate that it was probably made by Horace Lord in late 1847. The use of gun metal or brass for the frame was a common practice for Colt's model makers as it was a much easier material to work with than iron. The pattern of the frame, cylinder, barrel lug and loading lever catch all conform to designs developed by Colt or Lord from late 1847 to early 1848.
Alfred M. McCauley Collection. (Loan to Cody Firearms Museum)

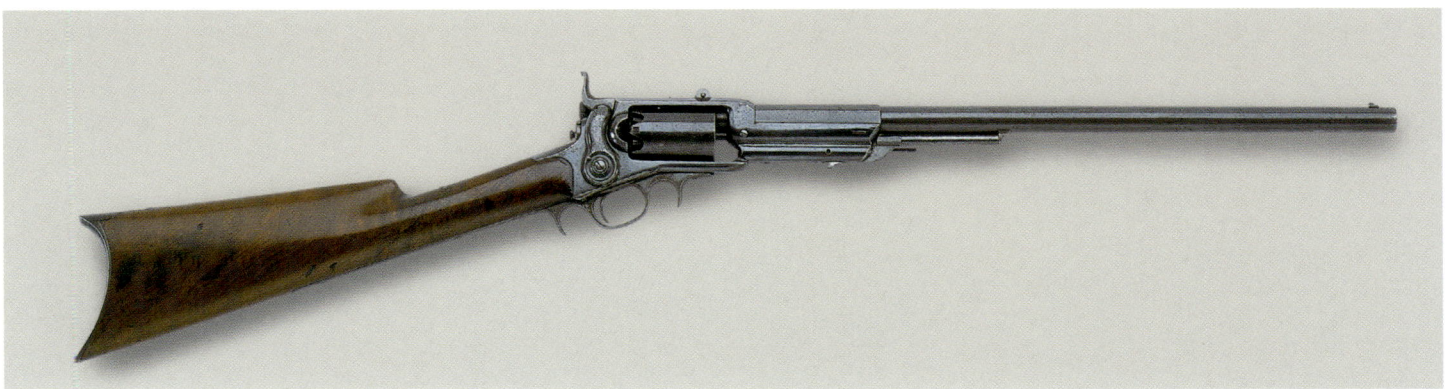

Colt New Model Sporting Rifle, .36 caliber, 24" barrel, serial number 132. The first production longarm to be manufactured by Colt at his Hartford factory was the New Model Sporting Rifle. Introduced in 1856, approximately 1,000 were made before the model was discontinued in 1859. This model is easily identified by the absence of a wood forearm and the presence of the Colt's patent oiler on the left side of the barrel lug.
C. John Blickhan Collection.

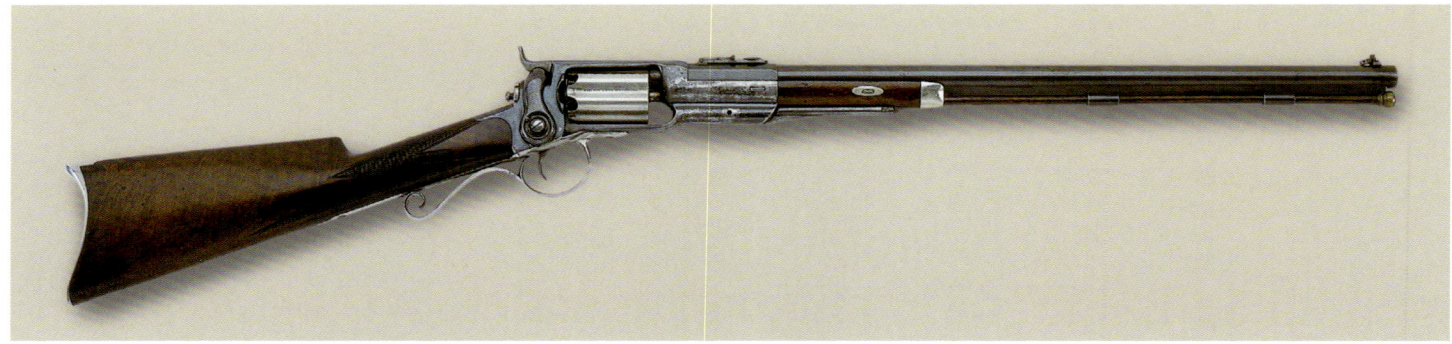

Colt New Model Sporting Rifle, .36 caliber, 27" barrel, serial number 1227. In 1857, Colt modified the design of the New Model Sporting Rifle by adding a conventional forearm. The resulting half-stock rifle was manufactured from 1857 until approximately 1864. During that period, fewer than 1,500 were made in .36, .40, .44, .50 and .56 caliber.

C. John Blickhan Collection.

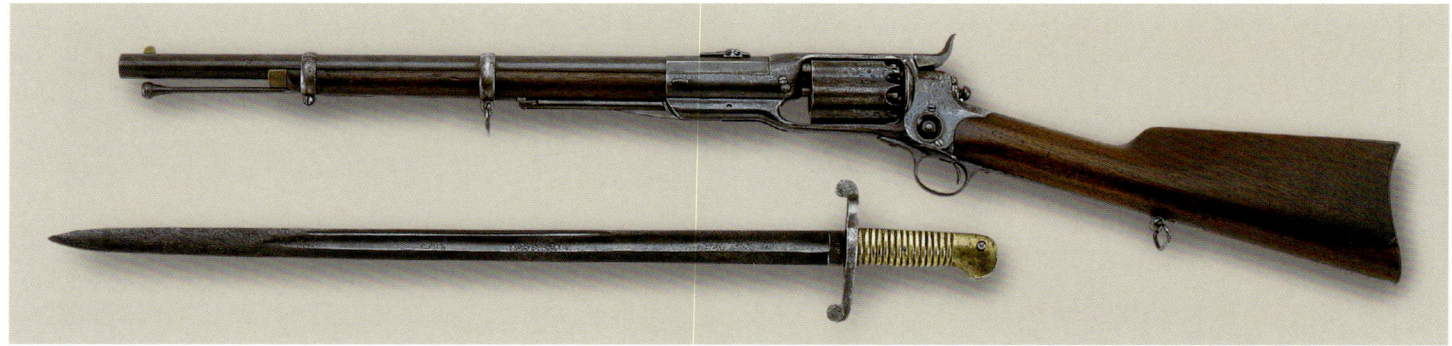

Colt New Model Artillery Carbine, .56 caliber, 24" barrel, serial number 1274. Fewer than 130 carbines of this type were sold by Colt between 1858 and 1860. Of that number, 64 were purchased by the United States Army Ordnance Department and an additional 64 were ordered by states under the provisions of the 1808 Militia Act. The carbine is accompanied by the proper saber bayonet furnished with this model which is serial numbered 4219.

C. John Blickhan Collection.

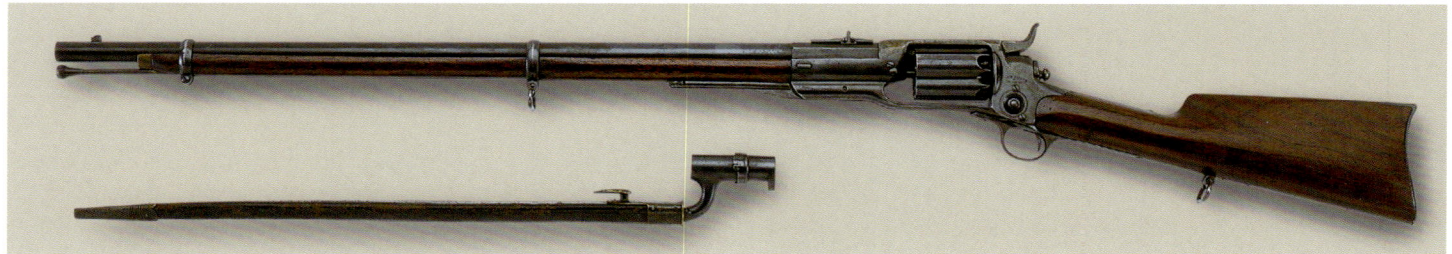

Colt New Model Navy Revolving Rifle Musket, .64 caliber, 31.125" barrel, serial number 14. In July of 1859, Colt submitted a sample .65 caliber Revolving Rifle Musket for testing to the United States Navy Bureau of Ordnance. After it successfully completed a series of trials, the Navy ordered an additional 100 rifles of the same caliber complete with socket bayonets and accessories. These arms, of which the present example was one, were shipped to the Washington Navy Yard on January 21, 1860.

C. John Blickhan Collection.

Colt New Model Sporting Rifle, .56 caliber, 31.25" barrel, serial number 2984. First made in 1858, fewer than 200 rifles of this pattern were manufactured prior to 1864. Though resembling a full-stock military rifle, the civilian sporting rifle is fitted with a gutta-percha cleaning rod and does not have any provision for a bayonet.

C. John Blickhan Collection.

Sample Colt Model 1854 Russian Contract Rifled Musket, .69 caliber, 42" barrel, serial number 8. In 1853 Colt and Charles Law purchased 25,000 U.S. Model 1816 Flintlock Muskets for resale. These arms were altered to percussian cap and rifled. In 1855 Colt bought out his partner and then entered into negotiations with the Imperial Russian Government for their sale. While approximately 3,000 were shipped to Russia, the balance remained in Hartford. These rifled muskets eventually were sold to Giuseppe Garibaldi in 1860.

Karl Kohlhorst Collection.

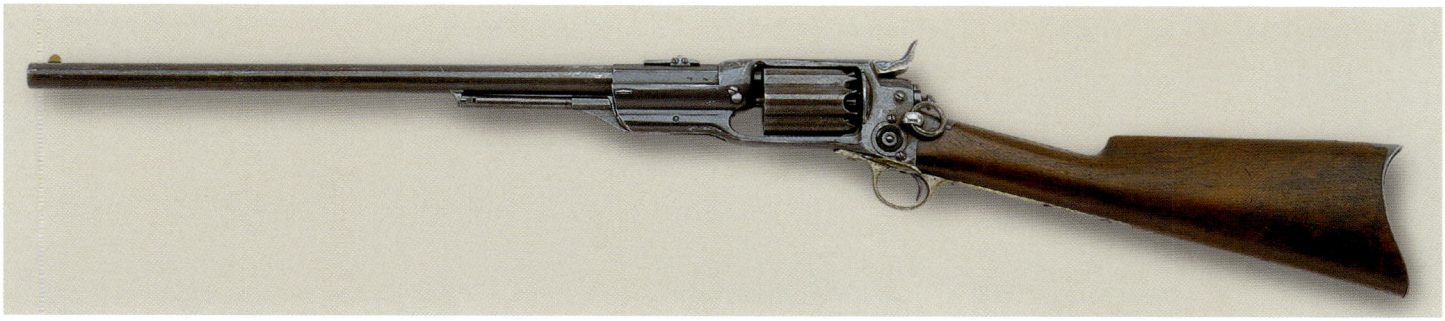

Colt New Model Revolving Cavalry Carbine, .56 caliber, 21" barrel, serial number 11649. Between 1858 and 1864, the Colt company shipped approximately 175 New Model .56 caliber Carbines to their London Agency. All of these arms were fitted with a sling swivel ring on the left side of their frames. Though designed for military use, no record has been found that would indicate these arms were purchased by the British Government for issue to any standing units. Consequently, it must be assumed they were sold commercially.

C. John Blickhan Collection.

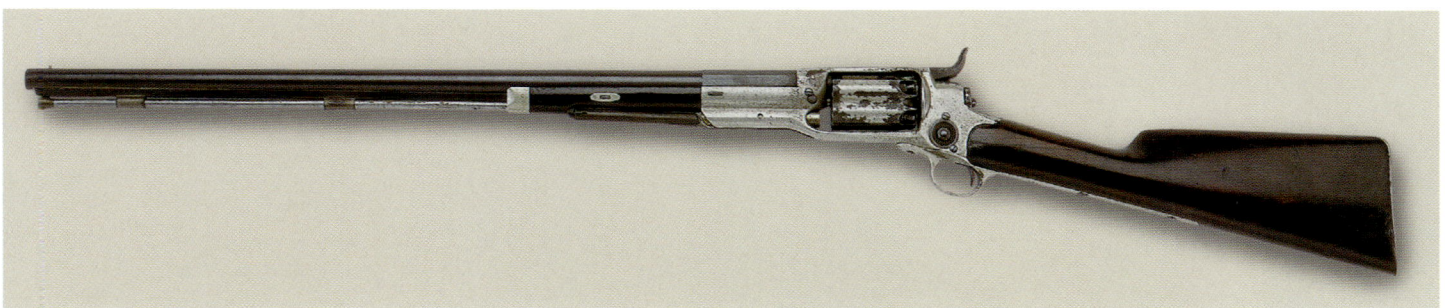

Colt New Model Revolving Shotgun, .60 caliber, 26.875" barrel, serial number 125. Introduced in late 1859, approximately 500 shotguns of this bore were manufactured up to 1861 when the model was discontinued due to lack of sales. A substantial number of these shotguns remained in the company's inventory well into the late 1860's. It is likely that this example was finished sometime during the latter period as it has a nickel-plated cylinder and frame.

C. John Blickhan Collection.

Colt New Model Revolving Shotgun, .75 caliber, 27" barrel, serial number 944. While this model was brought into production in 1860, manufacture was suspended during the Civil War. As a result, most of the approximately 600 made were assembled in the years between 1865 and 1870.

C. John Blickhan Collection.

While the Colt Single Action Army Revolver is the quintessential cowboy pistol, it was not the first cartridge Colt to be used in the West. That distinction belongs to the various alterations of the Colt New Model Army Pistol of Civil War fame. Following the introduction of self-contained metallic cartridges, large numbers of the percussion New Model Army were altered to the new ignition system. Large numbers of these pistols were shipped west where they quickly established the Colt company's reputation for making reliable cartridge revolvers.

The prevalence of urban crime during the 1870s and 80s, prompted many city dwellers to arm themselves. The Colt company met the needs of many with their deringers and small pocket pistols. It is interesting to note that one of the more influential books of the time, The Pistol as a Weapon of Self Defense in the House and on the Road (New York: 1875), recommended the Colt House Pistol as an ideal sidearm.

Early Colt Cartridge Pistols:
Conversions, New Line, Clover Leaf & Deringer Pistols
by John Blickhan

Although Samuel Colt recognized that the future of his firm would depend upon its development of revolvers using self-contained metallic cartridges, it was not until four years after his death that serious attention was paid to the problem.

Beginning in 1865, the Colt company began investigating a variety of cartridge systems which did not infringe upon the rear loading, bored-through cylinder patent held by Smith & Wesson. Numerous inventors, such as Hiram Berdan, Silas Crispin and Charles E. Sneider, offered their designs to the company but all were rejected. Instead, the firm decided to use a front loading system developed by one of its chief designers, F. Alexander Thuer. The major advantage of Thuer's design was that it only involved substituting a cartridge cylinder in place of the percussion one. Consequently, the basic construction of Colt's revolvers did not need to be altered.

Following the expiration of Rollin White's bored-through cylinder patent that had been licensed to Smith & Wesson, the Colt company immediately introduced altered revolvers based upon that design. Developed by Charles B. Richards, as well as William Mason, Colt's conversion system structurally altered the firm's pistols. It had the benefit of reducing Colt's inventory of completed, as well as incomplete, percussion revolvers. While popular, these alterations were rapidly replaced by the company's revolvers which had been specifically

Cased Colt Old Model Pocket Thuer Metallic Cartridge Pistol, .31 caliber, 4" barrel, serial number 306737. F. Alexander Thuer's cartridge revolver was designed in such a way as to allow the continued use of a percussion cylinder if needed. The cartridge cylinder was constructed in two parts: the forward section containing the chambers, and a rear ring that housed the firing pin, as well as ejector. Thuer patent cartridges were tapered so that they could be inserted into the chamber from the front, thereby evading the Rollin White patent. While production figures are unknown, relatively few were made in .31 caliber.

C. John Blickhan Collection.

designed for metallic cartridges.

As would be expected, many owners of percussion revolvers had them altered to metallic cartridge by local gunsmiths. Though some of the field conversions are somewhat rough in form, they functioned nevertheless. Better quality alterations were also carried out by major arms retailers, such as Schuyler, Hartley & Graham of New York City.

The first model to be introduced was the House Pistol now popularly known as the Colt Cloverleaf due to the form of its four-shot cylinder. Designed by Charles B. Richards, this revolver was chambered for the .41 rimfire cartridge. Manufactured from 1871 to 1876, slightly fewer than 10,000 were made.

The second revolver to be introduced was a .22 rimfire caliber seven shot Pocket Pistol that is now known as the Colt "Open Top" as it lacks a top strap to the frame. During its production life of 1871 to 1877, approximately 114,200 were made.

The most successful series of early cartridge revolvers were the Colt New Lines. Designed by William Mason, these pistols were produced in .22, .30, .32, .38 and .41 rimfire calibers. First marketed in 1873, the .32 rimfire caliber version remained in production until 1884. During that period a total of just over 55,000 New Line Pistols were made in .22 rimfire caliber; 11,000 in .30 rimfire; 22,000 in .32 rimfire; 5,500 in .38 rimfire, and; about 7,000 in .41 rimfire caliber.

The New Line series was replaced by the .38 or .41 centerfire caliber New House Pistol in 1880. Over its six-year production run, approximately 4,000 were made.

In 1882 Colt introduced a companion revolver in .32, .38 and .41 centerfire caliber that was called the New Police Revolver. Like the New House Pistol, this model did not generate much attention and only about 4,000 were made before the model was discontinued in 1886.

Without question the most popular of Colt's early cartridge pistols were the deringers. Manufactured in three distinct styles, the First and Second Models were based upon patents issued to Daniel Moore. First sold under the Colt name in 1870, approximately 6,500 of the First Model (all metal construction) were produced before it was discontinued. In addition, 9,000 of the Second Model which had detachable walnut grips were made. The Colt New Patent Deringer now called the Third or Thuer Model was by far the most popular. Introduced in 1875, this .41 rimfire caliber pistol was advertised until 1912. Over that period approximately 45,000 were made.

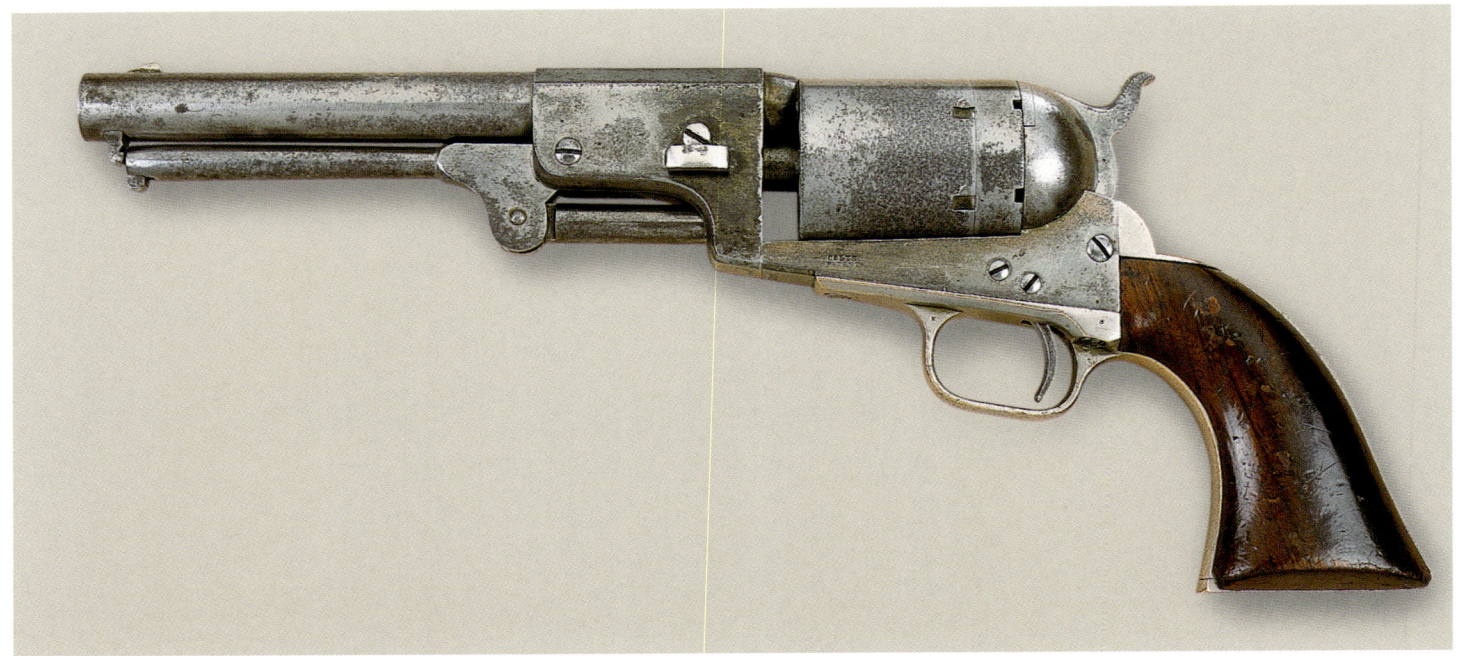

Sample Colt Third Model Holster Pistol Metallic Cartridge Alteration, .44rf caliber, 8" barrel, serial number 15703. In 1859 and 1860, the Colt company altered a number of revolvers to determine the efficacy of chambering them for metallic cartridges. While those made using Dreyse needle-fire and Lefaucheux pinfire cartridges showed little commercial promise, the bored-through cylinder revolvers, of which this is an example, appeared viable. Unfortunately, Samuel Colt was not able to evade or license the Rollin White patent covering that design and the project was abandoned.
C. John Blickhan Collection.

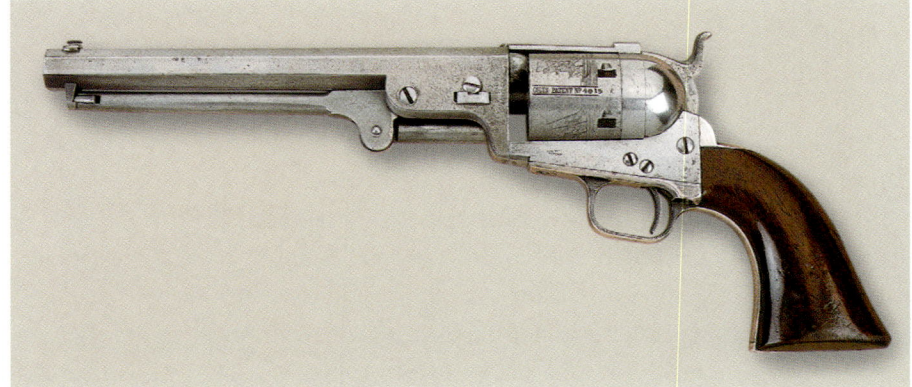

Colt Navy Model Thuer Metallic Cartridge Pistol, .38cf caliber, .36 caliber, 7½" barrel, serial number 4015. During the development phase of what was to become the Colt company's first metallic cartridge pistol, F. Alexander Thuer built several samples which had firing pins mounted in the rear of shoulders of the cylinder. When it was determined that this design was impractical, it was abandoned in favor of the two-piece cylinder discussed below.
C. John Blickhan Collection.

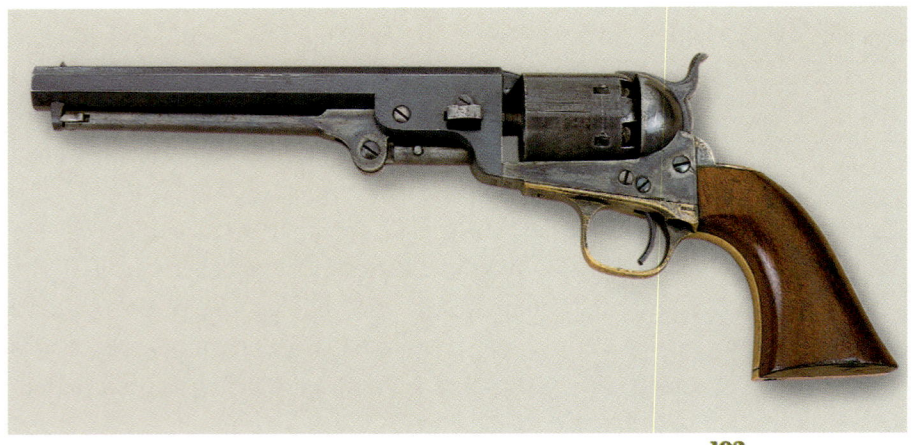

Sample Colt Navy Pistol Metallic Cartridge Alteration, .36 caliber, 7½" barrel, serial number 157097. Based upon the construction of this revolver, its design can be attributed to Hiram Berdan. In 1866 the Colt company produced several sample pistols incorporating cylinders of this type at Berdan's request. While Berdan claimed that his needle-fire cartridge was patentable, it essentially was a copy of a pre-existing design patented by Johannes von Dreyse. As a result, when Berdan offered the Colt company the opportunity to manufacture cartridge pistols of this type, the firm wisely declined.
C. John Blickhan Collection.

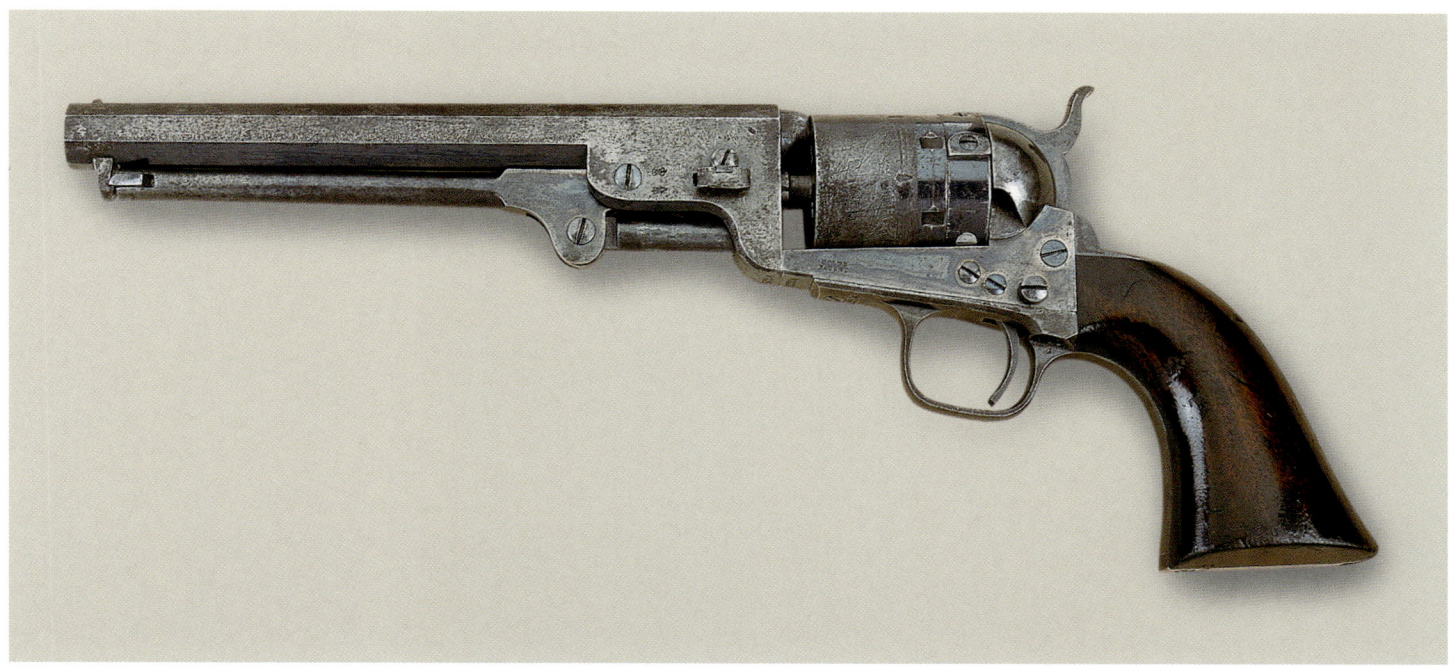

Colt Old Model Navy Thuer Metallic Cartridge Pistol, .36 caliber, 7½" barrel, serial number 125504. Although the first shipments of altered Navy revolvers were made in October of 1868, full-scale production of the cylinders they required did not begin until March of 1869.

C. John Blickhan Collection.

Colt New Model Army Thuer Metallic Cartridge Pistol, .44 caliber, 8" barrel, serial number 178316. By far the most commonly encountered Thuer alteration is that of the New Model Army. Production of this arm began in the late autumn of 1868 and continued until 1871. Though marketed in the United States, the model achieved a much higher degree of popularity in the British colonies. Consequently, a significant percentage of the production was shipped to the Colt company's London Agency.

C. John Blickhan Collection.

Engraved Colt New Model Navy Thuer Metallic Cartridge Pistol, .36 caliber, 7½" barrel, serial number 35123. Based upon the construction and quality of the engraving found on this silver-plated revolver, it is likely that the work was executed by either Gustave Young or Herman L. Ulrich. The ivory grips are carved in high relief on an-as-yet unidentified coat-of-arms incorporating a five-pointed star.

C. John Blickhan Collection.

Colt Metallic Cartridge Six Shot Army Revolving Pistol (Richards Conversion), .44cf caliber, 8" barrel, serial number 20681. Charles B. Richards's system for altering percussion revolvers by the attachment of a fixed plate to the interior face of the frame's recoil shield which contained a retractable firing pin was patented. The upper edge of this piece had an extension which was machined to form the rear sight. The right side of this plate was fitted with a pivoted loading gate to allow the insertion and extraction of cartridges from the rear. In addition, these revolvers were equipped with an ejector rod mounted on the right side of the barrel. In 1871 approximately 1,200 percussion cap New Model Army Pistols were altered on the Richards system for use with metallic cartridges at the Springfield Armory. These pistols can be identified by the presence of conversion numbers beneath their original Colt serial numbers and the "U.S." ownership stamp on the left side of their barrels forward of the breech.
Michael Ward Collection.

Colt Metallic Cartridge Six Shot Army Revolving Pistol (2nd Model Richards), .44cf caliber, 8" barrel, serial number 200787. An undetermined number of early Richards alterations were fitted with cylinders having 12 locking bolt stops machined into the cylinder rebated periphery. While this was intended to insure that the cylinder could be positively locked in the half or full position, in practice, the system left much to be desired. As a result it was abandoned relatively quickly after it was introduced (ca. 1871).
C. John Blickhan Collection.

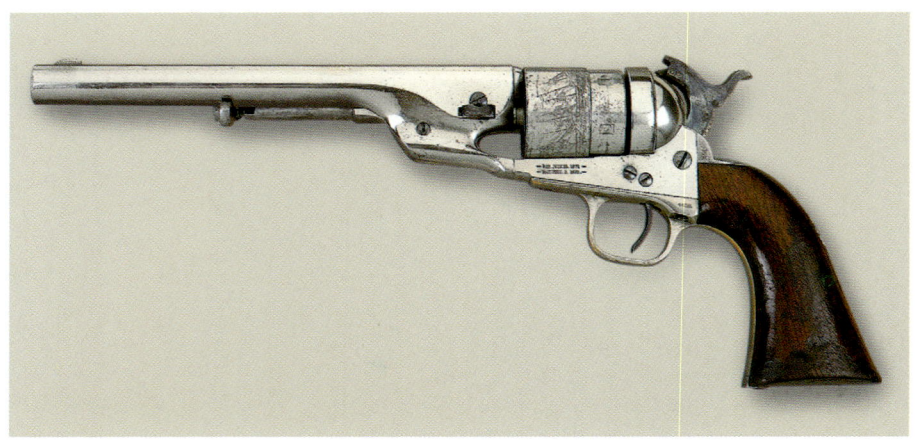

Colt Metallic Cartridge Six Shot Army Revolving Pistol (snd Model Richards Conversion), .44cf caliber, 8" barrel, serial number 195465. This revolver illustrates the alteration system developed jointly by Charles B. Richards and William Mason. In place of the firing pin being housed in the breech plate, it is attached to the hammer's nose. As a result of this repositioning, the upper section of the breech plate is cut away to allow the hammer's passage.
C. John Blickhan Collection.

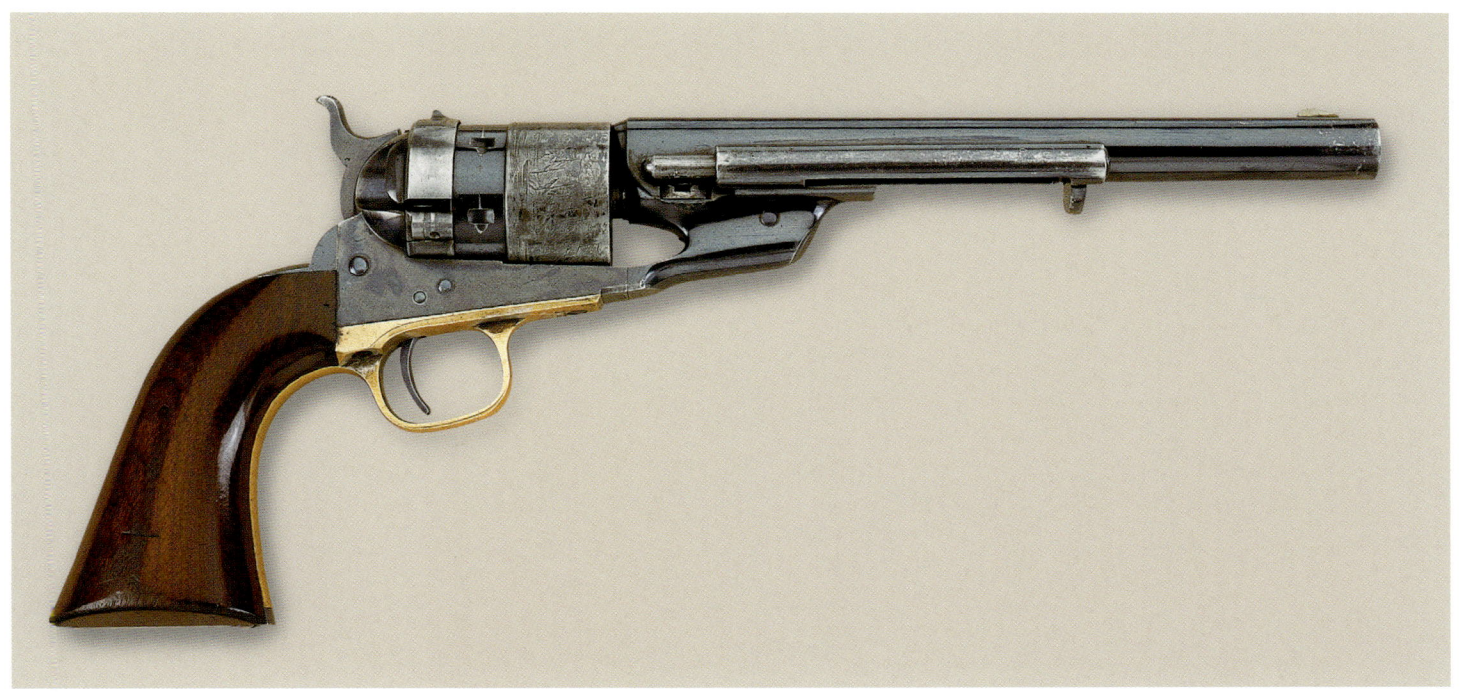

Colt Metallic Cartridge Army Six Shot Revolving Pistol (Richards Patent), .44cf caliber, 8" barrel, serial numbers 3733/2892. In contrast to the preceding pistols, this example was originally made as a cartridge pistol using parts left over from the company's percussion New Model Army Pistol production run.

Michael Ward Collection.

Colt 1851 Navy- Field Conversion. This gun, serial number 61728, represents the early contract conversion from the percussion for the Navy. Conversion number 1728. This Navy is marked "R.W.M." and "U.S." The iron backstrap and triggerguard indicate that it was shipped as a percussion gun and then returned to the factory for conversion. Known as a New York Navy Yard Conversion. The initials "R.W.M." stand for Richard W. Meade, and he was the Navy Inspector.

C. John Blickhan Collection.

Colt Metallic Cartridge Navy Six Shot Revolving Pistol (Richards-Mason Conversion), .38cf caliber, 7½" barrel, serial number 3789. It is estimated that approximately 3,500 New Model Navy revolvers were altered on the Richards-Mason system for use with metallic cartridges between 1873 and 1876. While those made for the U.S. Navy were chambered for .38 centerfire cartridges, the majority of those made for the commercial market were .38 rimfire.

C. John Blickhan Collection.

Colt New Model Pocket of Navy Caliber Five Shot Revolving Pistol (Richards-Mason Patents), .38 caliber, 6½" barrel, serial number 11552. Sales of the percussion New Model Pocket of Navy Caliber never reached the levels the Colt company had anticipated for the pistol following its introduction in 1865. Consequently, in the early 1870s, the majority of these pistols were altered for use with metallic cartridges. In addition, existing parts inventories were also used to build cartridge revolvers with new barrels such as that found on this pistol.

C. John Blickhan Collection.

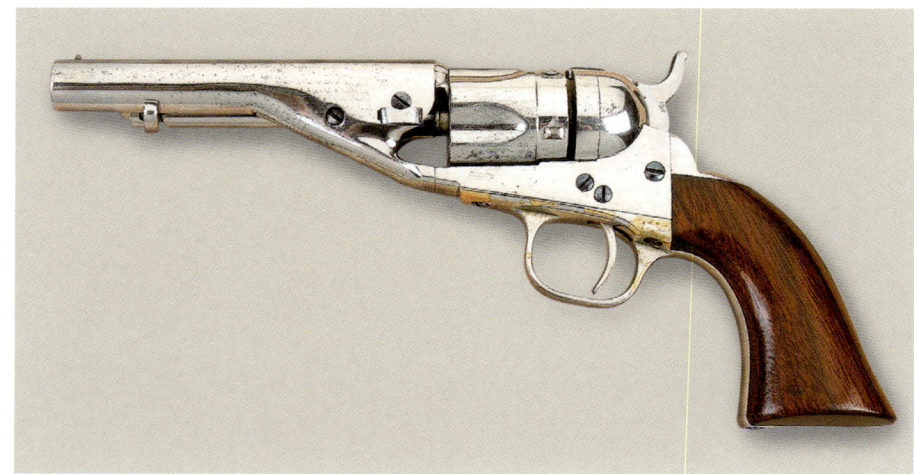

Colt New Model Police Five Shot Revolving Pistol (Richards-Mason Patents), .38 caliber, 4½" barrel, serial number 3036. From approximately 1873 to late 1876, the Colt company manufactured about 19,000 New Model Police cartridge pistols. While the majority had round cylinders, a number were built using modified fluted cylinders originally made for percussion arms.

C. John Blickhan Collection.

Colt Metallic Cartridge Army Six Shot Revolving Pistol (Richards-Mason Patents), .44cf caliber, 8" barrel, serial number 6108. Originally made as a cartridge revolver, this pistol is fitted with a barrel having a solid stepped lug, instead of altered percussion barrel with a plugged loading rod aperture. The majority of these revolvers were made in 1877 and 1878.

Michael Ward Collection.

Colt First Model Holster Pistol Conversion, .44rf caliber 5⅝" barrel, serial number 7163. This after-market conversion was achieved by cutting off the rear of the cylinder to allow the insertion of cartridges, as well as the installation of a breech plate, to take up the space between the original recoil shield and the breech face of the cylinder.

C. John Blickhan Collection.

Colt Whitneyville-Walker Holster Pistol Conversion, .44rf caliber, 7¼" barrel, serial number A Company 150. As pistols were not inexpensive, many owners had them converted for use with cartridges by local gunsmiths. The example illustrated here represents a rare conversion of a Whitneyville-Walker Holster Pistol.

C. John Blickhan Collection.

Colt Old Model Navy Pistol Conversion, .38rf caliber, 7½" barrel, serial number 21283. This revolver was converted rather simply by cutting off the rear face of its cylinder and removing the percussion nipples so that the hammer could strike the exposed rims of chambered cartridges.

C. John Blickhan Collection.

Colt New Model Pocket Pistol Conversion, .32rf caliber, 3½" barrel, serial number 12684. Through the installation of a two-piece cylinder, this revolver was effectively made into a cartridge revolver. The retention of the loading rod assembly suggests that it could also have been used as a percussion pistol if the need arose.

C. John Blickhan Collection.

Colt Old Model Navy Pistol Conversion, .38cf caliber, 7½" barrel, serial number 168244L. It appears that this revolver was altered for use with metallic cartridges in England using the Richards system. Whether or not the work was carried out by the Colt company's London Agency is open to speculation but the quality of the work suggests that might have been the case.

C. John Blickhan Collection.

Engraved Colt New Model Army Pistol Conversion, .44rf caliber, 8" barrel, serial number 114721. It is believed that alterations of this type using a straight full-length cartridge cylinder were commissioned in the late 1870s by one of the major New York City retailers. The most likely candidates for their manufacture are either J. P. Moore & Sons or, the Hartley & Graham Company.

Michael Ward Collection.

Colt New Model Revolving Military Rifle Conversion, .38rf caliber, 31⅜" barrel, serial number 144. In the mid-1870's the New York City firm of Schuyler, Hartley & Graham had a number of obsolete percussion Colt rifles altered to cartridge by Herman Boker, as well as B. S. Moulton. These arms were fitted with sharply fluted cylinders and the capping cutouts on their right recoil shields were enlarged to allow the insertion of cartridges into the cylinder.

C. John Blickhan Collection.

Colt New Model Revolving Sporting Rifle Conversion, .38rf caliber, 21" barrel, serial number 512. This field conversion was carried out by attaching a new breech plate to the interior face of the recoil shield and modifying the original cylinder so that it could be used with metallic cartridges.

C. John Blickhan Collection.

Colt New Model Revolving Sporting Rifle Conversion, .44rf caliber, 27" barrel, serial number 2367. This field conversion was constructed using the original cylinder with its rear face removed and a new breechplate.

C. John Blickhan Collection.

Colt Army Six Shot Revolving Pistol, .44rf caliber, 7½" barrel, serial number 2487. As this model was one of the first large bore cartridge pistols made by Colt, it was eagerly sought-after by emigrants heading to the American West. As a result, most of the surviving examples, such as the one illustrated here, display evidence of extensive use.

C. John Blickhan Collection.

Colt Army Six Shot Revolving Pistol, .44rf caliber, 7½" barrel, serial number 47. In 1871 the Colt company introduced a .44 caliber revolver which had been specifically designed for use with metallic cartridges, rather than an alteration of pre-existing percussion arms. Commonly referred to today as the Model 1871/72 Open Top Revolver, approximately 7,000 were produced before the pistol was replaced by the Single Action Army Pistol in 1873. The example seen here is fitted with a Navy Pistol pattern grip and an earlier canteen shoulder stock..

C. D. Terry Collection.

Engraved Colt Army Six Shot Revolving Pistol, .44rf caliber, 7½" barrel, serial number 1970. This attractively engraved revolver was probably made in late 1872. Unlike serial number 47, this example is fitted with Army Pistol pattern grips.

C. D. Terry Collection.

Engraved Colt New Model Army Pistol Conversion, .44rf caliber, 8" barrel, serial number 157649. Long referred to as "Mystery Conversions," revolvers altered in the fashion seen here, are now believed to have been made by Schuyler, Hartley & Graham. When it became apparent that the firm's inventory of percussion New Model Army Pistols had little chance of being sold in their original form, Schuyler, Hartley & Graham had them altered to metallic cartridge by B. S. Moulton. Interestingly, the majority of the pistols altered by Moulton were engraved examples which had been held in stock by Schuyler, Hartley & Graham for some time.

C. John Blickhan Collection.

Colt Seven Shot Revolving Pistol, .22rf caliber, 2⅜" barrel, serial number 4. Commonly called the "Open Top" pocket pistol due to its lack of a top strap over the cylinder, this model was introduced in 1871. By the time it was discontinued in 1877, approximately 114,200 had been made.

Bernard F. Oakes Collection.

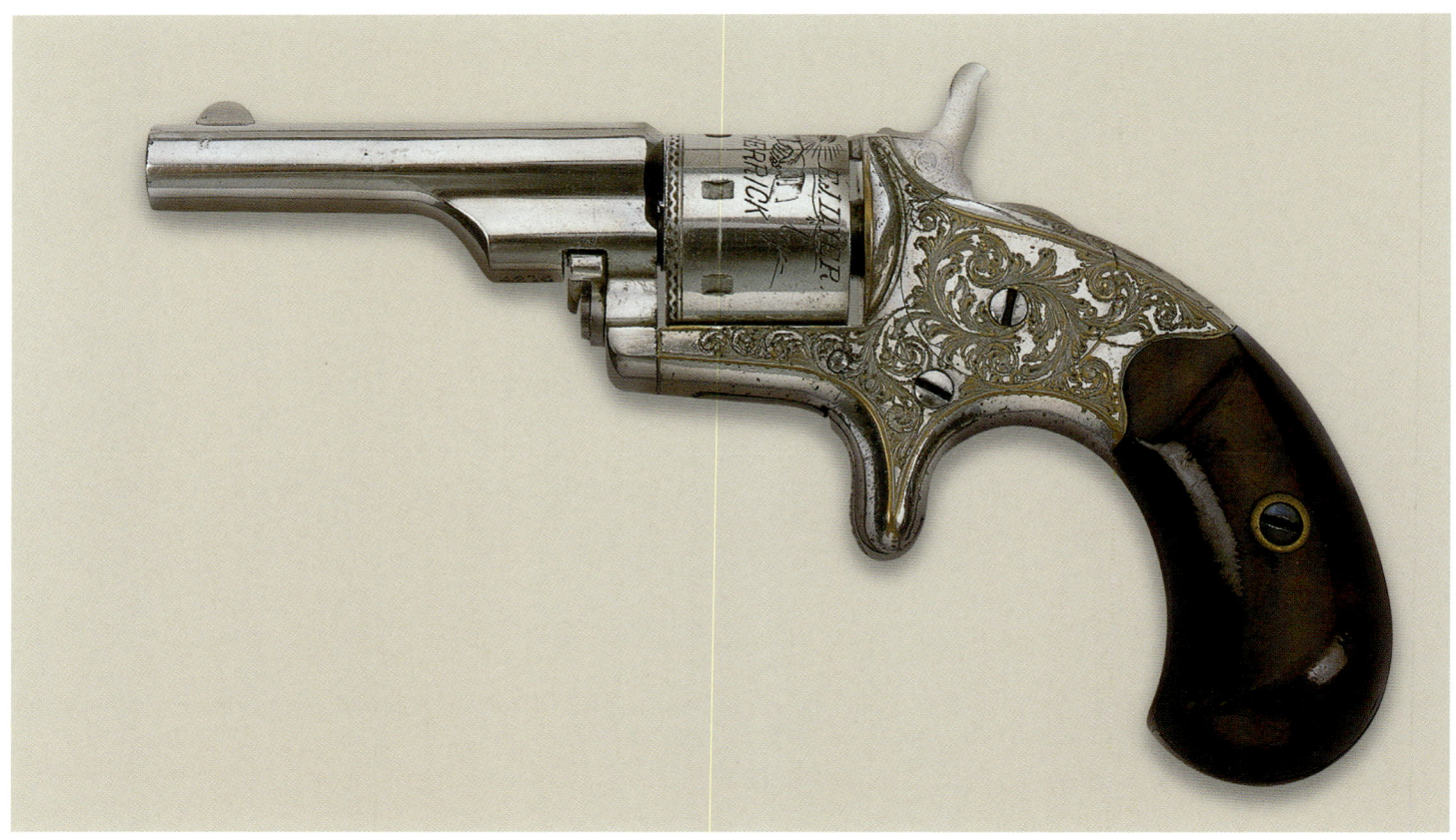

Engraved Colt Seven Shot Revolving Pistol, .22rf caliber, 2⅛" barrel, serial number 4316. While the frame of this nickel-plated revolver is engraved with finely cut foliate scrollwork, the cylinder is inscribed with a presentation inscription ("PRESENTED to HENRY HERRICK By E. J. Dyer") accompanied by Masonic symbols.

Fred Sweeney Collection.

Colt Seven Shot Revolving Pistol, .22rf caliber, 2⅛" barrel, serial number 1637.

Bernard F. Oakes Collection.

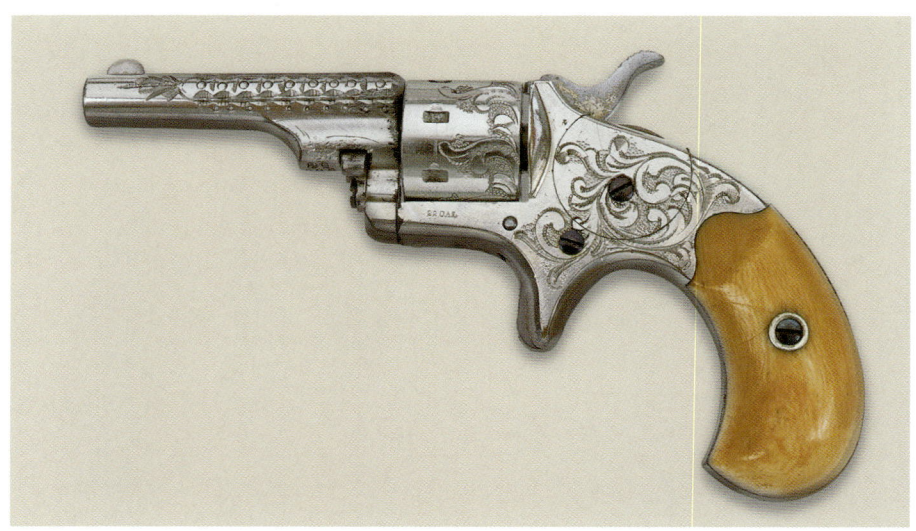

Engraved Colt Seven Shot Revolving Pistol, .22rf caliber, 2⅛" barrel, serial number 91825. In contrast to the majority of engraved Seven Shot Revolving Pistols which were modestly decorated, this example is embellished with foliate scrollwork on its frame, cylinder and barrel. To highlight the nickel-plated finish and ivory grips, the screw heads are all fire blued. Factory records indicate that it was shipped to New York City retailers Hartley & Graham, in October 1888.

Fred Sweeney Collection.

Engraved Colt's Patent House Pistol, .41rf caliber, 3" barrel, serial number 2178. The House Pistol is now usually referred to as the "Cloverleaf Model" due to the form of its four-shot cylinder. The model was introduced into the Colt company's product line in 1871 and was discontinued in 1876. Total production is estimated to have been approximately 10,000 pistols. The rather sparse scrollwork engraved on this revolver's frame is typical of the decoration used for this model.
                                              Fred Sweeney Collection.

Colt's Patent House Pistol, .41rf caliber, 2⅝" barrel, serial number 9722. Toward the end of the House Pistol's production, its signature four-shot cylinder was replaced by a conventional round five-shot version. At the same time, the ejector rod which had been a feature of the earlier variation, was abandoned. The brass frame of this pistol was originally silver-plated.
                                              Fred Sweeney Collection.

Boxed Colt Seven Shot Revolving Pistol, .22rf caliber, 2⅝" barrel, serial number 63142. This standard production nickel-plated and walnut gripped pistol is unusual in that it is still accompanied by its original paper box labeled: COLT'S / SEVEN SHOT PISTOL / .22 Caliber / For Long or Short Cartridges.
                                              William D. Bluver Collectin

Cased Colt Seven Shot Revolving Pistol, .22rf caliber, 2⅛" barrel, serial number 730. This standard production nickel-plated pistol was retailed through the Colt company's London Agency. Prior to sale, it was boxed in a walnut case which has the agency's trade label affixed to the interior lid.
Fred Sweeney Collection.

Colt's Patent House Pistol, .41rf caliber, 3" barrel, serial number 6847. While the majority of House Pistols were nickel-plated, it was offered with a fully blued finish such as that seen on this pistol.
Fred Sweeney Collection.

Colt's Patent House Pistol, .41rf caliber, 1½" barrel, serial number 7301. One of the more uncommon variations of the House Pistol are those fitted with 1.5" barrels.

Fred Sweeney Collection.

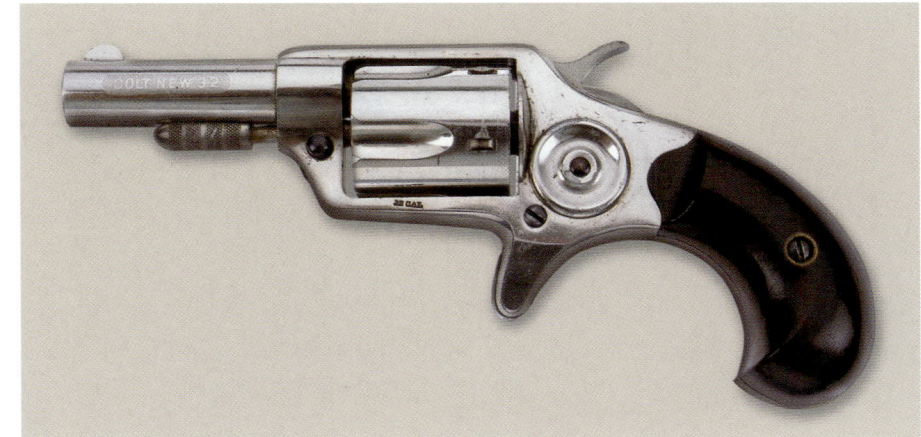

Colt New Line .32rf Caliber Revolving Pistol, 2¼" barrel, serial number 7634. Approximately 22,000 New Line .32 rimfire caliber revolvers were manufactured from 1873 to 1884. During the model's final year of production, it was also made available in .32 centerfire caliber.

Fred Sweeney Collection.

Cased Colt New Line .22rf Caliber Revolving Pistol, 2¼" barrel, serial number 24298. Later production New Line .22 caliber revolvers, of which this is an example, had extended flutes machined into the exterior surface of their cylinders over the chamber shoulders.

Fred Sweeney Collection.

Cased and Engraved Colt New Line .22rf Caliber Revolving Pistol, 2½" barrel, serial number 13465. The New Line series of revolvers was introduced in 1873. The first model was a .22 rimfire caliber revolver that was made until 1877. Typical of those pistols made during the initial production run, this pistol's cylinder has relatively short flutes along the chamber shoulders. Fittingly, this Helfricht-engraved revolver is boxed in a presentation style case which is lined in satin and velvet.

Pete Holder Collection

Engraved Colt's Patent House Pistol, .41rf caliber, 1½" barrel, serial number 7232. The construction and style of the foliate scrollwork found on this pistol suggests that it was probably engraved by Cuno A. Helfricht. Helfricht was employed as the Colt company's primary engraver from approximately 1871 to 1921.

Robert Funk Collection.

Colt New Line .30rf Caliber Revolving Pistol, 1¾" barrel, serial number 2227. The .30 caliber variation of the New Line was introduced in 1874 and discontinued in 1876. During those three years, it is estimated that about 11,000 were made. The example illustrated here has a blued and casehardened finish similar to that found on the company's Single Action Army revolver of the same period. The grips are unusual in that they are carved with a rampant colt at the top and foliage along their base.
Fred Sweeney Collection.

Cased Colt New Line .30cf Caliber Revolving Pistol, 2¼" barrel, serial number 7149. This blued, casehardened and ivory gripped revolver was probably made in either late 1875 or early 1876. It is boxed in a typical American-made Colt case of the period.
Fred Sweeney Collection.

Engraved Colt New Line .41rf Caliber Revolving Pistol, 2¼" barrel, serial number 2834. The .41 rimfire caliber New Line was made from 1874 to 1879. Based upon the construction, as well as the form, of the scrollwork engraved on the barrel and cylinder, the work can be attributed to Cuno A. Helfricht.
Robert Funk Collection.

Engraved Colt New Line .38rf Caliber Revolving Pistol, 2¼" barrel, serial number 6209. After production of this model was underway, the cylinder design was modified so that the locking stop recesses were cut into its breech face. Concurrently, the length of the cylinder flutes was substantially increased. The present example displays a rare combination nickel and gold-plated finish, as well as engraved scrollwork by Herman L. Ulrich.
Fred Sweeney Collection.

Colt New Line .38rf Caliber Revolving Pistol, 2¼" barrel, serial number 430. Between 1874 and 1880, an estimated 5,500 New Line revolvers were made in this, as well as .38 centerfire caliber. Pistols made shortly after the model was introduced were fitted with cylinders having abbreviated flutes, as well as locking stop recesses cut into their exterior circumference.
Fred Sweeney Collection.

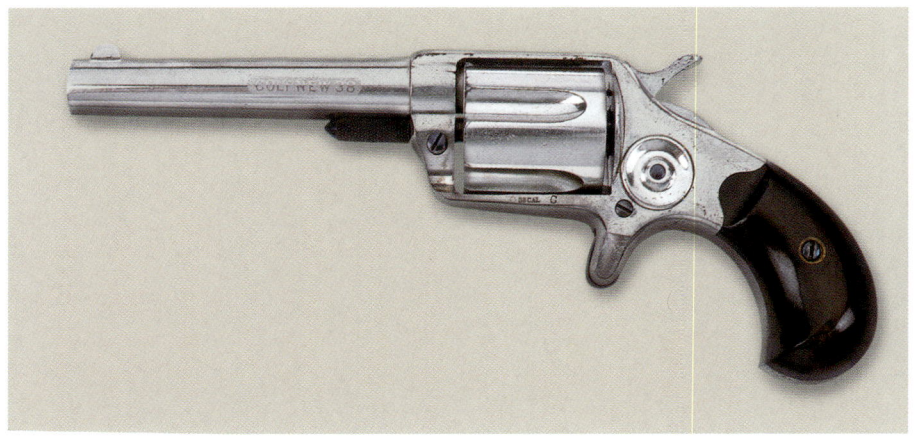

Colt New Line .38cf Caliber Revolving Pistol, 4" barrel, serial number 8846. The centerfire version of the New Line .38 was introduced relatively late in the model's production life. Unlike previous variations, the example illustrated here is fitted with a pivoted loading gate on the right side of the frame to the rear of the cylinder.
Fred Sweeney Collection.

Cased Colt New Line .41cf Caliber Revolving Pistol, 2¼" barrel, serial number 8715. This blued and casehardened revolver was originally shipped to the Colt company's London Agency. Prior to sale it was boxed in a standard British case made of walnut. A copy of the Agency's trade label is glued to the interior surface of the case lid.
Fred Sweeney Collection.

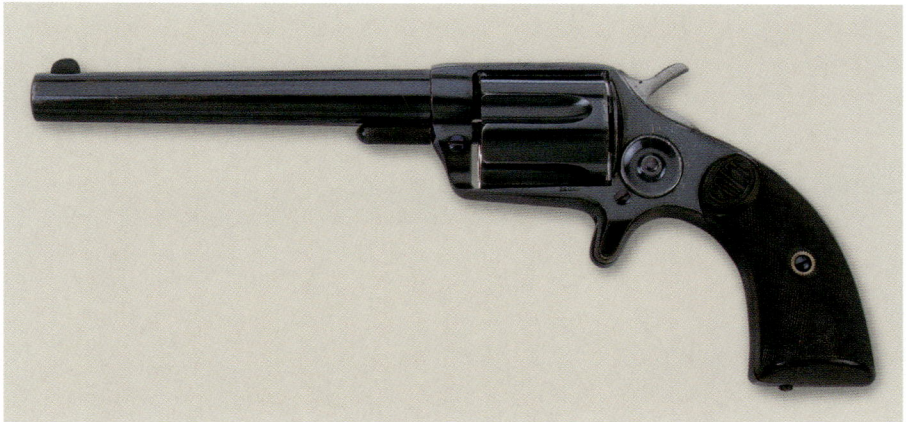

Colt's Patent New House Pistol, .32cf caliber, 5" barrel, serial number 22211. The New House series of revolvers was made from 1880 until 1886. During that period, an estimated 4,000 were produced in .32 centerfire, .38 centerfire and .41 rimfire caliber. While structurally resembling the New Line models, the New House Pistols had flattened butts, as well as hard rubber grips embossed with the name "COLT."
Fred Sweeney Collection.

Cased Colt's Patent New House Pistol, .38cf caliber, 2¼" barrel, serial number 14336. The style and configuration of the case accompanying this revolver suggests that it was sold by an English retailer.
Fred Sweeney Collection.

Colt New Police Pistol, .38cf caliber, 2¼" barrel, serial number 21802. Commonly referred to as the "Cop & Thug Model" due to the scene cast in the hard rubber grips, this model was introduced in 1882. By the time production was discontinued in 1886, approximately 4,000 had been manufactured.

Fred Sweeney Collection.

Cased and Engraved Colt National Number 1 Deringer, .41rf caliber, 2½" barrel, serial number 3971. This blued and silver-plated pistol was evidently shipped to the Colt company's London Agency and then exported to India where it was retailed by P. Orr & Sons of Madras. Between 1870 and 1890, approximately 6,500 Number 1 Deringers were manufactured by the Colt company. Though made by the Colt, this model was originally produced by the National Arms Company of Brooklyn, New York. The latter company was purchased by Colt in 1869.

Fred Sweeney Collection.

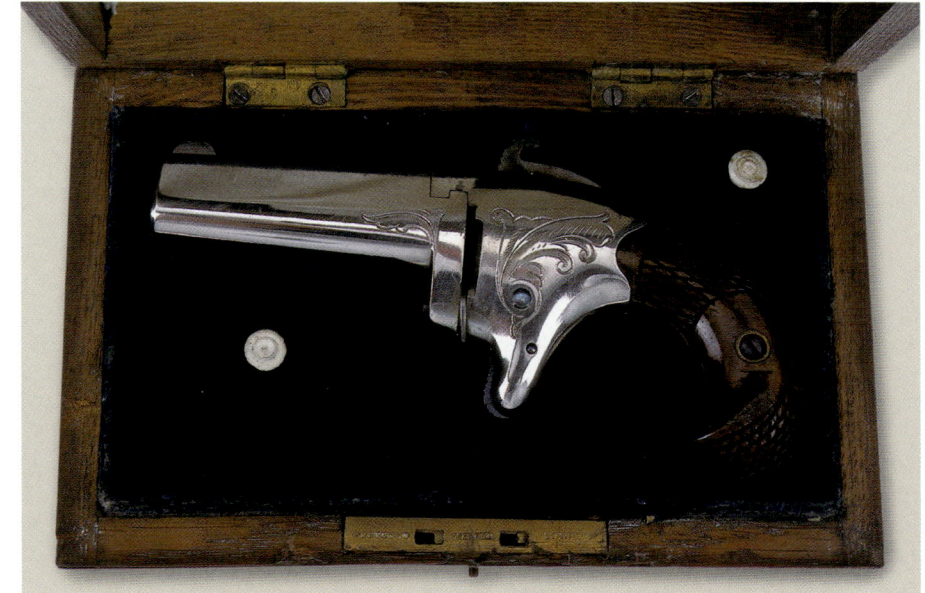

Cased and Engraved Colt National Number 2 Deringer, .41rf caliber, 2½" barrel, serial number 2493. This nickel-plated pistol illustrates the typical form of the Number 2 Deringer. The frame and barrel breech are engraved with loosely constructed foliate scrolls, while the walnut grips are somewhat coarsely checkered. It is boxed in an English style walnut case.

Fred Sweeney Collection.

Colt New Patent Deringer Pistol, .41rf caliber, 2½" barrel, serial number 25054. Although the majority of those pistols made after that the barrel pivot bolster had been abandoned had gently angled grips, a small number were produced with sharply curved grip profiles, as well as low-slung hammer spurs. Most, if not all of these arms were made by I. C. Brezina, who worked as an assembler for the Colt company from 1880 to 1926.

Fred Sweeney Collection.

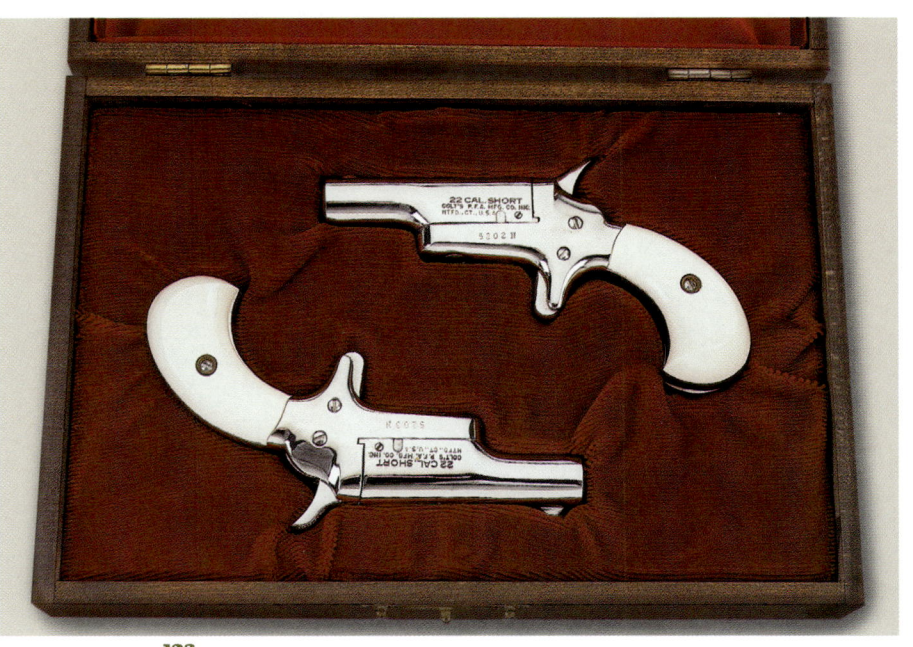

Pair of Colt Fourth Model Deringers, .22rf caliber, 2½" barrels, serial numbers 5202N and 5203N. These nickel-plated and ivory gripped pistols are accompanied by tooled leather holsters made by John Bianchi. The Fourth Model Deringer was introduced in 1959 and production continued until 1963. Pistols having an "N" suffix to their serial number were nickel-plated.

Karen Green Collection.

Cased Pair of Colt Fourth Model Deringers, .22rf caliber, 2½" barrels, serial numbers 8000N and 8001N. This pair of nickel-plated and ivory gripped pistols made in 1960 are cased in a book style case. The book's spine is gilt stamped "Colt Deringers / Limited Edition / by / Colt" and the front cover "A / Limited / Edition / by / Colt."

Karen Green Collection.

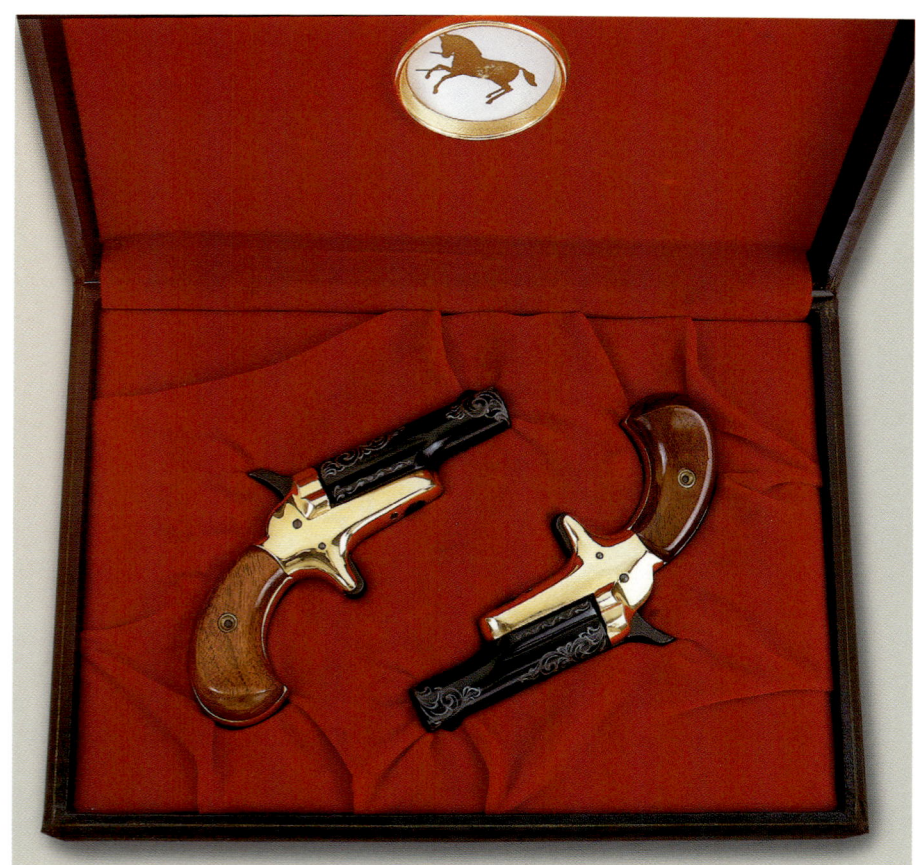

Cased and Engraved Pair of Colt Lady Model Deringers, .22rf caliber, 2½" barrels, serial numbers 10547DER and 10548DER. Cased in a Swedish leather box lined in red velvet, these pistols have gold-plated frames, blued barrels and walnut grips. They were engraved with foliate scrollwork by Alvin A. White.

Karen Green Collection.

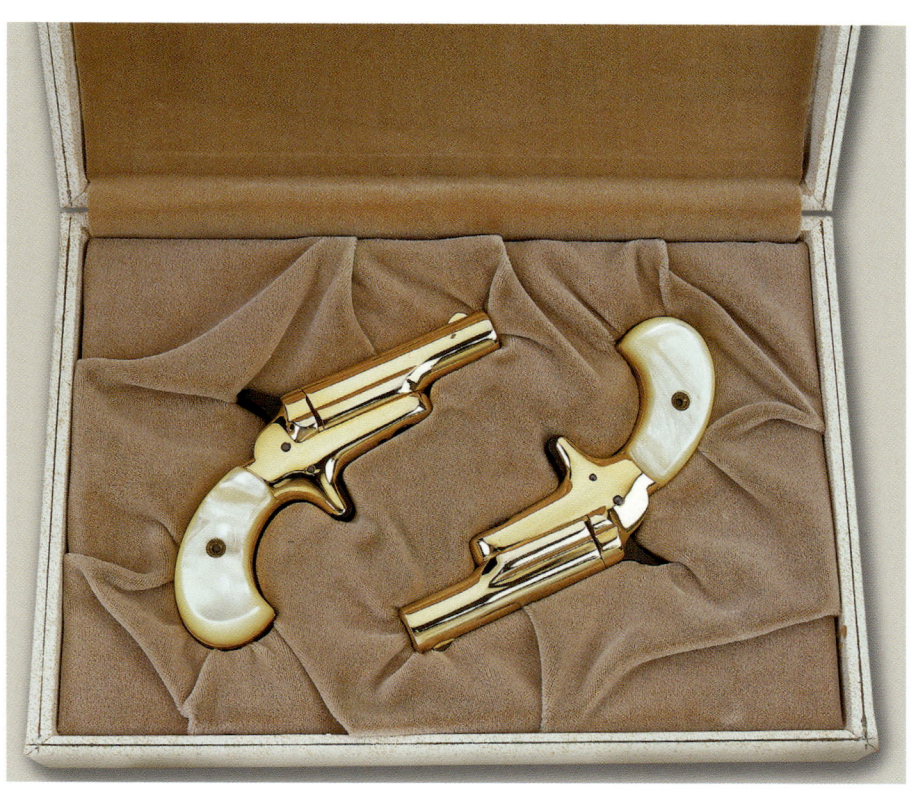

Cased Pair of Colt Lady Model Deringers, .22rf caliber, 2½" barrel, serial numbers 15673DER and 15674DER. Finished in full gold plate and fitted with pearl grips, this pair of deringers are cased in a Swedish-manufactured leatherette box having a beige velvet lining. The Lord and Lady series of Colt deringers were introduced in 1970 and made until 1976.

Karen Green Collection.

Cased Pair of Colt Lord & Lady Model Deringers, .22rf caliber, 2½" barrels, serial numbers 2417LDR and 2418LDR. While the Lord Model has a gold-plated frame and blued barrel with walnut grips, the Lady Model is finished in full gold plate with pearl grips. Their Swedish-made case is covered in maroon colored leatherette and lined with red velvet.

Karen Green Collection.

Designed by William Mason, the .38 and .41 caliber Colt's Self-Cocking Double Action Pistols are now commonly referred to as either the Lightning or Thunderer Colt revolvers depending upon their caliber (.38 and .41 respectively). These trade names were given to this model by B. Kittridge & Co. of Cincinnati, Ohio, in a successful attempt to increase their sales. Favored by bank guards, lawmen and outlaws, both revolvers saw extensive use in the Frontier West.

Following the success of the .38 and .41 caliber Double Action Lightning Revolvers, the Colt company introduced a larger version in 1878. Now popularly known as the Model 1878, these pistols proved to be quite popular. In addition to be used by countless sportsmen, cowboys and the like, a significant number were also purchased by the U.S. Army. Though produced in a variety of calibers, by far the greatest number were chambered for the .45 Long Colt cartridge. In common with the .38 and .41 caliber Double Action revolvers, this model was christened the "Omnipotent" by B. Kittridge & Company of Cincinnati.

Model 1877 & 1878 Double Action

By Kurt House

The Models of 1877 and 1878 were Colt's first venture into the double action revolver market and were a direct response to the pleas of Colt's London Agent, Frederick von Oppen, and the European need for a dependable Colt in the more advanced rapid fire mode. Shooters in Europe had been acquainted with double action firing since shortly after the American Civil War, because of the double action products of other makers, notably Adams, Tranter, Webley and other English gunmaking firms. In numerous letters, Colt's London agent at the time stressed that if he were to compete with the English firms with a Colt product, then the company must produce a double action or "self cocking revolver." While Colonel Colt claimed to have used the double action in his first experiments with the revolving cylinder, the earliest concrete evidence was in 1842 and another version in 1858. After the invention of metallic cartridges, Colt Armory Superintendent William Mason designed both the Models of 1877 and 1878.

Colt's first response to this market was the Model of 1877, chambered in only three calibers: .32, .38 and .41 which were promptly named by Benjamin Kittridge, one of Colt's six major distributors (or "Allies"), as the "Rainmaker, Lightning and Thunderer" models respectively. The .32 caliber is rare, with only about 200 produced.

As a further response to the need for the same larger calibers used by the Single Action Army, Colt introduced in the next year the Model of 1878, or "Frontier" revolver as it is sometimes known. In America and else-

Cased Pair Colt Double Action Self-Cocking Revolvers (Model 1877), .38 caliber, 3½" barrels, serial numbers 16 and 17. Although no shipping record has been found for number 16, serial number 17 was shipped by the Colt company to B. Kittredge & Company, Cincinnati, Ohio, on May 2, 1877. In common with many early production revolvers of this type they have a blued and casehardened finish, as well as one-piece, checkered rosewood grips.

James Parks Collection.

where too, both of these Colt models became popular due to the scarcity of a similar double action competitor, with 166,849 of the 1877 Model and 51,210 of the large frame Model 1878 being produced. Production of these two fixed cylinder models continued until 1905 for the large frame (1878) and 1909 for the small frame (1877) when they were replaced by the swing-out cylinder double action models of 1889 and 1894. The attraction of the large frame 1878 was in its similarity to the popular Single Action, indeed using the same barrel and ejector housing, and because its calibers were the same as used by the Single Action Model.

Nevertheless, the Models of 1877 and 1878 were immensely popular in their time and are associated with much of the same illustrious history as the Single Action Army. Widely preferred by both lawmen and outlaws alike because of their fast shooting ability, the models were also employed in many of the first western movies. Notable among those who employed the models were outlaws Rowdy Joe Lowe, Billy The Kid and John Wesley Hardin, various companies such as the Pacific Mail Steamship Company (marked PMSS Co.), American Express and Wells Fargo, as well as famous personalities like Frederic Remington, Captain Jack Crawford, Pawnee Bill, W. F. "Buffalo Bill" Cody and numerous sheriffs and lawmen including Pat Garrett.

In addition to the role played by both models in the winning of the American West, the Models of 1877 and 1878 were used extensively in other conflicts, such as the Boer War in South Africa, the Canadian Riel Rebellion and by the Royal Canadian Mounted Police, and during the Philippine Insurrection. This latter American conflict, in fact, caused a major variation in the 1878 when the United States military placed an order for "5,000 Colt revolvers, six inch barrel, .45 caliber, double action, latest model, rounded butt with sling." This variation of the Model 1878 has become known as the 1902 or "Philippine Model" and is distinguished by its enlarged trigger and guard. It bears the inspector's stamp "RAC" on the left side above the grip and "U.S." on the right side as well as "1902" above the grip. Although the reasons for the enlarged trigger and guard were speculated upon by many authors, Author Don Wilkerson has shown without a doubt the true explanation to be that the weak hammer fall on the standard Model 1878 could not be depended upon to consistently explode the primers of the standard government .45 cartridge, and thus the leverage of the trigger had to be increased, thereby necessitating the larger guard.

When the amount of variation of these two fixed cylinder double action revolvers produced by Colt is considered, and as collectors realize their colorful history, the value of and demand for both the Model 1877 and the Model 1878 can be expected to continue to increase.

Inscribed Pair Colt Double Action Self-Cocking Revolvers (Model 1877), .41 caliber, 5" barrels, serial numbers 82961 and 86966. Shipped on March 14, 1893 (86966) and April 4, 1893 (82961) to the Simmons Hardware Company of St. Louis, Missouri, both of these revolvers are engraved on their grip straps (inset) "H. C. LINDSEY / CHIEF / TOPEKA KAN." Henry C. Lindsey (died January 1927) served in the Union Army during the Civil War. In 1867 he received a captain's commission and saw action during the Indian Wars. In the late 1870s, he became a lawman and served as Deputy Marshal and in 1893 was appointed Chief of Police in Topeka, Kansas. Lindsey also was a friend of James B. (Wild Bill) Hickok.

James R. Parks Collection.

Colt Double Action Self-Cocking Revolver (Model 1877), .38 caliber, 4½" barrel, serial number 49463. Although no shipping record has been located for this revolver, it was at one time owned by a member of the Greensburg, Kentucky Police Department.

Robert P. Palazzo Collection.

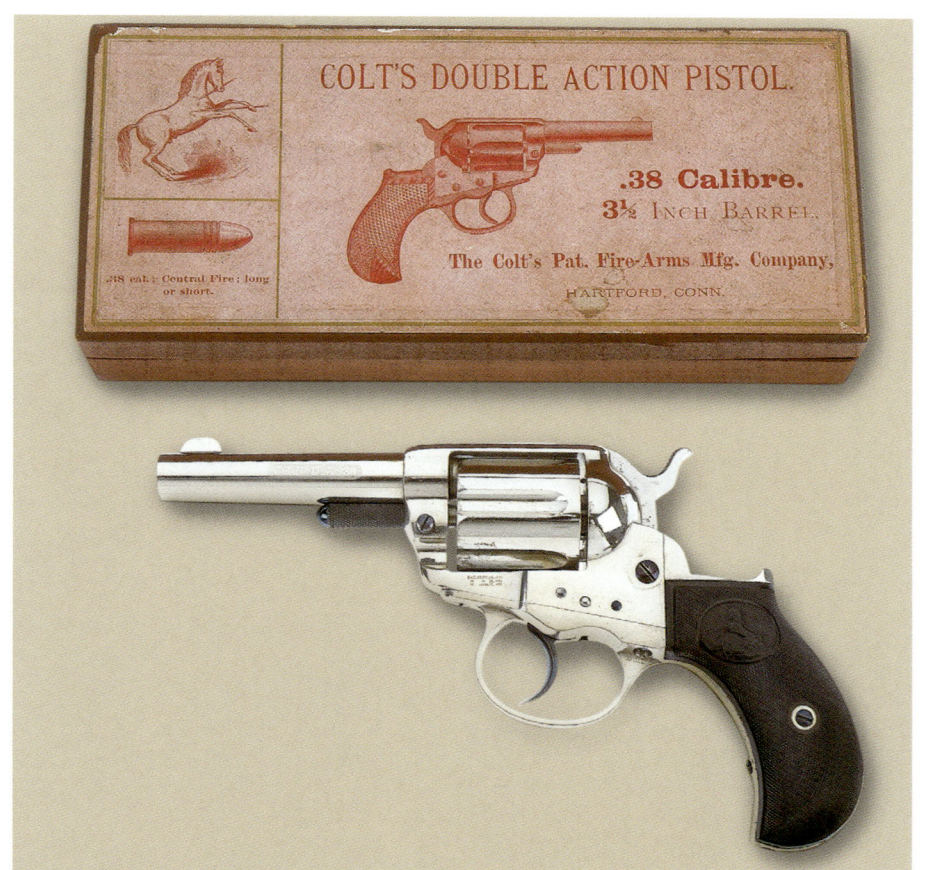

Colt Double Action Self-Cocking Revolver (Model 1877), .38 caliber, 3½" barrel, serial number 6339. This nickel-plated pistol was probably made in 1878 and is fitted with two-piece hard rubber grips used from the early autumn of 1877 until the model was discontinued. The revolver is still accompanied by its original shipping box, the cover of which has a pink label imprinted with a line engraving the Lightning Model.

Paul Frederick Collection

Engraved Colt Double Action Self-Cocking Revolver (Model 1877), .41 caliber, 4½" barrel, serial number 42994. This revolver was most likely engraved by Cuno A. Helfricht. It was originally fitted with hard rubber grips and records indicate it was shipped to the Simmons Hardware Company of St. Louis, Missouri, on April 30, 1883.

Ed Cox Collection.

Engraved Colt Double Action Self-Cocking Revolver (Model 1877), .38 caliber, 4½" barrel, serial number 66659. This striking revolver is not only engraved, but also, has a gold-plated finish and two-piece pearl grips. Between 1877 and 1897, only 31 Double Action .38 caliber revolvers were shipped with a full gold-plated finish.

Dale Ring Collection.

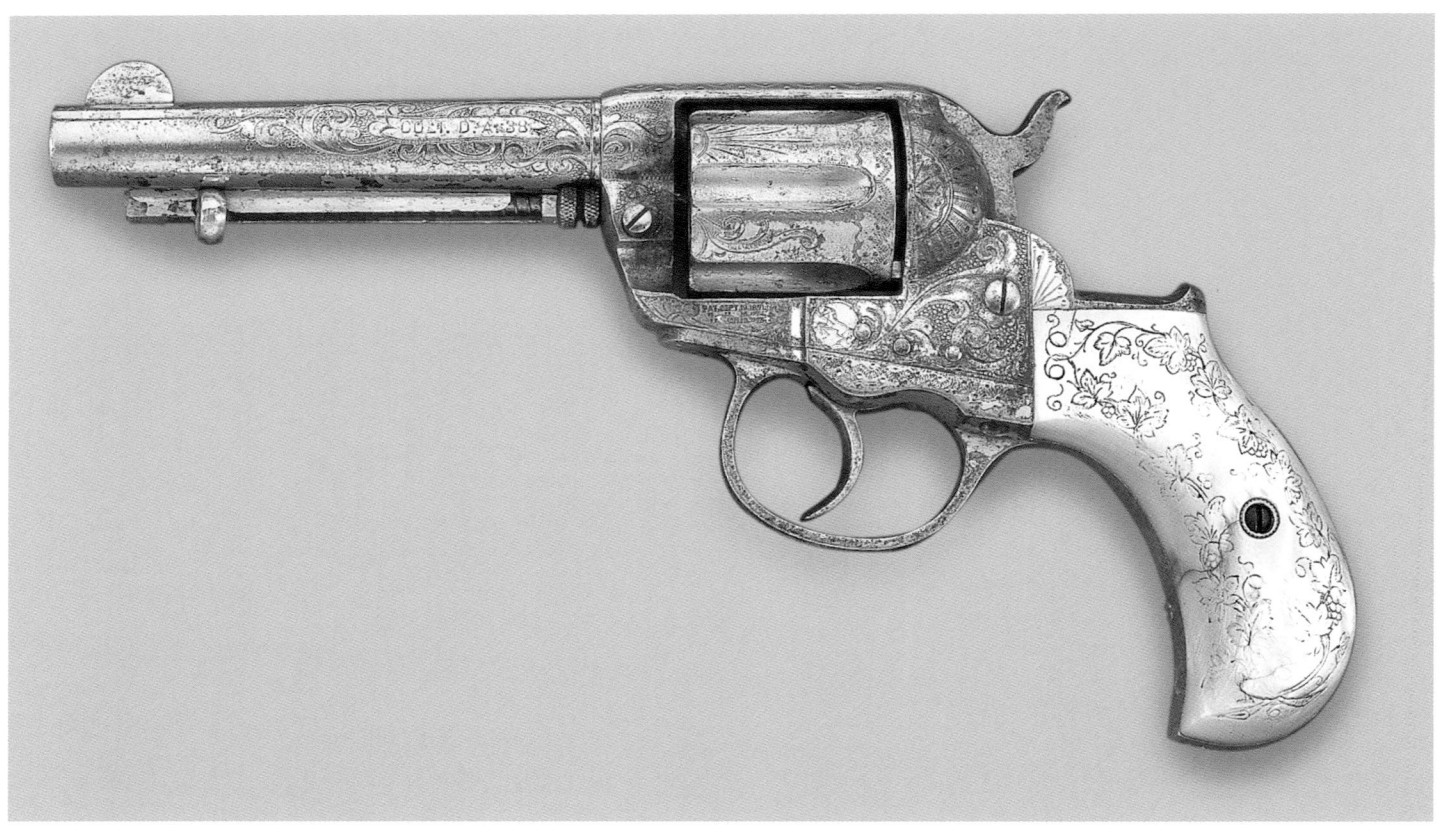

Engraved Colt Double Action Self-Cocking Revolver (Model 1877), .38 caliber, 4½" barrel, serial number 98716. This gold and nickel-plated revolver was probably engraved by Cuno A. Helfricht. It is also likely that Helfricht engraved the scrolling vine foliage cut in the pearl grips. Between 1877 and 1897 only five revolvers of this type were shipped with mixed finishes. This example was originally shipped on September 4, 1894 to J. F. Schmelzer & Sons in Kansas City, Kansas.

Gary Erb Collection.

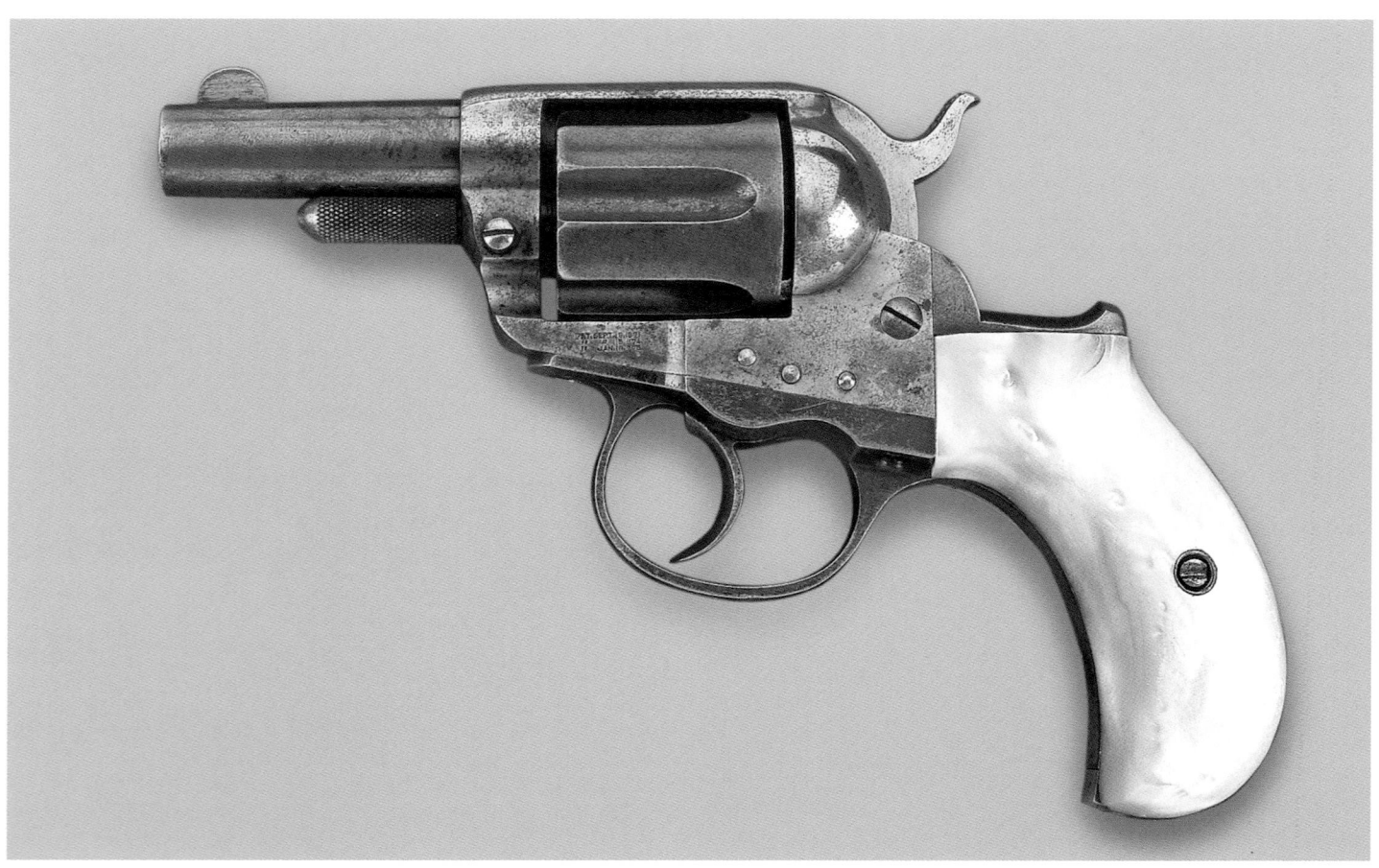

Colt Double Action Self-Cocking Revolver (Model 1877), 2½" barrel, .41 caliber, serial number 69697. Relatively few .41 caliber Double Action Self-Cocking revolvers were fitted with 2½" barrels during the model's production life.

Ed Cox Collection.

Engraved Colt Double Action Self-Cocking Revolver (Model 1877), .41 caliber, 5½" barrel, serial number 78780. This revolver was engraved with finely cut foliate scrollwork by Cuno A. Helfricht prior to being shipped on October 9, 1890 to the Colt company's agency in San Francisco, California. The interior of the pearl grips are inscribed with the name "F. Hammer," who may have been the original owner.

Gary Erb Collection.

Inscribed Colt Double Action Self-Cocking Revolver (Model 1877), .38 caliber, 4½" barrel, serial number 98138. This revolver was ordered by William Read & Son of Boston, Massachusetts for the American Express Company. It was shipped to Read & Son for C. E. Seaton, Superintendent of the American Express Company in Chicago, Illinois, on July 23, 1894. The backstrap (pictured below) was roll engraved prior to shipment with the inscription "AM EXP CO No. 16".

Robert P. Palazzo Collection.

Engraved Colt Double Action Self-Cocking Revolver (Model 1877), .38 caliber, 4½" barrel, serial number 108599. This modestly engraved revolver was ordered by G. P. Clark and shipped to him in care of the Simmons Hardware Company of St. Louis, Missouri, on February 12, 1898.

Gary Erb Collection.

Colt Double Action Self-Cocking Revolver (Model 1877), .32 caliber, 4½" barrel, serial number 112933. Between 1877 and 1897 only 214 Double Action Self-Cocking Pistols were made in .32 caliber.

Lewis E. Yearout Collection.

Colt Double Action Self-Cocking Army Pistol (Model 1878), .45 caliber, 5½" barrel, serial number 33. This revolver was presented by the Colt's Patent Fire Arms Manufacturing Company to Captain Otho E. Michaelis, Ordnance Inspector in the Dakota Territory. Records indicate that it was charged to the firm's "Presentation Account" and shipped on June 9, 1878.

Richard E. Burdick Collection.

Inscribed Colt Double Action Self-Cocking Revolver (Model 1877), .38 caliber, 3½" barrel, serial number 158706. Originally shipped to E. K. Tryon, Jr. & Company of Philadelphia, Pennsylvania, on June 19, 1905, this revolver later was owned by the Wells Fargo Company who stamped the frame with their ownership marking (pictured below) "W. F. CO. EX. 118."

Robert P. Palazzo Collection.

Colt Double Action Self-Cocking "Omnipotent" Army Pistol (Model 1878), .45 caliber, 7½" barrel, serial number 344. The "Omnipotent" revolvers were so marked at the request of the Cincinnati, Ohio, retailer N. Kittredge Company. Kittredge marketed the .38 caliber Colt Double Action Pistol under the name "Lightning" and the .45 Model 1878 as the "Omnipotent" model. Approximately 174 revolvers were marked in this manner. This example was shipped to Kittredge on August 17, 1878 as part of the second shipment of revolvers bearing the "Omnipotent" inscription.

Kurt House Collection.

Colt Double Action Self-Cocking Pistol (Model 1878), .450 Eley caliber, 5½" barrel, serial number 564. Given the popularity of double action revolvers in Great Britain, it is not surprising that Colt's large frame version gained quick acceptance there. In all, a total of 2,390 pistols of this caliber were made for export. This example was shipped to the firm's London Agency on September 26, 1878.

Kurt House Collection.

Engraved Colt Double Action Self-Cocking Army Pistol (Model 1878), .45 caliber, 8" barrel, serial number 4205. During the production life of this model, between 1878 and 1907, only one Double Action Army Pistol was fitted with an 8" barrel. Fitted with pearl grips, this engraved and silver-plated revolver was shipped to Marcellus Frotall on July 19, 1880.

Kurt House Collection.

Engraved Colt Double Action Self-Cocking Army Pistol (Model 1878), .45 caliber, 4" barrel, serial number 5942. Only 27 ejectorless and engraved .45 caliber Double Action Army Pistols were made by the Colt company between 1878 and 1907.

Lewis E. Yearout Collection.

Colt Double Action Self-Cocking Army Pistol (Model 1878), .45 caliber, 7½" barrel, serial number 1574. This nickel-plated revolver was fitted with hard rubber grips of the type used shortly after the model was introduced. Records indicate that it was shipped from the factory on March 5, 1880. The back strap is engraved with the name "W. L. Hunter," possibly its original owner.

Kurt House Collection.

Colt Double Action Self-Cocking "Omnipotent" Army Pistol (Model 1878), .45 caliber, 7½" barrel, serial number 4795. The "Omnipotent" Colt Double Action revolvers were sold by B. Kittredge Company of Cincinnati, Ohio. This example was shipped to that firm on January 22, 1881.

Lewis E. Yearout Collection.

Engraved Colt Double Action Self-Cocking Army Pistol (Model 1878), .45 caliber, 4¾" barrel, serial number 12484. Approximately 250 Model 1878 revolvers in all calibers and barrel lengths were engraved during the model's production life from 1878 to 1907. Of that number, however, only seven were engraved, nickel plated and fitted with pearl grips. This example was originally shipped to Peter Bergerson, City Marshal of Cheyenne, Wyoming.

Kurt House Collection.

Engraved Colt Double Action Self-Cocking Pistol (Model 1878), .38-40 caliber, 8½" barrel, serial number 22277. This Helfricht-engraved .38-40 revolver has the distinction of being the only one made with a 8½" barrel. In addition, it should be noted that during the model's production life, only seven pistols of this caliber were engraved. The present example was shipped on January 18, 1890 to the E. C. Meacham Company of St. Louis, Missouri.

Kurt House Collection.

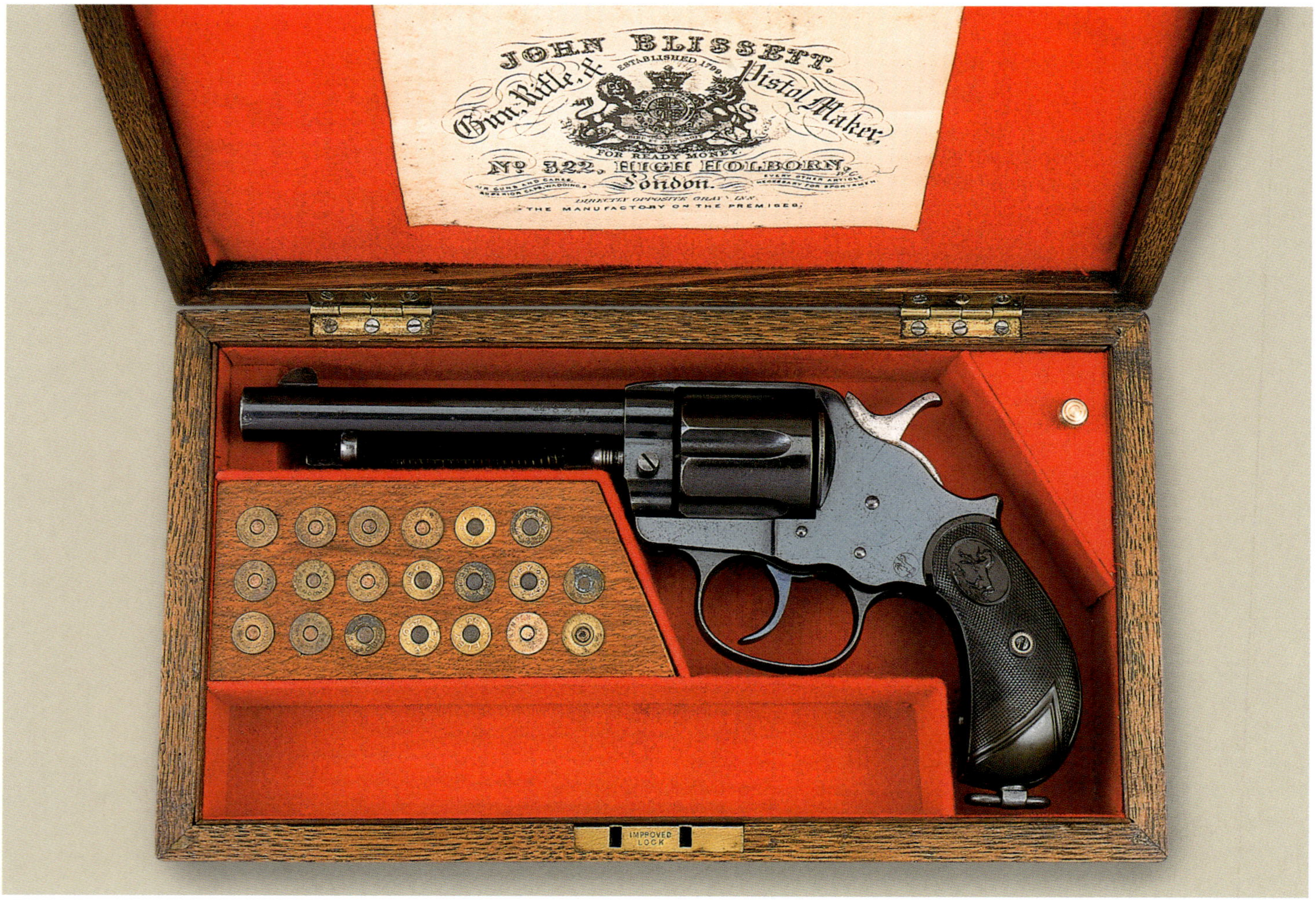

Cased Colt Double Action Self-Cocking Frontier Pistol (Model 1878), .44S&W (Russian) caliber, 5½" barrel, serial number 27,720. During the Model 1878's production, only 728 revolvers were made in this caliber. This revolver was originally shipped to Luigi Colombo in Genoa, Italy. It is presently housed in a case supplied by the London gunmaker John Blissett.

Kurt House Collection.

Colt Double Action Self-Cocking Army Pistol (Model 1878), .45 caliber, 4¾" barrel, serial number 17245. Approximately 705 revolvers of this barrel length were finished in full nickel plate by the Colt company. Factory records indicate that this particular pistol was shipped to Fisk & Van Uoxem in Chicago, Illinois, on August 23, 1886.
Craig A. Blancett Collection.

Colt Double Action Self-Cocking Army Target Pistol (Model 1878), .45 caliber, 7½" barrel, serial number 1. Although numbered 1, this revolver was made as a product verification sample for a series of special order target pistols made in 1889. In common with other Colt pistols used for this purpose, it was finished in the white.
Kurt House Collection.

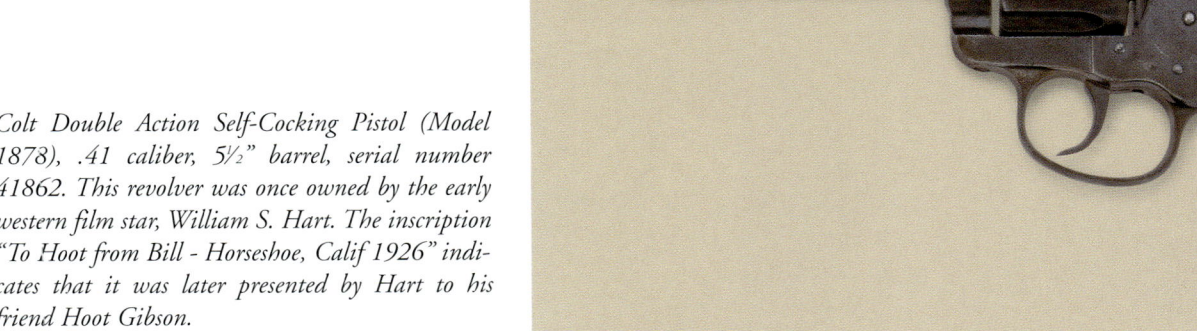

Colt Double Action Self-Cocking Pistol (Model 1878), .41 caliber, 5½" barrel, serial number 41862. This revolver was once owned by the early western film star, William S. Hart. The inscription "To Hoot from Bill - Horseshoe, Calif 1926" indicates that it was later presented by Hart to his friend Hoot Gibson.
Ed Cox Collection.

Cased Colt Double Action Self-Cocking Pistol (Model 1878), .476 Enfield caliber, 5½" barrel, serial number 30184. Originally shipped to the Colt company's London Agency, this revolver was subsequently retailed by Edward M. Reilly & Company whose trade label is affixed to the interior face of the case lid. The popularity of the .476 caliber cartridge with British buyers is demonstrated by the fact that the Colt company made 2,458 during the model's production life.

Kurt House Collection.

Colt U.S. Model 1902 Double Action Self-Cocking Army Pistol (Model 1878), .45 caliber, 6" barrel, serial number 46616. In 1902 the U.S. Army Ordnance Department ordered 5,000 revolvers having elongated triggers and expanded trigger guard bows for the Philippine Constabulary. This example was shipped to the Springfield Armory on October 8, 1902.

Craig A. Blancett Collection.

Colt U.S. Model 1902 Double Action Self-Cocking Army Pistol (Model 1878), .45 caliber, 6" barrel, serial number 47222. This pistol was purchased by the U.S. Government for issue to the Philippine Constabulary.

Lewis E. Yearout Collection.

Colt U.S. Model 1902 Double Action Self-Cocking Army Pistol (Model 1878), .45 caliber, 6" barrel, serial number 47270. This Philippine Constabulary pistol is illustrated with examples of the accessories that were originally issued with the revolver. The belt, cartridge pouch and pistol are from the collection of Kurt House, while the holster is from the collection of Ed Cox.

The U.S. Army and Navy purchased a large number of Colt Double Action .38 and .45 caliber revolvers during the late 19th and early 20th centuries. Their reliability and ease of use made them favorites with many servicemen even after the introduction of the Colt Model 1911 Government Model.

Among the most sought-after variations of all Colt's double action revolvers are those incorporating improvements designed by J. H. FitzGerald. Made in extremely limited quantities, the "Fitz Specials" feature cutaway trigger guard bows and bobbed hammers to allow their easy use.

Swing-Out Cylinder Double Action Revolvers
by Lynn Kvam

If the 19th century was the "Age of the Single Action Colt Revolver," the 20th century belonged to the "Double Action."

Designed so that a revolver could be cocked and fired simply by pulling the trigger, Colt double action pistols made their debut in 1877. It was not until 1889, however, that a truly reliable double action was introduced by Colt.

Chambered for the .38 and .41 caliber cartridges, the Colt New Navy, Double Action, Self-Cocking Revolver and its successors (the Model 1892, 1894, 1895, 1896, 1901, as well as 1903 New Army and Navy Revolvers), rapidly established Colt's name in the modern handgun market.

One key element of their design involved the mounting of the cylinder on an arm or crane which could be pivoted out of alignment with the frame. This allowed the cylinder to be swung to the side of the revolver for loading. When the cartridges had been inserted into the chambers, the cylinder could be moved back into its closed position in the frame and locked in place by a spring-loaded pin.

While the earliest Colt double action revolvers of this type had cylinders which turned counter-clockwise, or to the left, it was found that rotation direction put undue strain on the crane during firing. Consequently, in 1905 the turning direction was changed to a clockwise motion. This allowed Colt's engineers to chamber their revolvers for more powerful ammunition such as the .45 cartridge.

The popularity of the swing-out cylinder Colt revolvers is clearly demonstrated by the multitude of

Colt New Army Double Action Self-Cocking Revolver (Model 1896), .38 caliber, 6" barrel, serial number 98637. Production of this model began in 1896 and continued until 1901. During that period, approximately 291,000 were made. This revolver, manufactured in 1898, was presented to Harry A. Krumm.

Lynn Kvam Collection.

models that were made. Since the Colt New Navy was introduced in 1889 more than 35 distinct models have been produced. Among these are some of the 20th century's most famous handguns: the Banker's Special (introduced in 1928); Cobra (introduced in 1950); Detective Special (introduced in 1927); New Service Model (introduced in 1898); Officers Model (introduced in 1904); Official Police (introduced in 1927); Police Positive (introduced in 1905), and of course; the Python which entered the company's product line in 1955.

Although most of these models had long production runs or still are being manufactured, a few were short-lived. For example, only 926 .38 caliber revolvers were made for the U.S. Marine Corps in 1905, and fewer than 300 New Service Target Pistols were made with 6-inch barrels. Other rarities include the Fitz-Gerald Specials which featured spurless hammers and cut-away trigger guards; the Border Patrol Model of 1952 of which only 400 were made, and the 1951 Aircrewman which is rarer than a Paterson Colt due to the fact that most of the 1,189 made were destroyed.

The diversity of these revolvers makes them an ideal field of study. This is especially true of those models which were produced for many years and therefore incorporated sub-variations.

While the swing-out cylinder, double action Colt revolvers may not have as many historical associations as the Single Action Army or Government Model of 1911, they nevertheless are important in their own right. Furthermore, they contributed to the financial survival of the Colt company in a far greater measure than some of their more famous cousins.

Colt New Navy Double Action Self-Cocking Revolver (Model 1889), .41 caliber, 6" barrel, serial number 27089. Between 1889 and 1894, approximately 31,000 Model 1889 Double Action revolvers were manufactured by the Colt company. The example illustrated here was made during the last year of the model's production.

Lynn Kvam Collection.

Colt U.S. Model 1894 Double Action Revolver, .38 caliber, 6" barrel, serial number 103709. In 1894 the design of the Colt Double Action internal lockwork was changed by the addition of improved hammer and trigger locks. Revolvers supplied to the U.S. Army were fitted with plain walnut grips and were fitted with lanyard swivels on their butt straps.

Lynn Kvam Collection.

Colt U.S. Model 1901 Double Action Revolver, .38 caliber, 6" barrel, serial number 138093. This model differed from its predecessors only in the addition of a lanyard swivel mounted on the butt strap. It was manufactured from 1901 to 1903.

Lynn Kvam Collection.

Colt U.S. Model 1903 Double Action Revolver, .38 caliber, 6" barrel, serial number 209094. To improve accuracy, the Colt company reduced the bore diameter of its Double Action revolvers in 1903. At the same time the grip design was altered to improve the pistol's handling.

Lynn Kvam Collection.

Colt New Navy Double Action Self-Cocking Revolver (Model 1892), .38 caliber, 6" barrel, serial number 216429.

Lynn Kvam Collection.

Colt New Army Double Action Self-Cocking Revolver (Model 1892), .41 caliber, 4½" barrel, serial number 241927.

Lynn Kvam Collection.

Colt Officers Model Double Action Revolver, .38 caliber, 6" barrel, serial number 269362. Introduced in 1904, the Officer's Model was manufactured until 1943. The example illustrated here is typical of the first variation shortly after the model entered production.

Lynn Kvam Collection.

Colt Officers Model Double Action Revolver, .32 caliber, 6" barrel, serial number 410917. Made in 1916, this revolver was originally shipped to Albert Foster, Jr., the Colt company's sales representative in New York City.

Lynn Kvam Collection.

Colt Officers Model Double Action Revolver, .38 caliber, 6" barrel, serial number 412599. Based upon its serial number, this second variation of the Officers Model was made in 1916.

Lynn Kvam Collection.

Colt Officers Model Double Action Revolver, .22rf caliber, 6" barrel, serial number 20102. The third variation of the Officers Model chambered for the .22rf cartridge was made from 1930 to 1949. The longevity of its production was due to its popularity among target shooters.

Lynn Kvam Collection.

Colt Officers Model Special Double Action Revolver, .22rf caliber, 6" barrel, serial number 62566. The fourth variation of the Officers Model was introduced in 1949 and made until 1952. Designed for competition shooting, it was equipped with an adjustable Coltsmaster rear sight and an undercut front sight.

Lynn Kvam Collection.

Colt Double Action Officer's Model Match Revolver, .22rf caliber, 6" barrel, serial number 68066. This target pistol represented the fifth variation of the Officers Model to be made by Colt. It was introduced in 1952 as a replacement for the Officers Model Special and remained in production until 1969.

Lynn Kvam Collection.

Colt Double Action Officers Model Match III Revolver, .38rf caliber, 6" barrel, serial number J67280. The final variation of the Officers Model Match Revolver was the J-series Mark III which was produced during 1969 and 1970. It featured a ventilated sighting rib along the barrel and an integral ejector rod casing. During the two years of its production, only 496 were made.

Lynn Kvam Collection.

Colt U.S. Marine Corps Model 1905 Double Action Revolver, .38 caliber, 6" barrel, serial number 10395. The revolver adopted for issue by the U.S. Marine Corps differed from the New Navy Double Action Revolver only in the rounded shape of its butt and the use of checkered walnut for the grips. Numbered in its own series from 10001 to 10926, most of these revolvers were purchased by the Marine Corps.

Lynn Kvam Collection.

Colt Official Police Double Action Revolver, .22rf caliber, 4" barrel, serial number 24350. The .22rf caliber version of the Official Police was made from 1930 until 1969. During its production, over 30,000 were made. As its backstrap inscription demonstrates (inset), this example was originally purchased by the Federal Government for the use of the U.S. Customs Service during World War II.

Lynn Kvam Collection.

Colt Official Police Model Double Action Revolver, .38 caliber, 4" barrel, serial number 633310. This skeletonized revolver was made by the Colt company in 1939.

James Williams Collection.

Colt Official Police Model Double Action Revolver, .38 caliber, 2" barrel, serial number 849340. Although the standard barrel lengths offered for this model were 4", 5" and 6", it could be special ordered with uncatalogued shorter barrels such as the 2" type fitted to this revolver.

Lynn Kvam Collection.

Colt Model 1905 Double Action Revolver, .38 caliber, 6" barrel, serial number 10138. Although it could be supplied with a lanyard swivel as an extra cost option, the civilian version of the 1905 Marine Corps Revolver normally is not found with that accessory. The Marine Corps model was commercially advertised from 1905 until 1909.

Lynn Kvam Collection.

Colt Army Special Double Action Revolver, .32-20 caliber, 4" barrel, serial number 450764. This heavier version of the New Army and Navy series of revolvers was designed for use with more powerful cartridges, such as the .32-20 Winchester rifle round. Approximately 240,000 of these revolvers were manufactured from 1908 until 1927. The example shown here was made in 1920.

Lynn Kvam Collection.

Colt Official Police Model Double Action Revolver, .38 caliber, 5" barrel, serial number 582284. The Official Police was introduced in 1927 and remained in production until 1969. During that period, approximately 400,000 were produced.

Lynn Kvam Collection.

Colt Official Police Model Double Action Revolver, .38 caliber, 4" barrel, serial number 920528. This example, made in 1967, is typical of later versions of the Official Police.

Lynn Kvam Collection.

Colt New Service Model Double Action Revolver, .45 caliber, 5½" barrel, serial number 143065. This revolver was originally purchased by the Royal Northwest Mounted Police, the predecessor of the Royal Canadian Mounted Police, in 1919. As was customary at the time, a Mounted Police armorer stamped the backstrap of the pistol with the force's initials (inset).

William Bluver Collection

Colt Marshal Model Double Action Revolver, .38 caliber, 2" barrel, serial number 836847. Approximately 2,500 revolvers of this type were made between 1954 and 1956. The Marshal Model was essentially a variation of the Official Police with different model markings.

Lynn Kvam Collection.

Colt MK III Official Police Model Double Action Revolver, .38 caliber 4" barrel, serial number J91949. The J-series Official Police was introduced in 1969 and made until 1978.
Lynn Kvam Collection.

Colt MK III Metropolitan Model Double Action Revolver, .38 caliber, 4" barrel, serial number J19143. The Metropolitan model was a variation of the Official Police fitted with a heavyweight 4" barrel. It was manufactured from 1969 to 1978.
Lynn Kvam Collection.

Colt Commando Model Double Action Revolver, .38 caliber, 4" barrel, serial number 7904. Between 1942 and 1945, the Colt company produced 50,617 Commando Model revolvers for the U.S. Federal Government.
Lynn Kvam Collection.

Colt New Service Model Double Action Revolver, .44-40 caliber, 5½" barrel, serial number 4575. Introduced in 1898, the New Service Revolver was the first large bore swing-out cylinder pistol made by Colt. During its production run until 1944, over 356,000 were made. The example illustrated here was manufactured in 1900.
Lynn Kvam Collection.

Cased Colt New Service Target Model Double Action Revolver, .455 Eley caliber, 7½" barrel, serial number 57348. The New Service Target Model was manufactured from 1900 to 1940. This example made circa 1912, is fitted with ivory grips, carved on the right side in high relief with a spread eagle.

Lynn Kvam Collection.

Colt "Fitz Special" New Service Model Double Action Revolver, .45 caliber, 2" barrel, serial number 339282. Named after J. Henry Fitz-Gerald, who worked for the Colt company from 1918 to 1944, "Fitz Special" revolvers incorporated all of the following special order features: cut-away or open forward trigger guard bows; bobbed hammer spurs, and short barrels. This "Fitz Special" New Service Revolver was made in 1934.

Lynn Kvam Collection

Colt Model 1909 New Service Double Action Revolver, .45 caliber, 5½" barrel, serial number 44284. Produced under contract for the U.S. Army and Navy, the Model 1909 New Service was fitted with a lanyard swivel on the butt and plain walnut grips.

Lynn Kvam Collection.

Colt Model 1917 New Service Double Action Revolver, .45 caliber, 5½" barrel, serial number 131087. Approximately 151,700 revolvers of this type were made by the Colt company for the U.S. Government. The pistol differed from the Model 1909 in the length of its cylinder, barrel taper ad form of the cylinder stop lug.

Lynn Kvam Collection.

Colt Model 1917 New Auto Cartridge Service Double Action Revolver, .45acp caliber, 5½" barrel, serial number 335654. This revolver was designed for use with half-moon clips containing .45acp cartridges used in the Model 1911 semiautomatic pistol. This variation was made only in 1933.

Lynn Kvam Collection.

Colt New Service Model Double Action Revolver, .44-40 caliber, 4½" barrel, serial number 336452. It is believed that this piece parts revolver was made circa 1933.

Lynn Kvam Collection.

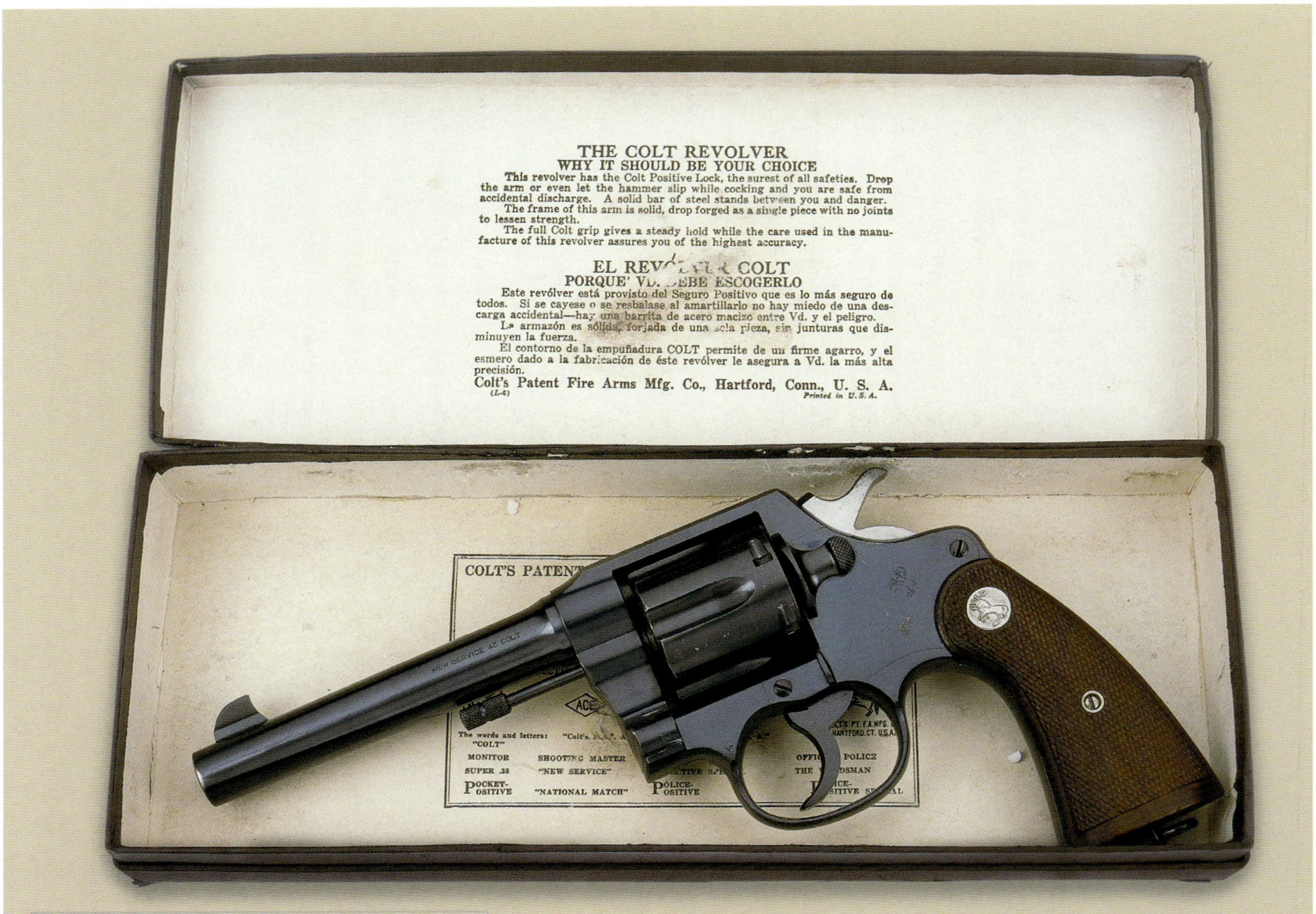

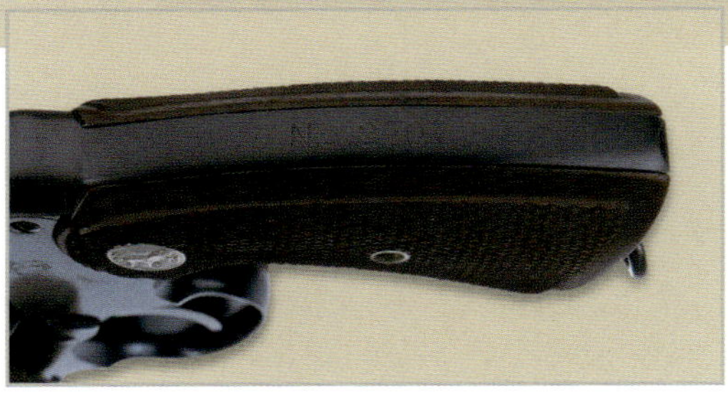

Colt New Service Model Double Action Revolver, .45 caliber, 5½" barrel, serial number 353656. Between 1904 and 1942, a total of 3,195 New Service Revolvers were purchased by the Royal Canadian Mounted Police. This revolver was among the last shipped to the RCMP in July of 1942 and is fully stamped with that force's ownership markings (inset). Interestingly, it is still accompanied by its original shipping box.

Craig A. Blancett Collection.

Colt New Service Target Model Double Action Revolver, .45 caliber, 6" barrel, serial number 337941. This example was probably made in 1933.

Lynn Kvam Collection.

Colt Pocket Positive Model Double Action Revolver, .32 caliber, 2½" barrel, serial number 155591. This short barrelled revolver was manufactured in 1937.

Lynn Kvam Collection.

Colt New Service Model Double Action Revolver, .45 caliber, 5½" barrel, serial number 342839. This revolver is believed to have been made in 1937.

Lynn Kvam Collection.

Colt New Service Target Model Double Action Revolver, .45 caliber, 7½" barrel, serial number 327921. This revolver was manufactured about 1927.

Lynn Kvam Collection.

Colt Shooting Master Model Double Action Revolver, .38 caliber, 6" barrel, serial number 333255. The Shooting Master variation of the New Service Revolver was produced from 1932 to 1941. The example shown here was made in 1932.

Lynn Kvam Collection.

Colt Police Positive Model Double Action Revolver, .38 caliber, 4" barrel, serial number 337809. This revolver, made circa 1930, was originally purchased by the Railway Express Company and is roll-engraved with its ownership marks on the backstrap (inset).

Lynn Kvam Collection.

Colt Police Positive Pequano Model Double Action Revolver, .32 caliber, 2" barrel, serial number 236154. The Pequano Model was made using parts left over when the Model B .32 caliber version of the Police Positive was discontinued. Sold primarily in Central and South America, this model was made from January of 1933 to September 1941. The exact production totals are unknown.

Lynn Kvam Collection.

Colt New Pocket Model Double Action Revolver, .32 caliber, 3½" barrel, serial number 32387. Introduced in 1893, the New Pocket Model was made until 1905. During that period, approximately 30,000 were produced.

Lynn Kvam Collection.

Colt Pocket Positive Model Double Action Revolver, .32 caliber, 3½" barrel, serial number 88585. The Pocket Positive replaced the New Pocket in Colt's product line in 1905. It remained in production until 1940, with approximately 130,000 being produced.

Lynn Kvam Collection.

Colt New Police Model Double Action Revolver, .32 caliber, 6" barrel, serial number 43071. The New Police Model was introduced in 1896 and remained in production until 1907. During that period, approximately 49,500 were manufactured. This example was probably made in 1906.

Lynn Kvam Collection.

Colt New Police Target Model Double Action Revolver, .32 caliber, 6" barrel, serial number 13374. Approximately 5,000 Target New Police Revolvers were produced between 1897 and 1905. The present example was manufactured in 1901.

Lynn Kvam Collection.

Colt Police Positive Model Double Action Revolver, .32 caliber, 4" barrel, serial number 343294. The .32 caliber version of the Police Positive was manufactured from 1907 to 1943. During that period, slightly fewer than 200,000 were made.

Lynn Kvam Collection.

Colt Police Positive Special Model Double Action Revolver, .38 caliber, 2" barrel, serial number 344824. The Police Positive Special was manufactured from 1908 to 1979. It differed from the standard model in the length of its frame and cylinder, which were longer to accommodate the cartridges used in this pistol. By the time it was discontinued over 750,000 had been made.

Lynn Kvam Collection.

Colt Police Positive Model Double Action Revolver, .38 caliber, 4" barrel, serial number 76920. Designed as the replacement for the Double Action Model 1877 Revolver, the Police Positive was added to the Colt company's product line in 1905 and remained in production until 1943. It proved to be quite popular and over 200,000 were made in .38 caliber. This skeletonized example was manufactured in 1914.

James Williams Collection.

Colt Police Positive Model Double Action Revolver, .38 caliber, 4" barrel, serial number 133226. Based upon its serial number, this pistol was made in 1921.

Lynn Kvam Collection.

Colt Police Positive Model Double Action Revolver, .22rf caliber, 4" barrel, serial number 214748. The second variation of the Police Positive Revolver was introduced in 1910 and is rare in .22rf caliber.

Lynn Kvam Collection.

Colt Police Positive Target Model Double Action Revolver, .22rf caliber, 6" barrel, serial number 6080.

Lynn Kvam Collection.

Engraved Colt Camp Perry Model Single Shot Pistol, .22rf caliber, 10" barrel, serial number 1. Prior to the general production of the Camp Perry Model, a series of approximately 63 sample pistols were produced by the Colt company for evaluation and testing. This pistol was presented by the president of the Colt's Patent Fire Arms Company, Samuel M. Stone, to Connecticut Governor John H. Trumbull in 1926 (see inset).
Mike McHugh Collection.

Camp Perry Model .22rf caliber, 10" barrel, serial number 244. This is a single shot built on a revolver frame. There were only 2488 made between 1926 and 1941.
Lynn Kvam Collection.

Colt Police Positive Special Model Double Action Revolver, .38 caliber, 4" barrel, serial number 58410M. This variation features a barrel with an integral extractor rod casing and more substantial grips than its predecessor.
Lynn Kvam Collection.

Colt Police Positive Target Model Double Action Revolver, .22rf caliber, 6" barrel, serial number 41317. The .22rf caliber Police Positive Target Model was introduced in 1910 and remained in production until 1941. This example was most likely made in 1935.

Lynn Kvam Collection.

Colt Police Positive Special Model Double Action Revolver, .32-20 caliber, 4" barrel, serial number 208931. This example illustrates the first variation of this model with a plain trigger.

Lynn Kvam Collection.

Colt Police Positive Special Model Double Action Revolver, .38 caliber, 4" barrel, serial number 371227. Sometime around 1929, the design of the Police Positive Special was slightly changed through the addition of checkering to the trigger bow and the stippling of the frame's top strap to reduce glare.

Lynn Kvam Collection.

Colt Police Positive Special Model Double Action Revolver, .38 caliber, 4" barrel, serial number 877982. The third variation of this model was built using Model D frame and the forward, as well as rear, contours of the butt are rounded instead of sharply angled.

Lynn Kvam Collection.

Colt "Fitz Special" Detective Special Model Double Action Revolver, .38 caliber, 2" barrel, serial number 408806. In common with other "Fitz Specials", this revolver has a bobbed hammer and a cutaway forward trigger guard bow. It is also fitted with pearl grips. Based upon its serial number, the pistol was probably manufactured in 1932.

Lynn Kvam Collection.

Colt Banker's Special Model Double Action Revolver, .38 caliber, 2" barrel, serial number 378004. In addition to being made in .22rf caliber, the Bankers Special was also offered in .38 Colt and .38 S&W caliber. The model was produced from 1926 until 1940.

Lynn Kvam Collection.

Colt "Fitz" Bankers Special serial number 368379 .22rf caliber. These models had a cutaway front triggerguard and a bobbed hammer. Only 25 to 50 were made in this configuration. This model was made in 1934.
Lynn Kvam Collection.

Colt Bankers Special 2" barrel, serial number 369008. The .22rf caliber was introduced in 1933 with a round butt. This model was made in 1934.
Lynn Kvam Collection.

Colt Police Positive Special MK V Model Double Action Revolver, .38 caliber, 4" barrel, serial number RD3839. Introduced in 1994, this model features ergonomic grips.
Lynn Kvam Collection.

Colt Aircrewman Model Double Action Revolver, .38 caliber, 2" barrel, serial number 3478LW. In 1951, the United States Air Force purchased 1,189 of these revolvers. Virtually all of these arms were subsequently destroyed due to the weakness of their light-weight alloy cylinders.
Lynn Kvam Collection.

Colt Cobra Model Double Action, serial number 2369LW .32 caliber with factory hammer shroud. This model is more commonly found in .38 caliber. Plastic grips were standard from 1950 to 1954. This model was made in 1951.
Lynn Kvam Collection.

Colt Aircrewman Model Double Action Revolver, .38 caliber, 2" barrel, serial number 18LW. Without question, one of the rarest 20th century Colt revolvers is the Aircrewman Model. Ordered by the U.S. Air Force in 1951, these revolvers were made with an alloy cylinder to reduce their weight. Unfortunately, tests indicated that the cylinders could not withstand the pressures generated by the .38 S&W Special cartridge for which they were chambered. As a result, virtually all of the 1,189 produced were destroyed.

Raymond Baldwin Museum of Connecticut History (Gift of the Colt's Patent Fire Arms Manufacturing Company)

Colt Aircrewman Model Double Action Revolver, .38 caliber, 2" barrel, serial number 7216LW. This revolver, which is fitted with an alloy cylinder, was originally shipped to the Western Cartridge Company in East Alton, Illinois, for ballistic testing.

Lynn Kvam Collection.

Colt Detective Special Model Double Action Revolver, .38 caliber, 2" barrel, serial number 412547. The Detective Special was introduced in 1927 and manufactured until 1986. While it closely resembles the Bankers Special, the Detective Special was essentially a Police Positive Special Revolver fitted with a 2" barrel. During the period it was produced, approximately 400,000 were made.

Lynn Kvam Collection.

Colt Border Patrol Model Double Action Revolver, .38 caliber, 4" barrel, serial number 823685. Approximately 400 revolvers of this type featuring a heavy weight 4" barrel were manufactured in 1952 for the U.S. Border Patrol. This model was never commercially advertised as they were made solely for the U.S. Department of the Treasury.

Lynn Kvam Collection.

Colt Detective Special Model Double Action Revolver, .38 caliber, 3" barrel, serial number A12399.

Lynn Kvam Collection.

Colt Detective Special Model Double Action Revolver, .38 caliber, 2" barrel, serial number C38291. The third variation of the Detective Special incorporated an integral ejector rod casing and improved grips.

Lynn Kvam Collection.

Colt Cobra Model Double Action Revolver, .22rf caliber, 3" barrel, serial number 173195. The Cobra was essentially a Detective Special Model built using a light-weight alloy frame. This .22rf caliber version of the Cobra was probably made about 1966.

Lynn Kvam Collection.

Colt Cobra Model Double Action Revolver, .38 caliber, 2" barrel, serial number F80196. In 1970, the serial numbers assigned to the Cobra Model were changed to an alpha-numeric system beginning with A60000. At the same time, the barrel design was changed to include an ejector rod casing.

Lynn Kvam Collection.

Colt Trooper Model Double Action Revolver, .357 Magnum caliber, 6" barrel, serial number 71225. The first variation of the Trooper Model was introduced in 1953 and was produced until 1969. It was serial numbered concurrently with the .357 Magnum revolver listed previously.
Lynn Kvam Collection.

Colt Trooper Model Double Action Revolver, .22rf caliber, 4" barrel, serial number 73697. This large frame pistol was designed primarily for target shooting.
Lynn Kvam Collection.

Colt Border Patrol Model Double Action Revolver, .357 Magnum caliber, 4" barrel, serial number J77492. The J-frame version of the Border Patrol Model was introduced into the Colt company's commercial product line in 1970.
Lynn Kvam Collection.

Colt Viper Model Double Action Revolver, .38 caliber, 4" barrel, serial number 98842M. This model, which is essentially a reduced weight variation of the Police Positive, was constructed using an alloy frame. It was only made during 1977.
Lynn Kvam Collection.

Colt .357 Caliber Double Action Revolver, 4" barrel, serial number 17389. Approximately 15,000 revolvers of this type were manufactured by Colt from 1953 until 1961. It was serial numbered in the same series as the Trooper Model discussed below.
Lynn Kvam Collection.

Colt Lawman MK III Model Double Action Revolver, .357 Magnum, 2" barrel, serial number J70765. The Mark III version of the Lawman was introduced in 1969 and remained in production until 1983.
Lynn Kvam Collection.

Colt Lawman MK V Model Double Action Revolver, .357 Magnum, 4" barrel, serial number 20854V. The final variation of the Lawman double action series of revolvers incorporating improved lockwork, was produced during 1984 and 1985.

Lynn Kvam Collection.

Colt Trooper MK V Model Double Action Revolver, .357 Magnum caliber, 6" barrel, serial number 12294V. The fourth variation of the Trooper Model was made from 1978 until 1982. In common with its predecessor, the barrel has an integral extractor rod casing.

Lynn Kvam Collection.

Colt Peacekeeper Model Double Action Revolver, .357 Magnum caliber, 6" barrel, serial number 66780V. The Peacekeeper was introduced in 1985 and discontinued in 1987. The model featured grips with finger cutouts on their forward surface to improve the pistol's handling characteristics.

Lynn Kvam Collection.

Colt Boa Mark V Model Double Action Revolver, .357 Magnum caliber, 6" barrel, serial number 43895V. The Boa was essentially a deluxe version of the Trooper Mark V Model. It was manufactured only during 1985.
Lynn Kvam Collection.

Colt Python Model Double Action Revolver, .357 Magnum caliber, 6" barrel, serial number 85262. Added to the Colt company's product line in 1955, the Python has proved to be one of its most successful double action revolvers. The degree of its popularity is perhaps best demonstrated by the fact that the model's name, Python, has become synonymous with Colt.
Lynn Kvam Collection.

Colt King Cobra Model Double Action Revolver, .357 Magnum caliber, 6" barrel, serial number C01095K. The King Cobra was only manufactured for five years (1986-2000). It differed from its earlier namesake in the design of its grip and the presence of a full-length ejector rod casing.
Lynn Kvam Collection.

Colt Anaconda Model Double Action Revolver, .44 Magnum caliber, 6" barrel, serial number MM818841. This model was introduced in 1990 and remained in production until 2000 when it was discontinued.
Lynn Kvam Collection.

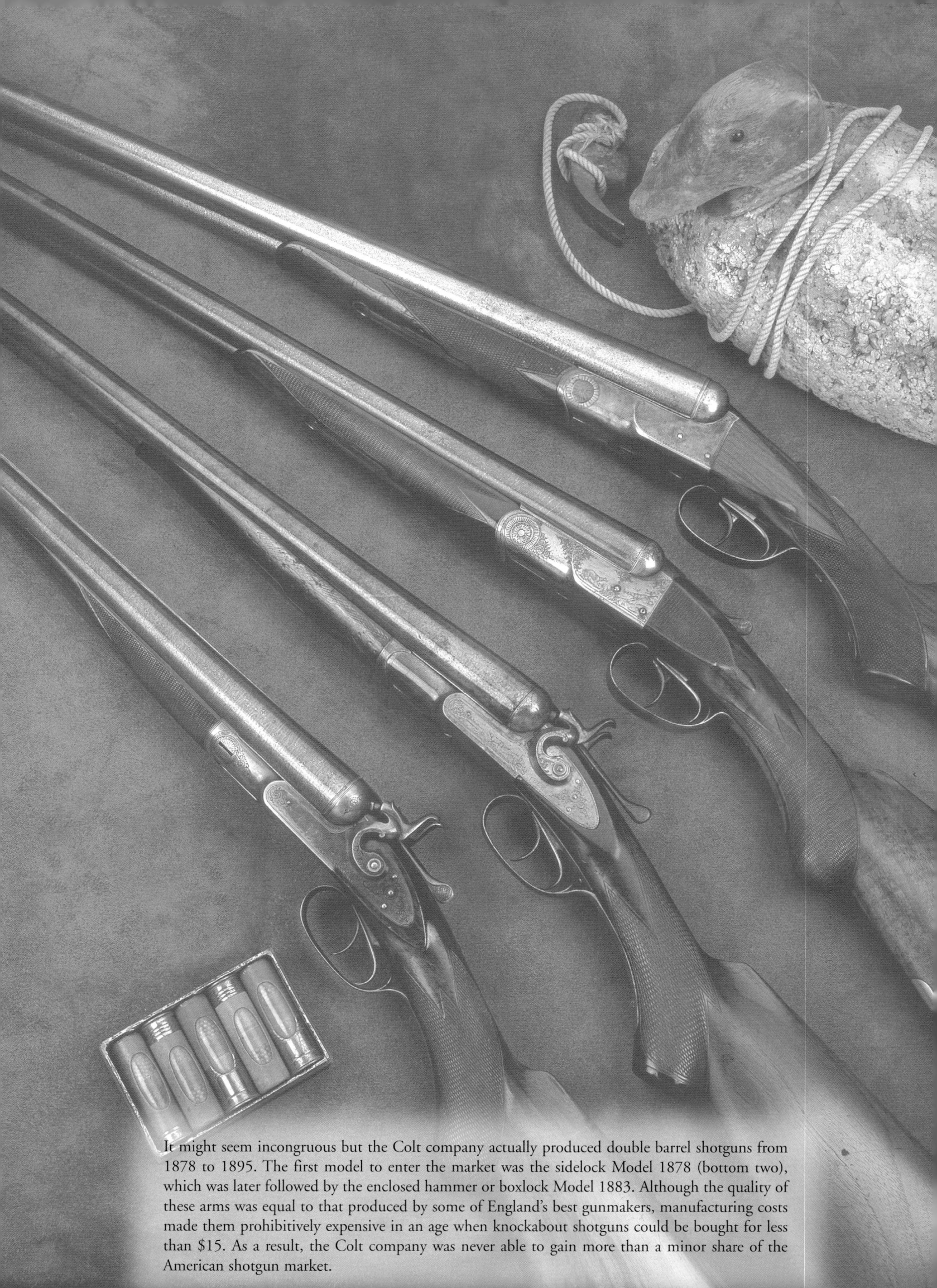

It might seem incongruous but the Colt company actually produced double barrel shotguns from 1878 to 1895. The first model to enter the market was the sidelock Model 1878 (bottom two), which was later followed by the enclosed hammer or boxlock Model 1883. Although the quality of these arms was equal to that produced by some of England's best gunmakers, manufacturing costs made them prohibitively expensive in an age when knockabout shotguns could be bought for less than $15. As a result, the Colt company was never able to gain more than a minor share of the American shotgun market.

The Colt Lightning Magazine Rifle was produced in a variety of calibers and frame sizes between 1884 to 1904. While the small and medium frame versions achieved a good deal of popularity, the large frame model (pictured on the left) was made in only limited quantities.

Berdan, Burgess and Lightning Rifles, Double Barrel Rifles, 1878 and 1883 Shotguns

by Richard R. Atkinson

By the end of the American Civil War it had become clear that firearms using loose powder and ball ignited by a separate percussion cap were obsolete. A new generation of single shot, as well as repeating, arms had demonstrated that the future lay with self-contained metallic cartridges which combined all the previous elements into one package.

While the Colt company had developed several experimental cartridge rifles before the war ended, the first production cartridge rifle was not made until 1866. That year 12,500 obsolete U.S. Special Rifle Muskets held in storage were altered by the company to the Snider breech-loading system for the government of Egypt. While the number of arms involved was not large, it was a beginning.

The second cartridge rifle to be made by the Colt company was also designed by an outsider, Colonel Hiram Berdan. Perfected between 1866 and 1868, 30,000 Berdan Rifles were eventually made under contract for the Russian Imperial Government. In addition, approximately 50 were commercially made for distribution by Colt.

The popularization of upland game bird hunting during the mid-1870s prompted the Colt company to enter the highly competitive shotgun market in 1878. Though both their sidelock and later boxlock shotguns were well received by the sporting public, price cutting by other manufacturers severely limited their sale. In all a total of 22,690 sidelock shotguns were made from 1878 to 1889, and 7,366 hammerless shotguns were produced between 1883 and 1895.

In an attempt to broaden the firm's product line in

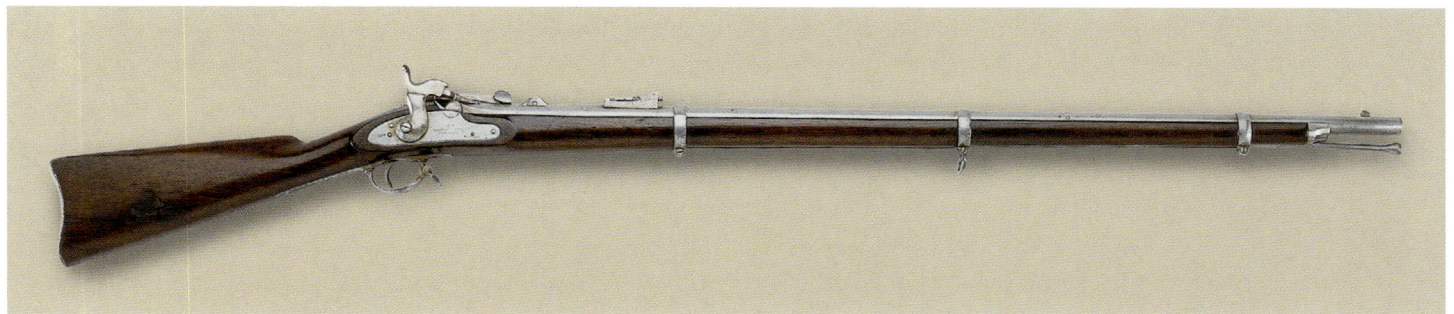

Sample Morgenstern Breechloading Rifle Musket, .58 caliber, 40" barrel, no serial number. The construction of this rifle musket's hinged breechblock and the fact that it is chambered for a modified pinfire cartridge, suggest that it is one of the samples made at the Colt works by William Morgenstern in 1867. Although the design was shown to the representatives of various European governments, it did not elicit any interest.

C. John Blickhan Collection.

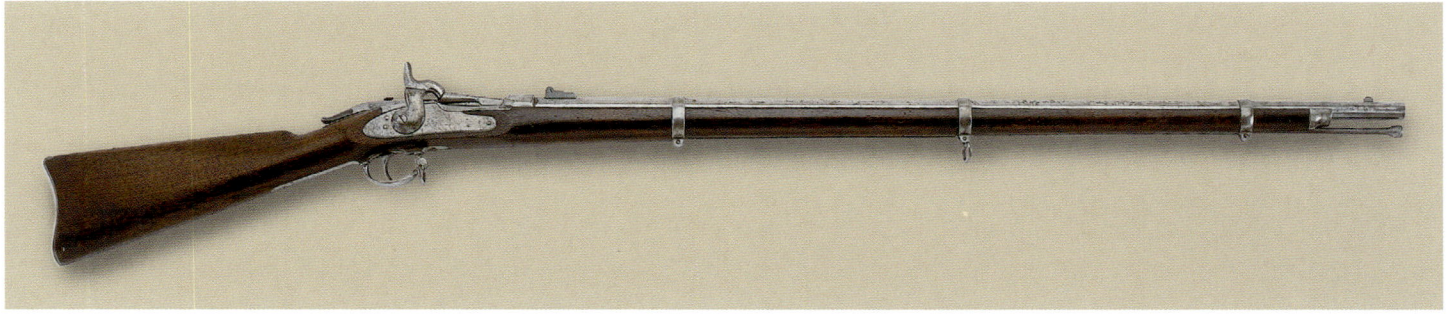

Sample Root & Lord Breechloading Rifle Musket, .58 caliber, 40" barrel, no serial number. A total of four sample breechloading rifle muskets incorporating E. K. Root's sliding breech bolt and Horace Lord's automatic cartridge ejector were made in 1866. While interest was expressed in the design by the Government of Spain, no orders were received for muskets of this design and the project was abandoned by the Colt company in December 1866.

Carl Kohlhorst Collection.

Sample Berdan Breechloading Rifle Musket, .58 caliber, 40" barrel, no serial number. On October 25, 1866, Hiram Berdan entered into an agreement with the Colt company to have samples of his breechloading rifle designs made in the firm's model shop. The first pattern to be built there incorporated a hinged two-piece breechblock that was set into a receiver housing which could be threaded onto a pre-existing barrel. This design was replaced shortly thereafter by one having a solid breech block such as that seen here. Based upon Colt company records, it is likely that this rifle musket was made sometime in May or June of 1867.

C. John Blickhan Collection.

1883, Colt decided to produce a lever action repeating rifle based upon patents issued to Andrew Burgess. This decision quickly led to an acrimonious trade war between Colt and the New Haven Connecticut-based Winchester Repeating Arms Company. After fewer than 6,500 Burgess rifles and carbines had been made, the model was dropped in January of 1885.

Colt then pursued the development of a slide-action repeating rifle that had been designed by William H. Elliot and Carl J. Ehbets. Named the Colt Lightning Magazine Rifle, this design was manufactured in three distinct frame sizes: the .22rf caliber small frame; .32, .38 and .44 caliber medium frame, and; the express caliber large frame. During its production life the medium frame Lightning Magazine Rifle was relatively successful with approximately 90,000 having been made between 1884 and 1902. In comparison, fewer than 6,500 large frame rifles were produced between 1887 and 1894. As might be expected, the .22 caliber version was the most popular. By the time it was discontinued in 1904, a total of approximately 90,000 thousand had been manufactured.

In addition to the above, the Colt company produced a few limited run longarms, such as the Laidley breechloading rifle in 1867; the special order sidelock double barrel rifle (1879-1885), and; the Franklin Magazine Rifle of 1887 and 1888.

Colt Berdan Russian Model 1868 Rifleman's Rifle, .42 caliber, 32½" barrel, no serial number. It is likely that this sample rifle was made in early December 1868. Actual delivery of production examples began on March 19, 1869 and the contract for 30,000 rifles was completed in May 1870.
Carl Kohlhorst Collection.

Colt Berdan Model 1868 Carbine, .42 caliber, 18¼" barrel, no serial number. During the design phase of the Berdan Model 1868 Rifleman's Rifle, consideration was also given to the manufacture of a carbine variant. While none were ever commercially made, approximately 25 design samples were produced for testing.
Carl Kohlhorst Collection.

Sample Colt Berdan Russian Model 1868 Rifleman's Rifle, .42 caliber, 32½" barrel, serial number 10. In keeping with normal manufacturing practices of the time, the Colt company retained a number of production examples from the Berdan rifle contract to use as product verification samples. These arms were selected at random and then fully gauged to insure that all parts met the specifications called for in the contract. Number 10 was later sold by the company to John R. Hegeman, Jr., an early twentieth century Colt collector.
J. Mike Peters Collection.

Colt Berdan Target Rifle, .44-77 Sharps caliber, 28" barrel, no serial number. During the early to mid-1870's, the Berdan patent rifle found considerable favor among members of the Colt company's rifle team. Produced on special order to the individual requirements of each member of the team, examples have been found in a variety of calibers and configurations. It is believed that fewer than 10 of these off-hand target rifles were made.
Carl Kohlhorst Collection.

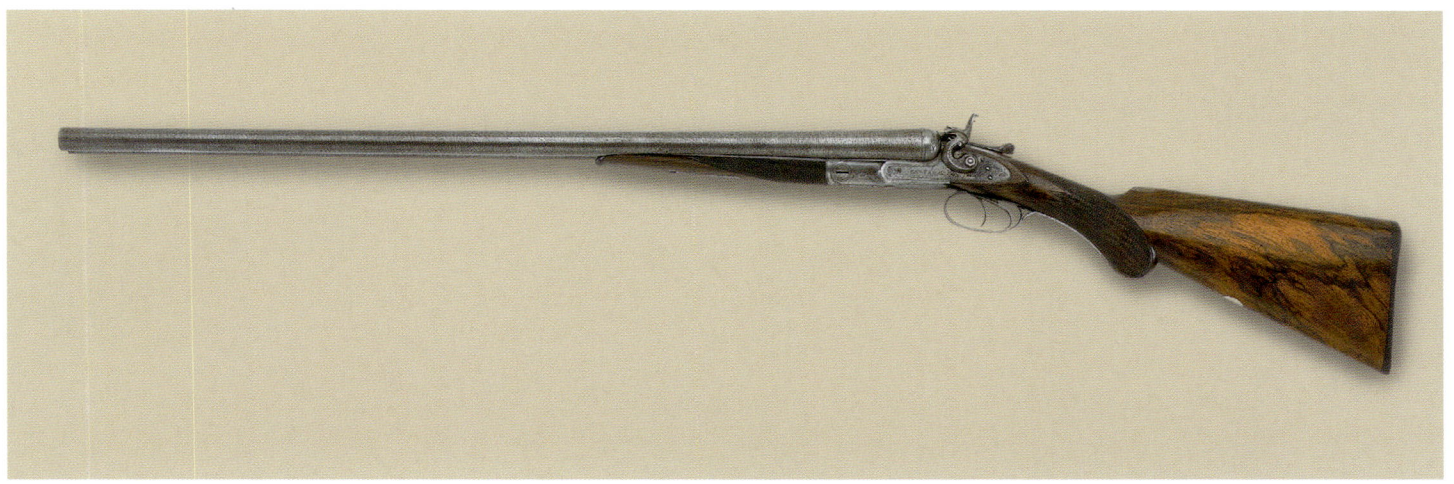

Colt Model 1878 Double Barrel Shotgun, 12 gauge, 30" barrels, serial number 15305. In an effort to capitalize on the increased interest in upland bird shooting during the late 1870's, the Colt company introduced a double barrel shotgun in 1878. Approximately 22,690 were made before the model was discontinued in 1889.

C. John Blickhan Collection.

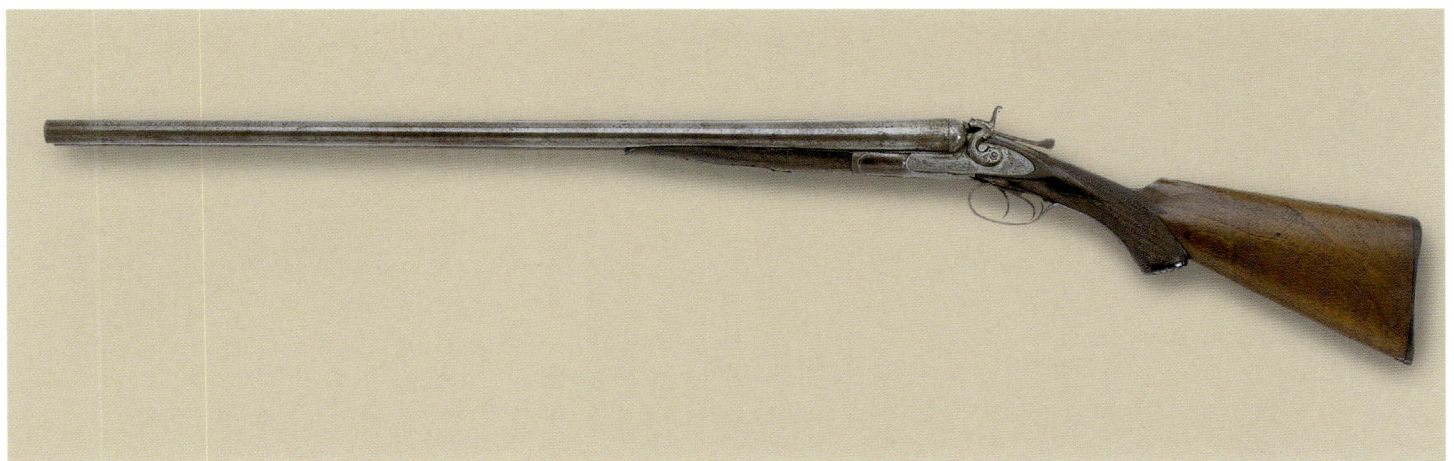

Colt Model 1878 Double Barrel Shotgun, 10 gauge, 32" barrels, serial number 18913. In addition to the 12 gauge, the Model 1878 Shotgun was also made available in 10 gauge. This bore size was particularly popular with geese hunters.

C. John Blickhan Collection.

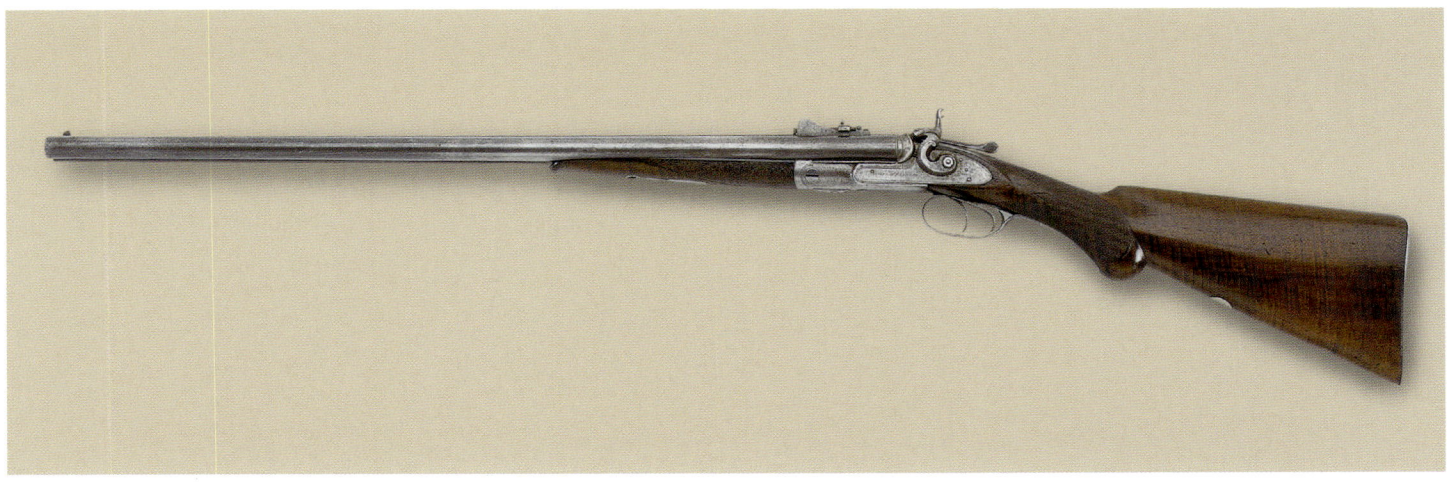

Colt Model 1878 Double Barrel Rifle, .45-85 caliber, 28" barrels, serial number 1. Between 1879 and 1885, the Colt company made approximately 40 double barrel rifles on a special order basis. Credit for their design and production goes to Samuel Colt's son, Caldwell Hart Colt, who had developed an affection for English rifles of this type. Fittingly, this particular example was originally owned by Caldwell Colt.

C. John Blickhan Collection.

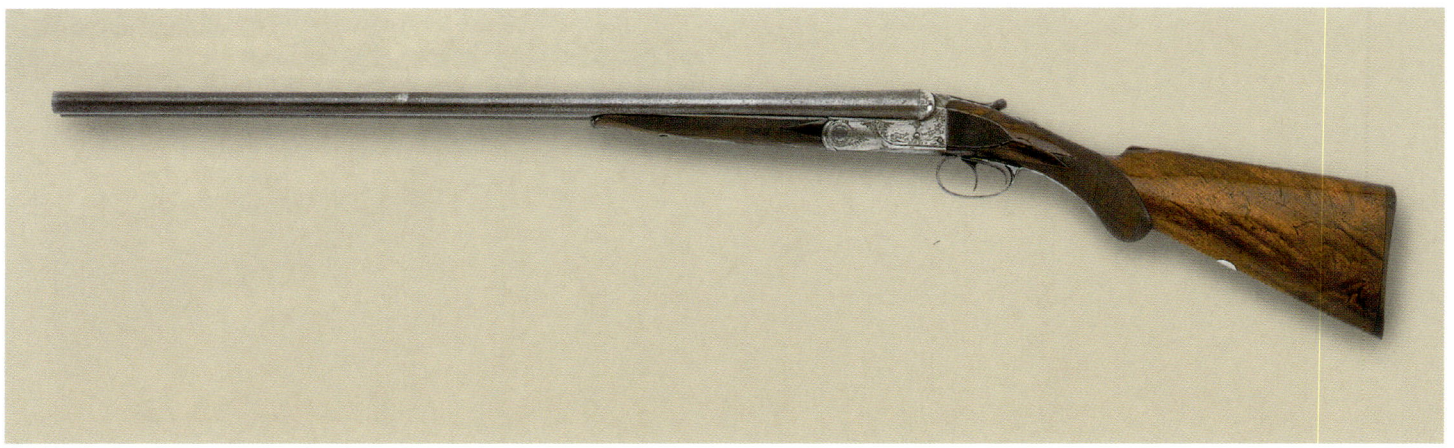

Colt Model 1883 Double Barrel Hammerless Shotgun, 12 gauge, 30" barrels, serial number 34. Designed by William Mason shortly before he left Colt for the Winchester Repeating Arms Company, the Model 1883 Shotgun was produced to compete with English arms then being imported into the United States in large quantities. It never achieved the popularity that the company had envisioned and only 7,366 were made before it was discontinued in 1895.

C. John Blickhan Collection.

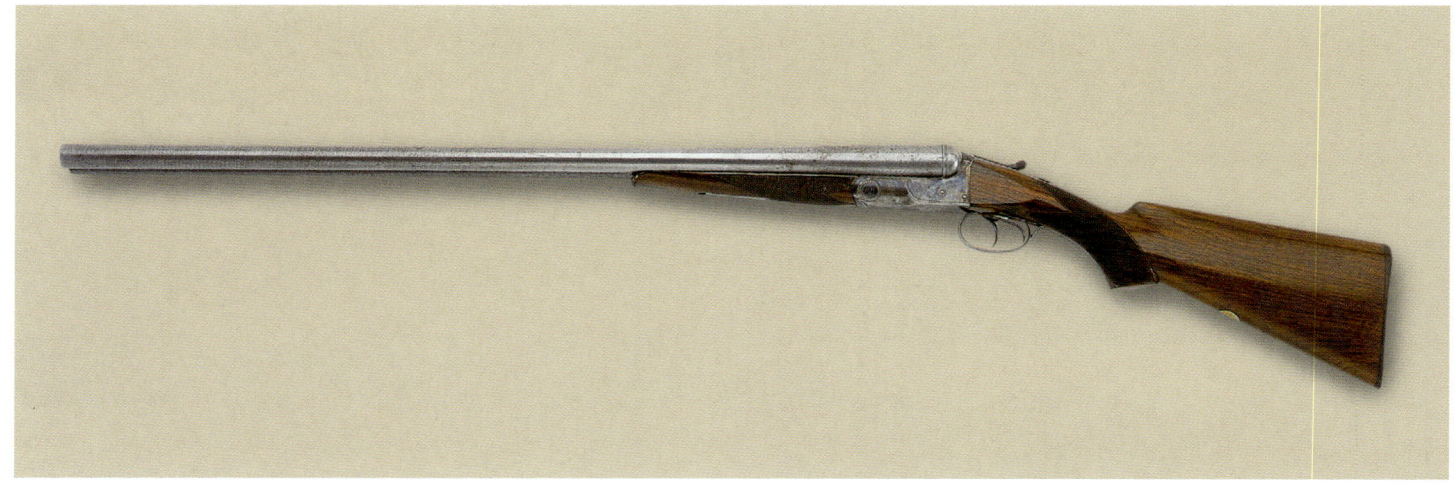

Colt Model 1883 Double Barrel Hammerless Shotgun, 10 gauge, 32" barrels, serial number 8328. This example illustrates the large bore version of the Model 1883 as made in the months before it was dropped from the Colt company's product line.

Richard Atkinson Collection.

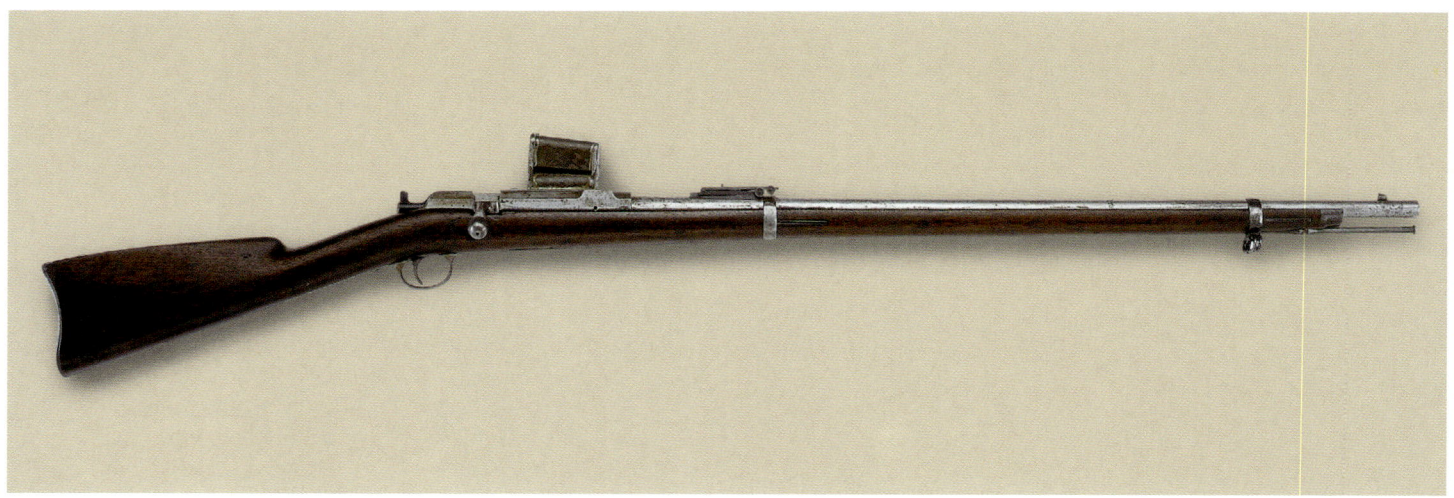

Sample Colt Franklin Patent Magazine Rifle Musket, .45-70 caliber, 32½" barrel, serial number 8. The vertical magazine on this Gras-pattern bolt action rifle was designed by William B. Franklin, vice president and general manager of the Colt company from 1865 to 1888. Fewer than 50 of these rifles were built in 1887 and 1888 for trial both in this country and abroad.

Carl Kohlhorst Collection.

Sample Colt Burgess Lever Action Rifle, .44-40 caliber, 25½" barrel, serial number M. In the 19th century it was standard practice for manufacturers to build model arms which were used as references in the production of both part and tooling drawings. The components of this example are marked both with the letter "M" as well as the word "Model" throughout.

Raymond Baldwin Museum of Connecticut History
(Gift of the Colt's Patent Fire Arms Manufacturing Company)

Colt Burgess Lever Action Carbine, .44-40 caliber, 20" barrel, serial number 1. This carbine was shipped to the New York retail house Hartley & Graham on May 18, 1883. As a Burgess Rifle bearing the same serial number was also shipped to Hartley & Graham (May 4, 1883), it is believed that the Colt company originally planned to number the carbines in a separate sequence from the rifles. This plan was apparently abandoned rather quickly, as subsequent carbines were numbered in the same series as the rifles.

Curtis L. Jones Collection.

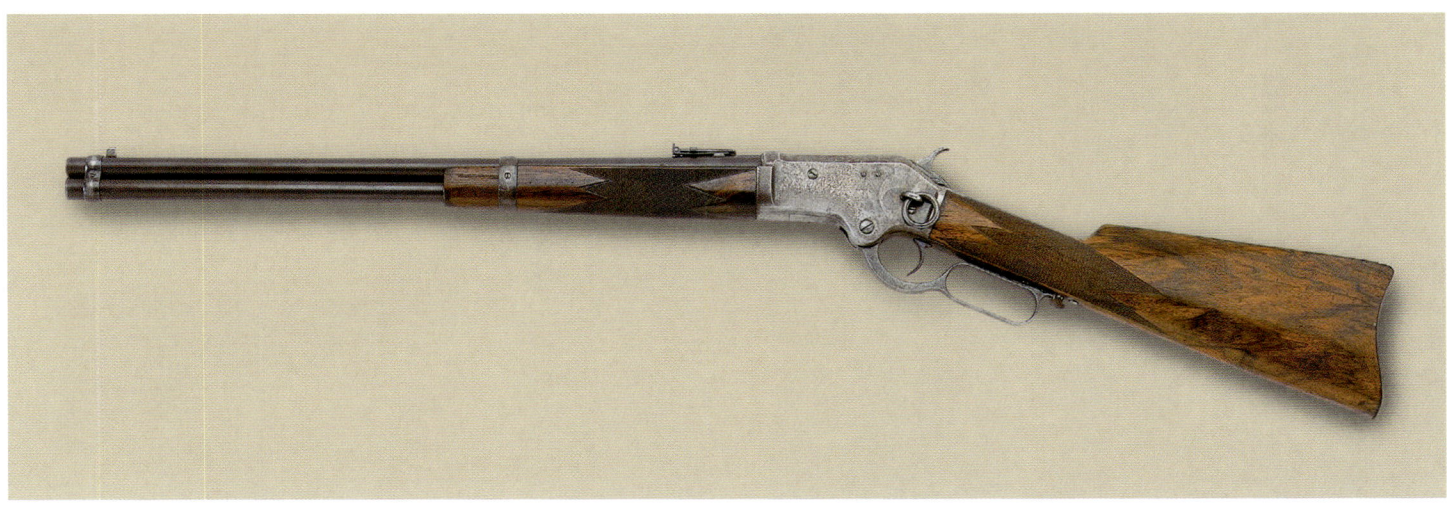

Colt Burgess Lever Action Sporting Carbine, .44-40 caliber, 20" barrel, serial number 5170. In an effort to capture some of the Winchester Repeating Arms Company's market, the Colt company began production of a lever action rifle based upon a design patented by Andrew Burgess in early 1883. In all a total of 2,593 Burgess carbines and 3,810 rifles were made before production was halted in January 1885.

C. John Blickhan Collection.

Colt Lightning Magazine Rifle, .44-40 caliber, 26" barrel, serial number 5832. The Medium Frame Colt Lightning Magazine Rifle was designed by W. H. Elliot and introduced into the company's product line in 1884. It proved to be a popular addition and remained in production until 1902. During that period a total of 89,777 were made in .32, .38 and .44 caliber.

Richard Atkinson Collection.

Colt Lightning Magazine Carbine, .44-40 caliber, 20" barrel, serial number 22084. The Medium Frame light weight Lightning Carbine was well regarded by sportsmen, as well as others, throughout the United States and a considerable number were made during the model's production life.

C. John Blickhan Collection.

Colt Lightning Magazine Rifle, .38-40 caliber, 26" barrel, serial number 29643. One of the options offered for the Lightning Rifle was a deluxe version having a well-figured walnut stock which featured a checkered pistol grip and slide handle.

C. John Blickhan Collection.

Colt Lightning Magazine Rifle, .40-60-260 caliber, 28" barrel, serial number 4824. In response to requests for a more powerful version of the Lightning Rifle, the Colt company introduced a Large Frame variation in 1887. Chambered for a variety of "Express" cartridges, this model had a limited market and only 6,496 were manufactured before it was discontinued in 1894. Relatively few deluxe examples, such as the one illustrated here, were produced by the Colt company during this model's production life.

C. John Blickhan Collection.

Colt Lightning Magazine Carbine, .40-60-260 caliber, 22" barrel, serial number 5226. Due to the recoil generated by the .38, .40, .45 and .50 caliber cartridges used in the Large Frame Lightning Magazine Rifle, few carbines were made in this frame size.

C. John Blickhan Collection.

Colt Lightning Magazine Rifle, .22rf caliber, 24" barrel, serial number 2526. The most popular Lightning Rifle made by Colt was the Small Frame variation chambered for the .22rf caliber cartridge. Introduced in 1887, it was manufactured until 1904. During that period a total of 89,912 were made.

C. John Blickhan Collection.

The Colt company reentered the longarm market in 1957 when it introduced the Colt 57 Bolt Action Sporting Rifle. Although that model and the Coltsman which followed it were built using Fabrique Nationale actions, the company later used Sako actions such as that seen on the bottom rifle.

Colt "57" Bolt Action Sporting Rifle, .30-06 caliber, 22" barrel, serial number C5418. Built by the Jefferson Manufacturing Company of North Haven, Connecticut, for Colt, the "57" rifle used a Fabrique Nationale Mauser action. The barrel, stock and all other fittings were manufactured in the United States. It is estimated that slightly more than 5,400 were produced in both .243 and .30-06 caliber during 1957.

Mike McHugh Collection.

Colt AR 15 Semiautomatic Rifle, .223 caliber, 21" barrel, serial number SP184941. This semiautomatic version of the U.S. M16 Rifle was manufactured by the Colt company from 1963 until 1998. Unlike most sporting armns of the period, it featured an ergonomic straightline form which reduced the effects of recoil upon a user. The rifle was also fitted with a synthetic stock which was unaffected by climate changes.

Gary A. Briggs Collection

Sample Colt Over/Under Double Barrel Shotgun, 12 gauge, serial number 1. This engraved and gold-inlaid sample was made for Colonel T. E. Bass, manager of the Colt company's European sales. The model designation assigned to this design was "Armsmear," the name of Samuel Colt's home in Hartford, Connecticut.

Mike McHugh Collection

found an immediate following among target shooters and sportsmen alike. More M-16/AR-15 rifles were produced than any other longarms in Colt's history.

In 1964 Colt added a semi-automatic .22 rimfire caliber rifle to its line-up: the Colteer. This was followed by two more versions: the Stagecoach, introduced in 1965 and the Courier in 1970. Made by Colt rather than an outside contractor, well over 50,000 were made before they were discontinued.

One of the more unusual rifles to be offered by Colt was its Sharps-Borchardt rifle of 1970. Evocative of the American frontier, these rifles were essentially custom-made. Intended for the high-end market, about 500 were built before the model was discontinued.

In 1973 Colt entered into an agreement with the Sauer arms company of Austria to market a centerfire bolt action to be called the Colt-Sauer.

The most recent longarm to be sold under the Colt name was a synthetic stocked lightweight hunting rifle produced by the Ultra Light Arms Company. This model was manufactured for slightly over a year.

As most of Colt's recent rifles and shotguns were made in limited numbers, they are rapidly becoming sought-after collectibles.

Colt Colteer 1-22 Bolt Action Rifle, .22rf caliber, 24" barrel, no serial number. In an effort to capture a portion of the juvenile rifle market, the Colt company introduced an inexpensive single shot bolt action rifle in 1957. As with the Model "57," these rifles were initially made by the Jefferson Manufacturing Company of North Haven, Connecticut. Toward the end of the model's production life, however, the Colt company assumed that responsibility. Despite sluggish sales, the model remained in the company's product line until 1966.

James C. Cassatt Collection.

Colt Colteer 1-22 Bolt Action Rifle, .22rf caliber, 22" barrel, no serial number. Sometime after the beginning the 1960s, the Colteer's barrel length was reduced from 24" to 22". Although the model was not serial numbered, it is believed that about 25,000 were produced.

James C. Cassatt Collection.

Colt Colteer 1-22 Bolt Action Rifle, .22rf Magnum caliber, 22" barrel, no serial number. In an effort to attract more customers, the Colt company offered the Colteer in .22rf Magnum

James C. Cassatt Collection.

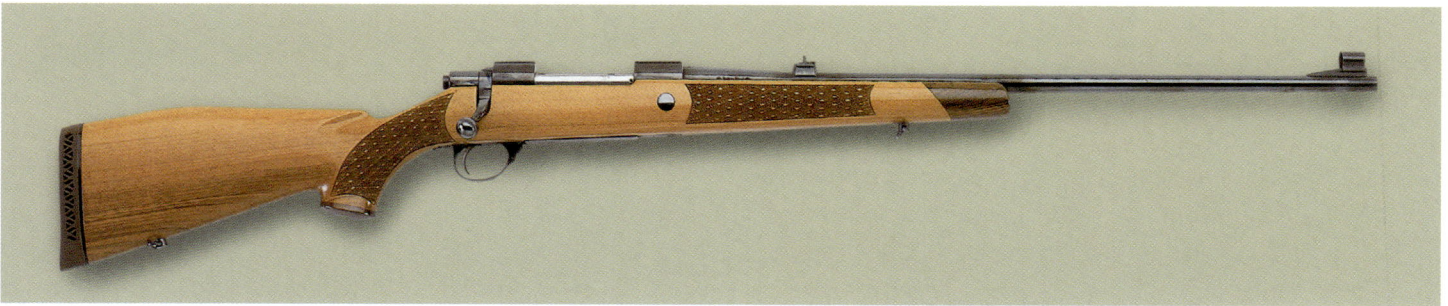

Colt Coltsman Custom Model Sporting Bolt Action Sporting Rifle, .30-06 caliber, 22" barrel, serial number 11905. In 1958, the name of the Colt "57" was changed to the Coltsman. In common with its immediate predecessor, the model was made using Fabrique Nationale Mauser actions. In 1962, the company began building rifles with an imported Sako action, such as that seen here. The Custom Grade was offered from 1962 to 1965 with a select walnut stock with hand cut checkering.

Mike McHugh Collection

Colt Standard Model Coltsman Sporting Bolt Action Rifle, .223 caliber, 22" barrel, serial number 75122. Approximately 5,000 standard grade Coltsman rifles with Sako actions were made in .223, .243, .264 and .308 caliber between 1962 and 1965.

Mike McHugh Collection

Colt Bolt Action Light Rifle, .30-06 caliber, serial number LR001022. Advances made in polymer chemistry during the 1950s and 60s benefited the American arms industry in a number of ways. Chief among these was the use of these materials in the construction of gun stocks. As the material was impervious to moisture, stocks could be made which did not warp when exposed to the elements. In addition they possessed a greater tensile strength than wood stocks, as well as the added advantage of much lighter weight.

Mike McHugh Collection.

Colt Colteer Semiautomatic Rifle, .22rf caliber, 19½" barrel, serial number SC16744. The Colteer was introduced into the Colt company's product line in 1964 and remained in production until 1976. The three variations of the model (the Colteer, Stagecoach and Courier) enjoyed relatively strong sales throughout their production and approximately 31,900 were made.

Gary A. Briggs Collection

Colt Stagecoach Semiautomatic Rifle, .22 caliber, 16½" barrel, no serial number. This variation of the Colteer featured the scene of a stagecoach hold-up (based upon the design originally found on the company's percussion era pocket pistols) roll-engraved on the left side of the receiver, as well as saddle ring and stud. The Stagecoach model was manufactured from 1964 to 1976. The example illustrated here was partially skeletonized for demonstration purposes

Gary A. Briggs Collection

Colt Courier Semiautomatic Rifle, .22rf caliber, 19¾" barrel, serial number SC18229. This model differs from the Colteer only in the fact that it had a pistol grip stock. It was produced from 1970 to 1976.

Gary A. Briggs Collection

Colt Sauer Bolt Action Sporting Rifle, .308 Winchester caliber, serial number CR10687. Introduced in 1973 and discontinued in 1985, the Colt Sauer rifle was made in Germany by J. P. Sauer & Sohn. While the shooting public recognized its intrinsic high quality, sales never reached the levels envisioned by Colt's management.

Mike McHugh Collection

Colt Sharps Single Shot Rifle, .22-250 Remington caliber, 26" barrel, serial number CS99. Reminiscent of the Sharps Borchardt rifle produced during the late 1870s, the Colt Sharps was a custom made sporting or target rifle manufactured by the firm's subsidiary, the Sharps Arms Company. It is estimated that approximately 500 were built during 1970 in a variety of calibers and barrel lengths. In common with the example shown here, all of these arms were cased.

Mike McHugh Collection

Colt Sauer Grand African High Grade Sporting Rifle, .458 Winchester caliber, 24" barrel, serial number CR15721. Stocked with bubinga wood, silver-plated and hand engraved, the Grand African rifle represented the Colt company's attempt to compete with the custom gunmakers of both America and Europe.

Collena McHugh Collection

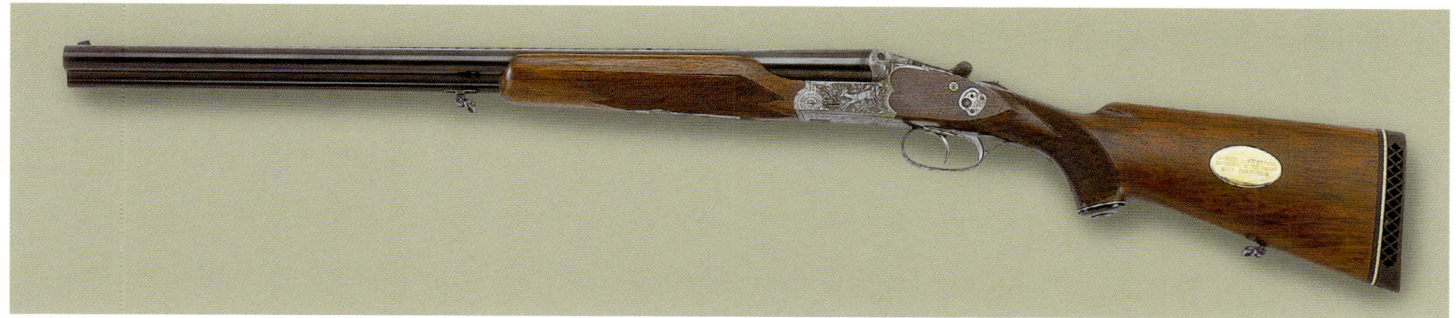

Colt Sauer Combination Rifle-Double Barrel Shotgun, .30-06 caliber by 12 gauge, 26" barrels, serial number G.A.S.1. This unique engraved and gold inlaid combination rifle/shotgun was made in 1976, for George A. Strichman, Chairman of Colt Industries from 1964 to 1985. Less ornate versions were offered to the public from 1974 to 1978.

Mike McHugh Collection

Colt Double Barrel Shotgun, 12 gauge, 30" barrels, serial number 469077. Approximately 50 Colt Double Barrel Shotguns were manufactured during 1961 and 1962 to test the potential market response to their possible introduction. All of these arms were made by Fabrication Mechanique, Carron Frette, in France.

Mike McHugh Collection

Colt Slide Action Repeating Shotgun, 12 gauge, 30" barrel, serial number 74267. This model was manufactured by the Jefferson (later Kodiak) Manufacturing Company of North Haven, Connecticut, using French made actions between 1961 and 1965. During its production life, approximately 2,000 were produced in 12, 16 and 20 gauge.

Mike McHugh Collection

Colt Semiautomatic Shotgun, 12 gauge, 28" barrel, serial number C010001. Approximately 5,293 shotguns of this type were manufactured by the Luigi Franchi of Brescia, Italy for Colt between 1962 and 1966. The serial number series for this model began with the shotgun illustrated here, number C010001.

Mike McHugh Collection

While the Model 1911 (top left) is the best known of all the Colt semiautomatic pistols to have been issued to U.S. servicemen and women, it wasn't the first. That distinction belongs to the Model 1900 (pictured at bottom) which was issued in limited numbers to both the U.S. Army and Navy in 1900. Following it, the government purchased other models in both .38 and finally .45 caliber.

With due apologies to Dashiell Hammett, the Colt pistols assembled here are "the stuff that dreams are made of." Pictured from far left are the unique .41 caliber Model 1903, serial number 8 Model 1905 with an experimental grip safety, a Model 1905 fitted with John M. Browning's grip safety, a Model 1907 pistol, a Model 1909 having the serial number 0, and, at top, the prototype Model 1910 pistol serial number 1.

Automatic Pistols
Model 1900 to Series 90's
by Lowell Pauli

The first semiautomatic pistol to be manufactured in the United States was the .38 caliber "Automatic Colt Pistol" introduced in 1900. Designed by John M. Browning in the late 1890s, this pistol marked the Colt company's coming of age.

Although the firm had hoped that the new model would be adopted for military service, testing revealed that it would not survive the rigors of field use. Consequently, Colt concentrated its marketing efforts on developing civilian sales. However, as with many groundbreaking ideas, public acceptance of the Automatic Colt Pistol was mixed and only about 3,500 were made before it was replaced by what is now known as the Model 1902.

The model of 1902 was also chambered for the .38 caliber cartridge. It was produced in two distinct variations: the seven shot "Sporting Model" and an eight shot "Military Model." Unlike their predecessor, both of these pistols did rather well. Over 7,500 Sporting Models were made before it was discontinued in 1908, and approximately 18,000 Military pistols were produced between 1902 and 1929.

The most successful of the early Colt self-loading pistols were the series of pocket models first marketed in 1903. Chambered for .25, .32 and .380 caliber cartridges, these models firmly established the Colt company as the premier manufacturer of semi-automatic sidearms. Produced in four different styles (the .38 caliber exposed hammer model of 1903; the hammerless .32 caliber version introduced the same year; a larger

Model 1900 Automatic Colt Pistol, .38 caliber, serial number 187, purchased by the U.S. Army in 1900. The left walnut grip plate is stamped with John T. Thompson's inspection cartouche, "JTT", and the acceptance date "1900." This pistol is one of 100 Model 1900 pistols purchased for field trials in May of the year they were introduced.

Edward S. Meadows Collection.

.380 caliber variation first sold in 1908, and a small .25 caliber pistol also put into production in 1908), they were remarkably popular. Over the years they were made, the Colt company produced approximately 1,145,000 pistols in these four calibers.

In 1905 the firm introduced a .45 caliber semi-automatic pistol that remained in production until 1911. Although only 6,100 were made, this model heralded Colt's most famous modern pistol: the Military Model 1911.

The Colt Model 1911, as it is now generally known, is without doubt the most famous semi-automatic pistol in the world. Designed by John M. Browning, the Model 1911 and its improved derivatives have been carried by countless American, as well as foreign, servicemen throughout the 20th century. On battlefields worldwide it has earned an unequaled reputation for reliability. The regard with which it is held is perhaps best demonstrated by the fact that more than 5,000,000 have been made by Colt, as well as other licensed contractors, since 1911.

Just as the phrase "Colt .45" meant a Single Action Army Revolver in the 19th century, today it signifies a Model 1911.

Although developed as a military weapon, the public purchased large numbers of the Model 1911. Calls for a smaller bore version led to the introduction of the Colt Super .38 pistol in 1929. Made in both a standard and target variations, this model remained in production until it was replaced by a new version in 1969. Over this period slightly more than 205,000 were made.

In 1931 the Colt company began production of a .22 rimfire caliber target pistol built on the Model 1911's frame, called the Ace. This model was followed in 1933 by a dedicated .45 caliber target pistol appropriately called the National Match model. Approximately 11,000 Ace pistols were made before it was discontinued in 1947, and 10,000 National Match Model 1911's were made between 1933 and 1941. In addition about 13,500 Service Model Ace pistols in .22 rimfire caliber were made from 1937 to 1945.

Model 1900 Automatic Colt Pistol, .38 caliber, serial number 1205, shipped to the Brooklyn Navy Yard on November 22, 1900. A total of 1,250 Model 1900 pistols were purchased by the U.S. Navy in 1900. The serial number sequence for these arms is from 1001 to 1250.

Lowell E. Pauli Collection.

Model 1900 Automatic Colt Pistol, .38 caliber, serial number 1695, purchased by the U.S. Army in 1900. As a result of recommendations made by the first review board, 200 additional Model 1900 pistols were ordered by the Ordnance Department with relocated slide serrations and thicker, as well as checkered grips. This pistol is accompanied by an original Rock Island Arsenal holster.

Edward S. Meadows Collection.

Model 1900 Automatic Colt Pistol, .38 caliber, serial number 386. Commercial versions of this pistol were manufactured from March of 1900 through May 1902. Of the total production of 4,274 pistols, approximately 3,000 were made with a sight safety.
Lowell E. Pauli Collection.

Presentation Model 1900 Automatic Colt Pistol, .38 caliber, serial number 2200. This gold inlaid pistol was given by the Colt's Patent Fire Arms Manufacturing Company to Lt. Charles A. Brand, the U.S. Navy's ordnance inspector stationed at the firm's Hartford factory, on March 30, 1901. Only three gold-inlaid Model 1900 pistols were made between 1900 and 1902.
Lowell E. Pauli Collection.

Model 1900 Automatic Colt Pistol, .38 caliber, serial number 4177. This commercial pistol is fitted with a modified sight safety and a round hammer typical of late production arms. Based upon its serial number, 4177 was made shortly before the model was discontinued in May 1902.
Lowell E. Pauli Collection.

Military Model 1902 Automatic Colt Pistol, .38 caliber, serial number 15006. The Military Model of 1902 can be readily differentiated from the Sporting version by its extended grip and eight-shot magazine. In July of 1902, the U.S. Army Ordnance Department purchased 200 Military Model pistols for field testing. These arms were serial numbered from 15001 to 15200.

Lowell E. Pauli Collection.

Sporting Model 1902 Automatic Colt Pistol, .38 caliber, serial number 4634. The Sporting Model was manufactured from May 14, 1902 to October 30, 1907 with serial numbers in sequence to the Model 1900. Identifiable by its seven-shot magazine, approximately 6,900 were made.

Lowell E. Pauli Collection.

Military Model 1903 Automatic Colt Pistol, .41 caliber, no serial number. During 1903, the Colt company produced approximately 5 Military Model 1902 which had been modified for use with an experimental .41 caliber rimless cartridge. Christened the Caliber 41 Rimless Smokeless Model 1903, these pistols were tested by the U.S. Ordnance Department during the controversy over whether a .38 or a .45 caliber sidearm should be adopted for service use.

Raymond Baldwin Museum of Connecticut History (Gift of the Colt's Patent Fire Arms Manufacturing Company)

Sporting Model 1902 Automatic Colt Pistol, .38 caliber, serial number 30065. This model was produced in two distinct serial number ranges: 4274-10999 and 30000-30190. Given its number, the present example was probably made in October 1907, shortly before the model was discontinued.
Lowell E. Pauli Collection.

Military Model 1902 Automatic Colt Pistol, .38 caliber, serial number 11653. The Model 1902's value was appreciated by governments other than that of the United States. In 1906 Chile ordered 500 pistols for its navy, of which this is an example. All of these pistols were shipped to the Colt company's London Agency on April 10, 1906 for trans-shipment to Chile.
Lowell E. Pauli Collection.

Military Model 1902 Automatic Colt Pistol, .38 caliber, serial number 42528. This commercial version of the Military Model was made in 1925, approximately three years before the model was discontinued. Approximately 18,000 pistols of this type were manufactured between July 1902 and December 1928.

Lowell E. Pauli Collection.

Automatic Colt .38 Caliber Exposed Hammer Pocket Model Pistol, serial number 19957. Introduced in December of 1903, this model was produced until December 1927. During its production, approximately 31,250 were made. The serial range for Exposed Hammer Pocket Pistol was from 16,000 to 47,226.

Lowell E. Pauli Collection.

Automatic Colt .38 Caliber Exposed Hammer Pocket Model Pistol, serial number 47226. This pistol has the distinction of having the highest serial number for its model. Factory records indicate that it was assembled on November 29, 1927.

Lowell E. Pauli Collection.

Special Order Automatic Colt .38 Caliber Exposed Hammer Pocket Model Pistol, serial number 29482, engraved on the backstrap (pictured below) with the original owner's monogram, "W.F.B." It is believed that this pistol which was shipped on August 5, 1911 to W. F. Burck, is the only factory inscribed Exposed Hammer Model 1903.

Michael McHugh Collection.

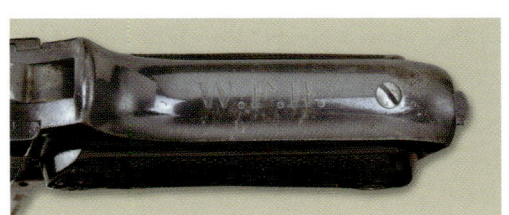

Special Order Automatic Colt .32 Caliber Pocket Hammerless Pistol, serial number 190407, made in 1915. In contrast to the vast majority of Model 1903 Hammerless pistols, this example was engraved with finely cut foliate scrollwork by Cuno L. Helfricht and fitted with pearl grip plates.
Mike McHugh Collection.

Sample Automatic Colt .32 Caliber Pocket Hammerless Pistol, no serial number. The basic design of what was to become the Model 1903 Pocket Automatic Pistol was submitted to the U.S. Patent Office by John M. Browning on April 3, 1902. In 1903, the Colt company produced this sample pistol to demonstrate the construction of the .32 caliber pistol which was to be put into production.

Raymond Baldwin Museum of Connecticut History (Gift of the Colt's Patent Fire Arms Manufacturing Company)

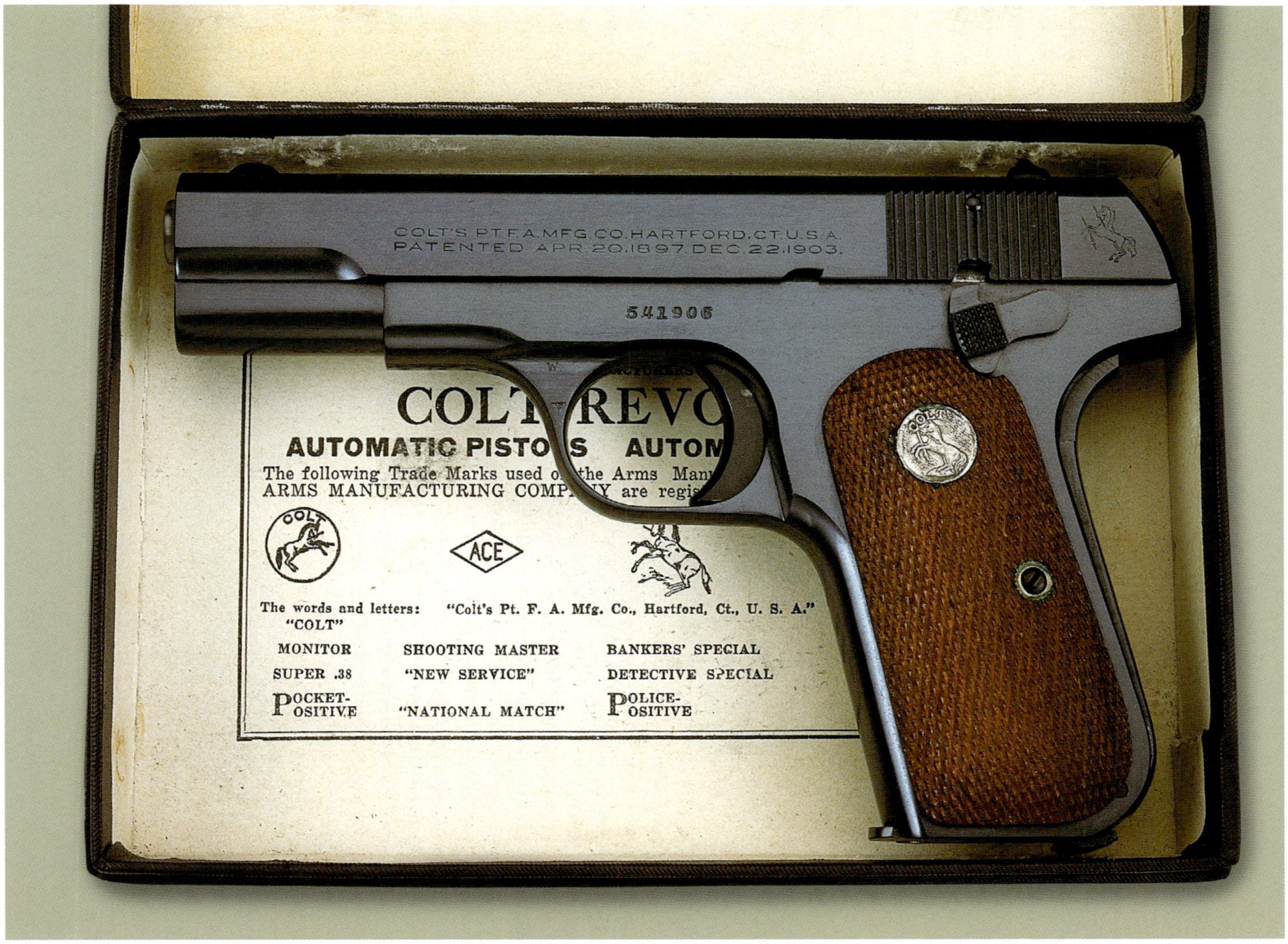

Automatic Colt .32 Caliber Pocket Hammerless Pistol, serial number 541906. Manufactured circa 1940, this late production pistol is accompanied by its original shipping box.

Lowell E. Pauli Collection.

Automatic Colt .32 Caliber Pocket Hammerless Pistol, .32 caliber, serial number 26309, manufactured in 1903. Approximately 527,200 Model 1903 Hammerless pistols were produced in this caliber from 1903 to 1945. Following the model's discontinuance, an additional 136 were assembled using leftover parts. The last of these was shipped in 1958.

Lowell E. Pauli Collection.

Colt Automatic Pistol Military Model Caliber .45 of 1905, serial number 4525, together with a combination attachable shoulder stock and holster. This pistol along with its rare optional shoulder stock and holster was shipped on February 28, 1910, to the Logan Hardware Company.
Lowell E. Pauli Collection.

Cased Colt Automatic Pistol Military Model Caliber .45 of 1905, serial number 2489. This pistol was one of 44 shipped to the Colt company's London Agency on May 9, 1907. It was subsequently sold to the Wilkinson Sword Company, who cased the pistol for resale. It was evidently purchased by a W. Gibbs of the 7th Hussars, whose named is stamped into the case's leather lid.
Lowell E. Pauli Collection.

Automatic Colt .32 Caliber Pocket Hammerless Pistol, serial number 570524. Although the U.S. Navy had purchased 200 of these pistols in 1917, it was not until World War II that Colt received any substantial contracts for the model. Between 1942 and 1945, slightly fewer than 17,000 were delivered to the government. Of these, 6,389 had blued and 10,527 had parkerized finishes.
Lowell E. Pauli Collection.

Colt Automatic Pistol Military Model Caliber .45 of 1905, serial number 121. Originally shipped in early 1906, this commercial Model 1905 was returned to the factory for a replacement slide sometime between 1916 and 1918.
Lowell E. Pauli Collection.

Colt Automatic Pistol Military Caliber .45 of 1905, serial number 8. Following the recommendations of the Board of Officers convened in 1906 to examine potential service pistols, the Colt company built several sample arms incorporating grip safeties. The presence of this device prevented the weapon from being fired unless the pistol was being securely held.
Raymond Baldwin Museum of Connecticut History (Gift of the Colt's Patent Fire Arms Manufacturing Company)

Colt Automatic Pistol Military Model Caliber .45 of 1907, serial number 121. Ordered for field trials in 1907, 200 of these pistols were delivered to the U.S. Army in March of 1908. All featured grip safeties, loaded chamber indicators and checkered walnut grips. This pistol was inspected by Major Kenneth Morton whose initials are stamped on the left forward edge of the trigger guard bow.

Edward S. Meadows Collection.

Colt Automatic Pistol Military Caliber .45 of 1905, serial number 2135. This pistol is fitted with the grip safety designed by John M. Browning. Unlike that developed by the Colt company's own engineers (Carl Ehbets, James Peard and George Tansley), Browning's design was remarkably simple. More importantly, it was also substantially stronger. In addition, this pistol has a loaded chamber indicator.
Raymond Baldwin Museum of Connecticut History (Gift of the Colt's Patent Fire Arms Manufacturing Company)

Automatic Colt .380 Caliber Pocket Hammerless Pistol of 1908, serial number 481. The .380 caliber Pocket Hammerless was manufactured from 1908 until June of 1945. A total of 138,009 were made during its production life. Early versions, such as this one, had a barrel bushing in front of the slide.

Lowell E. Pauli Collection.

Cased and engraved Automatic Colt .380 Caliber Pocket Hammerless Pistol of 1908, serial number 88037. This pistol was purchased by Captain Paul J. Roberts on September 29, 1925 during the National Matches at Camp Perry, Ohio. It is likely that the engraving was done by Wilbur A. Glahn.

Mike McHugh Collection.

Automatic Colt .380 Caliber Pocket Hammerless Pistol of 1908, serial number 90265. Manufactured in 1926, this pistol illustrates the care given in finishing by the Colt company to its products.

Lowell E. Pauli Collection.

Automatic Colt .380 Caliber Pocket Hammerless Pistol of 1908, serial number M137737. This General Officer's Pistol was issued to Brigadier General W. R. Gruber on March 3, 1947. A total of 3,128 pistols of this model were purchased by the United States Government during 1944 and 1945.

Lowell E. Pauli Collection.

Automatic Colt .25 Caliber Pocket Hammerless Pistol of 1908, serial number 88254. Introduced in 1908, the .25 caliber Pocket Hammerless Pistol was manufactured until 1941. During this time approximately 409,000 were made. This pistol was shipped on March 18, 1913 to the company's London Agency as part of a 50-pistol order.

Donald K. Morrison Collection.

Automatic Colt .25 Caliber Pocket Hammerless Pistol of 1908, serial number 93684. Accompanied by its original shipping box and instruction tag, this pistol has a nickel-plated finish, as well as pearl grips.

Donald K. Morrison Collection.

Cased and engraved Automatic Colt .25 Caliber Pocket Hammerless Pistol of 1908, serial number 382928. Featuring a blued finish and pearl grips, this pistol was shipped to the Phil B. Bekeart Company of San Francisco on October 29, 1929. The "Type A" engraving was probably done by Wilbur A. Glahn.

Mike McHugh Collection.

Automatic Colt .25 Caliber Pocket Hammerless Pistol of 1908, serial number 407534, stamped "U.S. Property." A limited number of .25 caliber pocket pistols were purchased on the open market or given to the U.S. Government by private citizens during World War II.

Lowell E. Pauli Collection.

Colt Automatic Pistol Caliber .45 Model of 1911, serial number 85. Made in December of 1911, this pistol was one of the first 100 delivered to the U.S. Army under its order of April 21, 1911.

Donald N. Ball Collection.

Colt Automatic Pistol Caliber .45 Model of 1911, serial number 4. The Model 1911 was approved for general use by the U. S. Army on March 29, 1911. On April 21, 1911, the Colt company received an order for 31,344 pistols. Serial number 4 was in the first shipment of these arms sent on January 4, 1912 to the Springfield Armory.

Edward S. Meadows Collection.

Colt Automatic Pistol Caliber .45 Model of 1909, serial number 0. Between January and mid-March of 1910, a total of 23 Model 1909 Pistols were made by the Colt company for testing and exhibition. Though well received by military authorities, the Model 1909 was only a stepping stone in the process of developing what was to become known as the Model 1911.

Raymond Baldwin Museum of Connecticut History (Gift of the Colt's Patent Fire Arms Manufacturing Company)

Colt Automatic Pistol Caliber .45 Model of 1910, serial number 1. Incorporating an improved thumb safety designed by John M. Browning, as well as a redesigned grip safety and angled grip, the Model 1910 physically resembles its successor, the Model 1911. During tests at Springfield Armory during November of 1910, it became apparent that the design of this pistol needed to be strengthened before it could be adopted for service.

Raymond Baldwin Museum of Connecticut History (Gift of the Colt's Patent Fire Arms Manufacturing Company)

Colt Automatic Pistol Caliber .45 Model of 1911, serial number 3991. This pistol was sold by order of the Chief of Ordnance on January 31, 1913, to Major General William Montrose Graham. Graham served in the regular army from 1855 to 1898 and was appointed Major General on the Retired List in 1915. He died on June 16, 1916.

Donald N. Ball Collection.

Colt Automatic Pistol Caliber .45 Model of 1911, serial number 576. Though identical to those issued to the U.S. Army, pistols delivered to the Navy were marked on their slides with the inscription "MODEL OF 1911 U.S. NAVY." In all, a total of 15,075 Model 1911 Pistols marked in this manner were delivered to the Navy between 1912 and 1915. This example was shipped to the Brooklyn Navy Yard on March 7, 1912.
Edward S. Meadows Collection.

Colt Automatic Pistol Caliber .45 Model of 1911 manufactured under license by the Remington Arms UMC Company of Bridgeport, Connecticut, no serial number. This skeletonized pistol was made to assist assemblers during the manufacture of the pistol by Remington during 1918 and 1919.

William E. Adams Collection.

Colt Automatic Pistol Caliber .45 Model of 1911, serial number 9699, manufactured under license by the Remington Arms UMC Company. Although the Remington company received a contract for 150,000 Model 1911 Pistols and later a revised contract for 500,000, the firm only produced 21,676 before the orders were cancelled due to the end of World War I. Number 9699 was shipped to the government on December 5, 1918.
Edward S. Meadows Collection.

Colt Automatic Pistol Caliber .45 Model of 1911, serial number 72571, manufactured under license by the Springfield Armory. Between 1914 and 1917, the Springfield Armory produced 25,767 Model 1911 Pistols. Serial number 72571 was the first pistol made at the Armory and was sent as a sample to the Office of the Chief of Ordnance in February 1914.
Edward S. Meadows Collection.

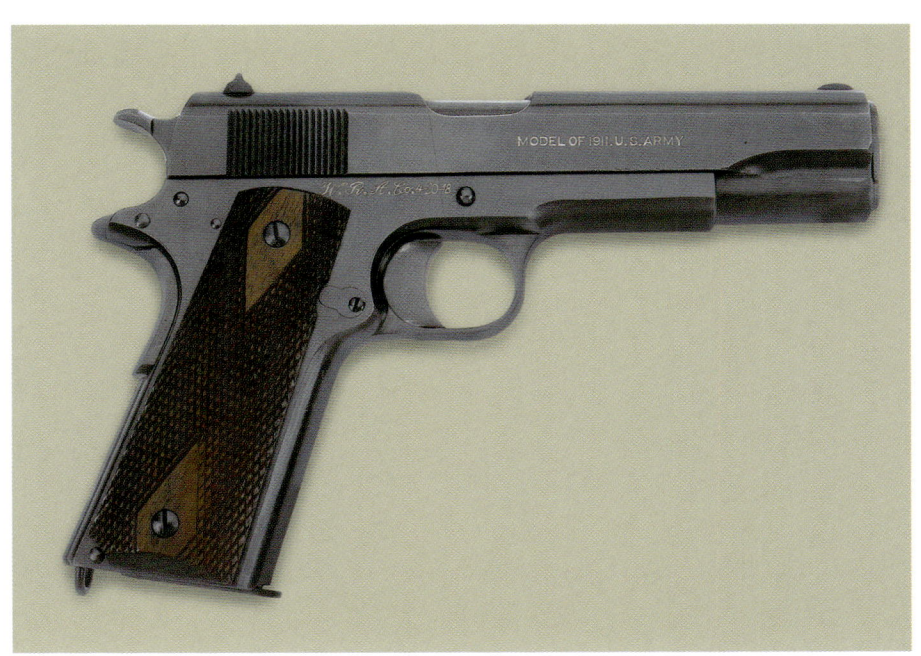

Colt Automatic Pistol Caliber .45 Model of 1911, without serial number. This pistol was sent as a sample to the Winchester Repeating Arms Company of New Haven, Connecticut, when that firm tentatively agreed to manufacture the Model 1911 under license for the U.S. Government. The right side of the slide is engraved with the inscription "W.R.A. 4-20-18" indicating the date it was received into the firm's ballistic laboratory collection.
Edward S. Meadow Collection.

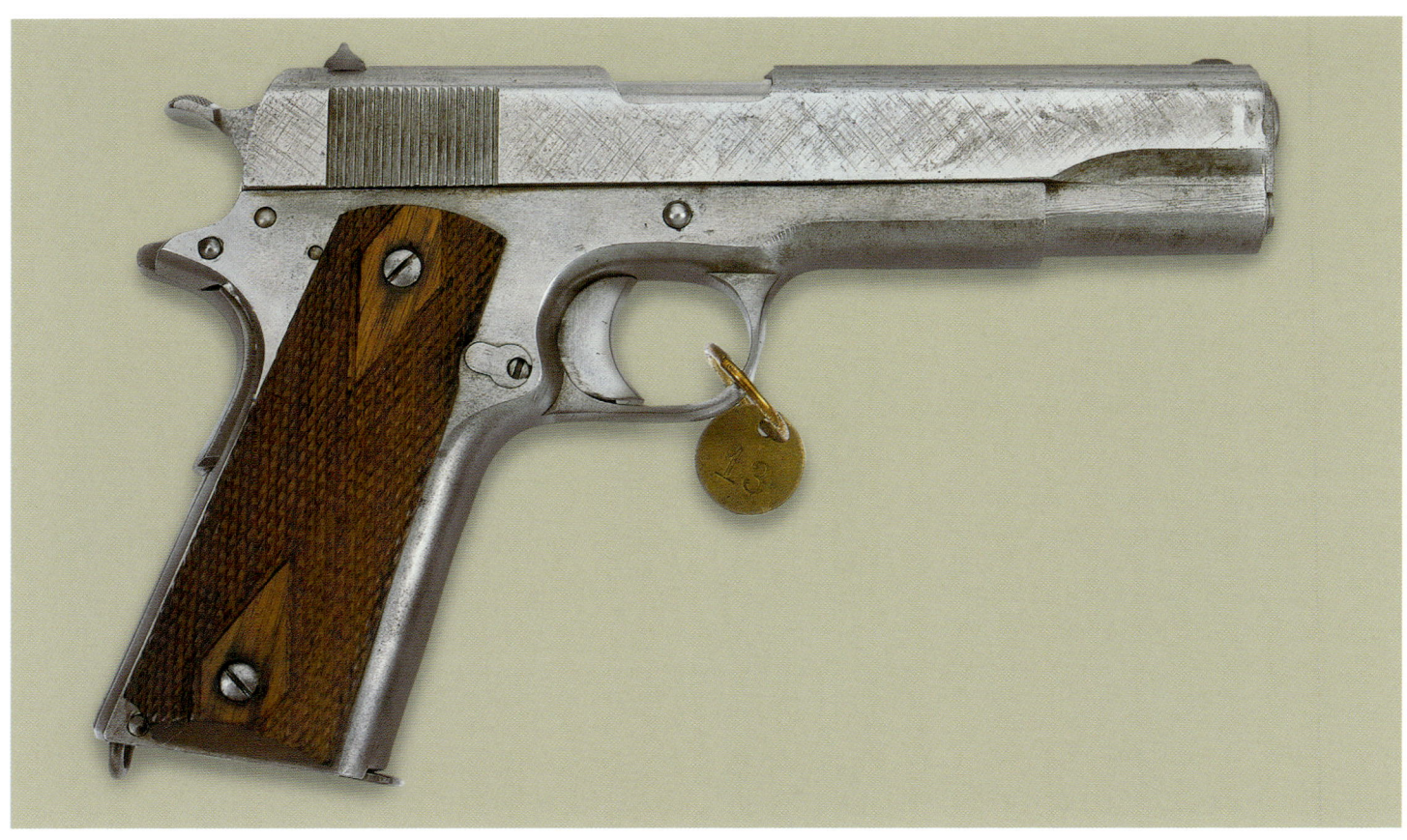

Sample Colt Automatic Pistol Caliber .45 Model of 1911 manufactured by the Winchester Repeating Arms Company, New Haven, Connecticut. Marked on the slide and receiver "G19P" (Gun 1919 [intended production year] Pistol), this is one of approximately 5 sample Model 1911 Pistols assembled by Winchester before their government contract for 500,000 was cancelled on December 24, 1918.

Edward S. Meadows Collection.

Colt Automatic Pistol Caliber .45 Model of 1911, serial number 30, manufactured under license by the North American Arms Company Ltd. of Quebec City, Quebec, Canada. Issued a contract for 500,000 pistols on July 1, 1918, the North American Arms Company delivered fewer than 100 before its contract was cancelled in December of 1918.

Lowell E. Pauli Collection.

Colt Automatic Pistol Caliber .45 Model 1911A1, serial number 708698. This transitional pistol embodies changes recommended by the Ordnance Department in 1923. The design alterations included shortening the trigger's length; extending the length of the grip safety; reworking the external contour of the mainspring housing; relieving the frame to the rear of the trigger, and; reworking the grip checkering. Number 708698 was delivered to the government in June of 1923.
Edward S. Meadows Collection.

Colt Automatic Pistol Caliber .45 Model 1911A1 U.S. Army, serial number 730958. Shipped to Springfield Armory on May 29, 1941, it was inspected by Colonel Robert Sears whose initials are stamped on the right side of the receiver in a rectangle.
Edward S. Meadows Collection.

Colt Automatic Pistol Caliber .45 Model 1911A1 U.S. Army, serial number 848050. During World War II the Colt company abandoned its standard blued finish in favor of a more durable phosphate process developed by the Parker Rustproof Company of Detroit, Michigan. Throughout World War II, Model 1911A1 pistols were delivered to the government with this "Parkerized" finish.
Edward S. Meadows Collection.

Colt Automatic Pistol Caliber .45 Model 1911A1, serial number S800456, manufactured under license by the Singer Manufacturing Company of Elizabeth Port, New Jersey. On April 17, 1940, the Singer Sewing Machine Company was awarded a special Educational Contract (W-ORD-396) to produce the tooling needed for the Model 1991A1, as well as 500 sample pistols. This contract was completed by December 1941 and the resulting arms were accepted for issue.

Donald N. Ball Collection.

Colt Automatic Pistol Caliber .45 Model 1911A1, serial number 922140, manufactured under license by the Remington Rand Corporation of Syracuse, New York. Setting aside business machines and typewriters for the war effort, Remington Rand manufactured 877,751 Model 1911A1 pistols between late 1941 and July of 1945.

Edward S. Meadows Collection.

Colt Automatic Pistol Caliber .45 Model 1911A1, serial number 1087471, manufactured under license by the Union Switch & Signal Company of Swissvale, Pennsylvania. This subsidiary of the Westinghouse Air Brake Company manufactured 55,000 Model 1911A1 pistols between January and October of 1943. It is unusual to find any wartime versions of the 1911A1 still accompanied by their original shipping cartons and spare magazines.

Edward S. Meadows Collection.

Colt Automatic Pistol Caliber .45 Model 1911A1, serial number 1864078, manufactured under license by the Ithaca Gun Company of Ithaca, New York. Ithaca manufactured 335,467 Model 1911A1 pistols during World War II. This example was shipped along with 1,499 others, on August 16, 1944, to the Royal Canadian Army Ordnance Depot at Longue Point, Montreal, Quebec.

William E. Adams Collection.

Colt Government Model .45 Caliber Automatic Pistol, serial number C14. The civilian version of the Model 1911 was assigned the name "Government Model" and given a serial number sequence having the "C" prefix. Number C14 was assembled on the first day of the model's production (March 9, 1912) and was shipped (with three others) on September 11, 1912, to early Colt collector J. R. Hegeman, Jr. of New York City.

Lowell E. Pauli Collection.

Colt Government Model .455 Webley Caliber Automatic Pistol, serial number W104740. The British Purchasing Commission bought 13,300 specially chambered Model 1911 pistols during World War I. To clearly identify that they were of a different caliber, these arms were assigned a "W" prefix to the serial number. This example was shipped to England in February or March of 1919. After World War II began, some of these pistols were taken from storage, refurbished if necessary and issued to Royal Air Force flight crews after being stamped "R.A.F."

William E. Adams Collection.

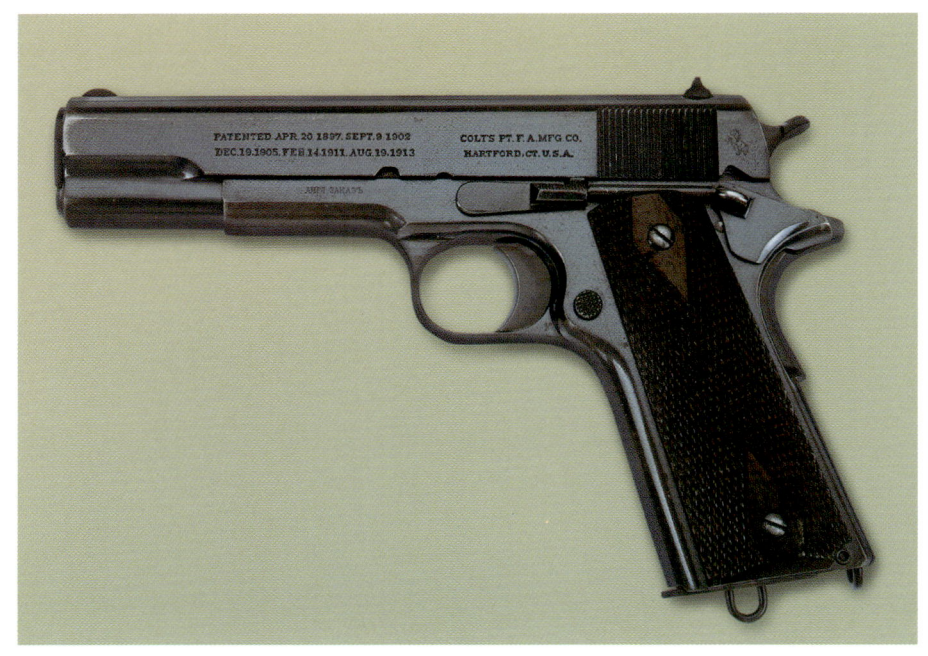

Colt Government Model .45 Caliber Automatic Pistol, serial number C50618. In 1914, the New York banking house J. P. Morgan & Company negotiated a contract with Colt for 51,100 Model 1911 pistols. This example was shipped to Russia on August 3, 1916.

William E. Adams Collection.

Engraved Colt Government Model .45 Caliber Automatic Pistol, serial number C135760. In addition to being engraved with finely cut scrollwork, this pistol is fitted with carved ivory grips, a special order Medium Patridge Rear Sight and a checkered trigger. It was shipped to T. B. Walton in care of Hibbard, Spencer Bartlett & Company, Chicago, Illinois, on March 27, 1923.

Mike McHugh Collection.

Colt Government Model .45 Caliber Automatic Pistol, serial number C138721. Immediately following the U. S. government's adoption of an improved version of the Model 1911, known as the Model 1911A1, the Colt company began making it commercially. This example was probably manufactured in 1924.

William E. Adams Collection.

Colt Government Model National Match Automatic .45 Caliber Pistol, serial number C163044. Between 1933 and 1941, the Colt company produced approximately 10,000 Model 1911A1 pistols designed specifically for target shooting. Aside from being fitted with special sights, these pistols had honed actions and barrels chosen for superior accuracy.

T. J. Mullin Collection.

Engraved Colt Government Model .45 Caliber Automatic Pistol, serial number C150250. This ivory gripped pistol was engraved by Wilbur A. Glahn with "Grade 2" style scrollwork. It was shipped to the Iver Johnson Sporting Goods Company of Boston, Massachusetts on August 20, 1926.
Mike McHugh Collection.

Pair of Gold Inlaid and Engraved Colt Government Model National Match .45 Caliber Automatic, serial numbers C201178 and C201184. This pair of highly decorated pistols was shipped to Sheriff J. E. Decker of Dallas, Texas, on November 22, 1940. In addition to their "Class C" engraving and extensive gold inlaid decoration by Wilbur A. Glahn, the pistols feature carved grips, cut-away trigger guards, special front sights, and 5-pound trigger pulls.

T. J. Mullin Collection.

Engraved Colt Government Model National Match .45 Caliber Automatic Pistol, serial number C163655. Engraved by Wilbur A. Glahn with "Grade B" scrollwork and fitted with ivory grips, this pistol was shipped to Abercrombie & Fitch of New York City on May 18, 1933. It was subsequently returned and reshipped to Abercrombie & Fitch on January 19, 1934.

T. J. Mullin Collection.

Colt Government Model National Match .45 Caliber Automatic Pistol, serial number C183279. Equipped with a Stevens pattern adjustable rear sight, this pistol was shipped to Lou J. Eppinger of Detroit, Michigan, on June 16, 1937.

T. J. Mullin Collection.

Colt Government Model .45 Caliber Automatic Pistol, serial number C221557. Manufactured in 1946, this pistol incorporates a number of small parts left over from the Colt company's wartime production.

William E. Adams Collection.

Engraved and Gold Inlaid Colt Government Model .45 Caliber Automatic Pistol, serial number 300000-C. Commissioned by William H. Goldbach, president of the Colt company's military division circa 1968, this pistol was engraved, as well as inlaid in gold and silver by Alvin F. Herbert. Among the decorative motifs found on this pistol are portrait busts of President Woodrow Wilson and General John J. Pershing; an artillery tableau, and; an infantry charge.

Raymond Baldwin Museum of Connecticut History
(Gift of William H. Goldbach)

Colt Government Model .45 Caliber Automatic Pistol, serial number 247297-C. Made in 1950, this pistol is one of 250 delivered to the State of New York's Arsenal in Brooklyn on December 16 of that year. All of these pistols in this order were roll-engraved on their slides with the inscription "PROPERTY OF THE STATE OF NEW YORK."

Lowell E. Pauli Collection.

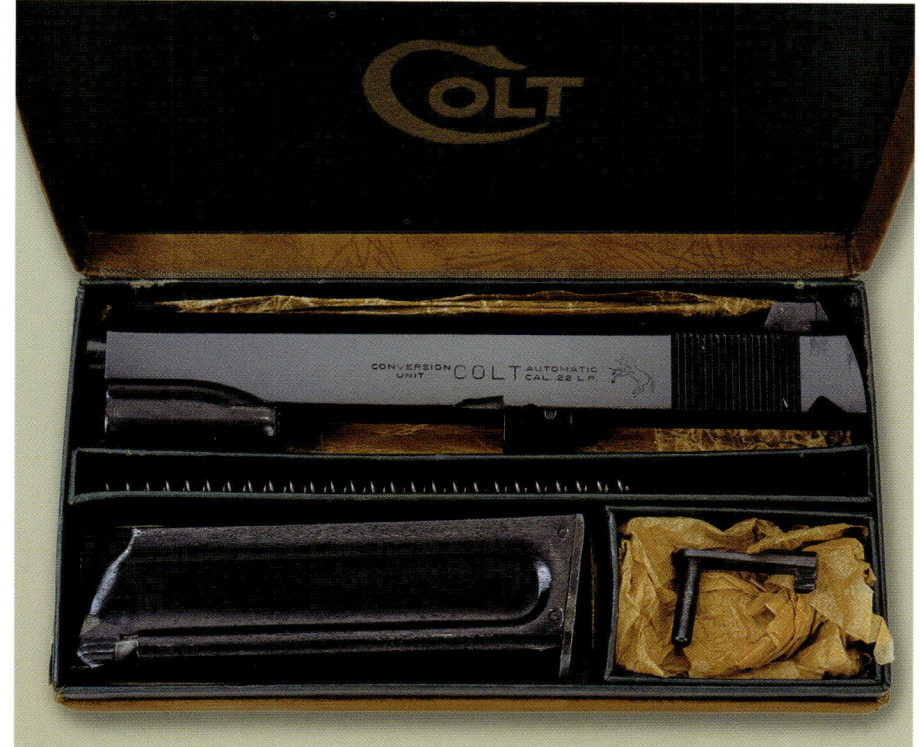

Colt .22-.45 Conversion Unit, no serial number. This kit containing a slide, barrel, magazine, barrel bushing, recoil spring and slide stop, allowed the .45 caliber Government Model to be used with .22rf caliber ammunition. Units of this type were manufactured from 1947 to 1954. This model was fitted with a Colt Master adjustable rear sight.

Lowell E. Pauli Collection.

Colt .38 AMU Automatic Pistol, serial number 158995. Initially developed for the Army Marksmanship Unit at Fort Benning, Georgia, relatively few .38 AMU Automatic Pistols were built by Colt. This example was originally shipped to Gil Hebard Guns of Knoxville, Illinois, on January 18, 1962.

Dan Duffy Collection.

Colt .38 Mid Range Automatic Kit Gun, serial number 00143-H. Manufactured from November 1963 through 1970, pistols of this type were shipped unassembled to purchasers. Number 00143-H was originally sold to Gil Hebard, who built the pistol illustrated here.

Lowell E. Pauli Collection.

Colt Super .38 Caliber Automatic Pistol, serial number 8200. Introduced in 1929, approximately 38,000 were manufactured prior to World War II. Built on the Model 1911A1's frame, the Super .38 was highly regarded by both sportsmen and target shooters. This example, still accompanied by its original shipping box and instruction sheet, was shipped to the H. & D. Folsom Company of New York City on July 26, 1930.

Craig Blancett Collection

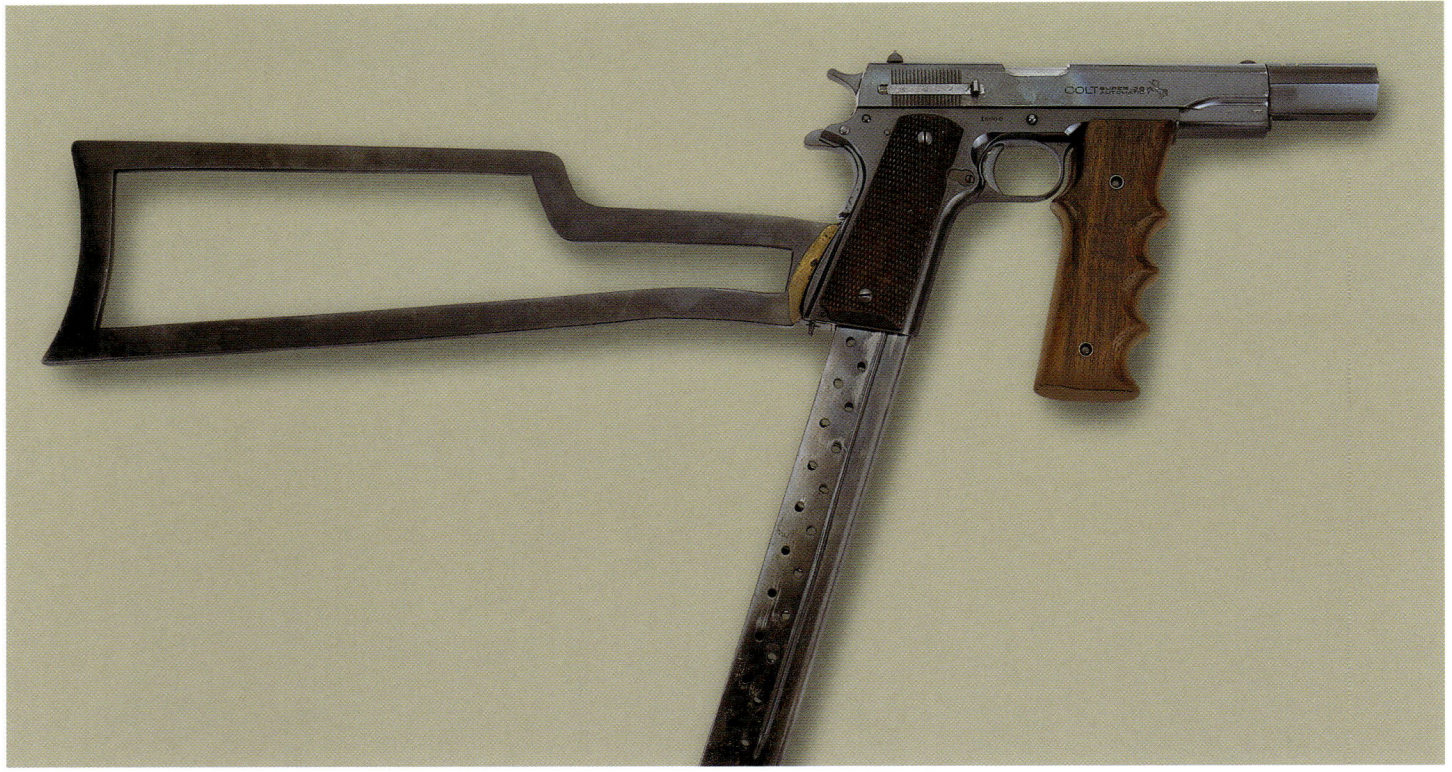

Colt Super .38 Caliber Selective-Fire Automatic Pistol, serial number 16000. This unique special order Super .38 was designed to function as both a semi and full automatic pistol. To assist the user's control during fully automatic fire, it was fitted with a forward pistol grip. The pistol also has an extended magazine and a shoulder stock. In anticipation of potential orders, it was submitted for testing in August of 1934 to the U.S. Department of Justice.

Lowell E. Pauli Collection.

Colt Gold Cup National Match Caliber .38 Mid-Range Automatic Pistol, serial number 2295MR. This target variation of the Model 1911A1 was built in 1961.

William E. Adams Collection.

Colt Government Model Gold Cup National Match .45 Caliber Automatic Pistol, serial number 9391NM. Manufactured in 1961, this target pistol is typical of those produced by Colt at the time.

William E. Adams Collection.

Engraved Colt Super .38 Caliber Automatic Pistol, serial number 16150. Shipped to the Powell & Clement Company of Cincinnati, Ohio, on August 10, 1934, this pistol was cut with "Class A" engraving by Wilbur A. Glahn.

Craig A. Blancett Collection.

Colt Super .38 Automatic Pistol, serial number 16331. This pistol is inscribed "E.P.D. No. 3" (inset) indicating that it was originally owned by the Escanaba (Michigan) Police Department. In all, that department purchased four Super .38 pistols for its officers in April of 1934.

Lowell E. Pauli Collection.

Colt Super Match .38 Caliber Automatic Pistol, serial number 19921. Approximately 3,900 Super Match .38 caliber pistols were made by Colt prior to World War II. Very few of them, however were fitted with ivory grips. This pistol was shipped to A. Novak & Company in Cicero, Illinois, on January 7, 1936.

Mike McHugh Collection.

Engraved Colt Super .38 Caliber Automatic Pistol, serial number 20066. Originally charged out to the loan account of the Colt company's sales manager H. W. Lidstone, on September 11, 1936, this "C Grade" engraved pistol was finally sold to W. E. Stager of Nashville, Tennessee and shipped on November 13, 1936.

Mike McHugh Collection.

Colt Super .38 Automatic Pistol, serial number 26286. During 1934, the City of St. Louis, Missouri, purchased 82 pistols of this type for its police force, all of which were engraved with the property mark "St.L.P.D."

Lowell E. Pauli Collection

Colt Super Match .38 Caliber Automatic Pistol, serial number 34994. Manufactured in the late 1930's, this pistol has a fixed rear sight typical of the model's early production.

Lowell E. Pauli Collection.

Engraved Colt Ace .22rf Caliber Automatic Pistol, serial number 6986. Engraved with "A Grade" scrollwork, this pistol was used as a display piece by the Colt company from December 29, 1936 through March 9, 1938. It was finally sold to the Cullum & Boren Company of Dallas, Texas and shipped on March 12, 1938.

Mike McHugh Collection.

Cased and Engraved Service Model Ace .22rf Caliber Automatic Pistol, serial number SM699, together with a .45-.22 Conversion Unit, serial number U4. This pearl gripped "B Grade" engraved pistol and conversion unit were shipped to Abercrombie & Fitch of New York City on November 10, 1938. Only eight Service Model Ace pistols and three other conversion units are known to have been engraved.

Mike McHugh Collection.

Colt Super .38 Caliber Automatic Pistol, serial number 37478. In April of 1945, the U.S. Government placed an order with Colt for 400 pistols of this type. While 24 were sent to Remington for ammunition testing, the balance, including this pistol, were shipped on July 20, 1945, to the Military Administration & Supply Division, Fowler Building, Rosslyn, Virginia. The Fowler Building is known to have been a storage facility for the Office of Strategic Services (O.S.S.) during World War II.
Lowell E. Pauli Collection.

Colt Ace .22rf Caliber Automatic Pistol, serial number 1039. The Colt Ace was introduced in 1931 and manufactured through 1947. In all, approximately 11,000 were made. This particular pistol was shipped to Colt's British agent, the London Armoury Company on August 5, 1931.
Lowell E. Pauli Collection.

Colt Service Model Ace .22rf Caliber Automatic Pistol, serial number SM727. The Service Model Ace was manufactured from 1935 to 1945. Designed for marksmanship training by the U.S. armed forces, few were sold commercially.
Lowell E. Pauli Collection.

Cased Service Model Ace .22rf Caliber Automatic Pistol, serial number SM821, together with a .45-.22 Conversion Unit, serial number U44. This set was manufactured in 1939 and is accompanied by its original form-fitted case.

Mike McHugh Collection.

Colt Service Model Ace .22rf Caliber Automatic Pistol, serial number SM3518. Marked "U.S. PROPERTY", this pistol was shipped to the Springfield Armory on December 19, 1942.

Lowell E. Pauli Collection.

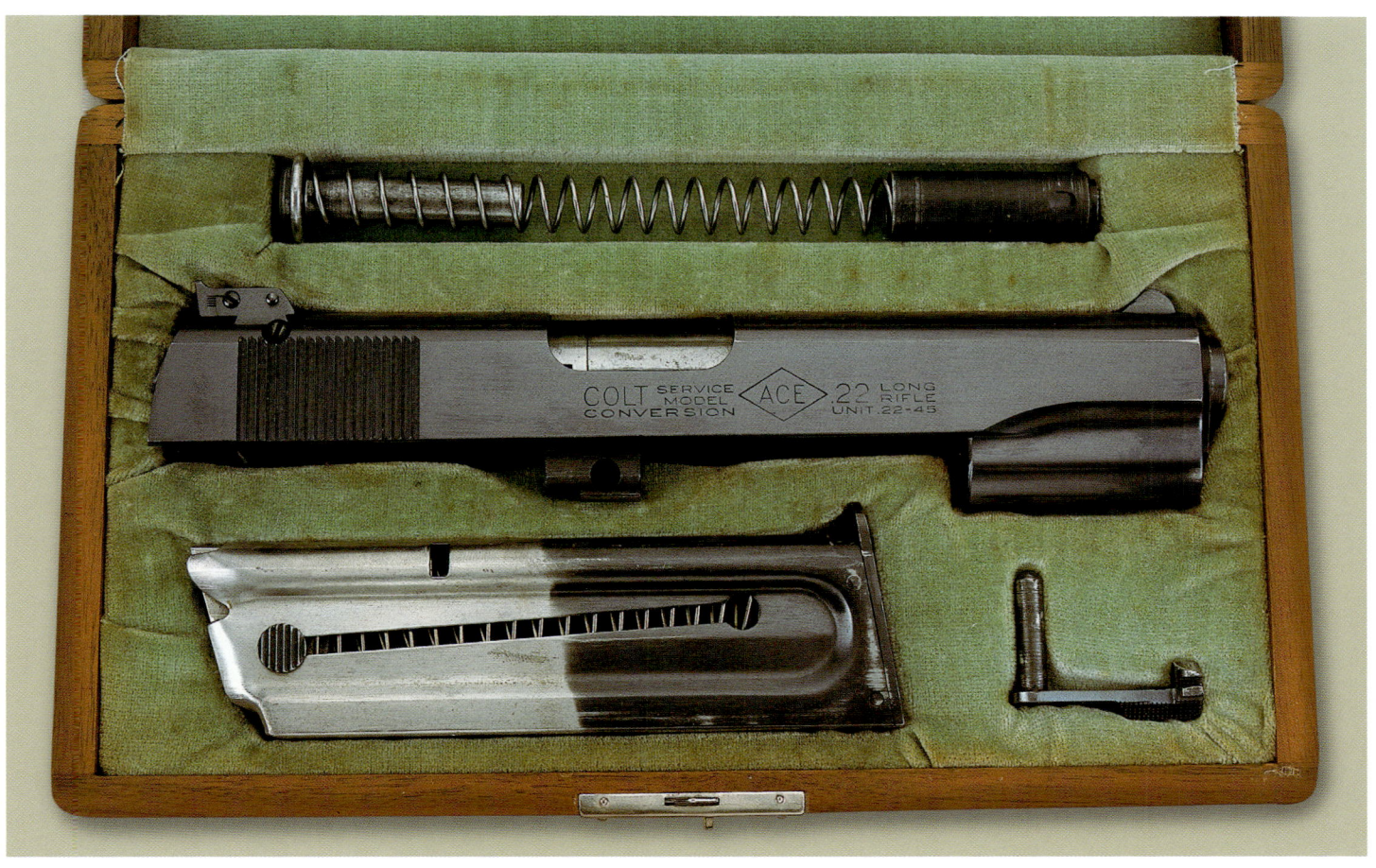

Cased Colt .22-.45 Conversion Unit, serial number U134. Approximately 1,758 of these units were produced prior to World War II. The case was offered as an extra charge option by the Colt company for $3.50.

Mike McHugh Collection.

Colt Service Model Ace .22rf Caliber Automatic Pistol, serial number SM10561. Typical of wartime production Colts, this pistol has a Parko-Lubrite finish. It was shipped on July 24, 1945 to the Naval Supply Depot located in Oakland, California.

Lowell E. Pauli Collection.

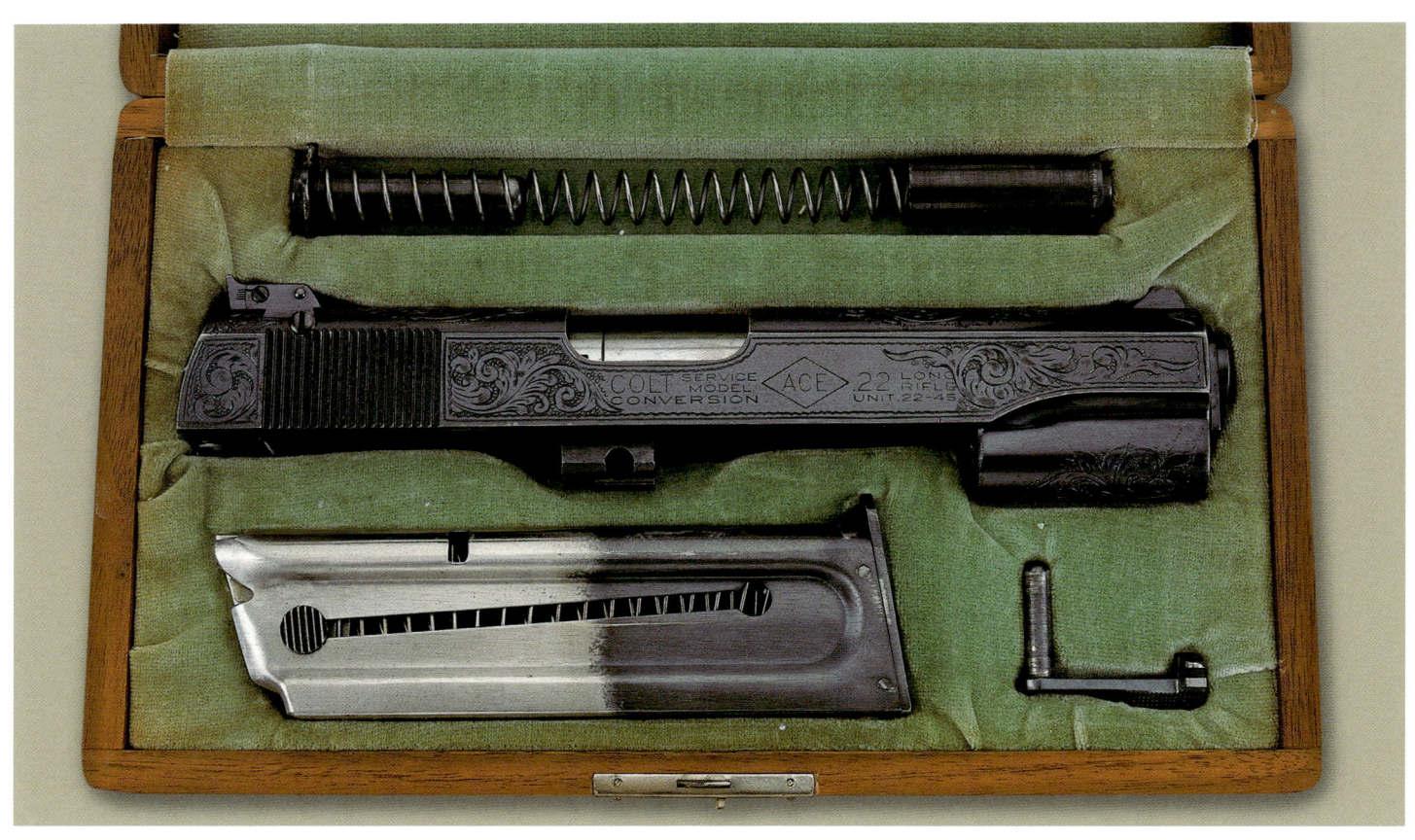

Cased and Engraved Colt .22-.45 Conversion Unit, serial number U102. First shipped to Marshall Field & Company of Chicago, Illinois, on November 9, 1938, this "B Grade" engraved unit was eventually sold to the same firm on October 31, 1939.

Mike McHugh Collection.

Colt Service Model Ace .22rf Caliber Pistol, serial number SM43737. In November of 1977, the Colt company reintroduced the Service Model Ace and continued its manufacture until early 1982. During this period, approximately 29,900 were made.

Lowell E. Pauli Collection.

Colt Mark IV Series 70 Goverment Model .45 Caliber Automatic Pistol, serial number 18309 B70. A total of 39,822 Series 70 Goverment Model Pistols were manufactured in 1979.
Lowell E. Pauli Collection.

Colt Light Weight Commander Model .30 Luger Caliber Automatic Pistol, serial number CLW010791. A total of 500 pistols of this type were manufactured in 1971 for Gugilemo De Marchi & Company of Turin, Italy. This particular pistol was shipped to that firm on October 1, 1971.
Lowell E. Pauli Collection.

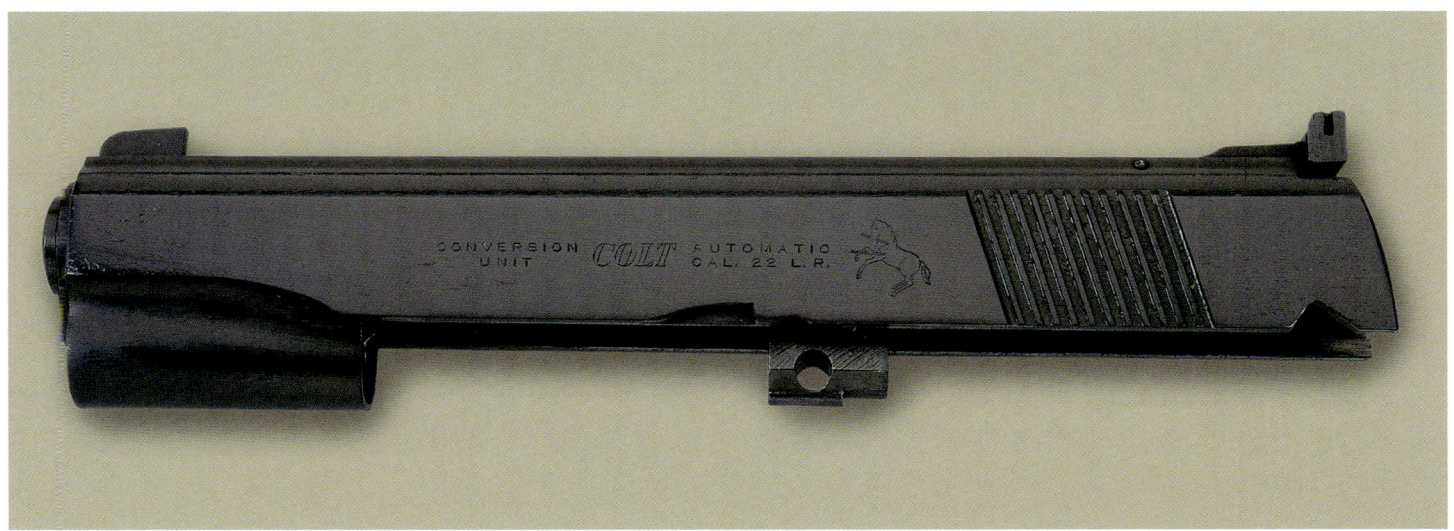

Colt .22-.38-.45 Conversion Unit, no serial number. From 1954 to 1983, conversion units of this type, fitted with Arco rear sights, were offered by the Colt company for use with its .38 Super or .45 caliber Government Model pistols.
Lowell E. Pauli Collection.

Engraved Colt Mark IV Series 70 Government Model .45 Caliber Automatic Pistol, serial number 70G97860. Engraved with "Class C" scrollwork, this nickel-plated pistol was shipped to the Northland Sports & Supply company of Minot, North Dakota on August 31, 1977.
T. J. Mullin Collection.

Engraved and Gold Inlaid Colt Mk IV Series 70 Government Model .45 Caliber Automatic Pistol, serial number WWII S-2. Commissioned by William H. Goldbach to commemorate his World War II service, this pistol was engraved and gold inlaid by Alvin A. White. Among the images which were inlaid are views of an aircraft carrier; Goldbach's pilot wings; a training aircraft. The left rosewood grip is inlaid with a gold shield-shaped escutcheon plate engraved with the "Screaming Eagle" insignia of the twentieth Air Force.
Raymond Baldwin Museum of Connecticut History
(Gift of William H. Goldbach)

Colt Combat Commander Model 9mm Caliber Automatic Pistol, serial number 70BS59304. Approximately 16,200 Combat Commanders were manufactured by Colt in 9mm, .38 Super and .45 caliber in 1977.

Lowell E. Pauli Collection.

Colt Mark IV Series 70 Gold Cup National Match .45 Caliber Automatic Pistol, serial number 70N95745. Made in 1981, this pistol features an electroless nickel-plated finish applied by the Nytex Corporation of Dallas, Texas, for the Colt Custom Shop.

Lowell E. Pauli Collection.

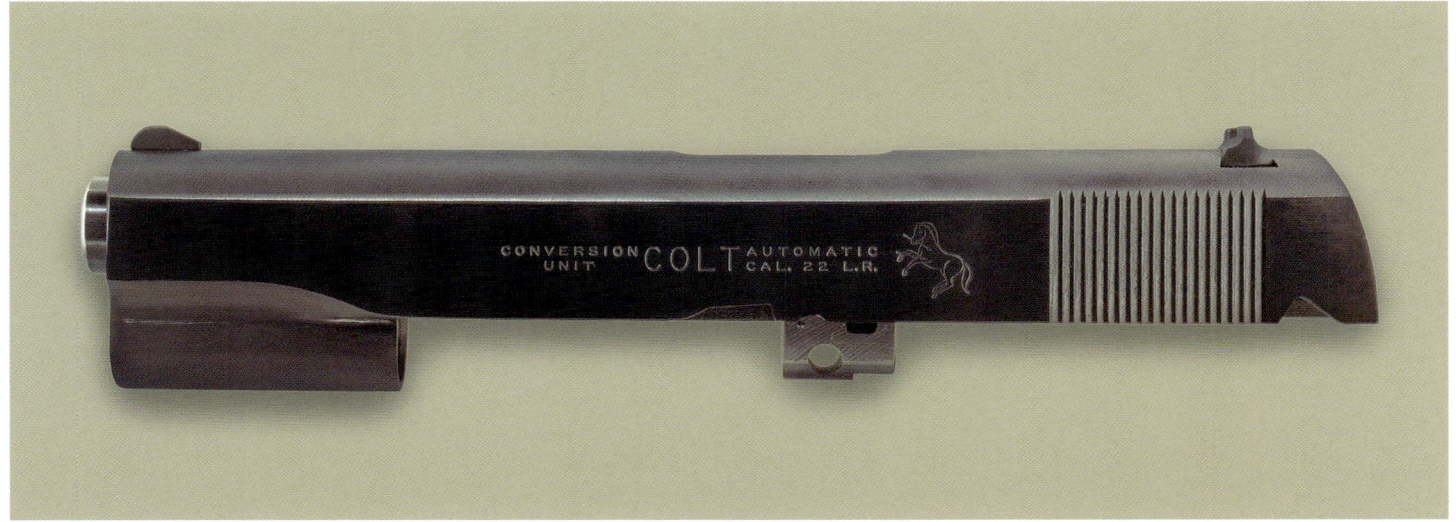

BBHC Photo

Colt Mark IV Series 70 .22rf Conversion Unit, no serial number. Fitted with a fixed rear sight, units of this type were produced by the Colt company from 1981 to 1983.

Lowell E. Pauli Collection.

Engraved Pair Colt Mark IV Series 80 Government Model .45 Caliber Automatic Pistols, serial numbers TJM1 and TJM2. These specially serial numbered, stainless steel pistols having "Class D" engraving and ivory grips were ordered by their owner in 1999. The engraving was executed by John Adams, Sr.

T. J. Mullins Collection.

Colt Mark IV Series 80 Government Model .45 Caliber Automatic Pistol, serial number FG05244. Manufactured in 1984, this pistol is fitted with a firing pin safety.

Lowell E. Pauli Collection.

Colt Mark IV Series 80 Government Model .45 Caliber Automatic Pistol, serial number SS10213. Made in 1985, this stainless steel model remained in production until 1991.
Lowell E. Pauli Collection.

Colt Mark IV Series 80 Commander Model .45 Caliber Automatic Pistol, serial number FL01722. This shorter version of the standard 1911A1 was manufactured from 1984 to 1991.
Lowell E. Pauli Collection.

Colt Mark IV Series 80 Combat Commander Model .38 Super Caliber Automatic Pistol, serial number FC12259. This model was manufactured from 1984 until 1991.
Lowell E. Pauli Collection.

Colt Mark IV Series 80 Gold Cup Commander Model .45 Caliber Automatic Pistol, serial number GCC0335. This stainless steel target pistol was made in 1991.

William E. Adams Collection.

Colt Mark IV Series 80 Gold Cup National Match .45 Caliber Automatic Pistol, serial number SN02388. Made circa 1987, this stainless steel pistol is fitted with Pachmayer grips.

William E. Adams Collection.

Colt Mark IV Series 80 Gold Cup Trophy .45 Caliber Automatic Pistol, serial number GCT09533. Manufactured during 1997 and 1998, the Gold Cup Trophy Pistol was an improved version of the Series 80 Gold Cup National Match pistol.

Lowell E. Pauli Collection.

Colt Mark IV Series 80 Officer's Model .45 Caliber Automatic Pistol, serial number FA15208. This shortened version of the Model 1911A1 was manufactured by Colt from 1985 to 1987

Lowell E. Pauli Collection.

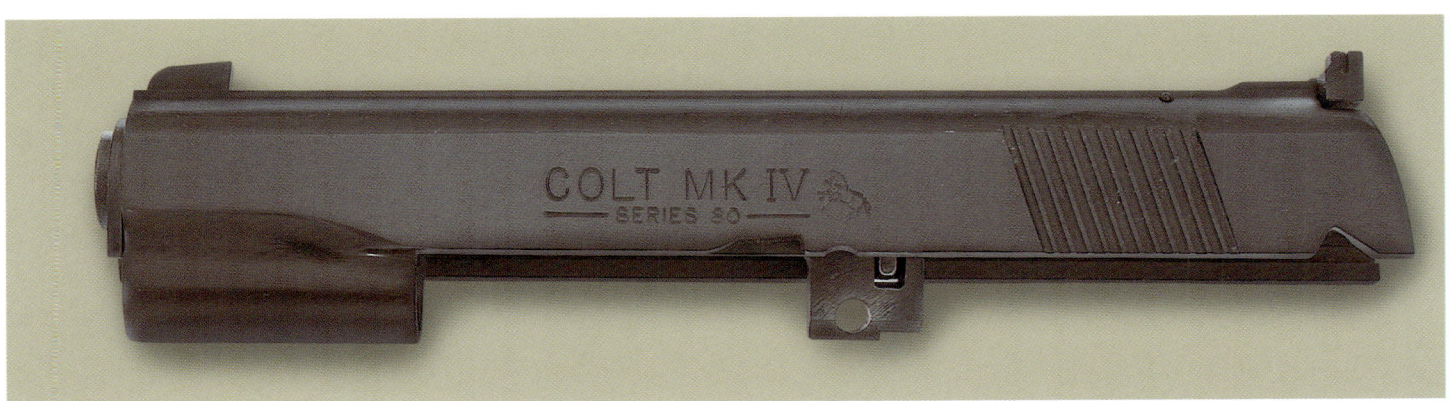

Colt Mark IV Series 80 .22rf Caliber Conversion Unit, no serial number. Units of this type, fitted with firing pin safeties and Arco adjustable sights, were made in limited quantities during 1983, 1984 and 1995.

Lowell E. Pauli Collection.

Colt Mark IV Series 80 Delta Elite Model 10mm Caliber Automatic Pistol, serial number DE30168. Essentially this pistol was a standard Mark IV Series 80 Government Model chambered for the 10mm cartridge. It was made from 1987 to 1991.

Lowell E. Pauli Collection.

Colt Mark IV Series 80 Government Model .380 Caliber Automatic Pistol, serial number RC37539. Produced in a variety of finishes, including blue, nickel plate and stainless steel, this reduced scale version of the Model 1911A1 was produced from 1984 to 1996.

Lowell E. Pauli Collection.

Colt Mark IV Series 80 Mustang .380 Caliber Automatic Pistol, serial number MU37337. This nickel-plated pocket pistol was made in 1989. The model was marketed by Colt from 1986 to 1998.

Lowell E. Pauli Collection.

Colt Mark IV Series 80 Mustang Plus II .380 Caliber Automatic Pistol, serial number RC96977. This model combined the Mark IV Series 80 .380 caliber frame with the Series 80 Mustang's shorter slide and barrel. Number RC96977 was manufactured in 1989.

Lowell E. Pauli Collection.

Colt Series 80 Model 1991A1 .38 Super Caliber Automatic Pistol, serial number 2794361. Very few .38 Super Model 1991A1 pistols were produced during the Series 80 program.

Lowell E. Pauli Collection.

Colt Series 80 Commander Model 1991A1 .45 Caliber Automatic Pistol, serial number CJ25640. Produced both in stainless steel, as well as a blued version, this model was produced from 1983 to 2000.

Lowell E. Pauli Collection.

Colt Series 80 Compact Model 1991A1 .45 Caliber Automatic Pistol, serial number CP36802. Manufactured from 1993 to 1998, the Compact Model 1991A1 featured a shorter barrel, slide and grip than those found on the standard 1991A1.

Lowell E. Pauli Collection.

Colt Series 80 Model 1991A1 .45 Caliber Automatic Pistol, serial number CV17337. The stainless steel version of the 1991A1 was manufactured from 1997 to 2002. Except for a very few made in 9mm and .38 Super, all of these pistols were chambered for the .45 cartridge.

Lowell E. Pauli Collection.

Colt Series 80 Commander Model 1991A1 .45 Caliber Automatic Pistol, serial number CJ28326. This stainless steel pistol was produced by Colt from 1997 to 2002.

Lowell E. Pauli Collection.

Colt Series 90 Pony .380 Caliber Automatic Pistol, serial number ML01616. This double-action pistol was made in 1997.

Lowell E. Pauli Collection.

Colt Mark IV Series 80 Government Model .45 Caliber Automatic Pistol, serial number SS17850E. First listed in the Colt company's 1983/1984 catalogue, the Series 80 pistols incorporated a firing pin lock that allowed the arm to be safely carried while loaded. The present example was used as a distributor's sample by Pacific Flyways Wholesale in Midvale, Utah, in 1996 and subsequently resold after its return to Colt to the Lew Horton Distributers, Inc., Westboro, Massachusetts.

Craig A. Blancett Collection.

Colt Mark IV Series 80 Combat Commander Model .45 Caliber Automatic Pistol, serial number FC24565E. This steel framed model has proved quite popular and remains in production as of this date.

Lowell E. Pauli Collection.

Colt Mark IV Series 80 Enhanced Combat Commander Model .45 Caliber Automatic Pistol, serial number FL04086E. This particular model was manufactured from 1992 to 1997.

Lowell E. Pauli Collection.

Colt Mark IV Series 80 Enhanced Government Model .45 Caliber Automatic Pistol, serial number SS29552E. This model can be differentiated from the standard Series 80 1991A1 pistols by its fixed front and rear sights; round top slide; upswept grip safety; finger cuts below the trigger; bevelled magazine aperture, and; internal changes.

Lowell E. Pauli Collection.

Colt Series 90 Double Eagle Model .45 Caliber Automatic Pistol, serial number DA10368. This double-action, stainless steel pistol was manufactured during 1991 and 1992.
Lowell E. Pauli Collection.

Colt Series 90 Double Eagle Combat Commander Model .45 Caliber Automatic Pistol, serial number DC02142. Produced from 1991 to 1996, most of the pistols made in this model were chambered for the .45 cartridge. A few, however, were chambered for the .40 Smith & Wesson round.
Lowell E. Pauli Collection.

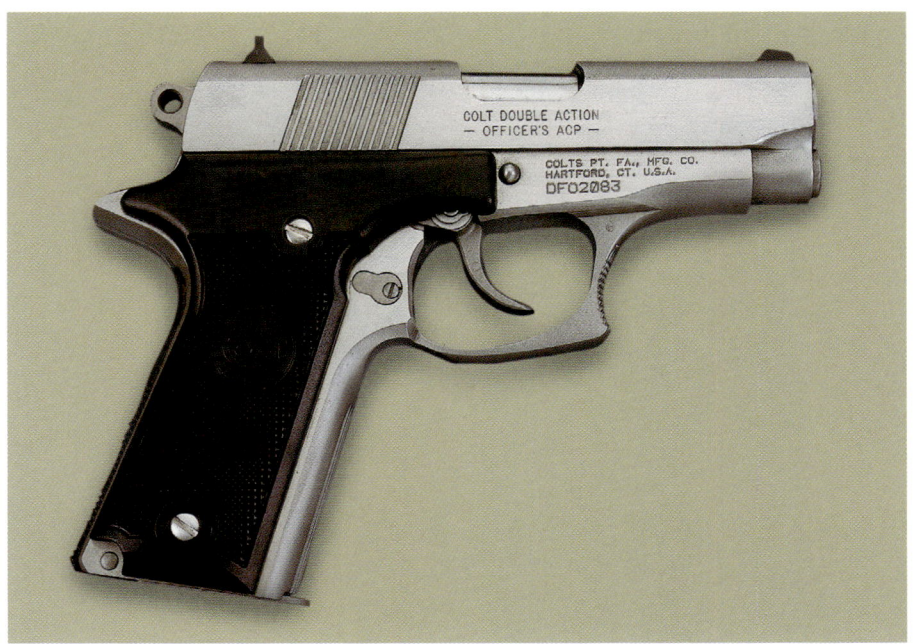

Colt Series 90 Double Eagle Officer's Model .45 Caliber Automatic Pistol, serial number DF02083. This model was made from 1991 to 1996.
Lowell E. Pauli Collection.

Colt Series 90 Double Eagle Light Weight Officer's Model .45 Caliber Automatic Pistol, serial number DL01557. This model was manufactured only during 1991.

Lowell E. Pauli Collection.

Colt All American 2000 9mm Caliber Automatic Pistol, serial number PF07599. Manufactured during 1992, this double-action model was the only Colt automatic pistol to have a polymer frame.

Lowell E. Pauli Collection.

Colt All American 2000 9mm Caliber Short Barrel Conversion 9mm Caliber Automatic Pistol, serial number RK02952. This pre-production version having an aluminum alloy frame, is fitted with a 4.25" barrel and shortened slide. Conversion units of this type were manufactured in extremely limited quantities.

Lowell E. Pauli Collection.

Colt Cadet .22rf Caliber Automatic Pistol, serial number CADET 038. Originally named the CADET and developed as a replacement for the Colt Woodsman, the Cadet model never entered production due to problems associated with its name as well as a lack of popularity.
Lowell E. Pauli Collection.

Colt Cadet .22rf Caliber Automatic Target Pistol, serial number 038 CADET. As with the pistol illustrated above, this example was intended to replace the Woodsman.
Lowell E. Pauli Collection.

Colt Mark IV Series 80 Concealed Carry Officer's Model .45 Caliber Automatic Pistol, serial number LF08382E. Manufactured only in 1998, this model was built using an Officer's Model frame and the Commander Model's slide with a 4.25" barrel.
Lowell E. Pauli Collection.

Colt Series 90 Defender Model .40 S&W Caliber Automatic Pistol, serial number GA01483. This compact version of the standard Government Model was produced in 1998.

Lowell E. Pauli Collection.

Colt Series 90 Pocket Nine Model 9mm Caliber Automatic Pistol, serial number NP02633. This pocket pistol was made by the Colt company in 1998.

Lowell E. Pauli Collection.

Sample Colt Pony .380 Caliber Automatic Pistol, serial number CPA001054. Although the Colt company announced the addition of this model to its product line in 1973, it never entered production. The existing test samples were manufactured for Colt by Firearms International, Incorporated.

Donald R. Morrison Collection.

Colt Junior .25 Caliber Automatic Pistol, serial number 841CC. This model was manufactured for Colt by Astra-Unceta S.A. of Guernica, Spain, during the late 1950s and early 1960s. It was also available in a .22rf caliber version under the same name.
Lowell E. Pauli Collection.

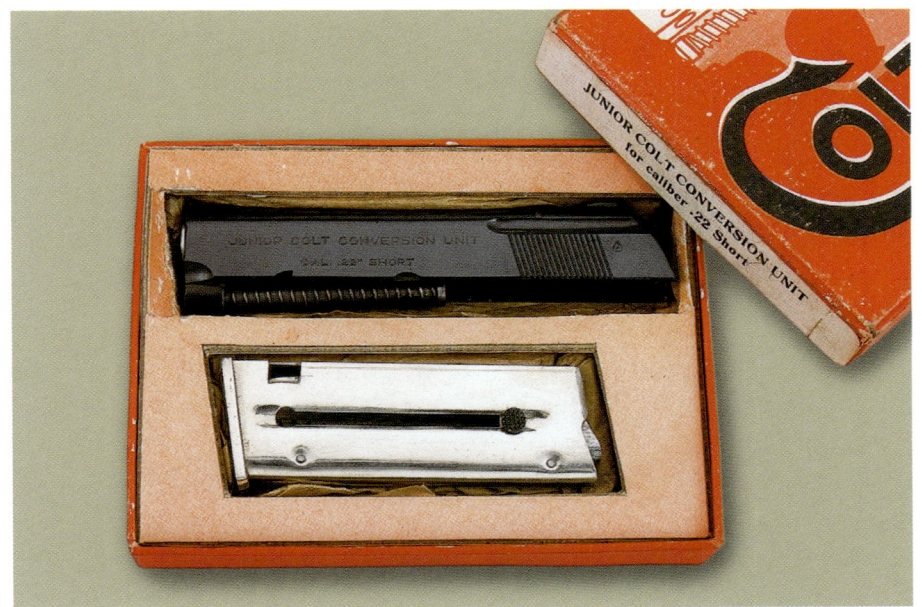

Colt Junior .22rf Caliber Conversion Unit, no serial number. This unit allowed the .25 caliber Junior to be used with .22rf ammunition.
Lowell E. Pauli Collection.

Colt .25 Caliber Automatic Pistol, serial number OD29212. Due to the provisions of the U.S. National Gun Control Act of 1968, the Colt company had to begin manufacturing the Junior Automatic Pistol in this country. Production of these arms began in 1970 and ended in 1973 after approximately 120,000 had been made.
Lowell E. Pauli Collection.

Among the most popular of all Colt semiautomatic pistols were the Woodsman series. These .22 rimfire handguns were made in a variety of configurations designed to meet the requirements of their intended use. Though they might differ physically, all were renowned for their accuracy and ease of use.

Throughout the production life of the Woodsman, the Colt company spent a substantial amount of time and money developing targeted advertising campaigns for the pistol. The two examples shown here were designed to appeal to target shooters and everyday outdoorsmen.

Woodsman Automatic Pistols
by Bob Rayburn

The original design for what was to become the Colt Woodsman was conceived by John M. Browning in 1912. Following a brief period of refinement, the "Colt Automatic Pistol Caliber .22 Target Model" was introduced in 1915.

Fitted with a 6⅝" lightweight barrel, the new Target Model was chambered for standard velocity .22rf Long Rifle ammunition. Reliable and inexpensive to use, the Colt .22 pistol was an instant success. This popularity endured over the 62 years of its production life. Before it was finally discontinued in 1977, several hundred thousand would be sold in numerous styles and configurations.

Although the earliest advertising issued by the Colt company promoted its use as a target pistol, the model quickly became a favorite of outdoorsmen and casual shooters. Perhaps because of this, the model was renamed "The Woodsman" in 1927.

In 1932 the pistol was re-engineered to accept high velocity .22rf Long Rifle cartridges, while continuing to function reliably with standard velocity rounds. The following year a Sport Model featuring a shorter barrel was introduced. Demands for an improved target version led to the production of a Match Target version having a heavier barrel and improved grips in 1938.

While the Colt company did not manufacture the Woodsman during World War II, an improved version was reintroduced in 1947. This model, known as the "Second Series," remained in production until 1955 when it too was replaced. The "Third Series" was manufactured for another 22 years until 1977.

All three series of Woodsman pistols were available

Engraved Pair Colt Woodsman .22 Caliber Automatic Pistols, 4.5" and 6.5" barrels, serial numbers 101992 (Sport Model) and 102052 (Target Model). This pair of pearl gripped pistols are engraved with Grade B scrollwork and foliage in a style that is associated with William H. Gough.
Robert J. Rayburn Collection

in Sport, Target and Match Target form. The Sport model had a 4½" round barrel, and the Target a 6" or 6⅝" barrel. The first Match Target pistols had a flat-sided 6⅝" barrel, while later versions featured slab-sided barrels measuring either 4½" or 6" in length.

Throughout the Woodsman's production, the Colt company never compromised its quality. As a result its production costs were rather high. Although this had not been a concern prior to World War II, in the years that followed the model faced ever-increasing competition from lower cost pistols produced by firms such as High Standard and Sturm, Ruger & Company. These challenges were met by the introduction of a series of economy models named the Challenger, Huntsman and Targetsman. Nearly identical to the Woodsman internally and equal in finish, these pistols used less expensive sights and were not equipped with such features as the automatic slide stop.

These measures were not enough to save the Woodsman, however, and in 1977 it was discontinued. The model's long production life and elegant design remain a tribute to John Browning's genius and the foresight of the Colt company to introduce a semi-automatic .22rf caliber pistol in 1915.

Colt Automatic Pistol, Caliber .22 Target Model, 6½" barrel, serial number 5. Manufactured during the first day of the model's production, this pistol displays all its salient features, such as the finely checkered walnut grips having a diamond panel surrounding the screw escutcheons; deep blued finish, and; carefully polished surfaces.

Robert J. Rayburn Collection

Colt Woodsman .22 Caliber Automatic Pistol, 4½" barrel, serial number 143832. Manufactured circa 1940, this pistol illustrates the construction of the standard production 4½" barrel Woodsman.

Richard Salerno Collection

Colt Woodsman Match Target .22 Caliber Automatic Pistol, 6½" barrel, serial number MT220. Introduced into the Colt company's product line in 1938, the Woodsman Match Target had a heavier barrel than the standard version. It also was fitted with extended checkered walnut grips, a straighter trigger and sights suitable for target shooting. This pistol was originally shipped to the noted ballistician and marksman, Lieutenant Colonel (later Major General) Julian Hatcher in 1938.

Robert J. Rayburn Collection

Colt Woodsman Match Target .22 Caliber Automatic Pistol, 6½" barrel, serial number MT15695. After the United States entered World War II, the Government purchased approximately 3,962 Match Target Pistols for training purposes. Most of these pistols, like the example illustrated here, which was made in 1943, were stamped at the factory "U.S. PROPERTY".

Robert J. Rayburn Collection

Colt Woodsman Second Series Match Target .22 Caliber Automatic Pistol, 6" barrel, serial number 2-S. Production of the Woodsman model was restarted by the Colt company in 1947. The post-war version, or second model, had a serial number sequence ending with the letter "S" and plastic grips in place of the earlier walnut ones. The Match Target variation had a heavy slab-sided barrel cut with weight reduction grooves along the axis of its bore.

Robert J. Rayburn Collection

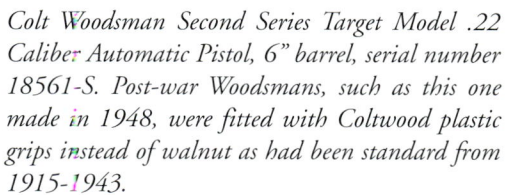

Colt Woodsman Second Series Sport Model .22 Caliber Automatic Pistol, 4½" barrel, serial number 14272-S. As re-introduced in 1948, the Sport Model and Target Model were identical except for their barrel lengths.

Robert J. Rayburn Collection

Colt Woodsman Second Series Target Model .22 Caliber Automatic Pistol, 6" barrel, serial number 18561-S. Post-war Woodsmans, such as this one made in 1948, were fitted with Coltwood plastic grips instead of walnut as had been standard from 1915-1943.

Robert J. Rayburn Collection

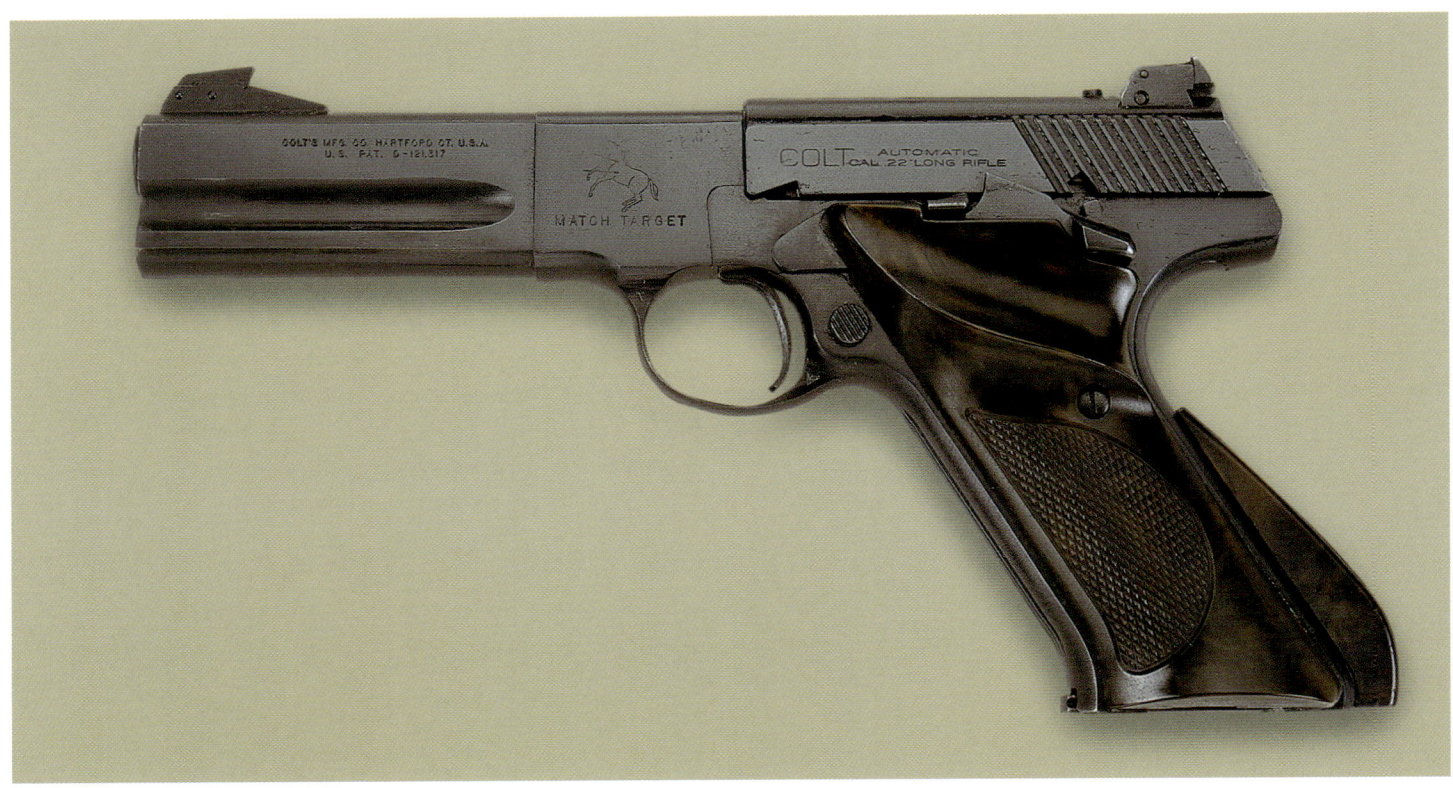

Colt Woodsman Match Target .22 Caliber Automatic Pistol, 4½" barrel, serial number 99518-S. Production of the Woodsman model was restarted by the Colt company in 1947. The first postwar version, or second series had a serial number sequence ending in the letter "S" and plastic grips in place of the earlier walnut ones. The Match Target variation had a heavy slab sided barrel cut with weight reduction grooves along the axis of its bore.

Robert J. Rayburn Collection

Colt Woodsman Third Series Target Model .22 Caliber Automatic Pistol, 6" barrel, serial number 228398-S. As a cost reduction measure, the design of the Woodsman's magazine release was changed in 1955. In place of the spring-loaded release that was located to the rear of the trigger previously used, a simple catch was installed on the bottom rear face of the butt. Pistols incorporating this change are now referred to as Third Series Woodsmans.

Robert J. Rayburn Collection

Colt Woodsman Third Series Match Target .22 Caliber Automatic Pistol, 6" barrel, serial number 035873S. Manufactured in 1972, this pistol illustrates the final configuration of the Match Target Woodsman fitted with checkered walnut grips.
Robert J. Rayburn Collection

Colt Woodsman Third Series Sport Model .22 Caliber Automatic Pistol, 4½" barrel, serial number 083273S.
Robert J. Rayburn Collection

Colt Woodsman Third Series Match Target .22 Caliber Automatic Pistol, 4½" barrel, serial number 302175S. This pistol, made in 1976, was manufactured shortly before the Woodsman series was discontinued.
Robert J. Rayburn Collection

Colt Challenger Model, .22 Caliber Automatic Pistol, 4½" barrel, serial number 6-C. The Challenger was introduced as a reduced cost variation of the Woodsman in 1950. It differs from the other second series models in having fixed sights; a magazine release located to the rear of the magazine well at the bottom of the grip and; the serial number suffix "C".
Robert J. Rayburn Collection

Cased Engraved Pair Third Model Colt Woodsman Sport and Match Target .22 Caliber Automatic Pistols, 4½" and 6" barrels, serial numbers PECEWS1141 (Sport Model) and PECEWS3162 (Match Target). This pair of pistols were engraved and gold inlaid for Charles E. Warren (insets), who served as president of the Firearms Division of Colt Industries, Inc., from 1975 to 1981.

Robert J. Rayburn Collection

Colt Challenger Model .22 Caliber Automatic Pistol, 6" barrel, serial number 75696-C. This pistol was made in 1955, shortly before the model's production was discontinued at serial number 77143-C.

Robert J. Rayburn Collection

Colt Targetsman Model .22 Caliber Automatic Pistol, 6" barrel, serial number 133667-C. Introduced 1959, the Targetsman Model can be identified by the presence of an adjustable rear sight. The pistol illustrated here was made in 1959.

Robert J. Rayburn Collection

Colt Huntsman Model .22 Caliber Automatic Pistol, 4½" barrel, serial number 118346-C. The Huntsman Model was introduced in 1955 and began at serial number 90001-C. This example was made in 1957 and is typical of the model in that it has a fixed rear sight.

Robert J. Rayburn Collection

Colt Huntsman Model .22 Caliber Automatic Pistol, 6" barrel, serial number 091606S. This late production example was made in 1976.

Robert J. Rayburn Collection

Long known as "The gun that made the twenties roar," the Thompson Submachine Gun was first produced by the Colt company. Favored by lawmen and gangsters alike, the Thompson became synonymous with the 1920s and the era of Prohibition. During World War II, its image was rehabilitated through its extensive service in virtually every theater of the war.

Held in great affection by all who have used it, the Browning Automatic Rifle has served this country with great distinction from late World War I to Vietnam. Designed by John M. Browning, the BAR, as it was most commonly referred to, was designed to provide a normal infantryman with the firepower of a machine gun. During the 1930s, a semiautomatic version (illustrated here) was produced for use by bank guards and police departments.

Machine Guns
by Tracie Hill

Webster's Dictionary defines "a machine gun" as "an automatic gun, often mounted, that fires repeatedly and rapidly." This is a rather poor definition of the term and an understatement, to say the least. Not since Henry V of England used massed archers at Agincourt in 1415 had the world seen such a devastating weapon.

With the invention of usable gunpowder, man's desire and dream of firing multiple projectiles started to come into focus. However, it wasn't until the American Civil War that the first successful "portable" means of firing multiple projectiles came into general use. It was the firearm designed by Dr. Richard Gatling, a farm implement designer, then living in Indiana.

The Gatling Gun is an arm with a series of several single shot firearms mounted to a central hub, which when rotated by the hand-cranked gear system, load, fire and unload. Dr. Gatling's design was first demonstrated in 1872 and with the addition of electricity and a motor, is still in use in almost every Western military.

Dr. Gatling's design was also the beginning of the Colt company's long tradition of building the best of what are now defined as "fully automatic firearms" or machine guns. While Gatling's firearm is not considered a machine gun, it laid the groundwork for what was to come.

The "Father of the Modern Machine Gun" was Hiram S. Maxim, born in Sangerville, Maine in 1840. Maxim designed his first working model of a fully automatic gun, a Winchester Model of 1873, to function with the recoil of the fired round. It was patented in 1883. By 1884, Maxim had operational his first gas-operated, belt-fed, fully automatic machine gun and it was being demonstrated all over Europe. By World War I the Maxim machine gun was the world standard. Colt's began building the Maxim and Vickers Machine guns in 1906 for the United States military.

Colt Model 1917 Browning Light Machinegun, .30-06 caliber, serial number 2899. One of John M. Browning's more famous designs, the water-cooled Model 1917 Machinegun was adopted for U.S. service at the beginning of World War I. By the end of that war, over 42,000 had been made by Colt, New England Westinghouse Corporation and Remington-U.M.C.

John Scott Collection.

Colt's first machine gun was designed by John Browning in 1891. This prototype led to the production of the Model of 1895, more commonly known as the "potato digger" due to the action of its toggle-link actuating arm.

John Browning continued to design new machine guns for Colt's. The 1917 water-cooled caliber .30 would become the standard American machine gun for the next 43 years.

When the United States Army decided in World War I that there was a need for a machine gun with better armor piercing power, Browning designed the M2 .50 caliber machine gun in 1917. This design was to become probably the greatest of Browning's machine guns. The M2 has been used in the air and on the ground, in water and air cooled versions, and is standard issue today, serving with US forces in Desert Storm and Afghanistan.

Another of Browning's designs, the Browning Automatic Rifle or B.A.R, was first prototyped in February 1917. Production by Colt's resulted in the first deliveries in July of 1917 as the Model of 1918.

The firearm that made the Twenties roar, the Thompson submachine gun, was first built by Colt's. It became a world standard and created a new category for firearms. The Thompson was first envisioned by John T. Thompson and designed by two young engineers, Theodore Eickhoff and Oscar Payne. General Thompson's company, Auto-Ordnance, contracted with Colt's in 1921 to produce 15,000 of the world's first sub machine gun.

Colt's reputation for building outstanding military hardware continues. Today's American soldier carries as his standard battle rifle a firearm whose early history was stormy, the M-16, part of a family of firearms designed by engineer Gene Stoner. With the help of General Curtis LeMay, Colt's produced the AR-15, which became an Air Force standard rifle. The M-16 and its current relatives are the standard battle rifles for many countries today.

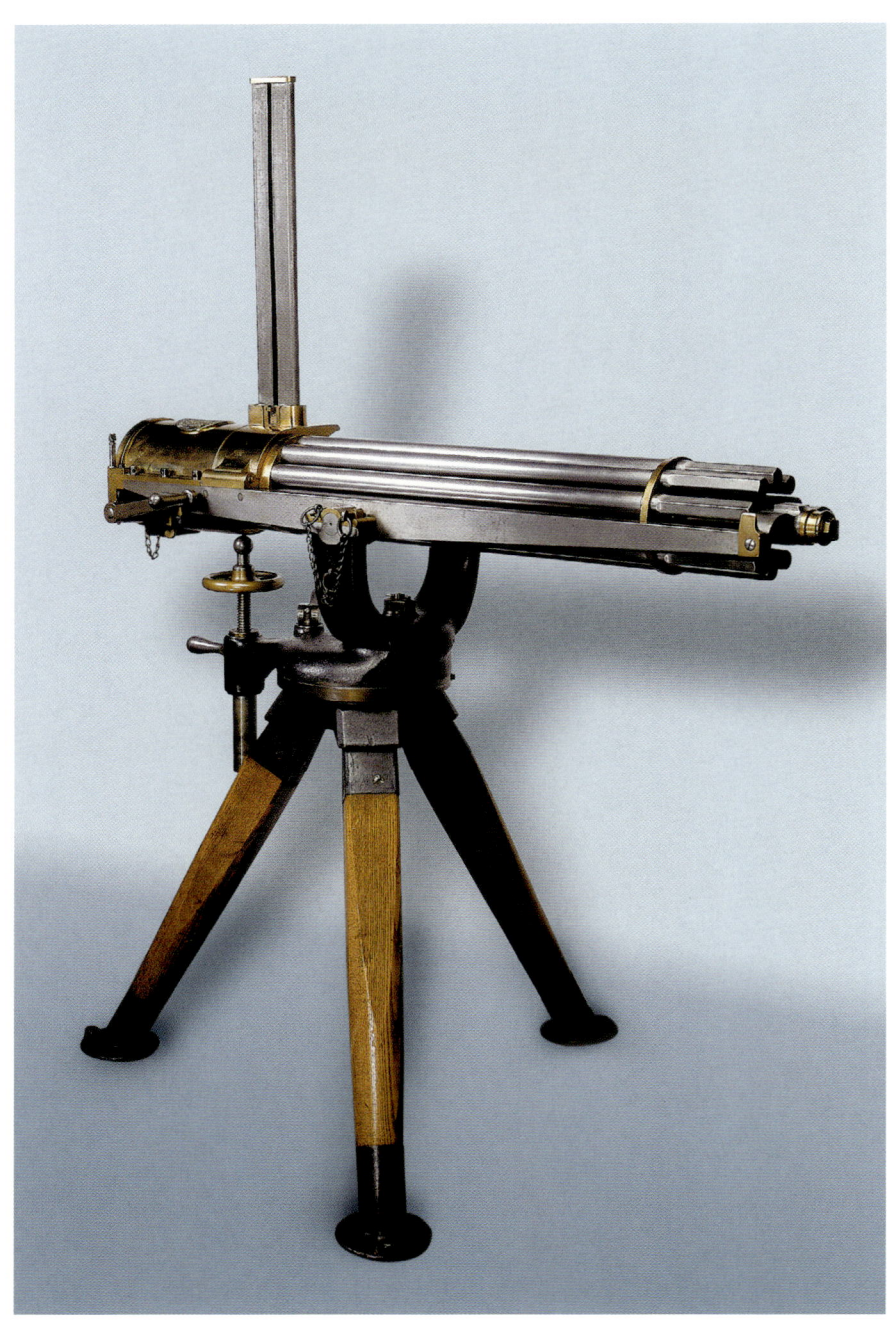

Colt Model 1875 Gatling Gun, .45-70 caliber, serial number 110. This ten barrel battery gun was originally sold to the State of New Jersey for militia use. After being declared obsolete, it was sold to the New York military surplus dealer, Francis Bannerman, from whose company Edwin Pugsley purchased it prior to 1940 for $27.50.

*Winchester Arms Collection
(Gift of Olin Corporation),
Cody Firearms Museum,
Buffalo Bill Historical Center*

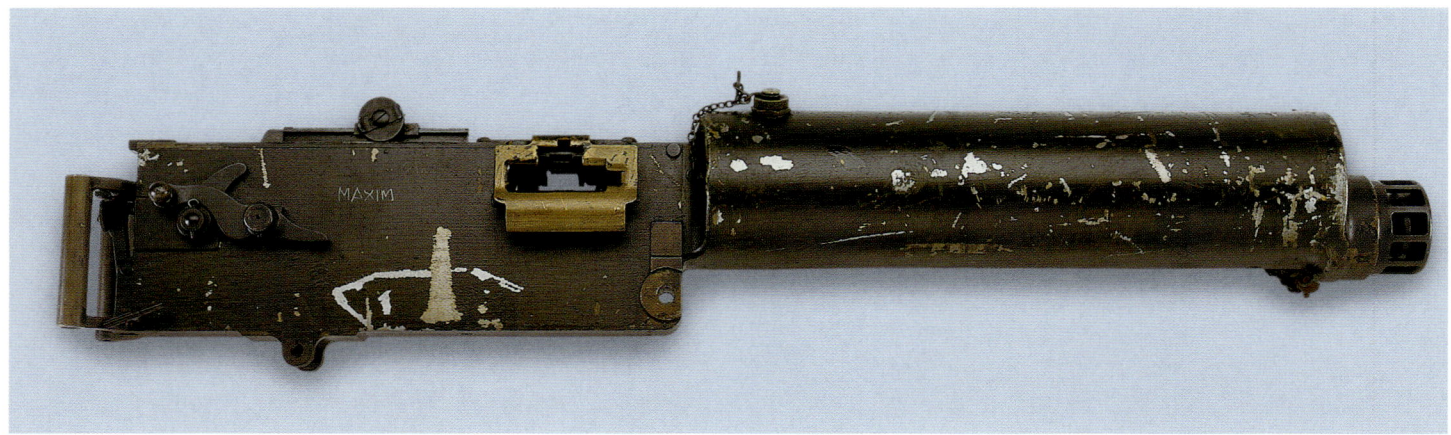

Colt Model 1904 Maxim Machine Gun, .30-06 caliber, serial number MCH2002. In 1904, the U.S. Army adopted a variation of the Model 1901 "New Pattern" Machine Gun made by Vickers Sons & Maxim Ltd. Officially designated the Model 1904, a total of 287 were delivered to the government between 1905 and 1908. Of that number, 197 were produced by the Colt company with the remainder having been supplied by Vickers-Maxim. While originally chambered for the .30-03 US Service Cartridge, virtually all were modified for use with the improved .30-06 round.

*Raymond Baldwin Museum of Connecticut History
(Gift of the Colt's Patent Fire Arms Manufacturing Company)*

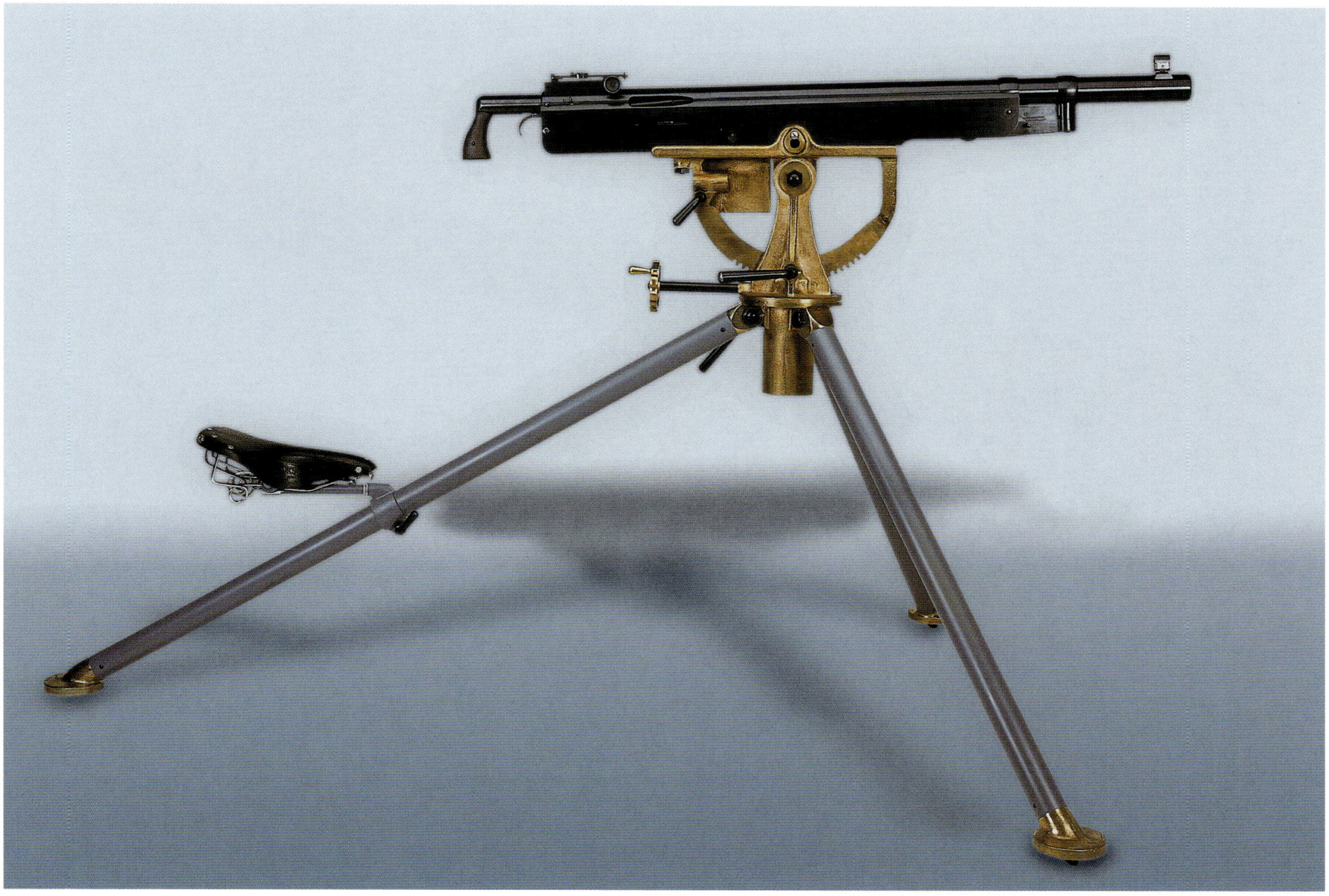

Colt Model 1895 Machinegun, .30-06 caliber, serial number 1011. Designed by John M. Browning, the Model 1895 Machinegun was adopted for service both by the United States Army and Navy. Initially the Army models were chambered for the .30-40 cartridge, however, after the .30-06 caliber round was adopted, they were rechambered for the new service cartridge.

Newell Graham Collection.

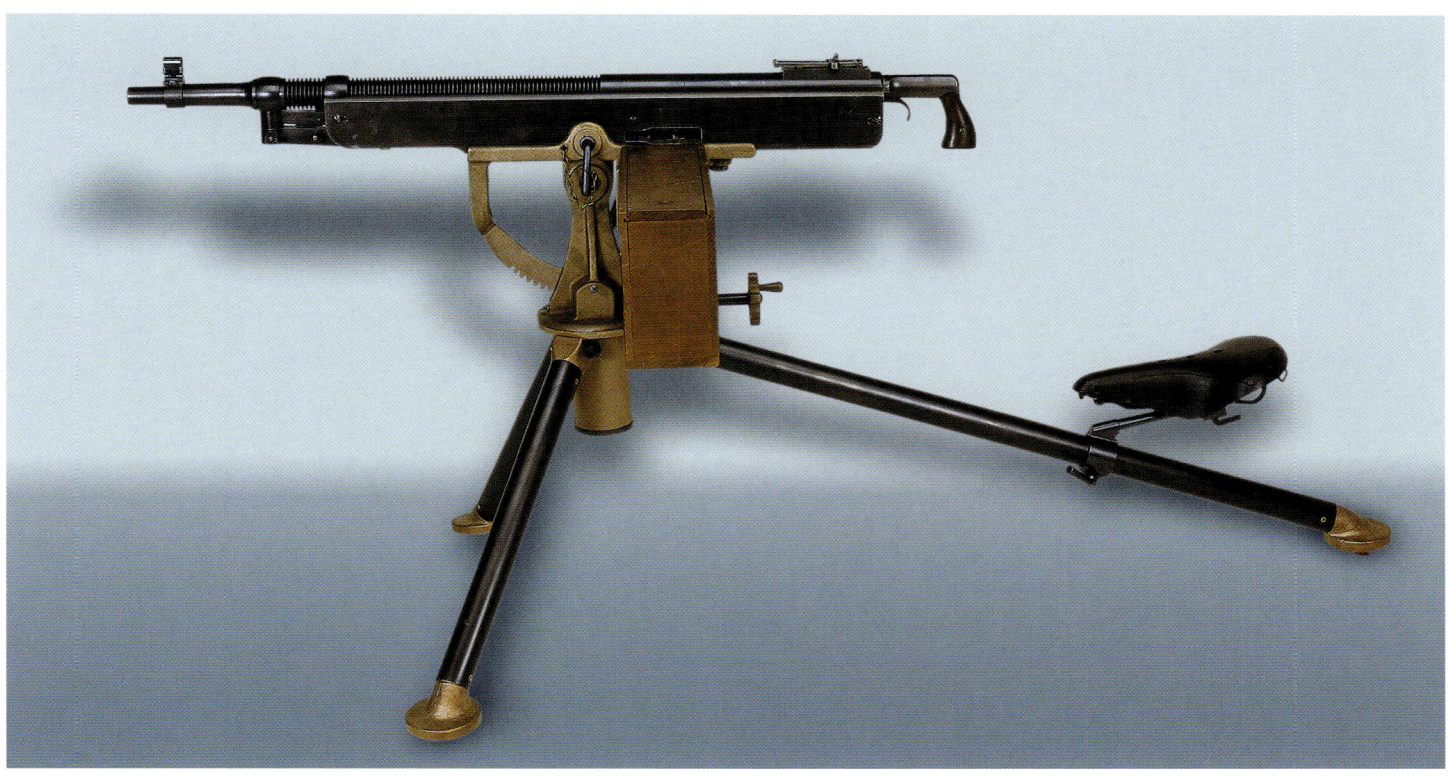

Colt Model 1914 Browning Light Machinegun, .30-06 caliber, serial number 14207. This improved version of John M. Browning's Model 1895 Machinegun was produced in a variety of calibers primarily for commercial sale abroad.

Lowell E. Pauli Collection.

Colt M2 Anti-aircraft Machine Gun, .50 caliber, serial number C2463w. Developed shortly before World War I ended, the water cooled Browning .50 caliber heavy machine gun entered U.S. service in 1921. Initially known as the Model 1921, the gun is fed by a belt entering the receiver from the left side. During its production life, the M2 was made in a variety of air and water cooled configurations.

Raymond Baldwin Museum of Connecticut History
(Gift of the Colt's Patent Fire Arms Manufacturing Company)

Colt Model 1909 Benet-Mercie Machine Rifle, .30-06 caliber, serial number 0. Adopted by the U. S. Army in 1910, the Benet-Mercie was an improved variation of the Model 1900 and 1907 Hotchkiss Light Machine Gun. Though the arm saw limited action during the Mexican border incursions of 1916, it received a great deal of criticism due to its awkward horizontal stripper clip loading system. Indeed, some wags christened it the "daylight gun" since it was difficult to use at night.

Raymond Baldwin Museum of Connecticut History
(Gift of the Colt's Patent Fire Arms Manufacturing Company)

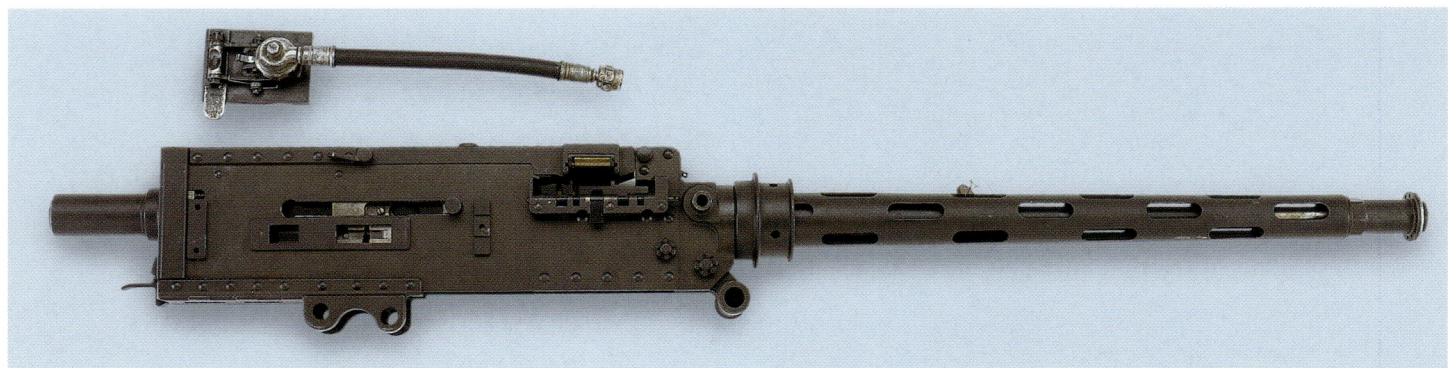

Colt Browning Light Machine Gun, .303 caliber, serial number C-107685. During World War II, the Colt company manufactured a substantial number of Browning Light Machine Guns for Great Britain and its Dominions (Australia, Canada, etc.). All of these arms were chambered for the .303 British service cartridge.

Raymond Baldwin Museum of Connecticut History
(Gift of the Colt's Patent Fire Arms Manufacturing Company)

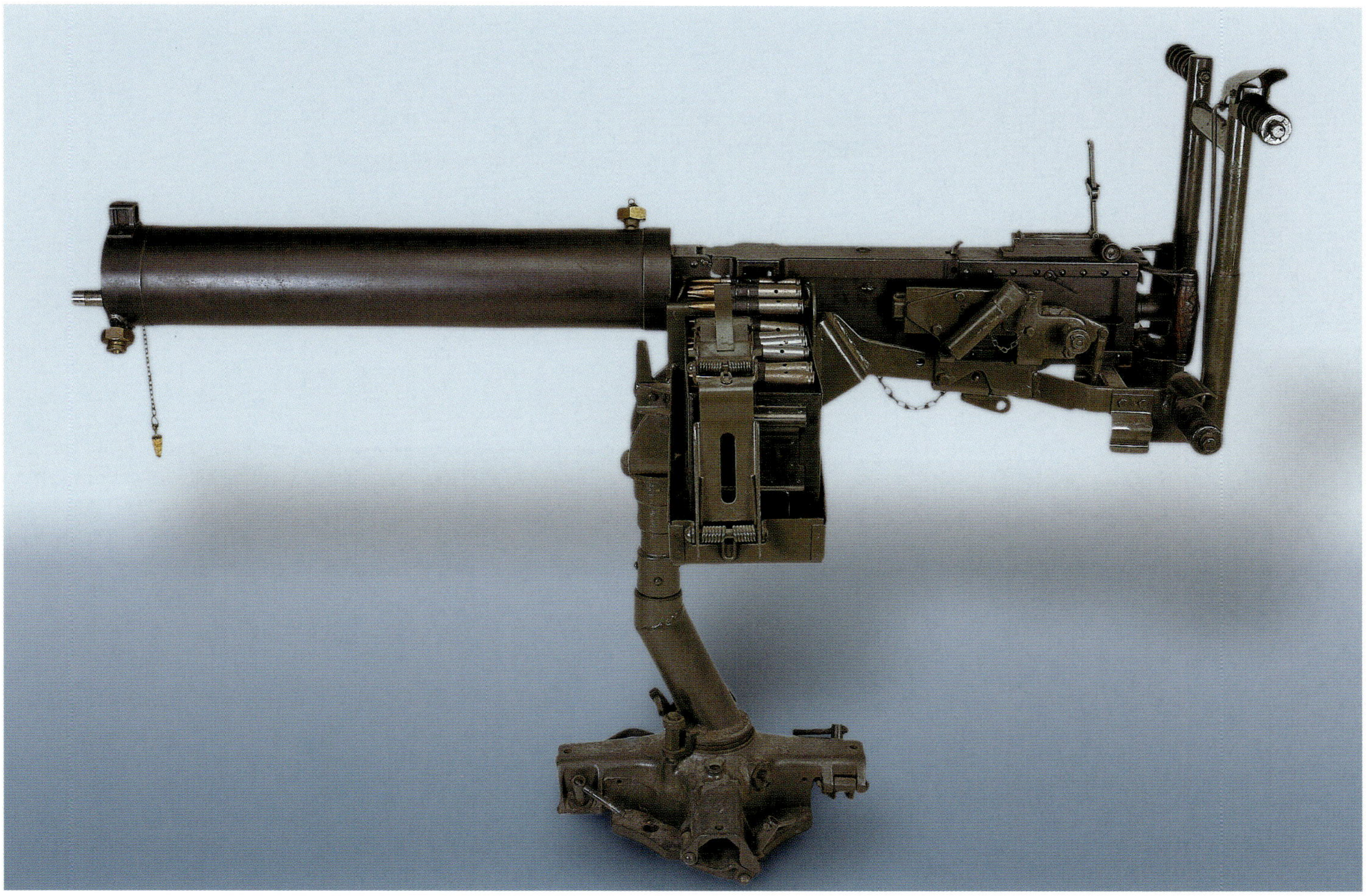

U.S. M2 Machine Gun, .50 caliber, serial number C-2240-w. This water-cooled Colt made Browning machinegun was originally shipped to the Winchester Repeating Arms Company in New Haven, Connecticut. It was used by that firm in its ballistics laboratory to insure that the company's .50 caliber ammunition would properly function in the weapon.

Cody Firearms Museum (Gift of Olin Corporation), Buffalo Bill Historical Center.

Colt Model 1921 Browning Heavy Machinegun, .50 caliber, serial number C7454. Although development of this model began in 1917, it was not commercially made until 1921. In 1933, the U.S. Government began placing orders with the Colt company for an improved version known as the U.S.M2.

John Scott Collection.

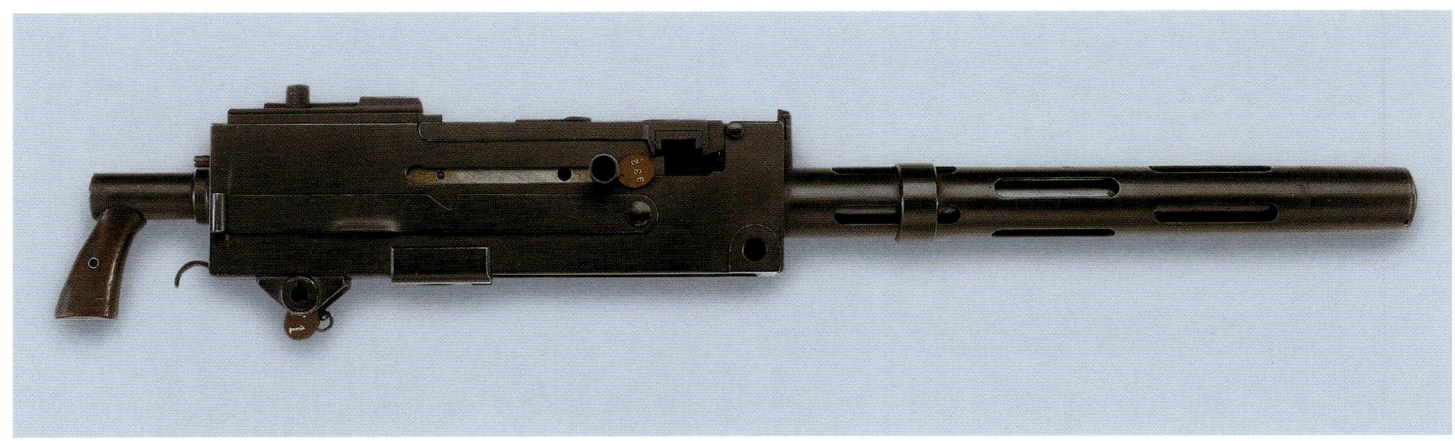

Colt Browning Light Machine Gun, .30-06 caliber, serial number 1259. One of the most popular and definitely the most widely used machine guns of the 20th century was the Colt Browning Model 1917. Adopted by the U.S. Army in 1917, the Browning .30 caliber gun was accurate, easy to use and above all else, reliable. In various forms and in various armies, it has seen service from World War I through the Gulf War of 1991.
Raymond Baldwin Museum of Connecticut History
(Gift of the Colt's Patent Fire Arms Manufacturing Company)

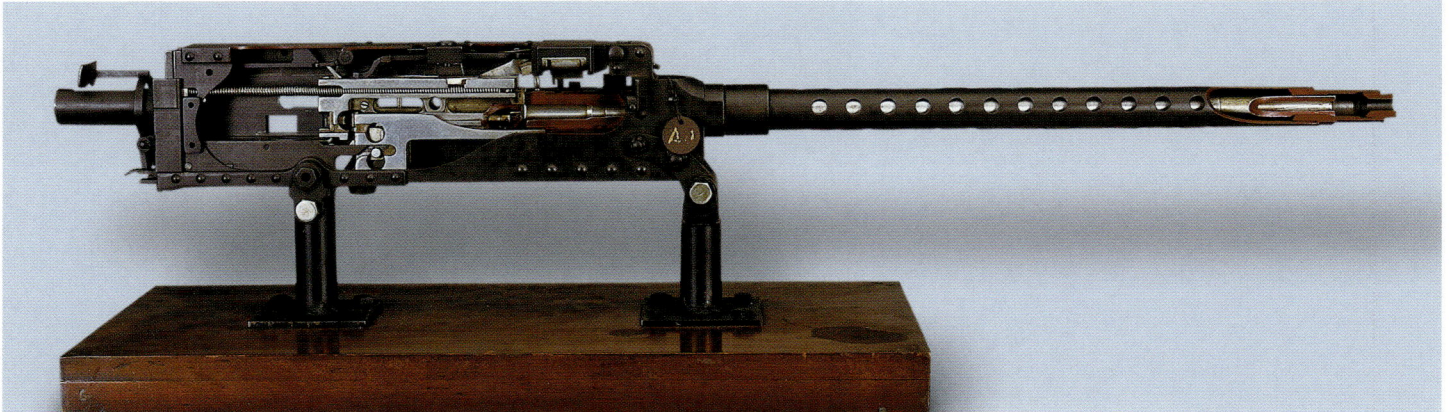

Colt M2 Machine Gun, .30 caliber. This aircraft gun has been skeletonized to show the construction and operation of its internal mechanism. Skeletonized arms were made primarily for training purposes. A few, however, were also used as exhibition or sales pieces.
Raymond Baldwin Museum of Connecticut History
(Gift of the Colt's Patent Fire Arms Manufacturing Company)

Colt M2 Machine Gun, .50 caliber, serial number SCRAP. This gun is fitted with an air cooled heavy barrel and was designed for use against lightly armored vehicles, such as scout cars, half-tracks and light tanks. Weapons of this type could be fired from fixed mounts in vehicles or from moveable tripod bases.
Raymond Baldwin Museum of Connecticut History
(Gift of the Colt's Patent Fire Arms Manufacturing Company)

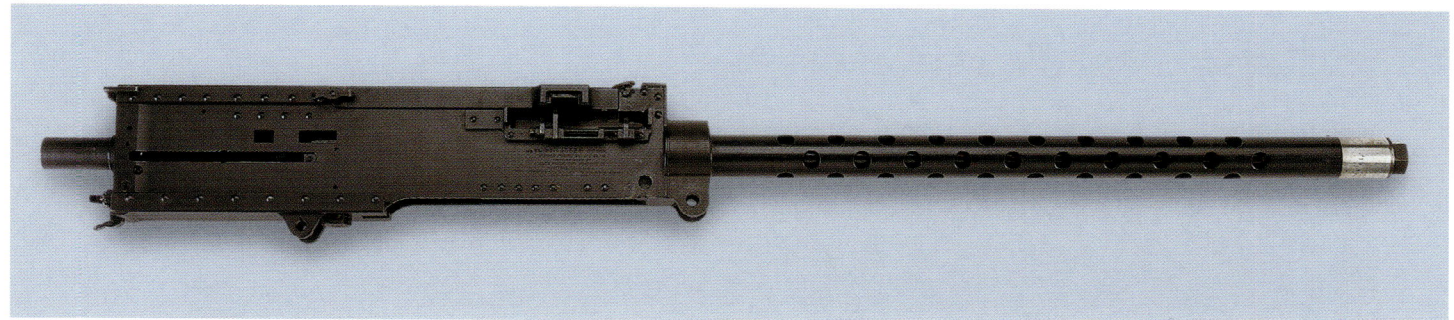

Colt M2 Aircraft Machine Gun, .50 caliber, serial number MG53-2C-10626. Developed shortly before World War I ended, the Browning .50 caliber heavy machine gun entered U.S. service in 1921. Initially known as the Model 1921, the gun is fed by a belt entering the receiver from the left side. During its production life, the M2 was made in a variety of air and water cooled configurations.

Raymond Baldwin Museum of Connecticut History
(Gift of the Colt's Patent Fire Arms Manufacturing Company)

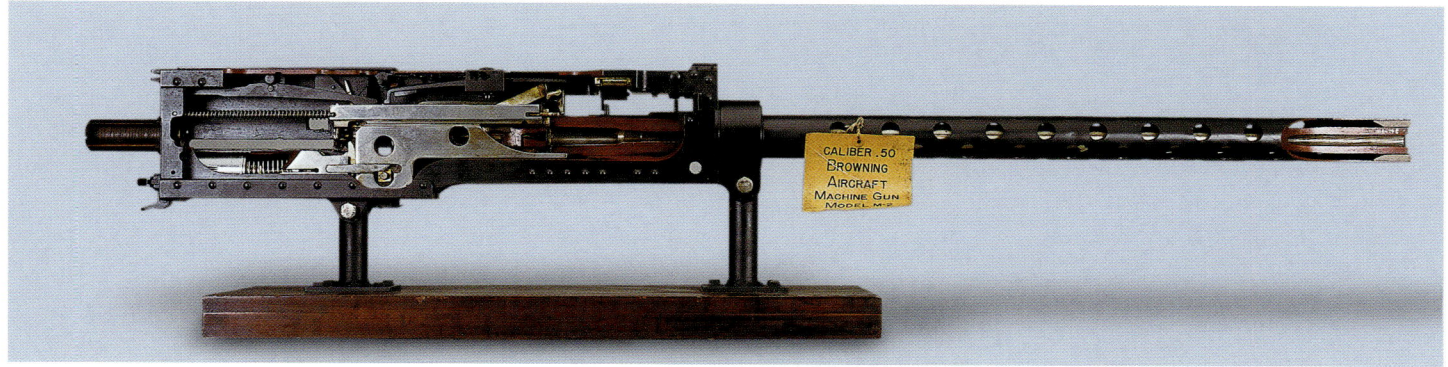

Colt M2 Aircraft Machine Gun, .50 caliber. This skeletonized arm was used to acquaint aircraft crew in the construction and servicing of the M2 Machine Gun.

Raymond Baldwin Museum of Connecticut History
(Gift of the Colt's Patent Fire Arms Manufacturing Company)

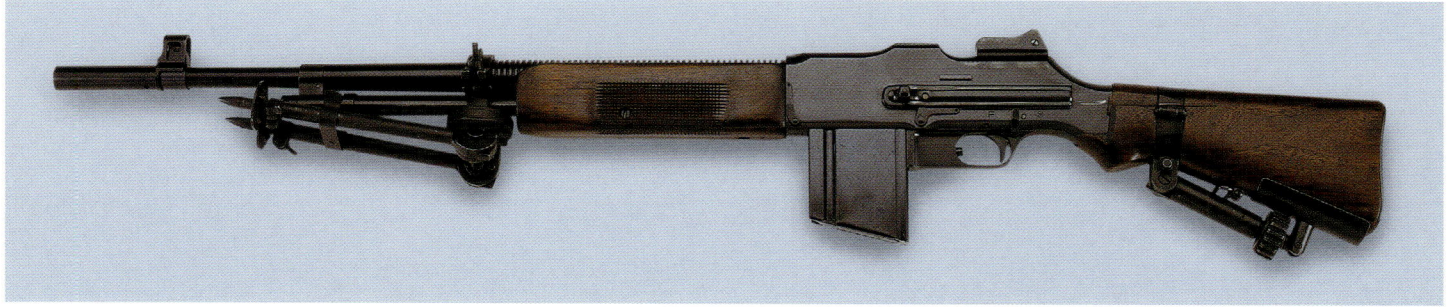

Colt Model 1922 Automatic Machine Rifle, .30-06 caliber, serial number C-1. Following World War I, the Colt company introduced a commercial version of the Model 1918 Browning Automatic Rifle, now commonly referred to as the BAR. Designed for full automatic fire, the Model 1922 was fitted with a folding bipod and a heavy ribbed barrel.

John Scott Collection.

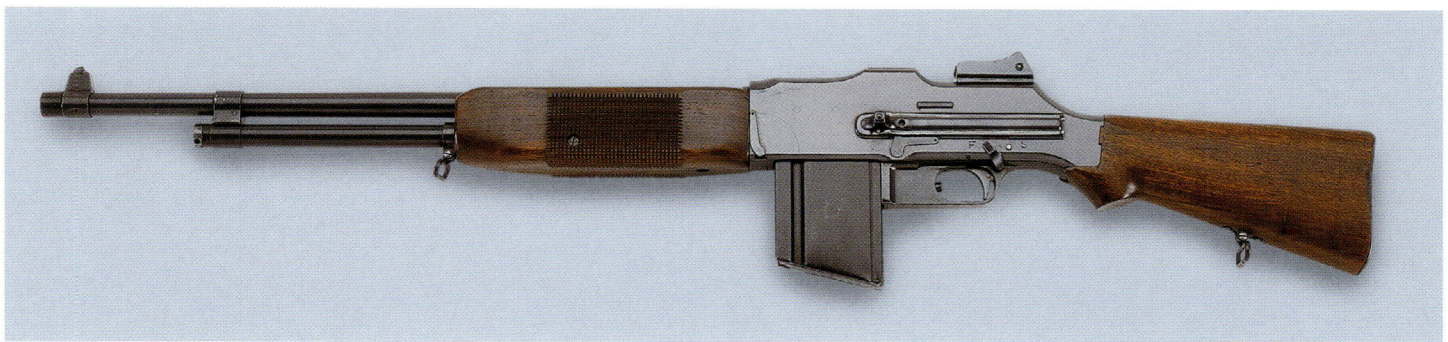

Colt Automatic Machine Rifle, .30-06 caliber, Model 1919, serial number C-100321. This is a commercial version of the standard U.S. Model 1918 Browning Automatic Rifle.

John Scott Collection.

Thompson Submachine Gun Model of 1921A, .45 ACP caliber, serial number 7916. This Thompson was shipped from Colt to Federal Laboratories, Incorporated, on December 12, 1921 as a "Sales Sample." It is accompanied by a "F.B.I."-style carrying case complete with Type "L" 50-round drum magazine, 4 Type "XX" 20-round box magazines, cleaning rod and metal spare parts kit..

Lowell E. Pauli Collection.

Thompson Submachine Gun Model 1923, .45ACP caliber, serial number 2059. Made on July 23, 1921, this Thompson was originally owned by General John T. Thompson and was given to Colonel Richard W. Cutts and is fitted with an experimental Cutts compensator to reduce muzzle rise. A Cutts compensator design was adopted by Auto-Ordnance and later used on several models of the Thompson Submachine gun.

Robert F. Lavender Collection.

Colt Model 1923 Thompson Autorifle, .30-06 caliber, serial number 18. Employing a retarded blowback action, John T. Thompson's Autorifle was developed in response to the U.S. Ordnance Department's call for self-loading rifle designs issued on August 15, 1919. Various forms of this rifle were made for or by the Auto-Ordnance Company and were produced from 1921 to 1929.

Tracie L. Hill Collection.

Colt Monitor Semiautomatic Rifle, .30-06 caliber, serial number C102823. Introduced in 1933, the Monitor was a full automatic and lighter weight version of the Browning Automatic Rifle. Designed for use by bank guards and police, it was made in very limited numbers during the 1930s. This particular example served the Terre Haute, Indiana Police Department.

John Scott Collection.

Colt AR-15 Rifle, .223 caliber, 21" barrel, serial number C00531. In a move which can only be called fortuitous, the Colt company purchased the exclusive manufacturing and marketing rights to the Armalite AR-15 Rifle from the Fairchild Engine & Aircraft Corporation. Although the rifle had been submitted for testing to the U.S. Government several years earlier, bureaucratic squabbling led to its rejection. The U.S. Air Force, however, recognized its merits and decided to adopt it for service. In 1963 the U.S. Army followed suit and the M16, as the military version is known, soon became a household word. For Colt, its adoption both here and abroad was an economic lifesaver.

John Scott Collection.

This well-worn Colt Single Action Army Pistol (serial number 131720) has the distinction of having been carried by Frank Cotton, a member of Theodore Roosevelt's Rough Riders (officially the 1st U.S. Volunteer Cavalry), at the Battle of San Juan Hill. Dennis Bovey Collection

Engraved Colt Single Action Army Revolver, .45 caliber, 4¾" barrel, serial number 183373. This engraved, nickel-plated and pearl gripped revolver was ordered through the A. F. Shapleigh Hardware Company in St. Louis, Missouri, for W. B. Jackson, whose name is inscribed on the backstrap. Jackson was a U.S. Deputy Marshal who was stationed at Gray Horse in the Indian Territory (present-day Oklahoma). It was shipped from the Colt factory on May 2, 1899.

Dick Burdick Collection.

Prewar Model 1873
Single Actions & Bisleys
by Bob Hartman

When most Americans hear or read the word Colt, the first image that comes to mind is that of a cowboy holding a Colt Single Action Army Revolver. This image has been ingrained in the country's psyche ever since the first illustrators traveled west to record life on the frontier. After the introduction of motion pictures, the presence of Single Action Army Revolvers in the hands of countless town marshals, outlaws and cavalrymen transformed the pistol into a symbol of the West.

The mystique surrounding this model was considerably enhanced by some of its popular nicknames: the "Equalizer" (no doubt drawn from the famous adage that while God had created man, "Colonel Colt made them equal"); "Frontier Six-Shooter" (an official tradename for the .44-40 caliber version), and the famous name, "Peacemaker." One enterprising Scottish emigrant agent of the 1880s even called it the "Shepherd's Friend," though it is highly unlikely that he told any of his clients why they might need a revolver in the American West.

Introduced in 1873, the .45 caliber Single Action Army Revolver was adopted for issue to the United States Army the same year. The vast majority of the approximately 358,000 made before the model was discontinued in 1940 were sold on the civilian market. The pistols were chambered for a wide variety of cartridges ranging from the diminutive .22 rimfire to the .476 Eley.

In 1894 the Colt company introduced a variation named after the Bisley shooting range in England. While it used the same barrel, frame and cylinder as the original Single Action, the Bisley model had a distinctive angled grip and broad-spurred hammer. Essentially designed as a target pistol, the Bisley could be ordered in any barrel length from 3 inches to 7½ inches. Made until 1914, this variation enjoyed moderate success with just over 45,000 being produced.

The Single Action Army Revolver's diversity and historical associations from the American frontier to the dark days of World War II, truly makes it "the stuff that dreams are made of."

Engraved Colt Single Action Army Revolver, .45 caliber, 7½" barrel, serial number 8928-E. Originally fitted with ivory grips, this nickel-plated and finely engraved revolver formed part of the Colt company's display at the 1876 Centennial Exhibition held in Philadelphia, Pennsylvania. The following year it was exhibited by the H. & D. Folson Company at the 1877 St. Louis Exposition. It was returned to the Colt company on October 15, 1877 and reshipped on February 12, 1878, to Henry Folson & Company of New York City for display. At some point after it was returned to the factory from New York, the revolver was fitted at the factory with checkered walnut grips as records indicate it was shipped to A. G. Spalding Brothers in Chicago, Illinois on September 12, 1897, with grips of that type. The pistol's final journey from the factory occurred on April 30, 1898, when it was shipped again to Spalding Brothers. Although the engraving is unsigned, the quality of the work suggests that it may have been done by either Herman L. Ulrich or Gustave Young, both of whom worked for Colt at the time the revolver was manufactured.

Dr. Joseph A. Murphy

Colt Single Action Army Revolver, .44 Smith & Wesson caliber, 7½" barrel, serial number 14. At the very beginning of this model's production, the sighting channel along the topstrap over the cylinder had a machined notch which formed the rear sight. As this had the appearance of the channel's sides being pinched together, revolvers of this type are referred to as the "pinched frame" models. About 100 revolvers were made with this style of sight. It was abandoned in favor of a simple notch cut at the rear of the channel.

Private Collection.

Colt Single Action Army Revolver, .45 caliber, 7½" barrel, serial number 23453. This commercially marketed revolver was shipped to the New York retailer, Spies, Kissam & Company on October 9, 1876, for resale. It was then engraved and fitted with cast bronze grips incorporating oval side panels that contain high relief Civil War battle scenes. Grips of this type were supplied by several New York dealers, most notably, Schuyler, Hartley & Graham.

Fred Lederman Collection.

Colt Single Action Army Revolver, .45 caliber, 5½" barrel, serial number 179. This is the earliest known Single Action Revolver to have been purchased by the United States Army for issue to the cavalry. Based upon its serial number, it is believed to have been made during the first week of the model's production in 1873.

John A. Kopec Collection.

Colt Single Action Army Revolver, .45 caliber, 7½" barrel, serial number 3474. Inspected by O. W. Ainsworth, this revolver was originally issued to Company K, 4th U.S. Cavalry, which served in the American West during the 1870s.

Frank D. Durrum, Jr. Collection.

Colt Single Action Army Revolver, .45 caliber, 7½" barrel, serial number 1825. Made in 1873, this revolver is stamped on the left side of the frame with the U.S. Army's acceptance mark "U.S." indicating that it was originally purchased by the government.

Logan Reed Collection.

Colt Single Action Army Revolver, .45 caliber, 4⅞" barrel, serial number 5099. Originally purchased by the U.S. Army, this revolver has had the "U.S." property marking removed and the barrel shortened by slightly more than 2.5 inches. While no records have been located concerning its issuance, the serial number is one digit away from an example recovered at the site of the Battle of the Little Big Horn.

John A. Kopec Collection.

Colt Single Action Army Revolver, .45 caliber, 7½" barrel, serial number 103741. A true memento of the American West, this revolver is stamped on its grip with the brand of the Pound Ranch. Owned by British interests, hence its name, the Pound Ranch was one of the larger late nineteenth century cattle operations in the Wyoming Territory.

Bob Funk Collection.

Colt Single Action Army Revolver, .45 caliber, 7½" barrel, serial number 34541. Withdrawn from U.S. Army service in 1893, this revolver was refurbished by the Colt company before being transferred to the State of New York for militia issue.

James S. Bryce Collection.

Colt Single Action Frontier Six Shooter, .44-40 caliber, 7½" barrel, serial number 45497. To identify the .44-40 caliber version of the Single Action Revolver, it was assigned the name "Frontier Six Shooter" which was etched (or later stamped) on the left side of the barrel. This example was shipped to Spies, Kissam & Company in New York City on June 1, 1878.

Paul I. Friedrich Collection.

Colt Single Action Army Revolver, .45 caliber, 4¾" barrel, serial number 36522. Originally fitted with a 7½" barrel, this pistol was apparently used to the point that the rifling had been thoroughly worn down. At that point it was replaced by a 4¾" barrel. The amount of wear seen on this example demonstrates the hard service it saw.

Les Gilman Collection.

Special Order Colt Single Action Army Revolver, .45 caliber, 7½" barrel, serial number 48484. This silver-plated revolver was fitted with "Double action configuration" grips of the style used on the Colt company's Double Action revolver introduced in 1877. Due to their angle, it was also equipped with sights 1/8 inch higher than normal. Factory records indicate that it was shipped on June 10, 1878 to a Mr. William Craps.

Blaine F. Miller Collection.

Colt Single Action Army Revolver, .45 caliber, 5½" barrel, serial number 56109. Originally shipped to the U.S. Army on May 19, 1880, this mixed serial number pistol was returned to the factory in 1903 for refurbishing and rebarrelling. It was then sent to the Springfield Armory on April 17, 1903.

Ray Meibaum Collection.

Colt Single Action Army Revolver, .45 caliber, 7½" barrel, serial number 62759. Shipped on June 4, 1883 to George J. Keyes, this pistol is one of 47 which were purchased privately to replace arms that had been stolen from the command of his brother, Captain A.S.B. Keyes, Troop D, 10th U.S. Cavalry.

Dr. James W. Watson Collection.

Engraved Colt Single Action Frontier Six Shooter, .44-40 caliber, 4¾" barrel, serial number 129108. Decorated by Cuno A. Helfricht with finely cut scrollwork, as well as overlapping scale ornament, this revolver originally belonged to William F. Cody, whose name is inscribed on the backstrap (inset). Cody, better known as Buffalo Bill, served as a scout during the Indian Wars and later toured the world with his Wild West show. This revolver was shipped to John P. Lower Sons, Denver, Colorado, in March 1889.

Dr. Joseph A. Murphy Collection

Colt Single Action Army Revolver, .45 caliber, 7½" barrel, serial number 82820. Made under contract for the U.S. Army, this pistol was inspected by Captain John W. Greer and David F. Clark. It was delivered to the government in 1882.

John Kopec Collection.

Colt Single Action Frontier Six Shooter, .44-40 caliber, 7½" barrel, serial number 106169. Factory records indicate that this revolver was shipped to the Boston retailer, William Read & Sons, on December 22, 1887.

Paul I. Friedrich Collection.

Colt Single Action Army Revolver, .45 caliber, 4¾" barrel, serial number 130048. This nickel-plated revolver was shipped on August 7, 1889 to the Simmons Hardware Company of St. Louis, Missouri. It is still accompanied by its original cardboard box having a pink label illustrating the Colt Single Action Revolver.

Paul I. Friedrich Collection.

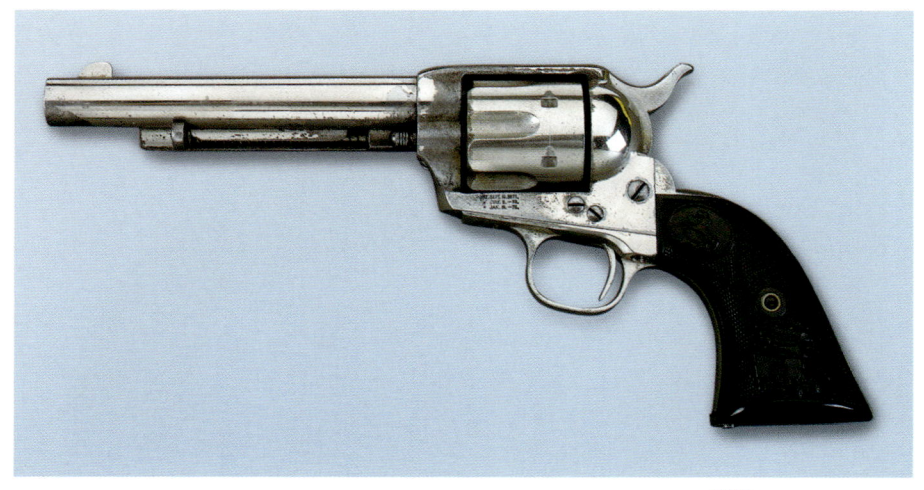

Colt Single Action Frontier Six Shooter, .44-40 caliber, 6" barrel, serial number 123370. During the entire production run of the Single Action Revolver, only 7 were produced with 6" barrels. Of that number only one was chambered for the .44-40 caliber cartridge.

Robert B. Hartman Collection.

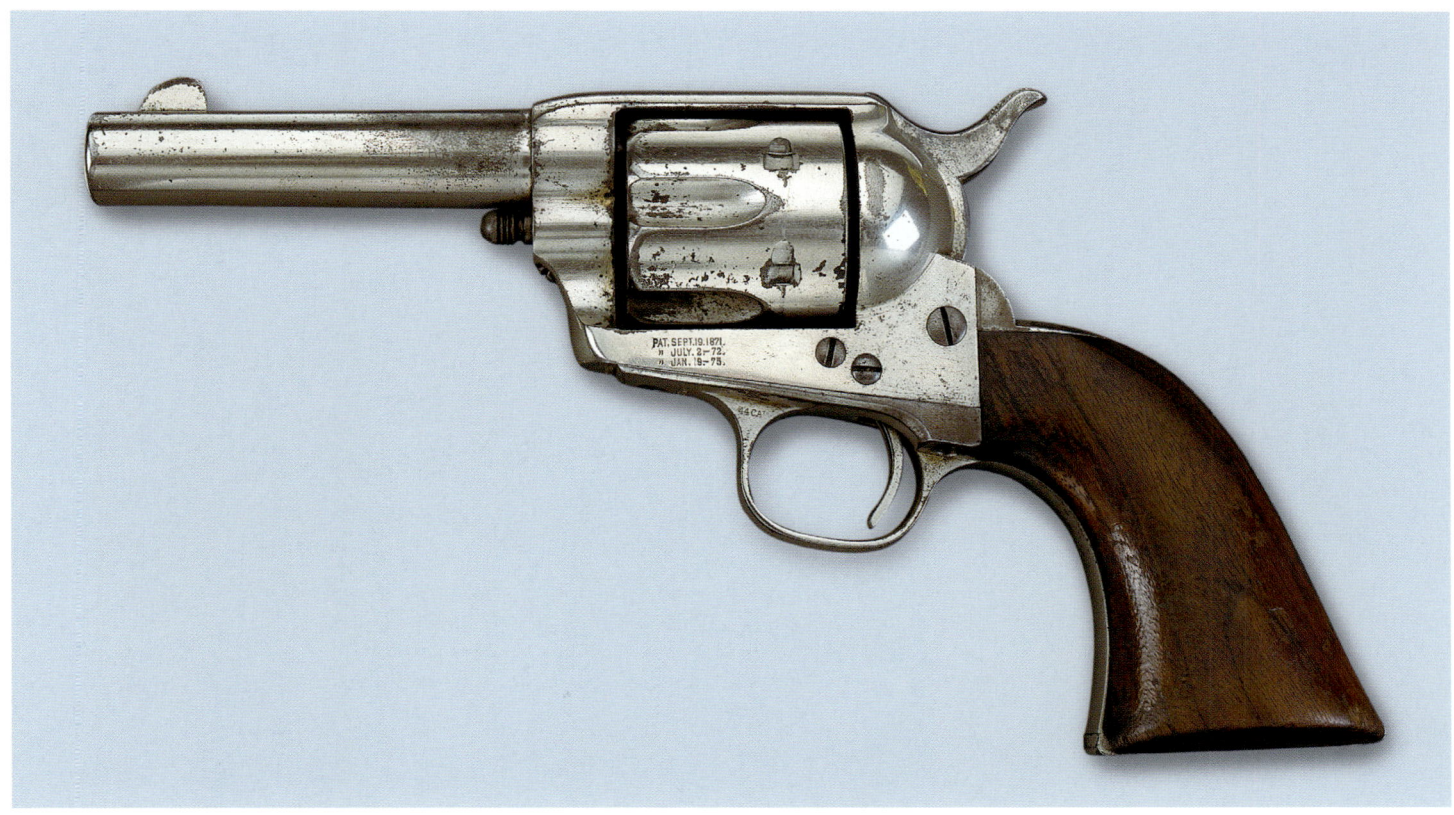

Colt Single Action Frontier Six Shooter, .44-40 caliber, 4" barrel, serial number 123366. The ejectorless 4-inch barreled version of the Single Action Revolver is commonly referred to as the "Sheriff's Model." Approximately 182 of these pistols were manufactured in .44-40 caliber from 1882 onward.

Robert B. Hartman Collection.

Skeletonized Colt Single Action Army Revolver, .45 caliber, 5½" barrel, no serial number. It is believed that this revolver was shipped to the Springfield Armory on January 31, 1896, as a model of the "new standard" or 5.5" barreled version of the Single Action Army adopted in 1895.

Dick Burdick Collection.

Colt Single Action Army Revolver, .45 caliber, 5½" barrel, serial number 131720. This refurbished revolver having a shortened barrel, was carried by a member of Theodore Roosevelt's Rough Riders during their charge up San Juan Hill in Cuba.

Dennis Bovey Collection.

Cased Colt Single Action Special Target Pistol, .450 Eley caliber, 7½" barrel, serial number 135348. While not advertised until 1890, the Special Target Pistol was first made by the Colt company in 1888. In contrast to the standard model it featured a "Flat-Top" frame and target sights. It could also be purchased on special order with elongated grips such as those seen here. This example was shipped on September 14, 1890 to the Colt company's London Agency.

Robert B. Hartman Collection.

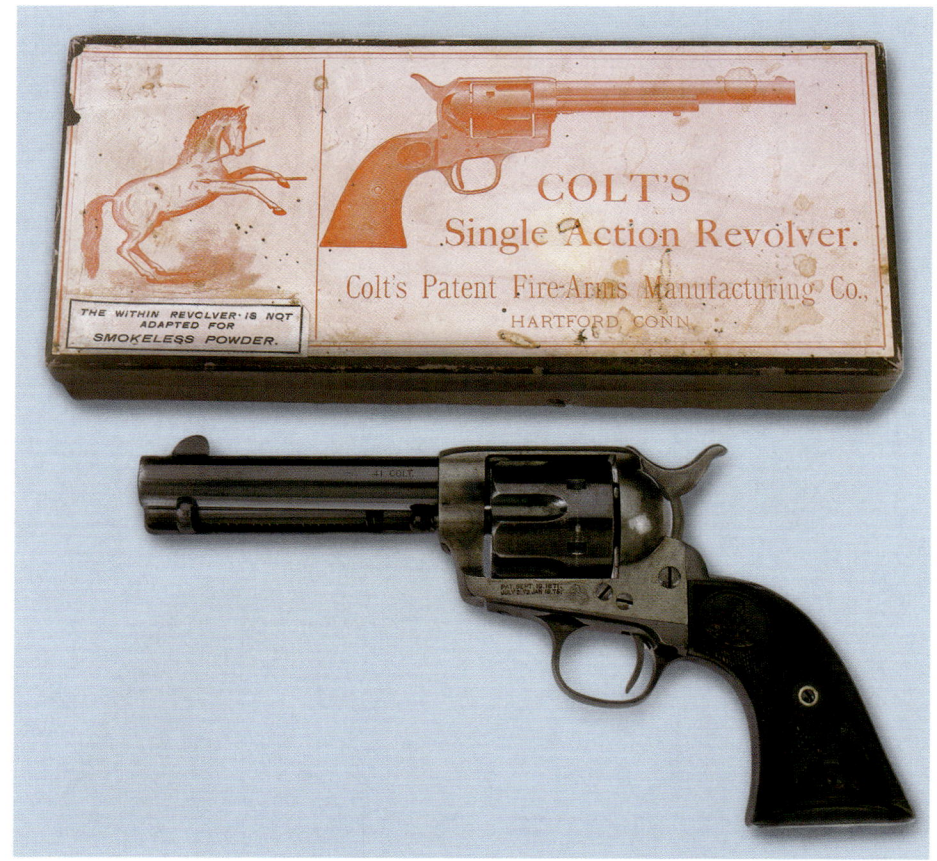

Colt Single Action Army Revolver, .41 caliber, 4¾" barrel, serial number 145450. One of the more popular of the Single Action Revolver's optional chamberings, was for the .41 Colt cartridge. In all, more than 19,000 were made in this caliber. The present example, still accompanied by its original box, was originally shipped to Montgomery Ward & Company of Chicago, Illinois, on March 31, 1892.

Jim Thorning Collection.

Engraved Colt Single Action Army Revolver, .45 caliber, 4¾" barrel, serial number 154018. This engraved, nickel-plated and pearl gripped revolver was ordered by Carl Kirchener and shipped to him in care of J. C. Petmecky in Austin, Texas. Corporal Kirchener was member of the Texas Ranger Frontier Battalion Company D stationed near El Paso. Kirchener family tradition related that the revolver was a present from the widow and father-in-law (Judge George Baylor) of Captain Frank Jones who commanded Company D.

Kurt House Collection.

Colt Single Action Army Revolver, .476 Eley caliber, 7½" barrel, serial number 140118. Of all the calibers offered by the Colt company for the Single Action Revolver, the largest was the .476 Eley. Most of these pistols, including that illustrated here, were made for the British trade. Records indicate that number 140118 was shipped to the company's London Agency on April 30, 1891.

Richard R. Atkinson Collection.

Colt Single Action Army Revolver, .45 caliber, 4¾" barrel, serial number 166985. This revolver was fitted at the factory with a special half-moon front sight and an ejectorless barrel. It was originally shipped to Hartley & Graham of New York City on January 7, 1898. It was later owned by Sheriff C. Norfleet Hill of Harris County, Texas, who died in 1942.

Paul Sorrell Collection.

Engraved and Gold-Inlaid Colt Single Action Army Revolver, .45 caliber, 5½" barrel, serial number 172485. Commissioned by Sears Roebuck & Company in Chicago, Illinois, this revolver represents one of Cuno A. Helfricht's finest efforts. In addition to having been engraved with exquisitely cut intertwining scrollwork, as well as strapwork panels, the barrel, cylinder and frame were inlaid with gold edging bands. The pearl grips were also carved by Helfricht with a high relief standing portrait of Columbia on their right side (inset). Following its shipment to Sears on October 23, 1897, it remained in that firm's inventory for a number of years. In the company's 1901 catalogue, it was advertised for sale as Item No. 34494 with the notation that while it had cost $60.00 to be made, the pistol could be purchased for $50.00 cash. Described by Sears in that catalogue as "...one of the nicest Cow Boy revolvers you ever saw...", number 172485 epitomizes the quality of Colt's best work at the end of the nineteenth century.

Dr. Joseph A. Murphy

Colt Single Action Frontier Six Shooter, .44-40 caliber, 5½" barrel, serial number 276842. In March of 1906, F.S. & H. Parrel purchased 50 revolvers through the American Trading Company of New York City, for use at their gold mines in Mexico. All of these pistols were inscribed on the backstrap (inset) with the legend "G.M.Parrel No. 1" through "G.M.Parrel No. 50." The revolver illustrated here is number 40 from that order.

Dick Burdick Collection.

Colt Single Action Army Revolver, .45 caliber, 5.5" barrel, serial number 252894. This nickel-plated and staghorn gripped revolver was used by the western movie star Rex Allen. Known as the "Arizona Cowboy," Allen appeared with the "Miracle Horse of the Movies," Koko, in 19 films produced by Republic Pictures between 1950 and 1954. He subsequently starred in the television series "Frontier Doctor" which was also known as "The Man of the West."

Bob Nelson Collection.

Colt Single Action Army Revolver, .45 caliber, 7½" barrel, serial number 246706. This special order Single Action Revolver is fitted with a smooth-bored barrel designed for use with cartridges loaded with shot, rather than a lead bullet. Popular with trick shooters, only 22 smooth-bored Single Actions were manufactured by the Colt company. This one was shipped from the factory on August 5, 1903.

Robert B. Hartman Collection.

Colt Single Action Army Revolver, .45 caliber, 7½" barrel, serial number 183327. It is fitted with pearl grips which are carved on the right side with a steer's head in relief. This revolver was originally shipped to Montgomery Ward & Company of Chicago, Illinois, on February 7, 1899.
Donald M. Yena Collection.

Colt Single Action Army Revolver, .45 caliber, 3½" barrel, serial number 253691. Specially ordered with an ejectorless 3.5" barrel, this pistol was originally owned by the Alaska Tredwell Gold Mining Company which was located on Douglas Island across the Gastineau Channel from Juneau. It is estimated that fewer than 50 revolvers of this type were made following the introduction of smokeless powder cartridges circa 1898.
Robert B. Hartman Collection.

Engraved Colt Single Action Army Revolver, .45 caliber, 5½" barrel, serial number 333575. Finished in full silver plate and fitted with ivory grips carved in relief with a steer's head, this pistol was made for Captain J. J. Sanders, who was a member of Company A of the Texas Rangers. Factory records indicate it was shipped to Colonel J. F. Stockton for Sanders on December 2, 1916. Marshal, Sheriff and Texas Ranger badges.
Paul Sorrell Collection.

Colt Single Action Army Revolver, .32-20 caliber, 4¾" barrel, serial number 272480. This nickel-plated and pearl gripped revolver was shipped to the Copper Queen Consolidated Mining Company in Bisbee, Arizona, on January 31, 1906. Given its finish and grips, it is likely it was ordered for the mine's general store or an employee of the company.
John Kopec Collection.

Colt Single Action Army Revolver, .45 caliber, 7½" barrel, serial number 289088. Originally shipped to Stauffer Eshleman & Company of New Orleans, Louisiana, on February 14, 1907, this pistol was later owned by William S. Speed of the Arizona Rangers. On August 5, 1908, Speed killed the outlaw Bill Downing, who had been a member of the Sam Bass Gang.
John Kopec Collection.

Engraved Colt Single Action Army Revolver, .45 caliber, 4¾" barrel, serial number 346731. Ordered by M. B. Couch, U.S. Inspector of Customs in Brownsville, Texas, this engraved, ivory gripped revolver also is gold inlaid with its owner's name on the backstrap. Factory records indicate it was shipped to Couch in care of the H. & D. Folsom Arms Company in New York City, on December 6, 1924.

Dick Burdick Collection.

Colt Single Action Army Revolver, .45 caliber, 4¾" barrel, serial number 308049. From 1887 to 1909, Wells Fargo & Company purchased a significant number of revolvers from the Colt company for its agents throughout the United States. This example was 1 of 24 shipped to the firm's New York City office on April 6, 1909. All of the revolvers in this shipment were marked "W F & Co" on their butt straps.

Mike Durhan Collection.

Engraved Colt Single Action Army Revolver, .45 caliber, 7½" barrel, serial number 342476. Fewer than a dozen Single Action Revolvers were finished in full gold plate. This one also was engraved and fitted with pearl grips carved in relief with an oxen's head. The backstrap is engraved with the original owner's name "W.R.Fogle, Jr." It was shipped to Mr. Fogle, a Ford Motor Company dealer in Minden, Louisiana, on August 30, 1921.
Kurt House Collection.

Colt Single Action Army Revolver, .45 caliber, 4¾" barrel, serial number 351098. In 1927, the City of San Antonio, Texas, purchased over 100 Single Action Revolvers for its Police Department. Each of these pistols was marked "S.A.P.D." together with a sequence number. This revolver is number 2 in the series.
Dick Burdick Collection.

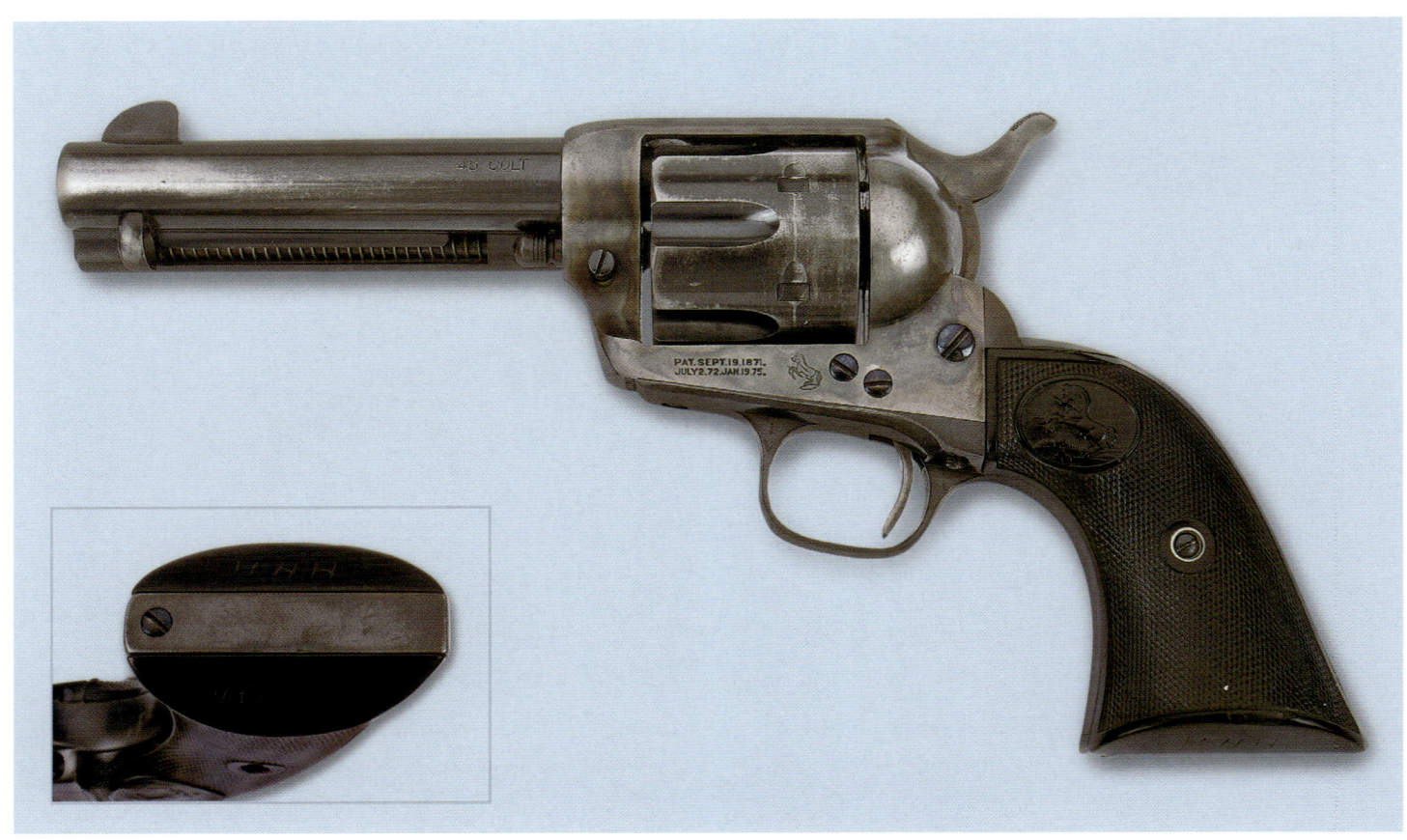

Colt Single Action Army Revolver, .45 caliber, 4¾" barrel, serial number 352983. Shipped on September 17, 1929, this revolver was ordered by Sheriff Frank Blackburn of Park County, Wyoming. First elected to that position in 1927, Blackburn served as the county's sheriff for 32 years.
William F. Welch Collection.

Colt Single Action Army Revolver, .38-40 caliber, 4¾" barrel, serial number 303524. In 1907, the Republic of Mexico purchased 74 revolvers of this type for its Customs Service. They were all inscribed on the barrel at the factory with the property mark "E de Mex.," prior to shipment to the Marcellus Hartley Company of New York City.
Dick Burdick Collection.

Colt Single Action Army Revolver, .45 caliber, 4¾" barrel, serial number 354919. Assembled on January 18, 1934, this revolver is fitted with special order checkered deluxe walnut grips having plain fleur-de-lis panels at their upper and lower edges. It was received in the factory's shipping room on January 24, 1934.

Robert B. Hartman Collection.

Colt Single Action Army Revolver, .45 caliber, 4¾" barrel, serial number 354388. Fitted with pearl grips carved in relief on their right side with the head of a longhorn steer, this silver-plated revolver was shipped to Sheriff Frank E. Hoegemeyer of Colorado County, Texas, in December 1930.

Robert B. Hartman Collection.

Colt Single Action Army Revolver, .38 caliber, 5.5" barrel, serial number 356157. This late production revolver was once owned by the actor Joel McCrea who starred in approximately 25 films between 1931 and 1962. Appropriately, given the venue of this exhibition, he played Colonel William F. Cody, opposite Maureen O'Hara's Annie Oakley in William A. Wellman's 1944 film "Buffalo Bill."

Ron Cantrell Collection.

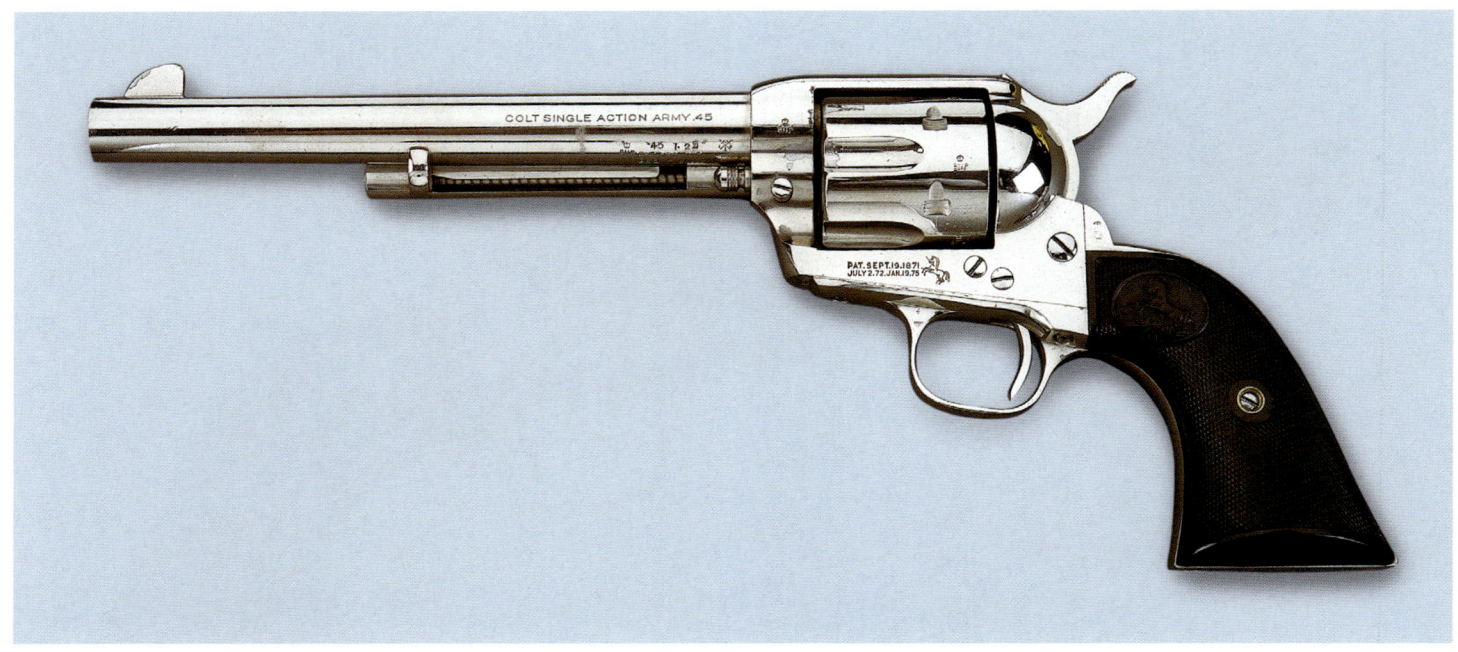

Colt Single Action Army Revolver, .45 caliber, 7½" barrel, serial number 356280. In anticipation of a possible invasion in early 1940, the British Government purchased 163 Single Action Revolvers for the Home Guard. Of this number, 52 had 7.5-inch barrels. Interestingly, over 38 percent of the total order was satisfied with nickel-plated pistols.

Robert B. Hartman Collection.

Engraved Colt Single Action Army Revolver, .38 Special caliber, 5.5" barrel, serial number 357330. Assembled on January 21, 1948, this pistol was shipped to the Colt company's historian, M. S. Huber, on October 19, 1972. It should be noted that this is the first arm engraved at the Colt factory by Leonard Francolini.

David Grunberg Collection.

Colt Single Action Army Revolver, .38 caliber, 5.5" barrel, serial number 357345. This postwar Single Action Revolver was engraved and gold inlaid to commemorate the opening of the Colt company's manufacturing plant in Singapore on January 28, 1969. It was originally owned by William H. Goldrach, president of the Colt's Weapons Division from 1969 to 1972.

Raymond Baldwin Museum of Connecticut History
(Gift of William H. Goldrach)

Engraved Colt Single Action Army Revolver, .45 caliber, 7½" barrel, serial number 357494. Used as a test sample for engraving, this fully blued revolver has the distinction of being the last Single Action Army to have been shipped from the Colt factory. Assembled on March 8, 1948, it was sold by Colt on February 2, 1980, at the Sahara Antique Arms Show.

Robert B. Hartman Collection.

Colt Single Action Army Revolver, .44rf caliber, 7½" barrel, serial number 487. In response to requests for a revolver chambered for the same cartridge as the Model 1866 Winchester Rifle, the Colt company introduced the .44 rimfire version in 1875. A total of 1,892 were made before the caliber was discontinued in 1887. Only 166 of that total were nickel-plated. Number 487 is believed to have been shipped to Francis De Gress of Mexico City, in 1875.

Robert Eder Collection.

Colt Single Action Bisley Target Model Revolver, .455 Eley caliber, 7½" barrel, serial number 185325. The Bisley Model was introduced in 1894. It differed from the standard Single Action Revolver in the form of its sharply angled grip and the broad thumbpiece of the hammer. The Target Model also had a flattened topstrap over the cylinder to accommodate the rear sight. Fitted with a military and bead front sight, this particular revolver was shipped to the Colt company's London Agency on April 24, 1899.

Terrence L. Hunt Collection.

Sample Colt Single Action Army Revolver, .45 caliber, 2" barrel, serial number 16534 OR 15430??. Without question, this is one of the most unusual Single Action Revolvers ever to have been made by the Colt company. Constructed sometime in the late 1870s, it features a swing-out cylinder and automatic cartridge case ejector designed by William Mason. Though the system was successfully applied to other Colt revolvers, such as the Model 1877 Lightning, it was never adopted for production.

*Raymond Baldwin Museum of Connecticut History
(Gift of the Colt's Patent Fire Arms Manufacturing Company)*

Colt Single Action Bisley Model Revolver, .38-40 caliber, 4¾" barrel, serial number 200650. This standard production revolver was shipped to Hibbard, Spencer, Bartlett & Company of Chicago, Illinois on October 27, 1900.

Terrence L. Hunt Collection.

Colt Single Action Bisley Model Revolver, .45 caliber, 5½" barrel, serial number 197681. Originally shipped as a .38-40 caliber revolver with a 4¾" barrel to Roberts, Sanford & Taylor of Sherman, Texas, this revolver has been extensively reworked. In addition, it is engraved with cattle brands (possibly by Weldon Bledsow).

Terrence L. Hunt Collection.

Colt Single Action Army Revolver, .22rf caliber, 7½" barrel, serial number 1734. In an attempt to reduce its existing supply of completed .44 rimfire pistols in 1887, the firm altered them for use with the .22 rimfire cartridge. It is believed that fewer than 90 were so altered. Number 1734 was shipped to either the Colt company's New York or San Francisco office on July 18, 1888.

Richard R. Atkinson Collection.

Colt Single Action Bisley Model Revolver, .38-40 caliber, 4" barrel, serial number 200651. Shipped on November 2, 1900, to the Winchester Repeating Arms Company, this ejectorless 4-inch barrelled revolver was fitted with a Winchester rifle front sight. It was subsequently shipped to the George Tritch Hardware Company in Denver, Colorado.

Robert B. Hartman Collection.

Colt Single Action Bisley Model Revolver, .38-40 caliber, 7½" barrel, serial number 318791. This standard production revolver was shipped to the T. B. Davis Arms Company in Portland, Maine, on September 1, 1911.

Terrence L. Hunt Collection.

Engraved Colt Single Action Bisley Model Revolver, .45 caliber, 4¾" barrel, serial number 304989. Engraved by Cuno L. Helfricht, this nickel-plated revolver is fitted with pearl grips carved on the right with a steer's head. It was shipped to the Van Camp Hardware & Iron Company of Indianapolis, Indiana, on March 6, 1908.

Terrence L. Hunt Collection.

Colt Single Action Bisley Model Revolver, .38-40 caliber, 5½" barrel, serial number 207936. This revolver was originally shipped to Hibbard, Spencer, Bartlett & Company in Chicago, Illinois, on March 29, 1901.

Terrece L. Hunt Collection.

Colt Single Action Bisley Model Revolver, .44-40 caliber, 4.75" barrel, serial number 250804. Typical of revolvers exported to Mexico, this Bisley bears evidence of hard and long service. This is particularly evident on the right side of the ivory grips where the Mexican eagle, which would have been originally carved in high relief, is now a mere shadow of its former self. The pistol is also accompanied by an equally well-worn Mexican holster.

Bob Eder Collection.

Colt Single Action Bisley Target Model Revolver, .38 caliber, 7½" barrel, serial number 308701. Only 96 Bisley Target Model Revolvers were chambered for the .38 Colt cartridge. This example which was fitted with checkered walnut grips, was originally shipped to W. S. Brown of Pittsburgh, Pennsylvania, on September 11, 1909.

Terrence L. Hunt Collection.

The widely divergent approaches taken to decorating modern Colt revolvers are clearly demonstrated in this assemblage. While some engravers continue to draw upon nineteenth century sources (e.g., the pistol middle right), others have adopted more contemporary approaches utilizing the extensive use of pictorial vignettes.

This pair of modern .45 caliber Single Action Army Revolvers (serial numbers SA26317 and SA51058), were used by the actor Kevin Costner in the 1985 film, Silverado. They are accompanied by a custom-made set of leather holsters and belt made by Arvo Ojala.

Mike Holloway Collection.

2nd and 3rd Generation Single Action Army, New Frontier, and Scouts

by Gurney Brown

Although production of the Model 1873 Single Action Army Revolver ceased in 1940, following World War II orders continued to be received sporadically for the model. These requests were fulfilled using leftover frames and other components that remained in the company's assembly room for the next decade and a half.

By 1954, however, the demand for the model had increased to a level that prompted the Colt's Manufacturing Company to seriously consider reintroducing the pistol into its product line.

The sudden popularity of the old Single Action Army Revolver was due in large part to television. The rapid acceptance of this new medium by the American public exposed countless thousands to "Westerns" broadcast across the country. As virtually every participant in these shows carried a Colt Single Action Army Revolver, or a close facsimile of them, it was natural that viewers would find them increasingly attractive. Realizing that a potential market existed for the revolver, the Colt company began its production again in 1955.

The reintroduced revolver, now known as the second generation Colt Single Action Army, mirrored its pre-war counterpart. It can be easily identified though by its use of the suffix "SA" following the serial number. While the largest number of these revolvers were cham-

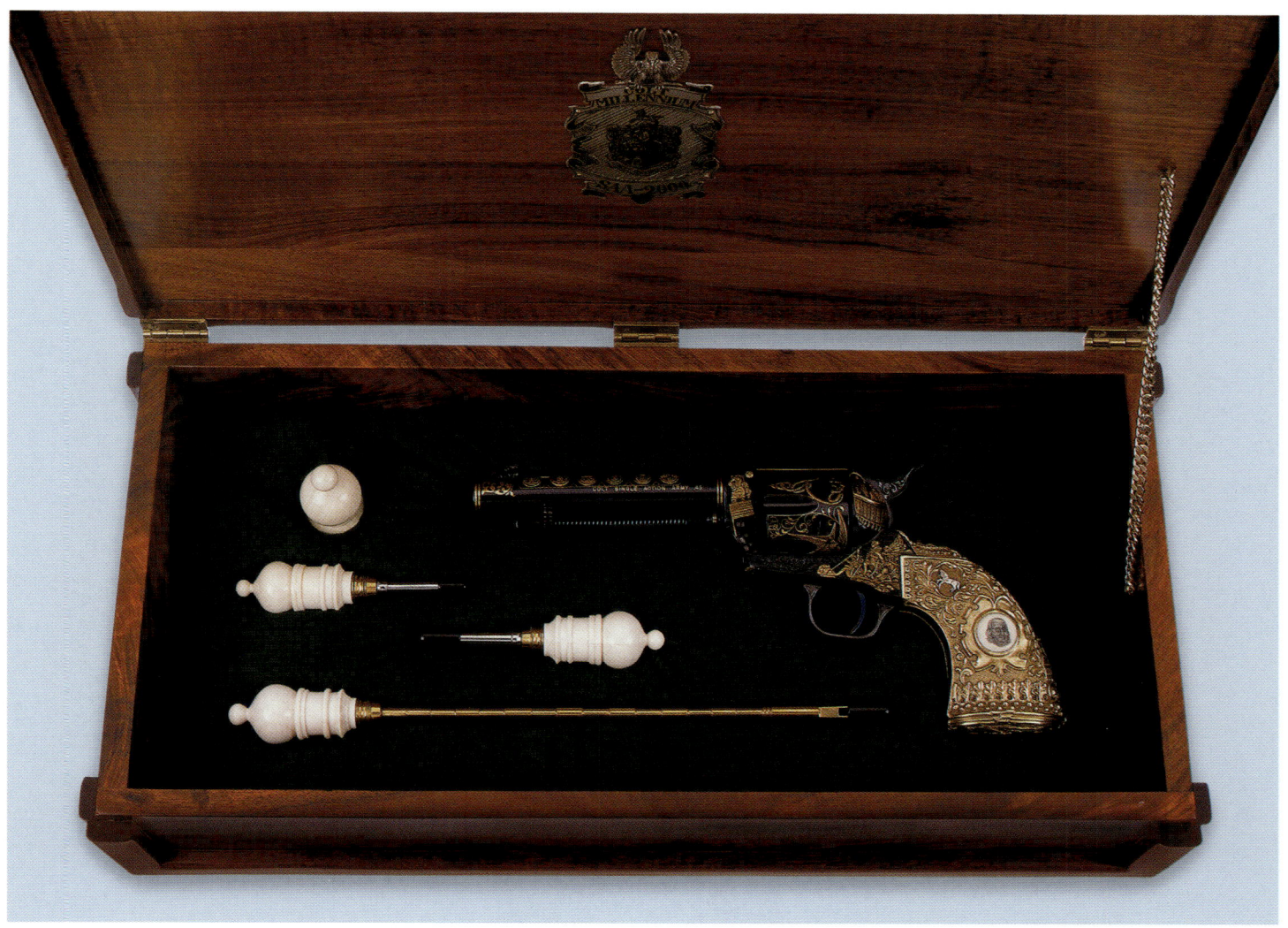

Cased and Engraved Colt Single Action Army Revolver, .45 caliber, 5½" barrel, serial number SAA2000. The "Colt Millennium" revolver was commissioned by its present owner to mark the beginning of the new millenium and was used by the Colt company as a special exhibition piece during 2000 and 2001. The engraved and gold inlaid ornament, executed by Bryson Gwinnell, includes the following motifs: the state seals of the original thirteen colonies (top of the barrel), the legend "MILLENNIUM" (cartridge ejector rod housing), the Colt dome (head of the cylinder pin), the inscriptions "The right to keep and bear Arms," "Amendment number two" and "Don't tread on me" accompanied by panels decorated with crossed muskets, serpents and the dove of peace (cylinder), the Lincoln assassination scene (left recoil shield), Paul Revere's ride (right side of the barrel bolster), the first moon walk (left side of the barrel bolster), driving the "Golden Spike" (right side of the frame; the Liberty Bell (loading gate), Washington crossing the Delaware River (left side of the frame). The grips are of solid 14kt gold cast and chased with the Statue of Liberty along the spine, as well as a standing portrait of a Minute Man on the buttcap. The sides of the grips are inlaid with ivory plaques carved in high relief with portrait busts of Thomas Jefferson (right side) and Benjamin Franklin (left side). The pistol is boxed in a koa wood case carved in relief on its lid with an American eagle. It was the first invoiced pistol to be shipped by Colt in the new millennium.

David Grunberg Collection.

bered for the .45 Long Colt cartridge, customers could also order it in .357 Magnum, .38 Special or .44 Special. As with the original Single Action, the standard barrel lengths were 4¾", 5½" and 7½." It should be noted, however, that other versions were produced. For example, the "Sheriff's Model" was fitted with a 3-inch barrel, while at the other end of the spectrum, "Buntline" pistols sported 12" or, in two instances, 16" barrels.

In February of 1976, the Colt company introduced a slightly redesigned Single Action Army Revolver, now commonly referred to as the Third Generation. Initially the serial numbers of this series continued the sequence of the Second Generation (five numerals followed by the letters "SA"). After 99999SA had been reached in 1978, the sequence changed to SA00001 through SA99999 and then to S00001A. As before, the model could be ordered in .357 Magnum, .44 Special, .44-40 or .45 Colt caliber with barrel lengths ranging from 2" to 12".

The continued popularity of the Colt Single Action Army Revolver in its modern form is due to the fact that it symbolizes not only the Colt name, but also the American frontier and the individualism of its original settlers. It furthermore provides a direct link to the past as it has been in production for almost 130 years. In an age when obsolescence is built into many product designs, this is truly a remarkable feat.

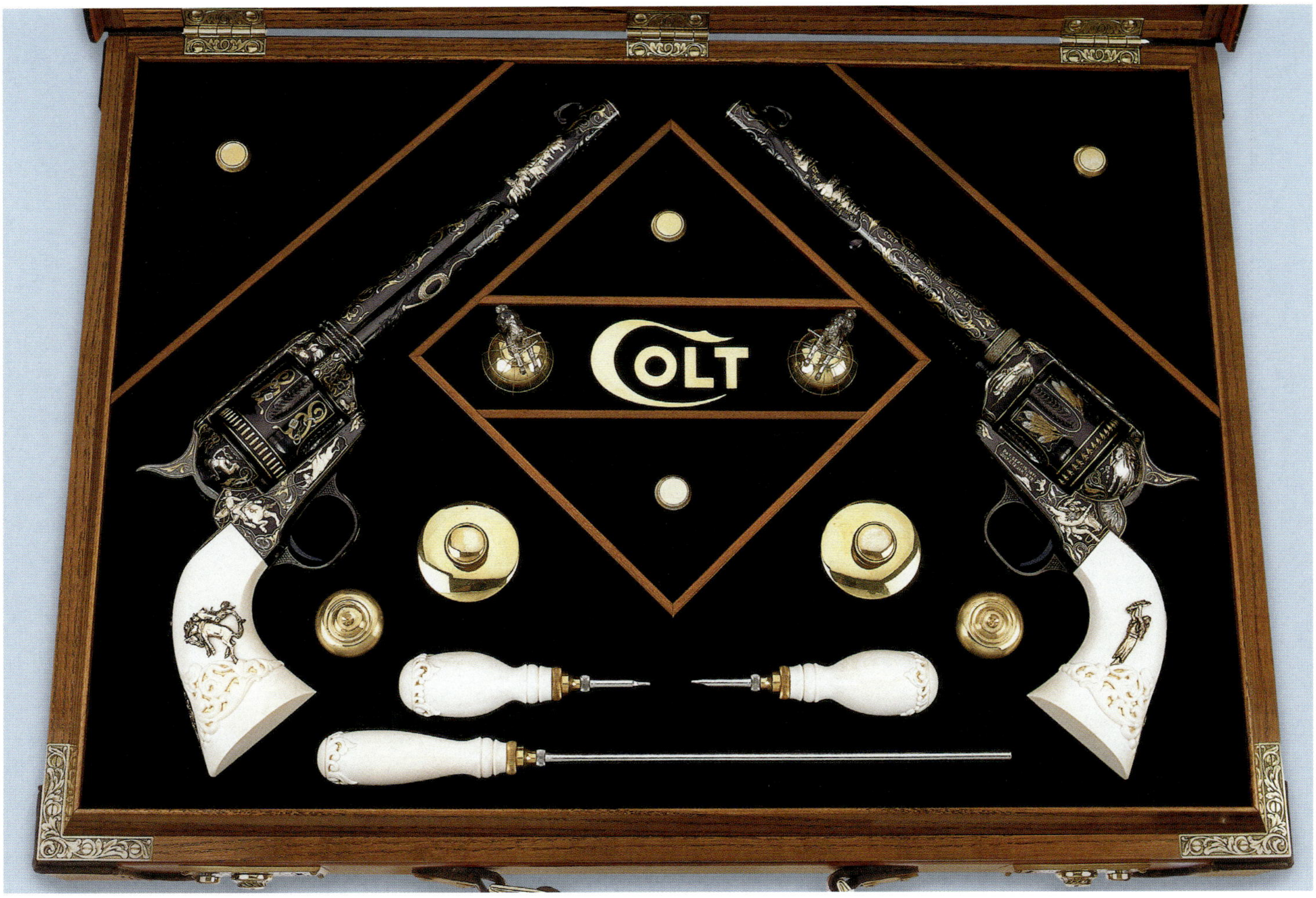

Cased and Engraved Pair of Colt Single Action Army Revolvers, .45 caliber, 7½" barrels, serial numbers 62338SA and 62339SA. Commissioned as a celebration of the American West, the "Cowboy & Indian" set of revolvers were extensively inlaid in gold with motifs representative of their namesakes by Leonard Francolini. Among the major motifs found on serial number 62338SA, the "Cowboy Revolver," are strands of barbed wire (barrel and cartridge ejector rod housing); a cattle drive scene (right forward side of the barrel); a frontier town scene (left side of the barrel); a holster and belt (trigger guard bow); spur, buckle, strap and bit (shoulder of the backstrap), and; a branding iron (expanded mid-point of the backstrap). The most ambitious work, however, is to be seen on the frame sides and buttcap. The right side of the frame is decorated with images of a cowboy bathing; another roping a steer, and a third, climbing up a rocky outcrop. The latter is cleverly done in that the cowboy's hand curves around the loading gate under which is hidden a coiled rattlesnake. The left side of the frame is inlaid with a mounted cowboy roping an Indian and a lynching scene on the barrel bolster. The buttcap is embellished with a detailed branding scene. The ivory grips are carved with scrollwork and inlaid with gold plaques cast and chased with a rodeo scene (right side), as well as a cowboy leaning against a vintage automobile (right side). Serial number 62339SA, the "Indian Revolver", is decorated with the following primary images: a wagon train under attack (right side of the barrel); a village encampment (left side of the barrel); the capture of an eagle and a buffalo hunting scene (right side of the frame); a chase scene (left rear side of the frame); and depiction of the sun ceremony (left barrel bolster); a war club (trigger guard bow); feathers (shoulder of the backstrap); quiver and arrows (expanded mid-point of the backstrap), and; an Indian sending smoke signals (buttcap). The ivory grips are carved with scrollwork and set with inlaid gold plaques cast and chased with a rendition of the "End of the Trail" (right side) together with an Indian woman worshipping the sun (left side). The set is housed in a leatherbound and suede-lined case with accessories decorated en suite.

David Grunberg Collection.

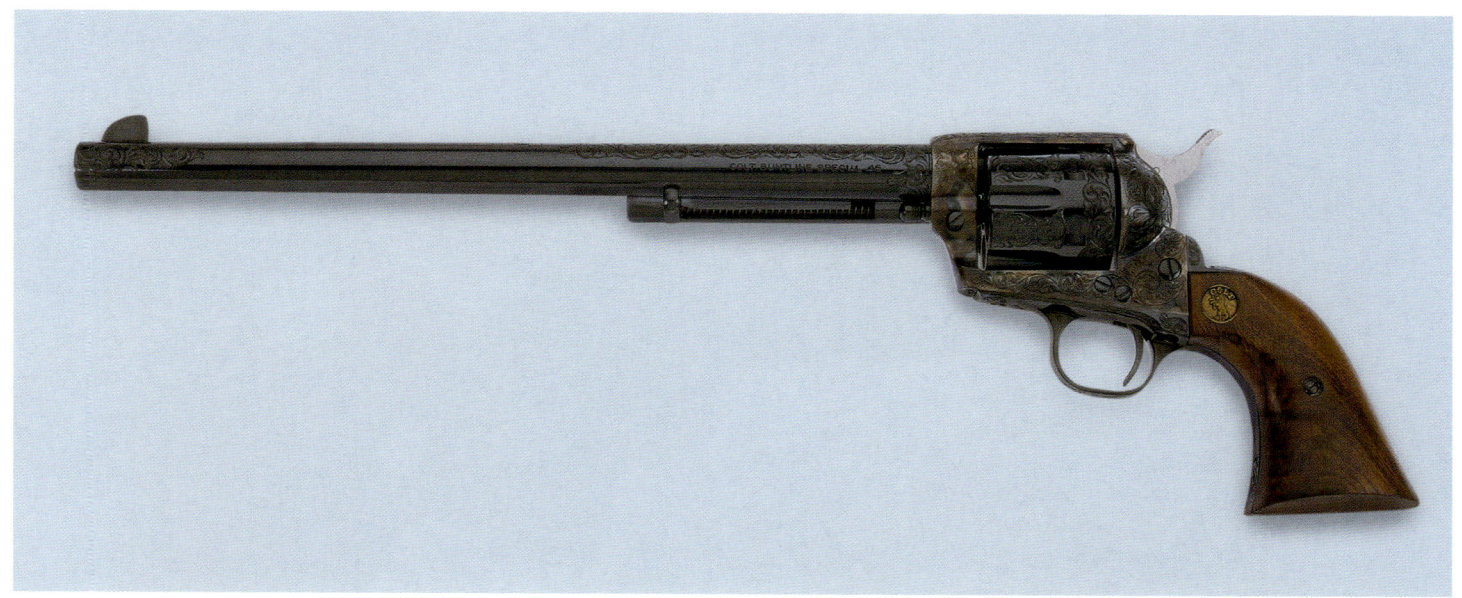

Engraved Set of Four Colt Single Action Army Revolvers. .45 caliber, 4¾", 5½", 7½", 12" barrels, serial numbers 61683SA to 61686SA. This series of consecutively serial numbered revolvers was shipped by the Colt company "In the White" (i.e., without any finish) to A. A. White Engravers, Inc., on November 14, 1972. They were then engraved by Alvin A. White with foliate scrollwork corresponding to the four styles of coverage offered by the Colt company. Serial number 61683SA displays the Style A pattern characterized by rather sparse and loosely constructed scrolls. Number 61684SA is decorated with the slightly more extensive scrollwork associated with Style B work. Number 61685SA exhibits the carefully cut scrollwork identified as Style C. The highest grade of engraving offered by the Colt company, Style D, is found on number 61686SA.
R. F. F. Collection.

Engraved Colt Single Action Army Revolver, .45 caliber, 4¾" barrel, serial number 45451SA. This fully blued revolver was engraved for the Colt company with finely cut scrollwork by Ogawa as a marketing sample. It was subsequently charged to the account of Al DeJohn of the Colt company's Custom Shop on April 14, 1969.

Marvin F. Essenmacher Collection.

Cased and Engraved Colt Single Action Army Revolver, .45 caliber, 7½" barrel, serial number 62379SA. Produced as a marketing sample, this blued and casehardened revolver was engraved for the Colt company by Oscar Flores. In addition, the pistol was also fitted with finely checkered walnut grips having silver medallions. Records indicate it was originally charged to the Loan Account of Don Mitchell, Colt's Marketing Manager, on May 5, 1972.

Marvin F. Essenmacher Collection.

Colt Single Action Army Revolver, .45 caliber, 7.5" barrel, serial number 66666SA. Perhaps the best known of all of the engraved and gold inlaid revolvers commissioned by William H. Goldrach while he was president of the Colt's Firearms Military Division is "The Colonel Samuel Colt Special." Decorated by Alvin A. White, it features gold inlaid vignettes depicting Samuel Colt, the original Hartford factory, and various firearms from the percussion era to the U.S. M16. The grips are inlaid with sheet gold plaques illustrating Colt's coat-of-arms (left side), and on the right, a Number 5 Paterson Revolver, Whitneyville-Walker Holster Pistol and the adorsed colt heads found on many Paterson longarms.
Raymond Baldwin Museum of Connecticut History (Gift of William H. Goldrach)

Colt Single Action Army Revolver, .45 caliber, 7.5" barrel, serial number 77778SA. This silver-plated revolver was engraved by Alvin A. White for William H. Goldrach.
Raymond Baldwin Museum of Connecticut History (Gift of William H. Goldrach)

Cased and Engraved Pair of Colt Single Action Army Revolvers, .45 caliber, 5½" barrels, serial numbers SA0001 and SA0002. Commissioned by Horace Greeley, IV, the decoration found on this pair of blued revolvers was designed by Al DeJohn and carried out by Steve Kamyk. Apart from the gold inlaid serial numbers and numerous margin bands, both pistols have inlaid rampant colt trademarks on the left side of their frames and fleur-de-lis ornament on the cylinders over each cartridge chamber. Upon completion they were boxed in a walnut case and then shipped to Mr. Greeley in care of the Service Armament Company of Ridgefield, New Jersey, on November 8, 1990.

Marvin F. Essenmacher Collection.

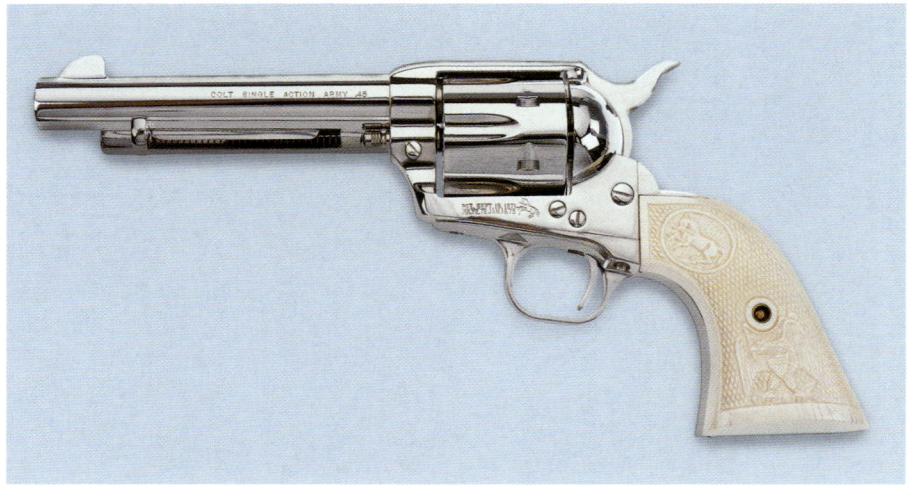

Colt Single Action Army Revolver, .45 caliber, 5½" barrel, serial number SA02600. Produced by the Colt Custom Shop in 1981, this nickel-plated revolver is unique because it was the only pistol made in this configuration to have been fitted with ivory carved with both the Colt company's rampant colt trademark and an American eagle. Records indicate that it was shipped by the factory to the Williams Gun Sight Company in Davison, Michigan, on November 4, 1981.

Craig A. Blancett Collection.

Engraved Colt Single Action Army Revolver, .45 caliber, 5½" barrel, serial number SA06408. In addition to being nickel-plated with fire-blued screws and external fittings, this revolver which was shipped on September 25, 1991, has a special order elongated grip. Factory records indicate that the Style B engraving was executed by John Adams.

Martin F. Essenmacher Collection.

Colt Sheriff's Model Single Action Revolver, .44-40 caliber, 3" barrel, serial number SA38694. It is estimated that approximately 1,275 blued and casehardened Sheriff's Model Revolvers were made between 1980 and 1993. This example was originally shipped to Aeromarine in Birmingham, Alabama on November 11, 1980.

Craig A. Blancett Collection.

Cased Pair of Colt Single Action Army Revolvers, .44-40 caliber, 4¾" barrels, serial numbers SA64907 and SA64908. Shipped on August 24, 1985, to Ashland Shooting Supplies in Ashland, Ohio, this nickel-plated pair of revolvers are fitted with special order checkered ivory grips, with fleur-de-lis terminal panels.

Craig A. Blancett Collection.

Colt Single Action Army Revolver, .357 Magnum caliber, 4¾" barrel, serial number SA54802. Originally shipped to Mathews & Boucher, Incorporated in Rochester, New York, on November 5, 1981, this revolver is finished in full nickel plate. During the production life of this model, approximately 500 revolvers were made in this style.

Craig A. Blancett Collection.

Cased Pair of Engraved Colt Single Action Army Revolvers, .44-40 caliber, 7½" barrels, serial numbers SA65247 and SA65248. Made for Stan Newman, manager of the Colt company's Parts Department, these pistols were engraved in four distinct patterns typifying work done from the firm's founding to date. Revolver number SA65247, which is gold-plated, was decorated by Dennis Kies, and the silver-plated number SA65248 exhibits the work of George Spring. The four patterns of scrollwork correspond to that cut by R. Henshaw during the 1830s, Louis D. Nimschke (ca. 1850-1900), Cuno A. Helfricht (ca. 1870-1921) and the contemporary styles used by the Colt Custom Shop. Upon completion they were boxed in a walnut case having a gold lid escutcheon engraved with the inscription "COLT ENGRAVING SAMPLERS." The pair was shipped to Richard Sherburne for Mr. Newman on December 15, 1989.

R. F. F. Collection.

Engraved Colt Single Action Army Revolver, .45 caliber, 7½" barrel, serial number SA68135. Produced as an engraving sampler by Howard Dove, this pistol is decorated with scrollwork typical of R. Henshaw (active during the 1830s), Louis D. Nimschke (ca. 1850-1900), Cuno A. Helfricht (ca. 1870-1921) and the contemporary work of the Colt Custom Shop. Factory records show that the piece was originally shipped to the Stacy Williams Company of Birmingham, Alabama, on October 24, 1987.

Craig A. Blancett Collection.

SA77770 - .44-40 caliber; 7½" barrel roll-engraved "COLT FRONTIER SIX SHOOTER," blued and casehardened finish, extended length cylinder flutes with bevelled forward edges, eagle pattern hard rubber grips.

Set of Ten Colt Single Action Army Revolvers, .44-40 and .45 caliber, 4" to 7½" barrels, serial numbers SA77770 through SA77779. As Geoffrey Chaucer wrote in his Canterbury Tales, "Pacience is an heigh vertu, certeyn" (The Franklin's Tale, line 773). First commissioned in 1988, this set of revolvers was not completed until September of 1995. During that period, the Colt company changed ownership three times, had four presidents and five different directors of its Custom Shop. Nevertheless, the project was eventually completed to everyone's satisfaction.

Paul D. Maxwell Collection.

SA77771 - as above with a 5½" barrel.

SA77774 - .45 caliber; 4¾" barrel; nickel-plated with blued screws and external fittings, Style D engraved scrollwork by Denise Thirion, ivory grips.

SA77772 - .45 caliber, 4" barrel, blued and casehardened finish, Style C engraved scrollwork by Dennis Kies, Model 1877 Double Action Revolver style backstrap, and checkered ivory grips.

SA77773 - .44-40 caliber; 4¾" barrel etched on the left side "colt frontier six shooter," blued and casehardened finish, Style D engraved scrollwork by John Adams, ivory grips.

SA77779 - .44-40 caliber; 7½" barrel etched on the left side "colt frontier six shooter," nickel-plated with blued screws and external fittings ivory grips engraved by Tom Freyburger.

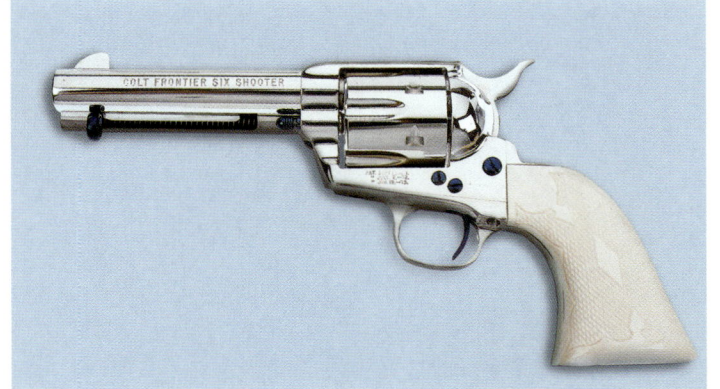 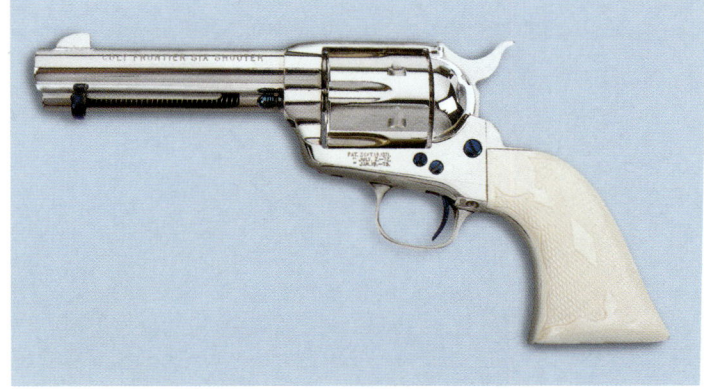

SA77777 & SA77778 - .44-40 caliber, Black powder frame, 4¾" barrels roll-engraved on their left sides "COLT FRONTIER SIX SHOOTER," nickel-plated with blued screws and external fittings, checkered ivory grips with plain fleur-de-lis terminal panels.

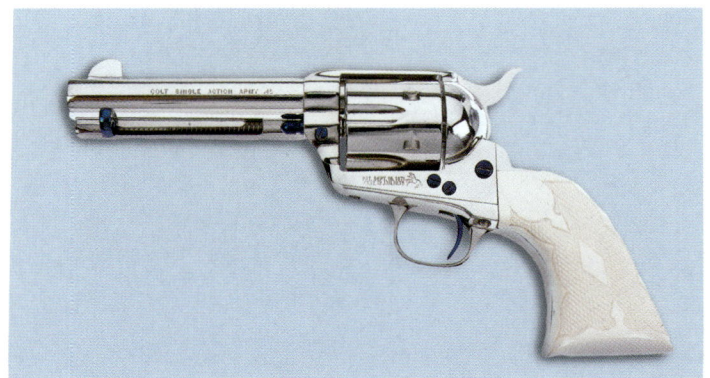 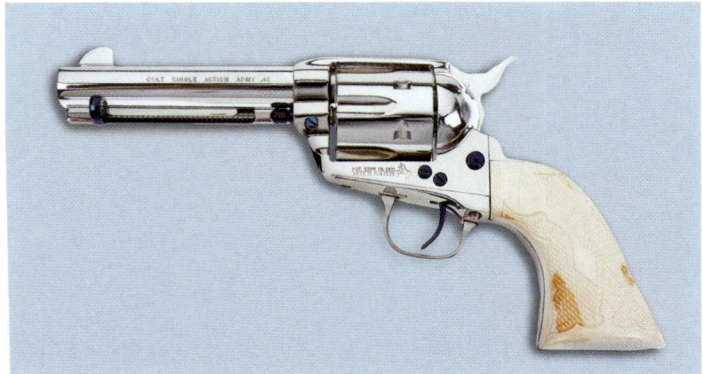

SA77775 & SA77776 - .45 caliber, 4¾" barrels, nickel plated with blued screws and external fittings, cross-bolt cylinder pin release catches, checkered ivory grips with plain fleur-de-lis terminal panels

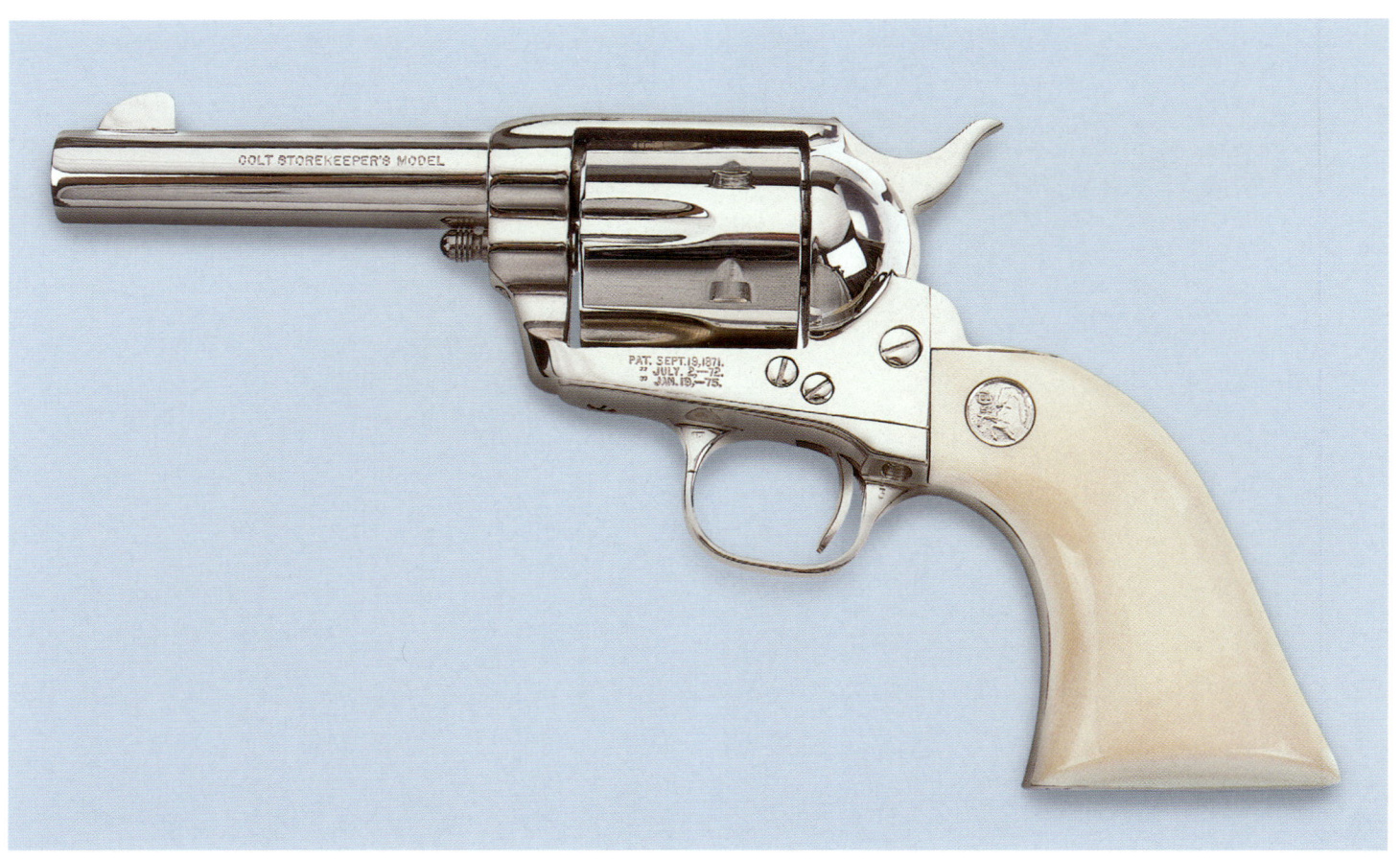

Colt Storekeeper's Model Single Action Revolver, .45 caliber, 4" barrel, serial number SA70978. This nickel-plated and ivory gripped revolver was shipped to the D.E.L. Supply Company of Tewksbury, Massachusetts on February 5, 1986. Only 96 pistols were made in this style during the model's production run from 1984 to 1993.

Craig A. Blancett Collection.

Colt Single Action Revolver, .45 caliber, 4¾" barrel, serial number SA71793. Finished in full nickel plate with blued screws and walnut grips, this revolver is skeletonized to reveal its internal mechanism, as well as construction. The tradition of the Colt company producing skeletonized arms can be traced back to the 1850s. While many were made solely for the training of the firm's assembly staff, others were used as exhibition pieces.

Craig A. Blancett Collection.

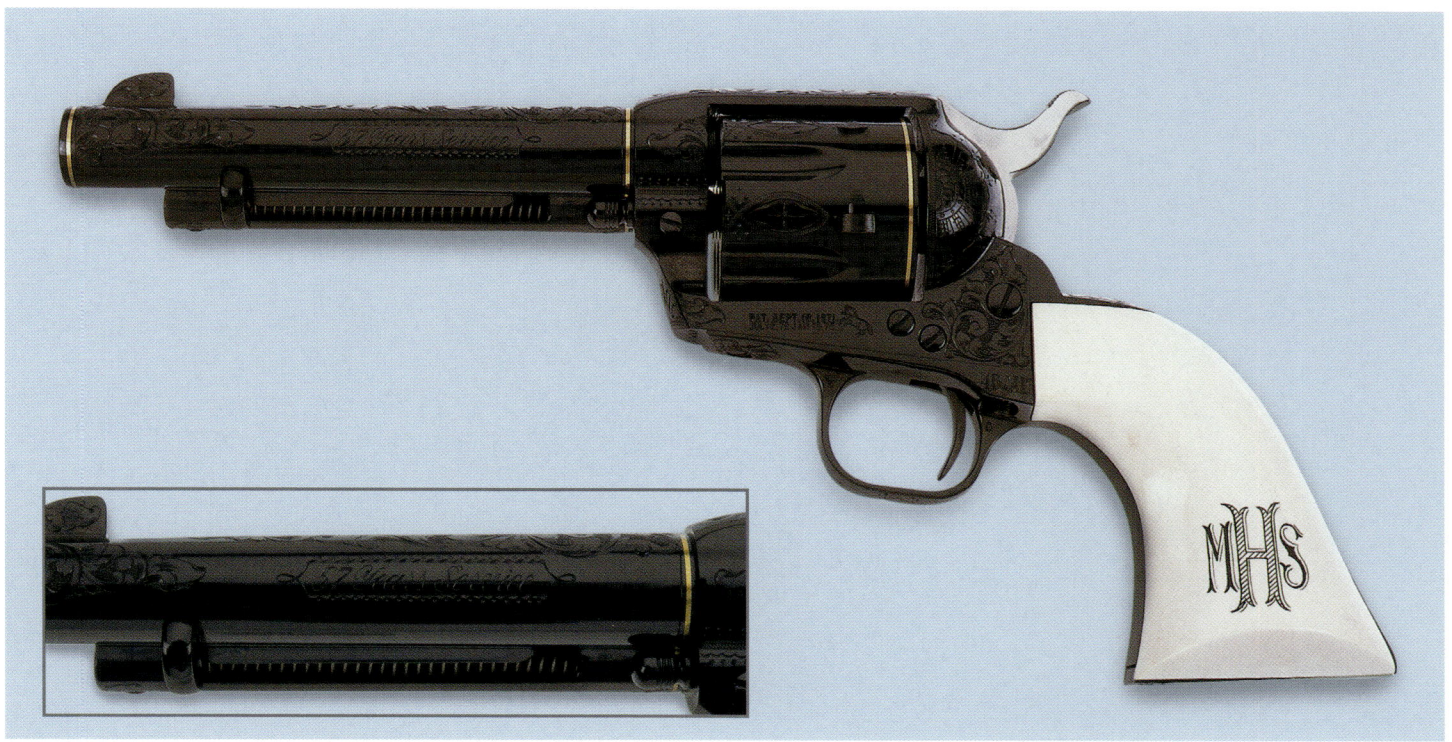

Cased and Engraved Colt Single Action Army Revolver, .45 caliber 5½" barrel, serial number S02406A. This fully blued revolver was presented to Martin S. Huber by the Colt's Manufacturing Company on June 17, 1993 as a retirement present. Huber joined the Colt company in 1936 and served as its chief historian from 1972 to 1993. In addition to the Type B "Helfricht Style" scrollwork engraved by Steve Kamyk, the pistol was decorated with the following special motifs: gold bands were inlaid on the barrel and cylinder, the barrel (inset) was roll-engraved on its left side "57 YEARS SERVICE," Huber's signature was engraved on the backstrap, and his retirement date "June 15, 1993" was inscribed on the butt strap. The ivory grips were engraved on their left side with the monogram "MSH." Prior to presentation the pistol was boxed in a walnut case with a lid escutcheon inscribed "Martin S. Huber / Historian Emeritus / 1936-1993."

David Grunberg Collection.

Engraved Colt Single Action Army Revolver, .45 caliber, 5½" barrel, serial number S06373A. Produced as a "Colt Show Gun" for exhibition at the Ohio Gun Collectors Association Show in Cleveland, Ohio, May 13-14, 2000, this nickel-plated revolver has a screwless frame. It was engraved with finely cut ink-filled Type C scrollwork by George Spring. The ebony grips are inlaid in silver with the serpentine Colt trademark on their right side. After being displayed in Ohio, the revolver together with a Colt black leather holster and belt was shipped to its present owner on June 15, 2000.

David Grunberg Collection.

Cased and Engraved Colt Single Action Army Revolver, .45 caliber, 4¾" barrel, serial number S18548A. This screwless frame, blued revolver was engraved with finely cut intertwining foliate scrollwork by Leonard Francolini in 1998. Throughout the decoration the artist accented his engraving with gold inlay work of the same pattern. In addition the patent dates and Colt trademark on the left side of the frame are inlaid in gold, as is the multi-colored image of an American eagle on the left recoil shield. The interior surface of the loading gate cut-out is inlaid in white and yellow gold with a cartridge set above the gold inscription "45LC." The hammer spur has been recontoured and engraved en suite with the remainder of the piece. The right side of the ivory grips are inlaid with a silver plaque cast in high relief with the bust of an American Bald Eagle.
David Grunberg Collection.

Cased and Engraved Colt Single Action Army Revolver, .45 caliber, 4¾" barrel, serial number S24930A. Decorated by Leonard Francolini in 2000, this screwless-framed revolver displays both intricately cut engraved scrollwork, as well as numerous gold inlays. In addition to the use of gold bands to highlight the margins of the major components, Francolini further embellished the pistol with a high relief depiction of the Colt company's trademark on the left side of the frame, an American Bald Eagle on the left recoil shield, and an American Bald Eagle on the top of the barrel surrounding the inlaid barrel inscription. The ivory grips are decorated on both sides with the Colt family's coat-of-arms inlaid in both gold and silver.
David Grunberg Collection.

Colt Single Action Army Revolver, .45 caliber, 7.5" barrel, serial number 1. This prototype for the Colt Centennial Model has silver gilt grips cast with western characters, and is inlaid in gold with vignettes illustrating the Colt factory, as well as the many nicknames given to the Single Action Army by its users (e.g., Hogleg, Plowhandle, Thumb-Buster). As with other revolvers commissioned by William H. Goldrach during his tenure as president of Colt's Firearms Division, this pistol was decorated by Alvin A. White.
Raymond Baldwin Museum of Connecticut History (Gift of William H. Goldrach)

Colt Single Action Army Revolver, .45 caliber, 4¾" barrel, serial number S28269A. This special order revolver has a combination blued and casehardened finish. In addition to the frame being casehardened, the pistol's hammer, trigger guard and backstrap are also likewise colored. Production of Colt Single Action Revolvers having serial numbers preceded by "S" and followed by "A" commenced in 1993.
Edward & Dominga Mullikin Collection.

Colt Single Action Army Revolver, .45 caliber, 7.5" barrel, serial number 2SC. Among the arms commissioned by William H. Goldrach while he was president of the Colt's Weapons Division were a series of Single Action Army Revolvers. The example shown here is an engraved and partially silver-plated Col. Saml. Colt Sesquicentennial Model produced in 1964.

Raymond Baldwin Museum of Connecticut History (Gift of William H. Goldrach)

Colt Single Action Army Revolver, .38-40 caliber, 3½" barrel, serial number S29966A. Manufactured in 1999, this nickel-plated revolver is unusual because it has a 3.5-inch barrel fitted with an cartridge ejector housing. Normally barrels of this length were not provided with this feature.

Craig A. Blancett Collection.

Engraved Colt Single Action Army Revolver, .45 caliber, 5½" barrel, serial Number CATALOG 97-1. This screwless-framed revolver was engraved and gold inlaid by Steve Kamyk for use in the Colt company's catalog, as well as display at 1997 Shot Show and Antique Arms Show both of which were held in Las Vegas, Nevada. In addition to scrollwork, the pistol has the following gold inlays: the rampant colt trademark in relief on the left side of the frame, the word "COLT" in relief on the loading gate, a portrait bust of Elizabeth Colt with her home Armsmear in the background on the right side of the frame, and a portrait bust of Samuel Colt together with a depiction of his factory on the left side of the frame. The ivory grips are fitted with gold Colt medallions.

R. F. F. Collection.

Engraved Colt Single Action Army Revolver, .45 caliber, 7½" barrel, serial number CCA1997. Produced for auction at the Colt Collectors Association annual meeting in 1997 which was held in St. Louis, Missouri, this revolver was engraved and gold inlaid by Dennis Kies. Befitting its sales venue, the gold work was designed to represent themes or scenes associated with St. Louis. The top of the barrel is decorated with a Hawken rifle and the inscription "S. Hawken," the sides of the barrel's muzzle are inlaid with 8 stars, the left recoil shield is inlaid with a peace token depicting clasped hands surrounded by the legend "Lewis & Clark 1804," a paddle wheel steamer is inlaid in relief on the right side of the frame, while a fiddle is inlaid in the same position on the left, a galena stone is set in the loading gate, the left and right sides of the frame's barrel bolster are inlaid with an outline map of Missouri and the monogram of the St. Louis Cardinal baseball team, and the backstrap is inlaid with the inscription "ST. LOUIS GATEWAY TO THE WEST."

David Grunberg Collection.

Engraved Colt Sheriff's Model Flattop Target Revolver, .41 caliber, 6" barrel, serial number CCA1999. Made for auction at the Colt Collectors Association annual meeting held in San Francisco, California, in 1999, this blued and casehardened revolver is decorated with various scenes of that city. In addition to engraved scrollwork by Tim and Christie George, in the style of Louis D. Nimschke and Gustave Young, the pistol was inlaid in gold as follows: the top of the barrel has a gold banner inscribed "CCA SAN FRANCISCO 1999," the right side of the barrel has a riband inscribed "THE CITY OF HILLS," the left and right side of the frame's barrel bolster are inlaid with an outline map of California and a California Quail, on the right side of the frame the Colt company's serpentine trademark is inlaid in gold, the loading gate is embellished with a spray of golden poppies, and the left recoil shield is inlaid with a rendering of the state's flag. The top strap of the frame is engraved and gold inlaid with an image of the Golden Gate Bridge disappearing into a fog bank. The left side of the ivory grips is carved in high relief with a nineteenth century port scene.

R. F. F. Collection

Cased and Engraved Colt Single Action Army Revolver, .45 caliber, 7½" barrel, serial number HISTORIAN NO. 1. Produced in 1986 for presentation by the Colt Collectors Association to Martin S. Huber, this blued revolver was engraved with Type C scrollwork and gold inlaid by Howard Dove after designs prepared by Al DeJohn. The barrel is inlaid with the following inscriptions: COLT HISTORIAN SPECIAL 45 (left side), 50 YEARS OF SERVICE (right side), the cylinder is inlaid with an image of the official seal of the Colt company's historian and an open shipping book, a quill pen and inkwell are found on the loading gate, and a facsimile of Huber's signature is inlaid on the backstrap. The ivory grips are engraved with Huber's monogram on their left side and the rampant colt trademark on the right. The pistol is housed in a glass top display case bearing the inscription "M. S. Huber, 50 Years of Service, 1936-1986."

David Grunberg Collection.

Cased and Engraved Colt Single Action Army Revolver, .45 caliber, 8" barrel, serial number Liberty No. 1. Commissioned by the Colt company as part of its "Great Moments of American History" series of highly embellished revolvers, Liberty No. 1 was engraved and gold inlaid by Alvin A. White. The left side of the barrel is inlaid with the series name and an American eagle in flight, while the right side is decorated with crossed pistols and the legend "Colt's Armory Hartford, Conn.," thirteen stars are inlaid on the cartridge ejector rod housing, a crowned imperial eagle with its wings displayed, as well as Lady Liberty's torch, are inlaid on the cylinder, a bust of Liberty is inlaid on the left recoil shield and the backstrap is inlaid with the inscription "Statue of Liberty Model." The left side of the grips is inlaid with a finely engraved plaque depicting the Statue of Liberty. The gold buttcap is cast and chiseled in high relief with the image of an American eagle. The pistol is cased in a leather-bound box by Arno Werner.
R. F. F. Collection.

Colt New Frontier Single Action Revolver, .38 Special caliber, 7½" barrel, serial number 4641NF. The New Frontier Revolver was first manufactured from 1961 until June of 1974. During its production life the standard finish for this series of pistols was a combination of blue and casehardening with walnut grips. Revolvers chambered for the .38 Special cartridge were only made from 1961 to 1963. As the construction of the pistol's sights suggests, the primary market envisioned for the New Frontier was target shooters.

Norm Green Collection.

Cased and Engraved Pair of Colt Single Action Army Revolvers, .45 caliber, 7½" barrels, serial numbers PBC-1 and PBC-2. The "Colt Philadelphia Bicentennial" pistols were engraved, as well as gold inlaid, jointly by Alvin A. White and Leonard Francolini. PBC-1 is inlaid with the attributes associated with the history of the United States: Molly Pitcher's cannon (left side of the frame), General Washington crossing the Delaware River (right side of the frame), an American eagle above a riband inscribed "E PLURIBUS UNUM" (left side of the barrel, an image of Independence Hall in Philadelphia, the Liberty Bell with the American flag set against the moon, a fife and drummers scene, and the inscription "200 / YEARS OF/ FREEDOM" on the cylinder. The shoulder of the backstrap is inlaid with a portrait bust of George Washington. The carved and engraved ivory grips are inlaid with an oval plaque cast and chased in high relief with a rampant colt. In addition, gold ribands decorated with fleur-de-lis are inlaid on either side of the grips. The gold buttcap is engraved with an American eagle and the inscription "AMERICA / 1776 / 1976." PBC-2 differs from the preceding in that the barrel is inlaid with a facsimile of John Hancock's signature on the right side of the barrel, an image of the U.S.S. Constitution appears on the left side of the frame, the right side of the frame is inlaid with a depiction of Paul Revere's midnight ride, and the shoulder of the backstrap is inlaid with a portrait bust of John Hancock. The pistols are boxed in a leather-bound case having a gold escutcheon engraved "American Revolution Bicentennial 1776-1976."

R. F. F. Collection.

Engraved Colt Single Action Army Revolver, .44-40 caliber, 5½" barrel, serial number RLS26CEO. Originally ordered by Ronald L. Stewart, President and Chief Executive Officer of Colt's Manufacturing Company, Inc., from July 1996 to September 1998, this revolver was not completed until he had left that position. Finished in full nickel plate, the piece was engraved by George Spring with Style D scrollwork highlighted with a baked ink. One of the more noteworthy features of the decoration is that Spring concealed the word "COLT" within the foliate scrolls in four different locations. The grips are of ivory set with silver Colt medallions.

David Grunberg Collection.

Cased and Engraved Colt Single Action Army Revolver, .45 caliber, 5½" barrel, serial number SAA1992. This fully blued, engraved and gold inlaid revolver was made for as a factory exhibition piece at the Colt Collectors Association annual meeting held in Hartford, Connecticut from October 2 to 4, 1992. It was engraved by Bryson Gwinnell with Style B scrollwork and inlaid in gold with the inscription "Colt An American Heritage" on the barrel, a portrait bust of Samuel Colt and the Armsmear crest on the cylinder, a rampant colt on the shoulder of the backstrap, and a facsimile of Samuel Colt's signature on the backstrap proper. The left side of the ivory grips was carved in high relief with an American eagle having a shield charged against its breast.

David Grunberg Collection.

Engraved Colt New Frontier Single Action Revolver, .44 Special caliber, 7½" barrel, serial number 5188NF. This revolver was engraved with foliate scrollwork by Bill Mains.

Norm Green Collection.

Cased and engraved Pair of Colt New Frontier Dual Cylinder Single Action Revolvers, .45acp caliber, 2½" barrels, serial numbers 1 ACP (5410NF) and 2 ACP (5411NF). Originally commissioned by David S. Woloch, this pair of revolvers was engraved and gold inlaid by Alvin A. White. In addition to Woloch's monogram on one recoil shield, his wife's, "J.L.W.", is inlaid on the recoil shield of the other. Factory records indicate that the scrollwork was of Class C style and that the pistols were inlaid with edging bands, the Colt company's name, as well as trademark on their frames and a facsimile signature of Samuel Colt on the topstraps. The grips and screwdriver handle are made of pieces from Connecticut's Charter Oak. Fittingly, White carved the grips with scrolling oak leaves which on the left side frame a gold escutcheon plate engraved with details concerning the tree's history. The spare cylinders are chambered for the .45 Long Colt cartridge.

R. F. F. Collection

Colt New Frontier Single Action Revolver, .45 caliber, 5½" barrel, serial number 7477NF. This blued and casehardened example was manufactured shortly before the model was discontinued in June of 1974. It is estimated that fewer than 70 third generation New Frontier revolvers of the type reintroduced in 1978 were made in 1974.

Edward & Dominga Mullikan Collection.

Engraved Colt New Frontier Single Action Revolver, .45 caliber, 7½" barrel, serial number 04136NF. In September of 1978, the New Frontier was reintroduced into the Colt company's product line with serial numbers beginning at 01001NF. The example illustrated here, which was engraved and gold inlaid by Leonard Francolini, was shipped to the Oshman's Sporting Goods company of Houston, Texas, on June 29, 1979. While the primary inlays consist of the figures of an American Black Bear on the left side of the frame and a Tule Elk on the right side, Francolini also decorated the pistol with inlaid foliate scrollwork, as well as edging bands. In addition, the barrel address was also inlaid in gold.

R. F. F. Collection.

Colt New Frontier Single Action Revolver, .45 caliber, 7.5" barrel, serial number 07713NNF.
Norm Green Collection.

BBHC Photo

Colt New Frontier Single Action Revolver, .45 caliber, 7½" barrel, serial number 10161NF. This standard production pistol manufactured in 1980, has a blued and casehardened finish, as well as walnut stocks inlaid with gold-plated Colt medallions. During the second period of its production life (1978-1984), approximately 7,400 pistols with 7.5" barrels were manufactured.

Edward & Dominga Mullikin Collection.

Colt New Frontier Single Action Revolver, .44-40 caliber, 4.75" barrel, serial number 14308NF. While the majority of the second production New Frontier Revolvers were made with 7.5" barrels, it is estimated that approximately 519 were fitted with barrels measuring 4.75" in length.
Edward & Dominga Mullikin Collection.

Colt Single Action Frontier Scout Revolver, .22rf caliber, 4¾" barrel, serial number 3294Q. Made in 1957, the first year of this model's production, the pistol shown here illustrates the "Duotone" finish employed at that time. While the barrel, ejector rod housing, cylinder and screws are blued, the alloy frame, trigger guard, as well as backstrap have a bright satin finish.
Dr. Thomas Covault Collection.

Colt New Frontier .22 Single Action Revolver, .22rf caliber, 4½" barrel, serial number G73371. Manufactured from November 1970 to 1986, the New Frontier Scout was sold with two cylinders: one chambered for .22rf Long Rifle cartridges, and; the second for .22rf Magnum. During its production life approximately 26,259 were made.
Dr. Thomas Covault Collection.

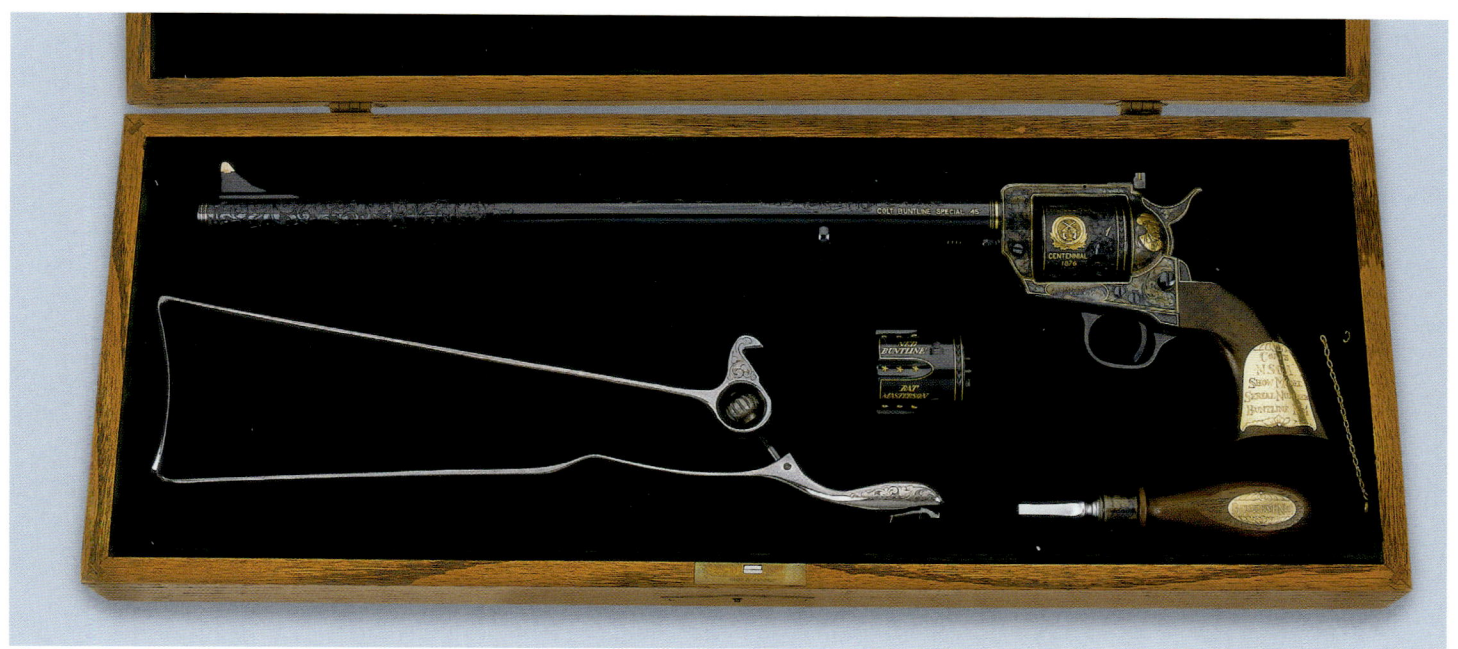

Cased and Engraved Colt New Frontier Dual Cylinder Buntline Single Action Revolver, .45 Long Colt and .45acp caliber, 16" barrel, serial number Buntline No. 1. This engraved and gold inlaid revolver was produced through the collaborative effort of Bob Burt, Leonard Francolini, Dan Goodwin and George Spring. Made for the Colt company's display at the 1976 National Sporting Goods Association Show, the pistol was decorated with Class C scrollwork and extensive gold inlays. Among the latter are portraits of Wyatt Earp (cylinder) and Ned Buntline (left recoil shield), Wyatt Earp's Dodge City Marshal's badge (loading gate), a pair of crossed revolvers surrounded by the legend "PHILADELPHIA / CENTENNIAL 1876" (cylinder), maker's details, and special serial number. The secondary cylinder is inlaid with the following names over the shoulder of each chamber: Ned Buntline, Wyatt Earp, Bat Masterson, Charlie Bassett, Bill Tilghman and Ned Brown. The silver-plated bronze shoulder stock is also engraved with scrollwork and the inscription "Colt's N.S.G.A. Show Model Serial Number Buntline No. 1." Following its use as a display piece, the revolver was shipped to Robert E. Hable on February 23, 1977.

R. F. F. Collection.

Colt Single Action Frontier Scout Revolver, .22rf caliber, 4.75" barrel, serial number 180608F. The second series of Frontier Scout Revolvers to be made had a "F" suffix to the their serial numbers. This change took place in 1958 and continued until production of the series ended in 1971.

Mark A. Green Collection.

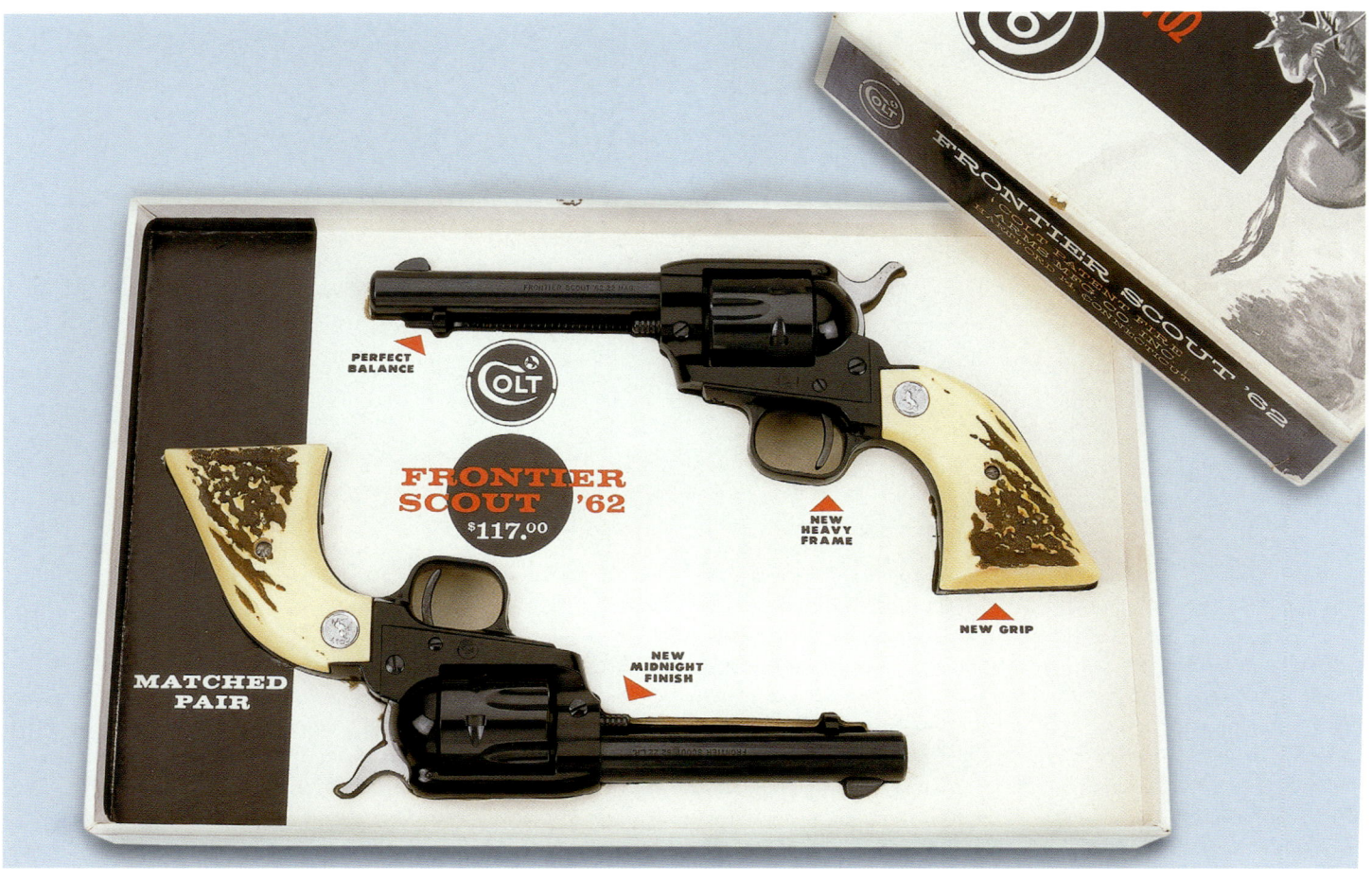

Colt Single Action Buntline Scout Revolver, .22rf Magnum caliber, 9½" barrel, serial number 24468K. Production of the "K" series of Frontier Scout Revolvers began in 1960 and continued until 1970. During that period approximately 43,987 were made. All the "K" series pistols were constructed using a heavy alloy frame. They were also all finished in full nickel plate.

Mark A. Green Collection.

Colt Single Action Buntline Scout Revolver, .22rf Magnum caliber, 9½" barrel, serial number 24468K. Production of the "K" series of Frontier Scout Revolvers began in 1960 and continued until 1970. During that period approximately 43,987 were made. All the "K" series pistols were constructed using a heavy alloy frame. They were also all finished in full nickel plate.

Mark A. Green Collection.

Colt Peacemaker .22 Buntline Single Action Revolver, .22rf caliber, 7½" barrel, serial number L08019. During 1974 the serial number prefix was changed to the letter "L". After about 23,900 revolvers had been made, the prefix was changed to the number "6". During the production run of the L-prefix series, approximately 1,195 Peacemaker Buntline revolvers having dual .22rf Long Rifle and .22rf Magnum cylinders were manufactured. All of these were made in 1974.

Dr. Thomas Covault Collection.

Colt New Frontier .22 Buntline Single Action Revolver, .22rf caliber, 7½" barrel, serial number G210968. The design of the New Frontier revolver was changed in 1982 by the addition of a cross-bolt safety located beneath the loading gate. Between 1982 and 1986, approximately 2,793 New Frontier Buntline Revolvers were made in this configuration.

Dr. Thomas Covault Collection.

Colt New Frontier .22 Single Action Revolver, .22rf caliber, 4¼" barrel, serial number G217780. The combination blue and casehardened finish seen on this pistol was standard during the first four years of this model's production.

Mark A. Green Collection.

Colt New Frontier .22 Single Action Revolver, .22rf caliber, 6" barrel, serial number G224528. Although the standard finish for this model had been blued and casehardened, problems arose with the casehardening process in 1985 which resulted in the adoption of a fully blued finish, such as that seen on this revolver.

Mark A. Green Collection.

It is likely that a great deal of the attraction held by Colt collectors for commemoratives is derived from their diversity of finish. From fully blued or nickel-plated versions to those having multiple finishes, commemoratives all delight the eye.

Authentic Colt Blackpowder Series Third Model Dragoon Pistol, .44 caliber, serial number 24609, cased with all accessories. Commissioned to celebrate the 50th Anniversary of Cherry's Sporting Goods in 1979, this reproduction Colt Third Model Holster Pistol was extensively engraved and gold inlaid by Leonard Francolini. Apart from gold bands on the barrel, cylinder and recoil shield, Francolini also inlaid the Cherry company's logo on the right side of the barrel lug. The accessories accompanying this pistol have also been engraved and many are ivory-mounted.

Kevin Cherry Collection.

2nd Generation Percussion Pistols

by Thomas A. Conroy

The success of Colt's Commemorative program during the 1960s encouraged the company to broaden its lineup of classic single action revolvers. In 1971, Colt reentered the percussion revolver market – a market dominated by company founder Samuel Colt from the 1830s to the 1860s - with commemorative versions of its famous "squareback" First Model Navy Pistol. The new revolvers honored Civil War generals Robert E. Lee and Ulysses S. Grant. The success of those offerings led to the introduction in 1972 and 1975 of standard versions of the Second Model Navy Pistol and the Third Model Holster Pistol (Third Model Dragoon). The two models and their variations were known, in house, as the C-series, the "C" prefix attesting to their commemorative origin.

The popularity of the early 1970s issues prompted Colt, in 1977, to announce an expanded lineup of 11 cap and ball models: the Whitneyville-Walker Holster Pistol, the First Model Pocket Pistol (Baby Dragoon), First through Third Holster Pistols (First through Third Dragoons), Old Model Navy Pistol (Model 1851 Navy), New Model Holster Pistol (Model 1860 Army) with rebated and fluted cylinders, New Model Navy Pistol (Model 1861 Navy), New Model Police Pistol (Model 1862 Police), New Model Pocket Pistol of Navy Caliber. They were known, collectively, as the Authentic

Pair of Authentic Colt Blackpowder Series Model 1851 Squareback Navy Revolvers, .36 caliber, serial numbers 29372S and 29373S, cased with all accessories. This pair of stainless steel reproductions were engraved with foliate scrollwork by Denise Thirion and fitted with ivory grips.
Dennis Russell Collection.

Colt Blackpowder Series™, with an "F" prefix to distinguish the new guns from earlier production. The original sub-contractor for Colt's C-series had been Val Forgett of Navy Arms. The new subcontractors for both the later C-series as well as the 2nd generation F-series pistols were Lou and Anthony Imperato of Iver Johnson.

Despite the success of the early reproductions and a strong demand for later versions, problems plagued the company. Rising production costs, marketing difficulties, quality control problems, sub-contractor squabbles and an increasingly uncertain U.S. economy during the "stagflation" period of the late 1970s and early 1980s forced Colt to call an abrupt halt to cap and ball production in 1982. Over an 11-year span, more than 88,000 2nd generation cap and ball Colts had been produced and shipped to Colt's Hartford, Connecticut, facility.

In 1993, Colt renewed the license of its previous sub-contractors, Lou and Anthony Imperato, who had founded the independent Colt Blackpowder Arms Company of Brooklyn. Production of 3rd generation percussion Colts began in 1994. For the first time in history, cap and ball Colts were assembled in New York City, a hitherto fictitious claim of many 19th century Colt barrel markings.

In addition to the 11 models produced earlier, Colt Blackpowder Arms added reproductions of the Model 1861 U.S. Rifle Musket in both standard and artillery versions, the Whitneyville-Hartford Holster Pistol, the Second Model Pocket Pistol, a short barrelled version of the New Model Police Pistol, and the No. 5 Paterson Holster Pistol in both deluxe and standard models, to its product line. A unique feature of the "Signature Series," as 3rd generation arms were named, was a facsimile of Samuel Colt's signature on either the musket trigger guard or revolver backstrap. All 3rd generation guns were shipped to the purchaser from the Brooklyn factory rather than through Colt's shipping department. More than 95,000 3rd generation guns had been produced by late 2002.

Regardless of when or where they were made, all modern percussion Colts authorized by Colt have common characteristics:

1. All were assembled, finished and inspected in the United States by Colt factory-trained craftsmen or by

Cased Authentic Colt Blackpowder Series Model 1851 Squareback Navy Revolver, .36 caliber, serial number 9479. This reproduction of the first pattern Colt Navy Pistol was manufactured from 1972 to 1982. Typical of early production examples assembled by Colt, this pistol features a lustrous blued and casehardened finish. The accessories accompanying this pistol include a powder flask, bullet mold, nipple wrench and cap box.
Jim Gefroh Collection.

Authentic Colt Blackpowder Series Model 1851 Squareback Navy Revolver, .36 caliber, serial number 25594, cased with all accessories. Built during the last period of the model's production life, this pistol was assembled and finished by Iver Johnson.
Jim Gefroh Collection.

Colt licensed sub-contractors from parts sourced abroad (principally Italy) and, to a lesser extent, the United States.

2. All feature proprietary Colt serial numbers and markings. In most cases, modern serial number ranges began again where the 19th century serial numbers had stopped.

3. Most models incorporate unique specifications (internal and external dimensions, screw thread types, nipple sizes and other manufacturing "telltales") which distinguish them from either 1st generation percussion Colts or other Colt-style reproductions.

4. All standard revolvers feature correct period-style color case-hardened frames, hammers, loading levers and plungers achieved by traditional bone and charcoal pack hardening.

5. All C and F-series guns and muskets "letter" from the Colt historian's office as genuine "Colts." No other Colt-style copies can make that claim.

2nd and 3rd generation percussion Colts are popular with shooters and collectors who appreciate their superior mechanical function, fit and finish. As replicas authorized by their original manufacturer, they are direct descendants of the famous 1st generation cap and ball Colts that made history during the mid-19th century.

Authentic Colt Blackpowder Series Model 1851 Squareback Navy Revolver, .36 caliber, serial number 29505, cased with all accessories. Approximately 500 stainless steel reproduction Model 1851 Navy Revolvers were made during the pistol's production life.

Jim Gefroh Collection.

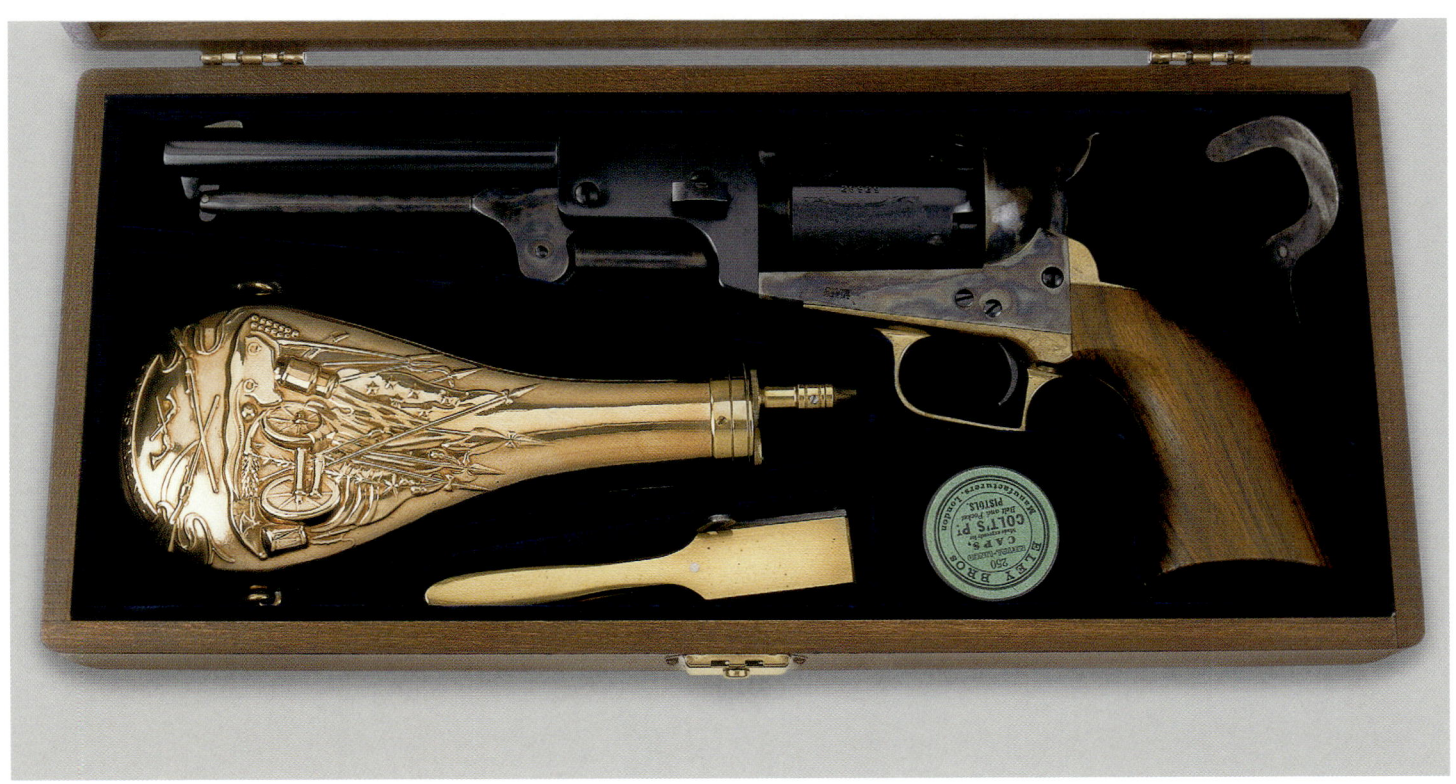

Authentic Colt Blackpowder Series First Model Dragoon Pistol, .44 caliber, serial number 26929, cased with all accessories. This reproduction of the first pattern Colt Holster Pistol is an example of the approximately 3,700 made under contract for the Colt company by Iver Johnson between 1978 and 1982.

Dennis Russell Collection.

Authentic Colt Blackpowder Series Third Model Dragoon Pistol, .44 caliber, serial number 25100, cased with all accessories. Later production pistols in this series, such as this example, were manufactured and finished by Iver Johnson for the Colt company.

Dennis Russell Collection.

Authentic Colt Blackpowder Series Fluted Cylinder Model 1860 Army Revolver, .44 caliber, serial number 207518, cased with all accessories. This reproduction of the first pattern Colt New Model Holster Pistol with a fluted cylinder was manufactured for Colt by Iver Johnson between 1978 and 1982. In all, fewer than 2,700 were made.

Dennis Russell Collection.

Authentic Colt Blackpowder Series Second Model Dragoon Pistol, .44 caliber, serial number 25745, cased with all accessories. As with the preceding example, this reproduction of the second pattern Colt Holster Pistol was made for Colt by Iver Johnson. Approximately 2,700 revolvers of this type were made between 1978 and 1982.
Dennis Russell Collection.

Authentic Colt Blackpowder Series Third Model Dragoon Pistol, .44 caliber, serial number 24067, cased with all accessories. Assembled and finished by the Colt company, this reproduction of the third pattern Colt Holster Pistol displays the lustrous blued and brightly casehardened finish commonly associated with Colt products. The Third Model Dragoon was produced between 1975 and 1982, with approximately 3,900 being made.
Jerry Bowe Collection.

Authentic Colt Blackpowder Series Model 1860 Army Revolver, .44 caliber, serial number 201835, cased with all accessories. This copy of the second pattern Colt New Model Holster Pistol having a rebated cylinder was made by Iver Johnson for Colt between 1978 and 1982. Approximately 6,300 pistols of this type were produced.
Dennis Russell Collection.

Authentic Colt Blackpowder Series Model 1860 Army Revolver, .44 caliber, serial number 211402S, cased with all accessories. During the manufacturing life of the reproduction second pattern Colt New Model Army Pistol, fewer than 1,600 examples were made in stainless steel for the Colt company by Iver Johnson.
Dennis Russell Collection.

Authentic Colt Blackpowder Series Model 1861 Navy Revolver, .36 caliber, serial number 41726. Manufactured by Iver Johnson for Colt, this revolver is accompanied by a presentation case fitted for the pistol alone. In all, slightly fewer than 3,200 New Model Navy Pistols of this type were made between 1978 and 1982.

Jerry Bowe Collection.

Authentic Colt Blackpowder Series Model 1862 Police Revolver, .36 caliber, serial number 51605, cased with all accessories. A total of 500 Colt New Model Police Pistols were produced by Iver Johnson in its 1 of 500 series.

Jerry Bowe Collection.

Authentic Colt Blackpowder Series Walker Revolver, .44 caliber, serial number 3867, cased with all accessories. A total of 2,920 reproduction Colt Whitneyville-Walker Holster Pistols were produced between 1978 and 1982.

Jerry Bowe Collection.

Sample Production Authentic Colt Blackpowder Series Model 1861 Navy Revolver, .36 caliber, serial number 43166S, cased with all accessories. In addition to the commercially available reproductions of the Colt New Model Navy Pistol Model marketed by the Colt company, a total of 6 stainless steel revolvers were manufactured by Iver Johnson for testing.

Dennis Russell Collection.

Pair of Colt Blackpowder Company Model 1849 Pocket Pistols, .31 caliber, serial numbers 49PKT and PKT49. This special order pair of reproduction Colt Pocket Pistols were assigned unique serial numbers and were engraved by Andrew Bourbon with the various styles of scrollwork typical of that found on Colt Pocket Pistols of the 1849 to 1860 period.

Tom Conroy Collection.

Authentic Colt Blackpowder Series Model 1862 Pocket Navy Revolver, .36 caliber, serial number 50855, cased with all accessories. A total of 500 Colt New Model Pocket Pistols of Navy Caliber were made by Iver Johnson for Colt with special black presentation cases.

Jerry Bowe Collection.

Authentic Colt Blackpowder Series Baby Dragoon Pistol, .31 caliber, serial number 16376, cased with all accessories. Only 500 reproductions of the Colt First Model Pocket Pistol were manufactured between 1978 and 1982.

Jerry Bowe Collection.

Authentic Colt Blackpowder Series Walker Revolver, .44 caliber, serial number PECEW-1. This reproduction of the Colt Whitneyville-Walker Holster Pistol was engraved by Alvin White for C. E. Warner, President of Colt Industries' Firearms Division from 1976 to 1981.
Tom Conroy Collection.

Authentic Colt Blackpowder Series Model 1860 Army Revolver, .44 caliber, serial number PECEW-1. This reproduction Colt New Model Army Pistol was specially engraved by Alvin White for C. E. Warner, President of Colt Industries' Firearms Division between 1976 and 1981.
Tom Conroy Collection.

Authentic Colt Blackpowder Series Model 1860 Army Revolver, .44 caliber, serial number PECEW-1. This reproduction of the Colt New Model Army Pistol with a rebated cylinder was engraved by Alvin White for C. E. Warner, President of Colt Industries' Firearms Division from 1976 to 1981.
Tom Conroy Collection.

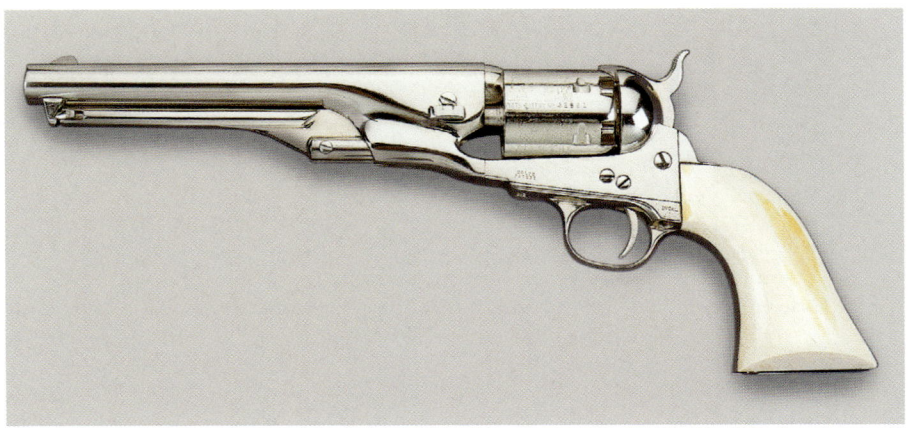

Authentic Colt Blackpowder Series Model 1861 Navy Revolver, .36 caliber, serial number 42591. This special order reproduction of the Colt New Model Navy Pistol is finished in full nickel plate and fitted with ivory grips. The backstrap is also engraved in English script with the legend: COLT'S PAT.F.A.MF.CO.
Tom Conroy Collection.

Colt Blackpowder Company Number 5 Paterson Holster Pistol, .36 caliber, serial number 4. Engraved with foliate scrollwork typical of the Paterson period, this revolver also is inlaid with gold bands on the barrel, cylinder and forward edge of the recoil shield. Fewer than 200 reproductions of this model were engraved.

Tom Conroy Collection.

Pair of Authentic Colt Blackpowder Series Model 1860 Army Revolvers, .44 caliber, serial numbers XFC6 and XFC7, cased with all accessories. This ivory-gripped pair of revolvers were engraved by John Adams, Sr., and finished in full nickel plate. Only ten reproduction Colt New Model Army Pistols were finished in this manner.

Jerry Bowe Collection.

Authentic Colt Blackpowder Series Model 1851 Squareback Navy Revolver, .36 caliber, serial number 24864, cased with all accessories. In addition to foliate scrollwork, Howard Dove engraved this reproduction Colt Second Model Navy Pistol with symbols associated with both the United States Navy and Marine Corps.

Jim Gefroh Collection.

Authentic Colt Blackpowder Series Third Model Dragoon Pistol, .44 caliber, serial number 20810. The decoration of this revolver was carried out by Tiffany & Company of New York City and executed by Leonard Francolini at the request of author R. L. Wilson. The motifs chosen were inspired by Native American artifacts in the Museum of the American Indian. The leather bound case was built by the late Arno Werner, a master bookbinder.

Tom Conroy Collection.

Cased Set of Authentic Colt Blackpowder Series Third Model Dragoon Pistol and a Colt Model 1851 Navy Revolver, .44 and .36 caliber, serial numbers 24863 and 24777. Engraved by John Adams, Sr., as well as gold inlaid with the Colt company's "Rampant Colt" trademark on their barrel lugs, these pistols are fitted with ivory grips.

Jerry Bowe Collection.

Authentic Colt Blackpowder Series Model 1851 Squareback Navy Revolver, .36 caliber, serial number 7143, cased with all accessories. This ivory-gripped reproduction was the first of this model to be engraved by Alvin White (ca. 1972) and is so marked on the grip.

Jim Gefroh Collection.

Cased Set of Authentic Colt Blackpowder Series Walker Revolver and Baby Dragoon Pistol, caliber .44 and .31, serial numbers 1902 and 16566. Produced to celebrate the Colt company's 150th anniversary, this set was engraved with four styles of engraving to reflect the work of R. Henshaw (1831); L. D. Nimschke (1850-1900); C. Helfricht (1871-1921), and; contemporary factory work. Both pistols are fitted with scrimshawed ivory grips.

Dennis Russell Collection.

Authentic Colt Blackpowder Series Walker Revolver, .44 caliber, serial number 2800, cased with all accessories. In addition to being engraved by Alvin White with finely cut scrollwork, the left side of the barrel lug features a buffalo hunting scene.

Dennis Russell Collection.

Colt Arizona Ranger Commemorative Frontier Scout Revolver, .22rf caliber, serial number 1590AR. Three thousand of these revolvers were manufactured in 1972, all of which were accompanied by a display case containing a replica Ranger's star. Barrels and cylinders were blued, while the frames were casehardened. The grips were made of walnut.

Tom Covault Collection.

Colt Commemoratives

By Kevin Cherry

Colt commemoratives first appeared on the scene in 1961 when Colt Firearms produced a special single action to commemorate the 125th Anniversary of the Colt Single Action Army revolver.

The project was very well received with Colt producing just under 7400 units. The pistols had a superior finish and were cased with a small commemorative key chain.

After such a successful project, Colt decided to offer its dealers the ability to order special roll marks, finishes and engravings on its production models in an effort to enhance sales. Two dealers stepped forward to try this new offering. Robert E.P. Cherry of Geneseo, Illinois, had Colt built a total of 104 .22 caliber deringers for the 125th anniversary of his hometown. Sig Shore of the Chicago, Illinois, area had Colt build 503 single action revolvers with short barrels in two styles of finish to commemorate the Sheriff's Model single action. Both projects were quite successful and thus the commemorative market was born.

The concept behind commemoratives, as it developed over a period of over 20 years, was to offer a good product at a fair price, limiting the production quantities to a level that was just a little less than the demand. As a result, there was an instant aftermarket on all new issues, as collectors who were unsuccessful in getting the most recent offerings immediately offered the new owners more money than they had paid for their new commemorative.

Another reason commemoratives were so successful was that they catered to the growing collectible market fueled by individuals who had ample discretionary

Colt Cherry's Sporting Goods, 35th Anniversary single action 45 and 22 scout pair was commissioned in 1964 with only 100 sets being produced. It was the only set ever made with 4" barrels on both guns and both guns being finished in an all gold plate. This particular set is serial number "2", REC2 and EPC2. The initials stood for Robert E. P. Cherry and Earl P. Cherry (founder of Cherry's in 1929). This is the lowest serial number in the hands of the general public. Each set was cased.

Kevin Cherry Collection.

income. The commemoratives offered these new collectors the opportunity to purchase an attractive weapon, in brand new condition, and with all the information they needed concerning its historical significance included in the package. The process presented far less risk than the chance of purchasing a potentially fraudulent antique piece.

These new projects offered Colt a new avenue of revenue as many collectors flocked to buy the commemorative firearms. As a result, Colt sought out the most knowledgeable dealers who dealt in commemoratives and created a commemorative committee in 1964 to discuss and offer advice on new issues. This committee continued until 1985 when it was finally dissolved.

As the late 1970s approached, Colt was faced, like many manufacturers, with lagging sales and the need to create more volume and revenue. The company began increasing the number of commemorative firearms produced in a year, as well as the quantities for each offering. As a result, there was a steady decline in commemorative collecting. Commemoratives made a large contribution to Colt's financial strength between 1961 and 1986. Colt produced over 250,000 guns during this period. In 1986, Colt built its last *bona fide* commemorative firearm.

Since that time, the excess commemoratives have disappeared and a whole new generation of collectors has evolved. Some have leaned towards antiques but many are coming back to commemoratives. With the advent of the Internet, many would-be-collectors with ample discretionary income can view these guns from the comfort of their homes and buy from the dealers who have web sites. This market continues to gain strength.

Colt Geneseo 125th Anniversay Fourth Model Deringer, .22rf caliber, serial number 87153D, together with its display case. Commissioned by Robert E. P. Cherry, the 104 Geneseo Anniversary Deringers are acknowledged today as the first commemoratives to have been commissioned by a dealer to be made by Colt.

Kevin Cherry Collection.

Colt Single Action Sheriff's Model Single Action Army Revolver, .45 caliber, serial number 0373SM. Commissioned in 1961 by Sig Shore, a Chicago arms dealer, a total of 478 blued and 25 nickel plated pistols of this type were made by the Colt company. Though not originally sold with display cases, special boxes were subsequently offered.

Earl Whitney Collection.

Colt 125th Anniversary Single Action Army Revolver, .45 caliber, serial number 1070AM. Manufactured in 1961, this was the first commemorative to be produced directly by Colt. During its production, a total of 7,390 were made. Revolvers in this series were blued with gold-plated trigger guards, backstraps and hammers. The grips were of walnut.
Bill Richman Collection.

Colt Rock Island Arsenal Single Shot Commemorative Pistol, .22rf caliber, serial number 180RIA. A total of 550 of these pistols were manufactured by the Colt company for Robert Cherry in 1962. Pistols in this series were blued and fitted with walnut grips.
Nancy Condry Collection.

Cased Set of Old Fort Des Moines Commemorative Colt Single Action Army and Frontier Scout Revolvers, .45 and .22rf caliber, both serial numbered 10. Manufactured in 1965, a total of 100 sets having gold-plated finishes and pearlite grips were produced.
Bill Richman Collection.

Cased Colt Wyatt Earp Commemorative Single Action Buntline Revolver, .45 caliber, serial number 10WYE. Featuring a 16" barrel and attachable shoulder stock, the Wyatt Earp Buntline special was produced in only limited numbers (500) in 1970. In keeping with the spirit of Earp, these commemoratives were blued and casehardened, as well as fitted with walnut grips.

Bill Richman Collection.

Authentic Colt Blackpowder Series Heritage Walker Revolver, .44 caliber, serial number 1752. Issued in conjunction with the publication of R. L. Wilson's The Colt Heritage, in 1980, approximately 1,850 revolvers of this type having a combination blued and casehardened finish with walnut grips were sold cased with Wilson's book.

Dennis Russell Collection.

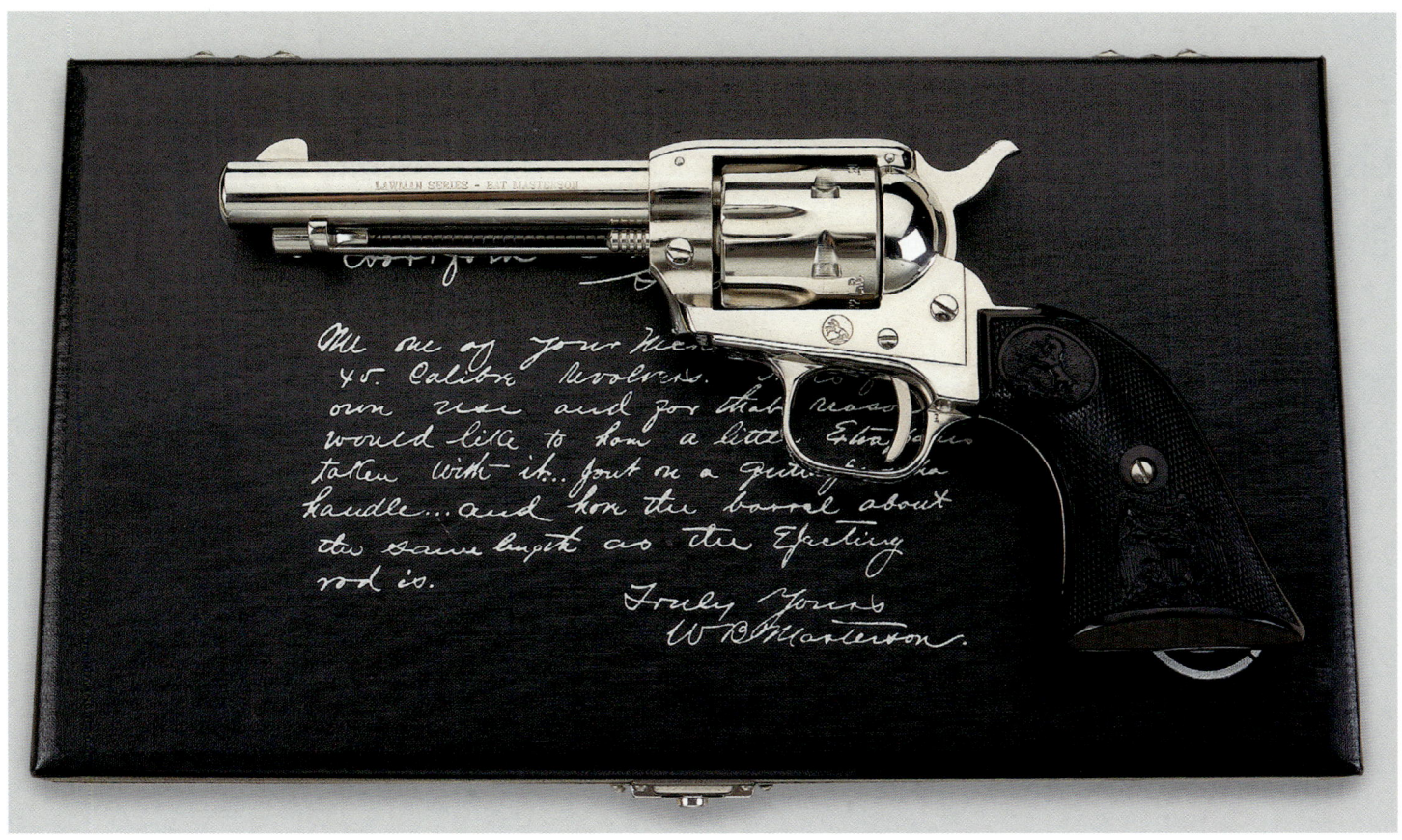

Colt Bat Masterson Commemorative Frontier Scout Revolver, .22rf caliber, serial number 1457LM. A total of 3,000 pistols in this caliber were produced in 1967. The standard finish was full nickel plate with hard rubber grips.

Tom Covault Collection.

Colt Bicentennial Three Pistol Set Consisting of a Single Action Army Revolver, Python and Authentic Colt Blackpowder Series Third Model Dragoon Pistol, .45, .357 Magnum and .44 caliber, serial numbers 909PM/PY and DG. Produced to celebrate the 200th Anniversary of the United States, a total of 1,776 Bicentennial sets were made in 1976. Cased in a three-tier case, these pistols were accompanied by a reprint of Armsmear, Henry Bernard's 1868 biography of Samuel Colt.

Bill Richman Collection.

200th Anniversary of the United States Cavalry Commemorative Authentic Colt Black Powder Series Model 1860 Army Revolvers, .44 caliber, serial numbers US1213 and 1213US. One of the few percussion commemoratives made, the 200th Anniversary U.S. Cavalry series was notable in that the pairs were accompanied by a walnut case, standard accessories and an attachable shoulder stock. Slightly over 2,974 were made in 1977.

Jerry Bowe Collection.

Colt National Rifle Association Commemorative Single Action Army Revolver, .45 caliber, serial number NRA4394. A total of 6,950 revolvers were issued to celebrate the N.R.A's. 100th anniversary in 1971. Available in either .357 Magnum or .45 caliber, these pistols were offered in three barrel lengths (4¾"; 5½", and; 7½").

Joe Pittenger Collection.

Colt Golden Spike Commemorative Frontier Scout Revolver, caliber .22rf, serial number 30GS. One of the most successful of Colt's commemoratives, a total of 10,965 Frontier Scout Golden Spike Revolvers were produced in 1969. Revolvers in this series were blued with gold-plated cylinders, trigger guards, backstraps, hammers and ejector housings. The grips were of pearlite.

Bill Richman Collection.

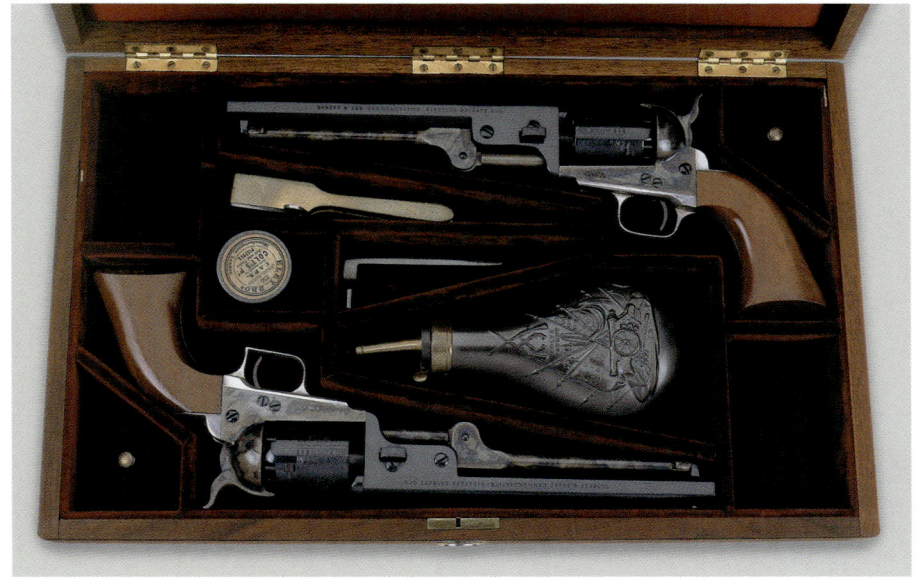

Cased Pair of Ulysses S. Grant and Robert E. Lee Commemorative Model 1851 Navy Pistols, .36 caliber, serial numbers 211GLP and 211LGP. While approximately 4,500 individual revolvers of this type were assembled and finished by Colt in 1971, only 250 sets were cased as pairs. The standard finish was blue with casehardened frames and walnut grips.

Jim Gefroh Collection.

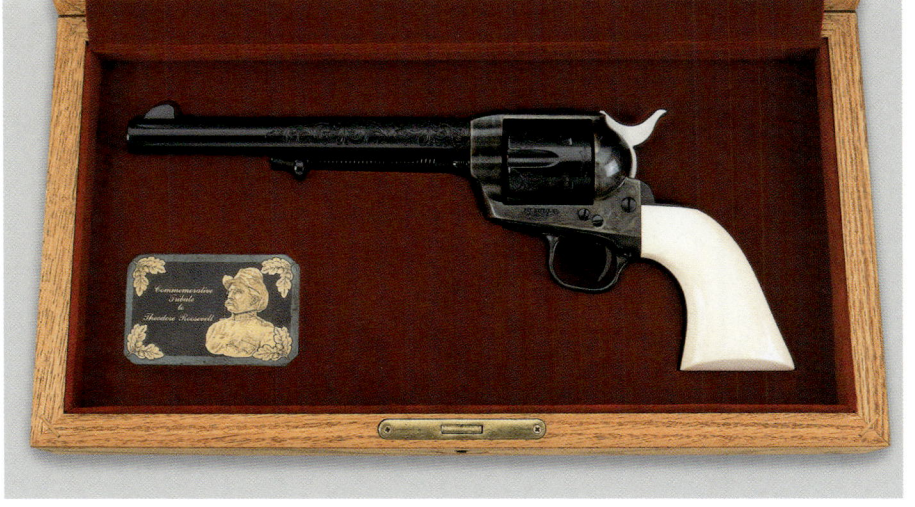

Colt Theodore Roosevelt Commemorative Single Action Army Revolver, .44-40 caliber, serial number TRC010. Produced in 1984, the 500 revolvers in this series all featured a blued and casehardened finish; factory engraving, and; ivory grips. They were also accompanied by an oak display case.

Rich Walker Collection.

Colt Kansas Statehood Commemorative Frontier Scout Revolver, .22rf caliber, serial number 006G. Produced in 1961, a total of 6,197 revolvers were made in this series which had a full gold-plated finish, as well as walnut grips.
Bill Richman Collection.

Colt New Mexico Golden Anniversary Commemorative Frontier Scout Revolver, .22rf, serial number NMA009. A total of 1,000 revolvers of this type were manufactured in 1962. Accompanied by a display case containing a medallion, this commemorative had a combination blued and gold-plated finish together with walnut grips.
Bill Richman Collection.

Colt West Virginia Statehood Commemorative Frontier Scout Revolver, .22rf caliber, serial number WV109. Issued in 1962, a total of 3,451 revolvers of this type with a combination blued and gold-plated finish were manufactured to honor the 100th anniversary of West Virginia's statehood.
Bill Richman Collection.

Colt Arizona Territory Centennial Commemorative Single Action Army Revolver, .45 caliber, serial number 594AC. Issued in 1963, only 1,264 revolvers were produced in this caliber. This model was furnished with a blued barrel and frame; gold-plated cylinder, trigger guard, backstrap and hammer; with pearlite grips.
Bill Richman Collection.

Colt Carolina Charter Tercentenary Commemorative Frontier Scout Revolver, .22rf caliber, serial number 400CT. A total of 550 revolvers were manufactured in 1963 to mark the 300th Anniversary of Carolina's original charter. In contrast to other commemoratives, a gold-plated finish was used to accent only the trigger guards, backstraps and hammers of this model.
Bill Richman Collection

Colt Idaho Territorial Centennial Commemorative Frontier Scout Revolver, .22rf caliber, serial number 0153TC. Issued in 1963, a total of 902 revolvers of this type were manufactured. All were accompanied by a display case.
Bill Richman Collection

Colt Nevada Statehood Commemorative Frontier Scout Revolver, .22rf caliber, serial number 1122NS. A total of 4,747 revolvers were manufactured in this series which was issued in 1964. This model was furnished with a combination blued and nickel-plated finish with pearlite grips and a display case.
Bill Richman Collection.

Colt Nevada Statehood Commemorative Single Action Army Revolver, .45 caliber, serial number 1122NC. Offered in several styles, the present example illustrates the standard .45 caliber version with a combination blued and nickel-plated finish of which 2,450 were made in 1964. All of the revolvers in this series were supplied with a display case containing a medallion.
Bill Richmann Collection.

Colt Montana Territorial Commemorative Frontier Scout Revolver, .22rf caliber, serial number 0749MF. Issued in 1964, the production run for this model totaled 2,296 revolvers, all of which had a combination blued and gold-plated finish with pearlite grips.

Bill Richman Collection

Colt Montana Territory Commemorative Single Action Revolver, .45 caliber, serial number 0749MA. A total of 850 revolvers of this type with a blued and casehardened finish were manufactured in 1964. Despite its low production, the model was shipped with two different styles of grips, pearlite and walnut.

Bill Richman Collection.

Colt Wyoming Diamond Jubilee Commemorative Frontier Scout Revolver, .22rf caliber, serial number 1220DJ. A total of 2,356 revolvers were made during the 1964 production run of this model. The standard finish consisted of a blued barrel and frame; nickel-plated cylinder, trigger guard, backstrap and hammer. The grips were made of pearlite.

Bill Richman Collection.

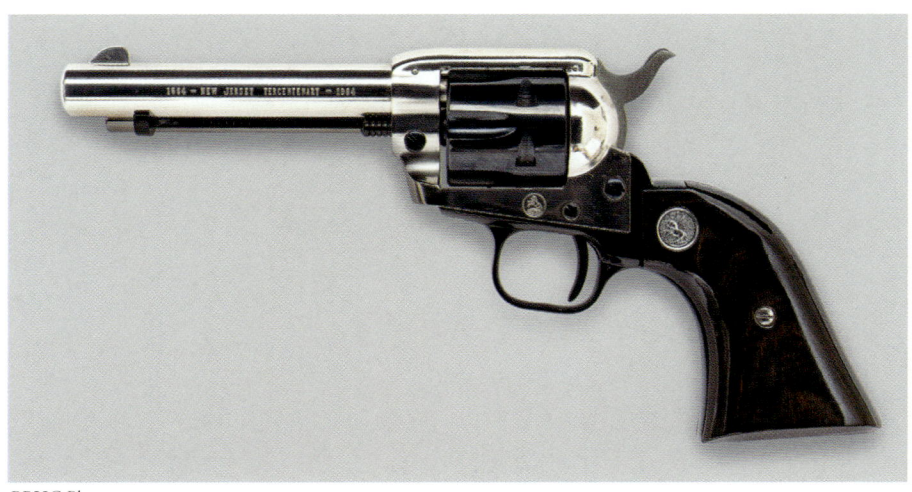

Colt New Jersey Tercentenary Commemorative Frontier Scout Revolver, .22rf caliber, serial number 0001NJ. This model was issued in 1964 and had a production run of 1,000 units, all of which had a combination nickel-plated and blued finish with laminated rosewood grips.

Bill Richman Collection

Colt St. Louis Bicentennial Commemorative Frontier Scout Revolver, .22rf, serial number 0078SL. Issued in 1964, this model had a total production of 1,051 revolvers. In common with other limited production pistols of this type, the St. Louis Frontier Scouts were supplied with a combination blued and gold-plated finish. Their grips were of imitation rosewood.

Bill Richman Collection

Colt Chamizal Treaty Commemorative Single Action Army Revolver, .45 caliber, serial number 0004CP. Issued in 1964 to recognize the treaty of Chamizal between the Mexico and the United States, only 100 revolvers were produced in this caliber. All had a combination blued gold-plated finish with pearlite grips.

Bill Richman Collection.

Colt Oklahoma Diamond Jubilee Commemorative Frontier Scout Revolver, .22rf caliber, serial number 1142OK. A total of 1,343 blued and gold-plated combination finish revolvers were built in this series which was issued in 1966. All were fitted with laminated rosewood grips and accompanied by display cases.

Bill Richman Collection.

Colt Dakota Territory Commemorative Frontier Scout Revolver, .22rf caliber, serial number 26DT. Manufactured in 1966, the production run for this model was limited to 1,000 revolvers. While the barrels, frames and cylinders were blued, gold plate was used to accent the trigger, trigger guard, backstrap and hammer. Grips were made of laminated rosewood.

Bill Richman Collection.

Colt Indiana Sesquicentennial Commemorative Frontier Scout Revolver, .22rf, serial number 1119IS. A total of 1,745 of these revolvers were manufactured in 1966 to celebrate the 150th Anniversary of Indiana's statehood. All were supplied with a display case.

Tom Covault Collection

Colt California Gold Rush Commemorative Single Action Army Revolver, .45 caliber, serial number 0006GP. A total of 130 of these gold-plated revolvers having simulated ivory grips were manufactured by Colt in 1966. In common with other commemoratives, they were accompanied by a display case.

Bill Richman Collection.

Colt Bat Masterson Lawman Series Commemorative Single Action Army Revolver, .45 caliber, serial number 90LMP. Issued as part of a series devoted to western lawmen, 500 Bat Masterson .45 caliber revolvers were manufactured in 1967. Standard finish was full nickel plate with hard rubber grips.

Bill Richman Collection

Colt Alamo Commemorative Single Action Army Revolver, .45 caliber, serial number 119A45. A total of 1,000 revolvers in this caliber were manufactured in 1967. The standard finish consisted of a blued barrel and frame with a gold-plated cylinder, trigger, trigger guard, backstrap and hammer.

Bill Richman Collection

Colt Nebraska Centennial Commemorative Frontier Scout Revolver, .22rf, serial number 65NEB. Commissioned in 1967, a total of 6,999 revolvers of this type having a combination blued and gold-plated finish with pearlite grips were produced for sale.
Bill Richman Collection

Colt Pat Garrett Lawman Series Commemorative Single Action Army Revolver, .45 caliber, serial number 10PGP. A total of 500 gold and nickel plated revolvers of this caliber were produced in 1968 as part of Colt's Lawman Series. All had pearlite grips and were sold with a display case.
Bill Richman Collection.

Colt Alabama Sesquicentennial Commemorative Frontier Scout Revolver, .22rf caliber, serial number 4AS. Manufactured in 1969, this model had a production run of 2,998 revolvers.
Bill Richman Collection

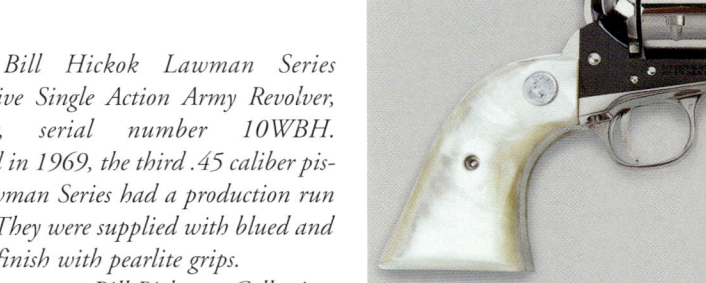

Colt Wild Bill Hickok Lawman Series Commemorative Single Action Army Revolver, .45 caliber, serial number 10WBH. Manufactured in 1969, the third .45 caliber pistol in the Lawman Series had a production run of 500 units. They were supplied with blued and nickel-plated finish with pearlite grips.
Bill Richman Collection.

Colt Texas Ranger Commemorative Single Action Army Revolver, .45 caliber, serial number 973TR. One of the more distinctive commemoratives produced by Colt, the 1970 Texas Ranger series are accompanied by a reverse cowhide bound history of the Rangers, as well as a ranger's badge imbedded in Lucite. A total of 1,000 were produced.
Tom Covault Collection.

Colt Maine Sesquicentennial Commemorative Frontier Scout Revolver, .22rf caliber, serial number 10MES. A total of 2,987 revolvers in this series were manufactured in 1970. The pistols in this series were made with a combination gold and nickel-plated finish. Included in their display cases was a gold-plated lobster paperweight honoring Maine's most famous seafood product.
Bill Richman Collection

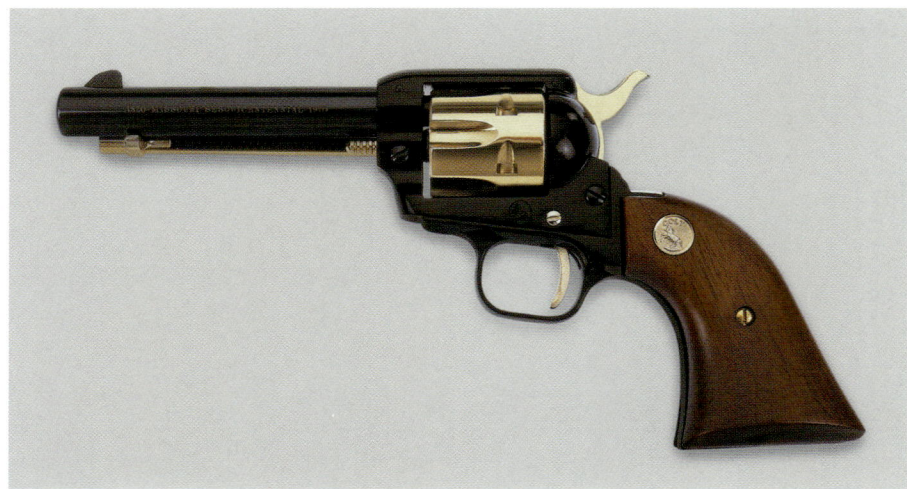

Colt Missouri Sesquicentennial Commemorative Frontier Scout Revolver, .22rf caliber, serial number 498MOS. Production of this model made in 1970 was limited to 2,975 pistols, all of which had a combination blued and gold-plated finish. The display cases made for this commemorative were of the vertical type and were supplied with a commemorative medallion.
Bill Richman Collection.

Colt Missouri Sesquicentennial Commemorative Single Action Army Revolver, .45 caliber, serial number P498MOS. A total of 888 revolvers with a combination blued and gold-plated finish were made in this caliber in 1970. A vertical display case accompanied these pistols instead of the normal flat type.
Bill Richman Collection.

Colt Florida Sesquicentennial Commemorative Frontier Scout Revolver, .22rf caliber, serial number 1824FLA. Featuring a distinctive casehardened frame and cypress grips, a total of 1,996 revolvers of this type were manufactured in 1972.
Tom Covault Collection

Colt John Wayne Commemorative Single Action Army Revolver, .45 caliber; serial number CJWC1984. Offered in Standard, Deluxe and Presentation grades, this example is one of the 3,100 standard production versions having a blued finish, as well as an oak display case. The John Wayne Commemorative was made in 1982.
Tom Covault Collection.

Colt Buffalo Bill Wild West Show Centenary Commemorative Single Action Army Revolver, .45 caliber, serial number CBBC0004. Only 283 revolvers were produced in this series which was issued in 1983. The standard finish was blued with a casehardened frame and walnut grips.
Bill Richman Collection.

Colt Texas Sesquicentennial Commemorative Single Action Army Revolver, .45 caliber, serial number TX0004. Fitted with ivory grips and accompanied by a presentation case, 1,000 revolvers of this caliber were manufactured in 1986.
Bill Richman Collection.

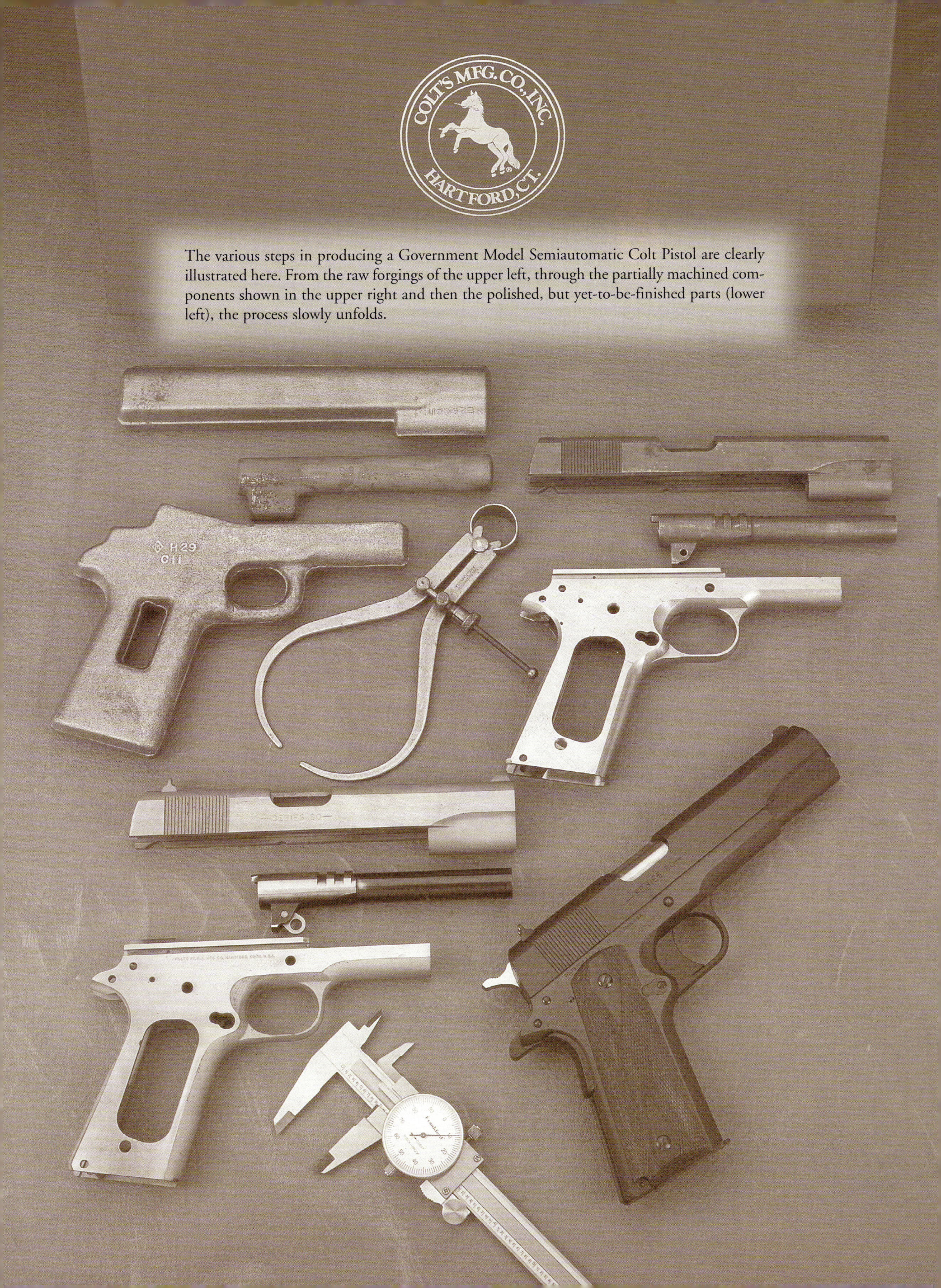

The various steps in producing a Government Model Semiautomatic Colt Pistol are clearly illustrated here. From the raw forgings of the upper left, through the partially machined components shown in the upper right and then the polished, but yet-to-be-finished parts (lower left), the process slowly unfolds.

At first glance it is difficult to imagine that the blued and casehardened revolver pictured at right started its life as a series of the rather ugly gray castings seen at left. Yet, it is from those castings that the Colt company works its magic in transmuting raw steel into a pistol having elegant lines and vibrant colors.

Current Production Models
by Kathleen J. Hoyt

Just as Samuel Colt's Hartford factory supplied arms to a broad spectrum of civilian and military clients, the Colt's Manufacturing Company of today continues that tradition. From its new home in West Hartford, Connecticut, not many miles from Samuel Colt's armory, the firm supplies customers worldwide.

One hundred and thirty three years after its introduction, the Colt™ Single Action Army® revolver remains in production, albeit in an improved form. Now in its third incarnation, the Single Action Army revolver is highly prized by recreational shooters, re-enacters and those who merely appreciate the revolver's long, as well as illustrious, history.

The company also manufactures a series of pistols based upon John M. Browning's Model 1911 Government Model® pistol. Available in various calibers, these pistols are marketed under the trade names Commander®, Defender™, Gold Cup™ and XSE™ series. Designed for personal defense and target shooting, these models have attracted a considerable following in the United States.

Another legendary model, the double action Python® revolver, likewise has been continued. Long-regarded as one of the finest centerfire handguns ever made, the Python is produced in a variety of forms meeting the requirements of competitive shooters, law enforcement officers and sportsmen in general.

The present Colt company also manufactures semi-automatic versions of the U.S. M4 and M16 series of rifles which were first made by Colt during the 1960s. Popular with police forces worldwide, light game hunters and marksmen, these models have proved to be a profitable addition to the firm's product line.

As in the past, Colt's Manufacturing Company emphasizes the production of quality products designed to meet the needs of a diverse clientele. In doing so it can be truly said that the firm meets the standards set by its founder, Samuel Colt.

Colt Single Action Army Revolver, .45 caliber, 4¾" barrel, serial number S33878A. This blued and casehardened revolver fitted with hard rubber grips embossed with the American eagle motif represents a direct tie to the Colt Manufacturing Company's past. Manufactured to the highest possible standards, the current production Single Action is a worthy successor to its illustrious predecessor.

Colt Archive Properties LLC Collection.

Colt Single Action Army Revolver, .45 caliber, 5½" barrel, serial number S33934A. Finished in the same manner as the original Single Action Army Revolvers, this pistol allows firearm enthusiasts of today the opportunity to own and fire a pistol that has become a symbol of America's past.

Colt Archive Properties LLC Collection.

Colt Cowboy Single Action Revolver, .45 caliber, 5½" barrel, serial number TF13487. Designed for use by re-enactors, as well as competition shooters, this revolver is an affordable and well-made reproduction of the original Colt Single Action Army Revolver.

Colt Archive Properties LLC Collection.

Colt Python Elite Double Action Revolver, .357 Magnum / .38 Special caliber, 6" barrel, serial number PE05104. Since the Python model was introduced in 1955, it has earned an enviable reputation for accuracy and durability. The current version, like the stainless steel and walnut gripped example illustrated here, demonstrates the Colt Manufacturing Company's commitment to continuing the tradition.

Colt Archive Properties LLC Collection.

Colt Government Model 1991 A1® Automatic Pistol, .45 caliber, 5" barrel, serial number 2807131. The latest version of the venerable Model 1911A1 has a matte black finish and is fitted with checkered rosewood grips.

Colt Archive Properties LLC Collection.

Colt Government Model 1991 Automatic Pistol, .45 caliber, 5" barrel, serial number CV22302. Constructed from stainless steel and fitted with hard rubber grips, this model represents a totally modern and utilitarian interpretation of the famous Colt Government Model.
    Colt Archive Properties LLC Collection.

Colt Government Model 1991 Automatic Pistol, .45 caliber, 5" barrel, serial number SS31136E. Introduced in 2002, this pistol features forward and rear sets of slide serrations; a reduced weight trigger; rounded hammer, as well as an ambidextrous safety. The use of stainless steel in conjunction with checkered rosewood also gives the pistol an aesthetically pleasing appearance.
    Colt Archive Properties LLC Collection.

Colt Special Combat Government Model Automatic Pistol, .45 caliber, 5" barrel, serial number SCGA2029. Designed to meet the needs of serious handgun users, this model is furnished with either a blued or satin nickel finish. The elongated slot hammer, extended ambidextrous safety, special grips and magazines with bumpers, all contribute to this pistol's effectiveness.
    Colt Archive Properties LLC Collection.

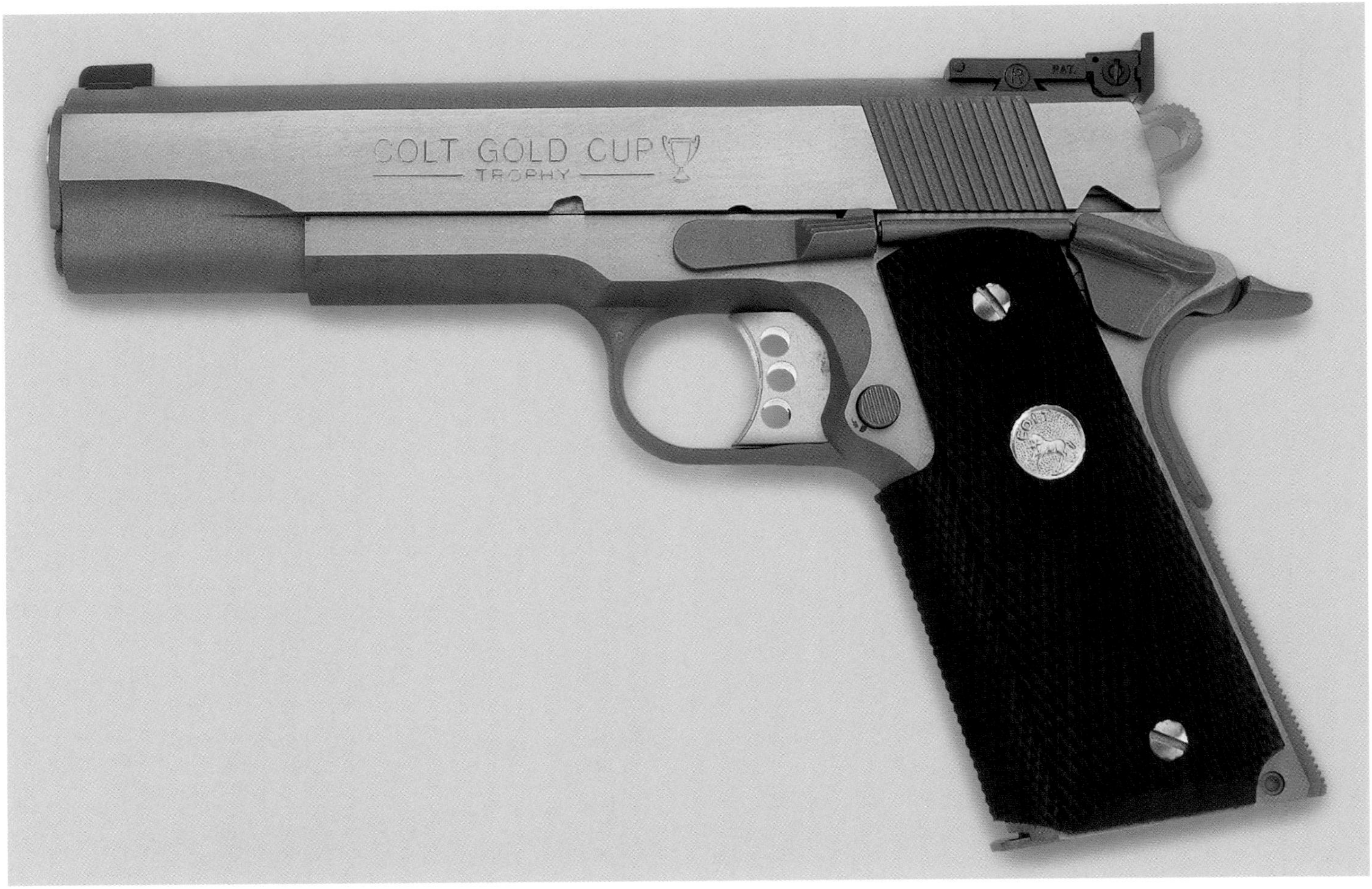

Colt Gold Cup Trophy Automatic Pistol, .45 caliber, 5" barrel, serial number GCT11689. This stainless steel pistol made by the Colt Custom Shop is an extremely accurate target pistol fitted with a Bomar-style rear sight.

Colt Archive Properties LLC Collection.

Colt Gold Cup Trophy Automatic Pistol, .45 caliber, 5" barrel, serial number GCT11584. Introduced in 1997, this blued version of the Colt company's famous Gold Cup series of pistols is made on special order by the Colt Custom Shop to insure the highest degree of accuracy.

Colt Archive Properties LLC Collection.

Colt Commander Model Automatic Pistol, .45 caliber, 4¼" barrel, serial number CJ30051. Introduced in 1999, this stainless steel pistol is a shorter version of the Government Model 1991 featuring a reduced length slide and barrel.
Colt Archive Properties LLC Collection.

Colt Commander Model Automatic Pistol, .45 caliber, 4¼" barrel, serial number FC26257E. This stainless steel pistol is a reduced size version of the Government Model 1991 having dual slide serrations, a reduced weight trigger, ambidextrous safety and slotted hammer.
Colt Archive Properties LLC Collection.

Colt Commander Model Automatic Pistol, .45 caliber, 4¼" barrel, serial number CJ30202. Finished in a matte black and fitted with Colt's signature double diamond checkered rosewood grips, this pistol was introduced into the company's product line in 1993.
Colt Archive Properties LLC Collection.

Colt Lightweight Commander Model Automatic Pistol, .45 caliber, 4¼" barrel, serial number FL08958E. Introduced in 2000, this pistol has a stainless steel finish, checkered rosewood grips, dual slide serrations and various weight reduction features.

Colt Archive Properties LLC Collection.

Colt Match Target® Competition H BAR® Semiautomatic Rifle, .223 Remington caliber, 20" barrel, serial number CCH033633. This heavy barrel version of the company's famous AR-15A2 is designed for competition target shooting. In contrast to the AR-15A2 it has a flattop receiver with a detachable carrying handle and nylon stock.

Colt Archive Properties LLC Collection.

Colt Defender Model Automatic Pistol, .45 caliber, 3" barrel, serial number DR24704. In 1998 the Colt company introduced this pocket-sized version of the Government Model that has wrap-around rubber grips with finger grooves.

Colt Archive Properties LLC Collection.

Colt AR-15®A3 Tactical Carbine, .223 Remington caliber, 16⅛" barrel, serial number LBD015751. Designed for police use, this compact firearm is fitted with a 4-position adjustable telescopic sight and a heavy weight short barrel.

Colt Archive Properties LLC Collection.

Collecting extends beyond guns for lovers of Colt. Coltiana or Colt memorabilia ranges from original Samuel Colt letters and instruction manuals to movie posters to bows and arrows. Collectors have accumulated photographs, comic books, and video tapes. It's an almost unlimited pursuit.

One of a set of 10 William Boyd lobby cards. The 1943 film Colt Comrades starred William Boyd as Hopalong Cassidy. Robert Mitchum also appeared in the film but wasn't a big enough star to appear on the lobby card.

Robert Hartman Collection.

Colt Memorabilia

by Karen Green

In common with most manufacturing companies, Colt has always concentrated its efforts on what the firm made, rather than how it did it. As a result, once a product line was discontinued, the general records concerning the specifics of that item or any programs associated with its sale were viewed as being of little significance. While some information was placed into the company's archives, most of what existed was consigned to the trash. In doing so, however, the firm inadvertently created a market for the material that survived.

Given the fugitive nature of paper records, be they advertising material, incoming and outgoing correspondence, engineering drawings or sales ledgers, it is not surprising that little has survived concerning Colt's 19th century operations. Yet, those pieces that do exist are highly sought-after as mementos of Samuel Colt's genius.

Particularly prized are those items that can be tied directly to the inventor himself. While few in number, pieces of his porcelain and silver services do remain in collectors' hands. Letters bearing his signature are more commonly encountered, though it should be noted that usually the bodies of those texts were written by his secretary. Nonetheless, they provide an immediate link to the man and his time.

Apart from material relating to Samuel Colt or his revolvers, collectors can also seek out memorabilia associated with the diverse products that were made in the

Ehbets patent, wood model circa 1880. *Connecticut State Library Collection.*

Colt works during the 19th century. In many ways this field is almost limitless as the Colt company either made or provided the space to independent contractors for the manufacture of such diverse items as lawn mowers, sewing machines, typesetters, tools, and steam engines, all of which were marked as having been built at the Colt armory.

Following World War I the Colt company diversified and began producing items made of thermoplastic bakelite. Items from this period, such as cigarette boxes, thermoses and electrical outlets, bearing the tradenames "Coltrock," "Coltstone" or just the Colt trademark, form a highly interesting class of collectibles.

The modern era has seen an increase in the number of pieces emblazoned with the Colt name. These items range from toy pistols made by the Hubley Company under license in the 1950s, to sporting goods manufactured by the Colt company itself in the 1960s. In addition, the name and rampant colt logo have been used on any number of other products that have been produced by firms catering to the collector market.

The study of "Coltiana" or Colt company memorabilia can provide students of the marque with countless hours of enjoyment. More importantly, it also provides a glimpse into the concern's past.

Due to the breadth and complexity of the field, collectors have become somewhat specialized. In general, enthusiasts now pursue items in the following broad categories.

1 - Personal items that belonged to Samuel Colt and his family, or letters and calling cards bearing his name.

2 - Factory related material such as correspondence; internal memoranda; newsletters; production dies, gauges and tools; or special awards.

3 - Advertising materials including broadsides; brochures; catalogues; dealer displays; operating instructions; posters, and; promotional items distributed by the company at trade shows.

4 - Commercially distributed collectibles bearing the Colt name.

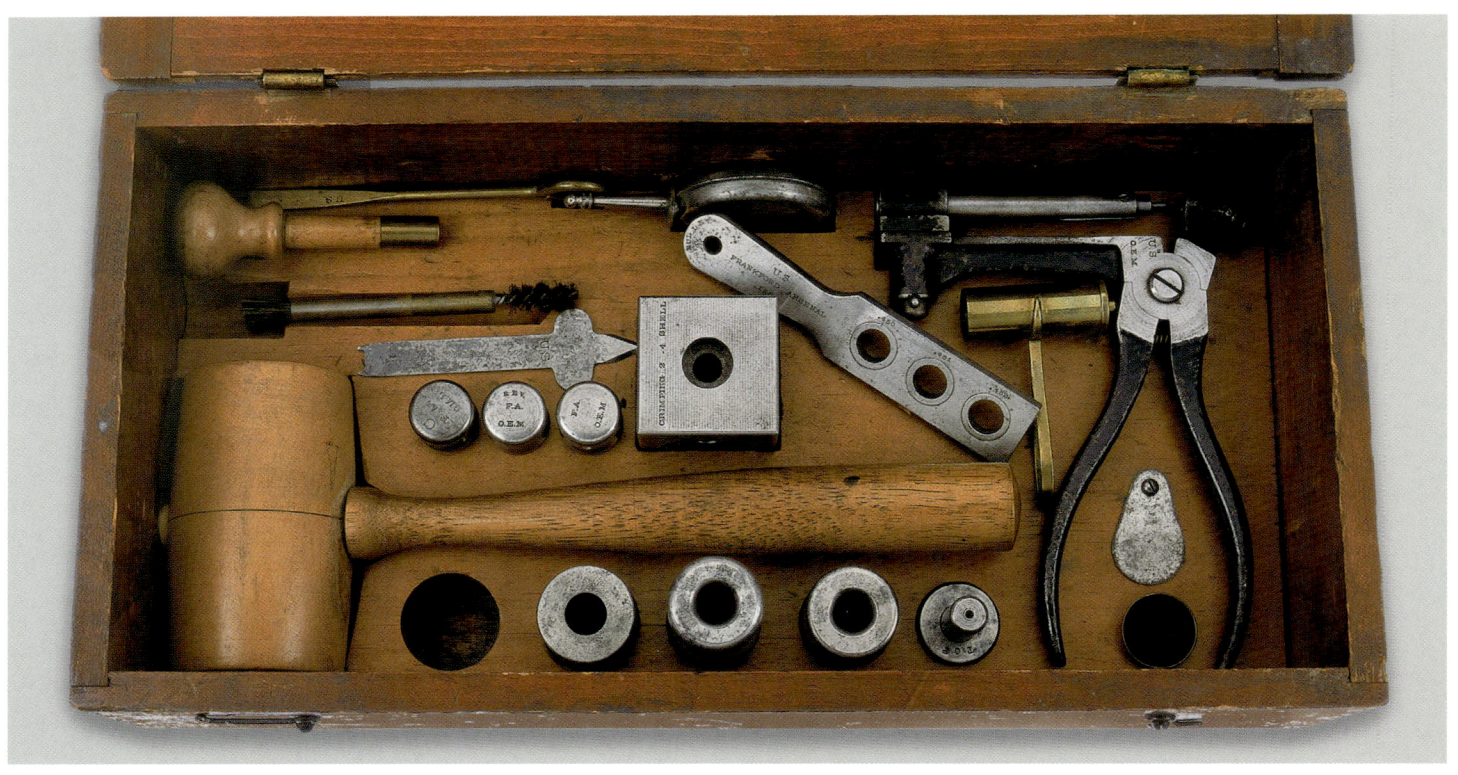

Model 1882 Frankford Arsenal Field Ammunition Reloading Kit. *Richard Burdick Collection.*

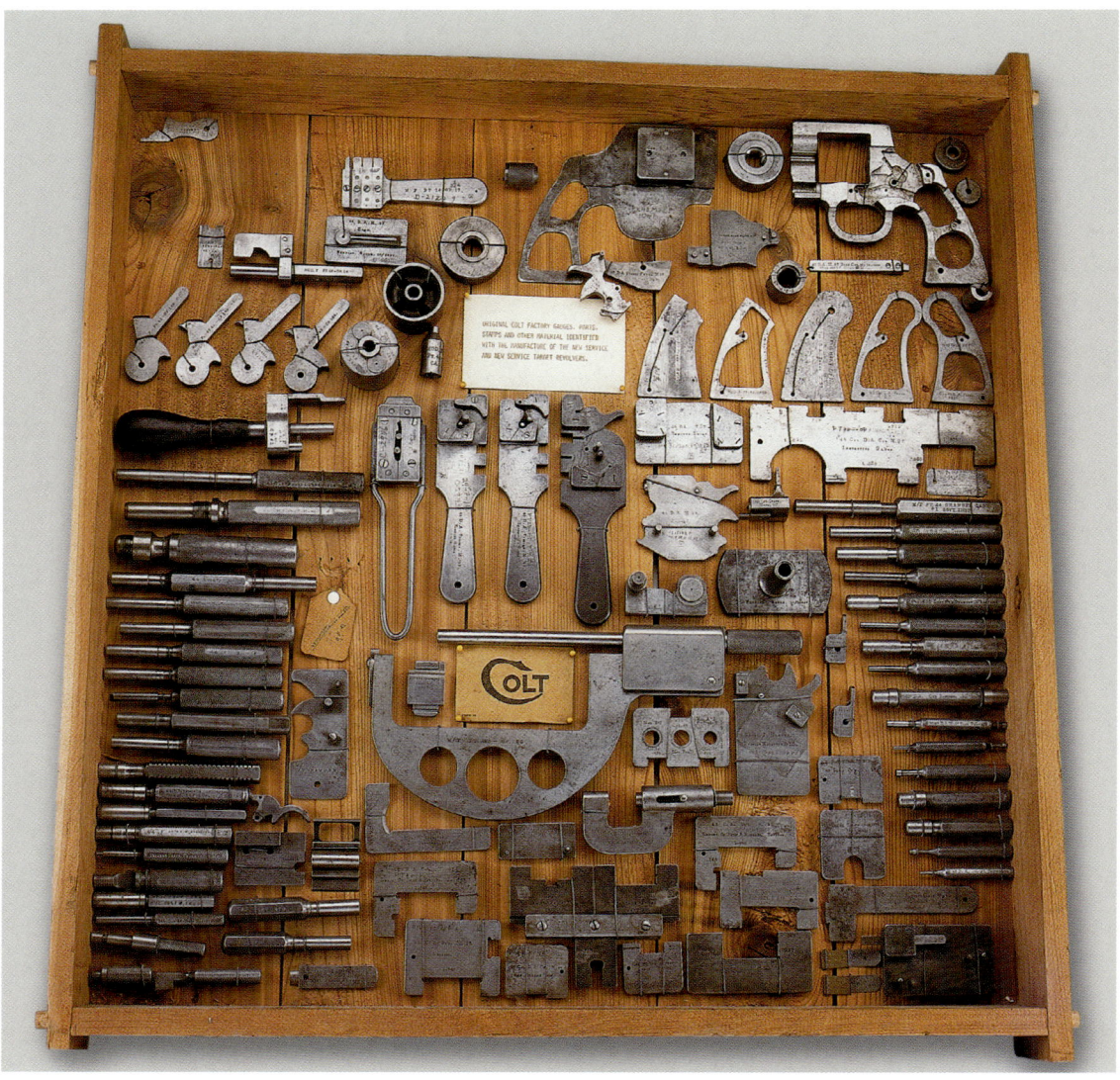

Inspection Gauges, for New Service Revolver. Partial assembled set. *Connecticut State Library Collection.*

Patent model revolver action submitted by E.K. Root to the U.S. Patent Office, 1855. *Dr. George Priestel Collection.*

Lockwork inspection Gauges, for 1877 Lightning. Connecticut State Library Collection.

Colt stock certificates. Robert Hartman Collection.

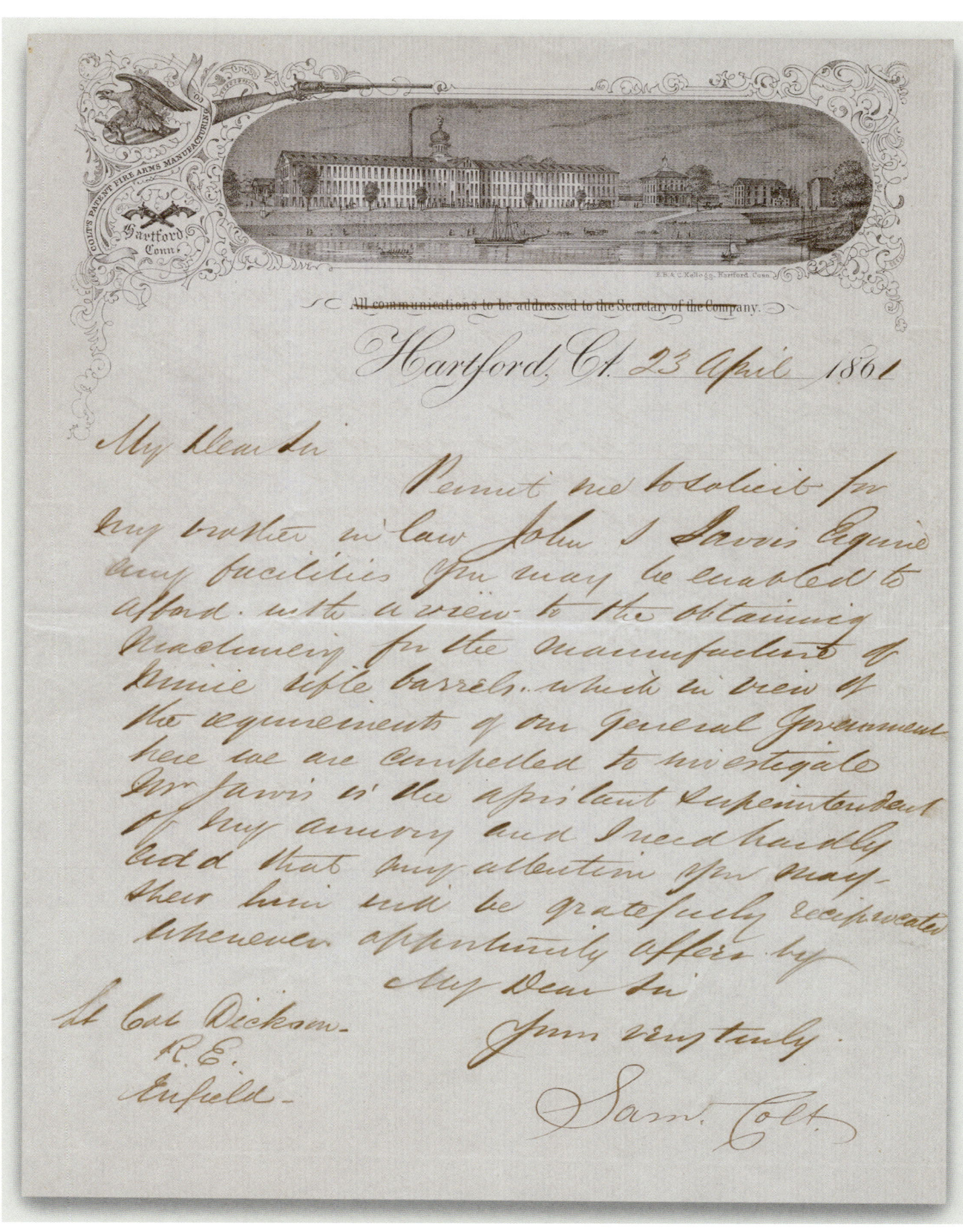

Letter from Samuel Colt to Lt. Colonel Dickson, 1861.   Dr. George Priestel Collection.

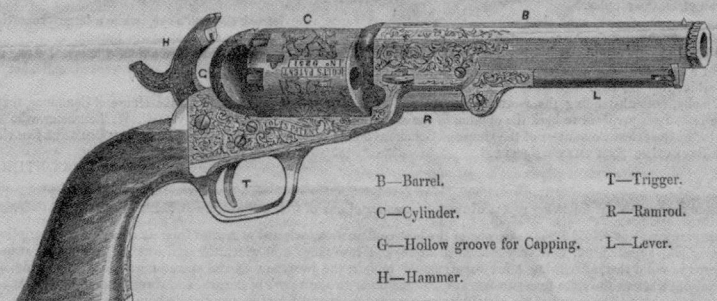

Samuel Colt's British Specification of 1835. Dr. George Priestl Collection.

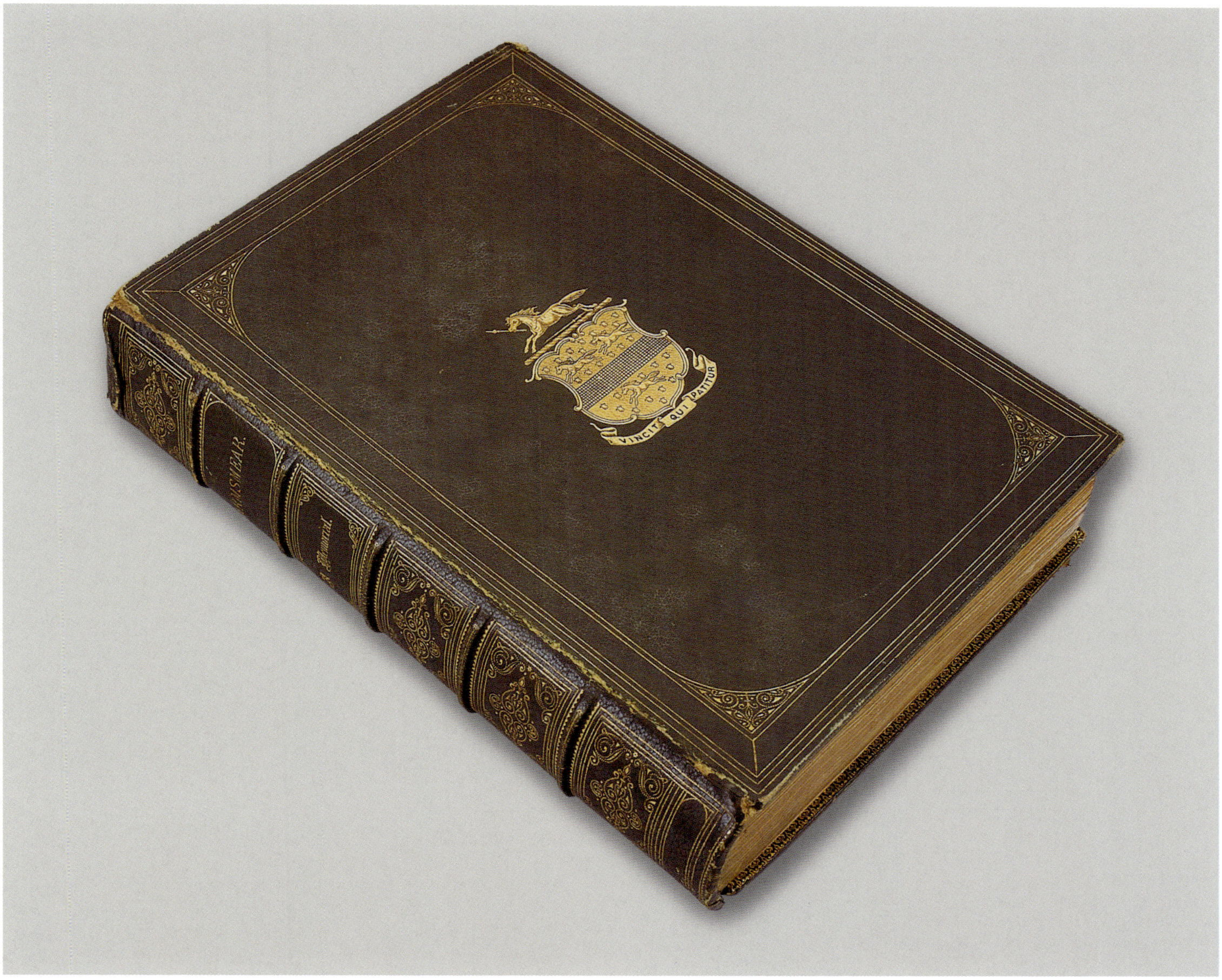

Original edition of Armsmear, 1866. *Dennis Russell Collection.*

Colt 125th Anniversary Limited Edition patch.
Dennis Russell Collection.

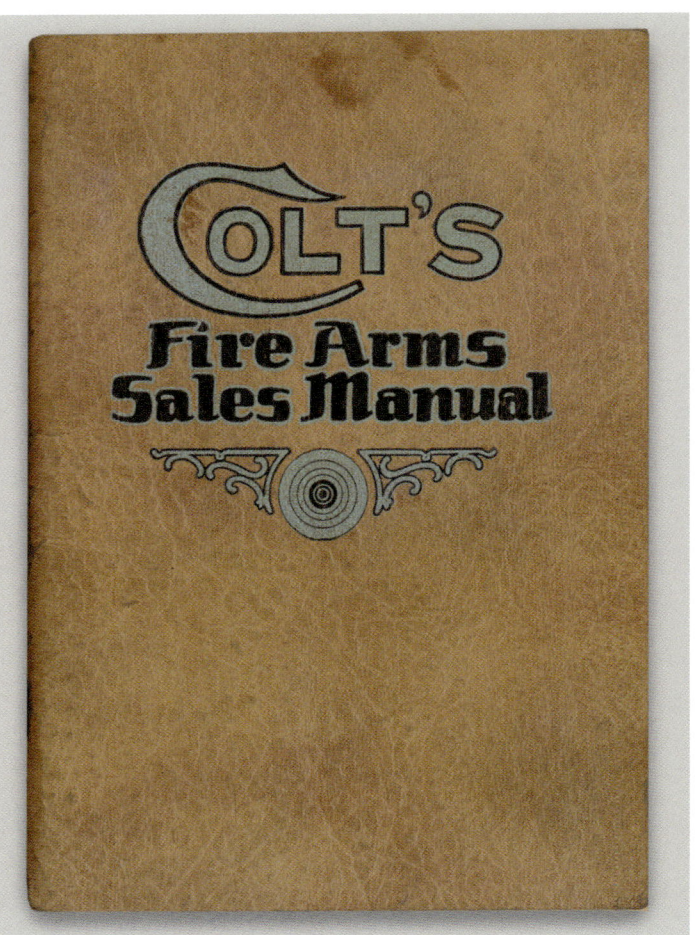

Collection of Colt instruction booklets. Top right: Colt Fire Arms Sales Manual *(1926) Top left:* Revolvers and Automatic Pistols *(1910) Bottom right:* Colt's Police Revolver Handbook *(1938) Bottom left:* Romance of a Colt *(1920)*

Lynn Kvam Collection.

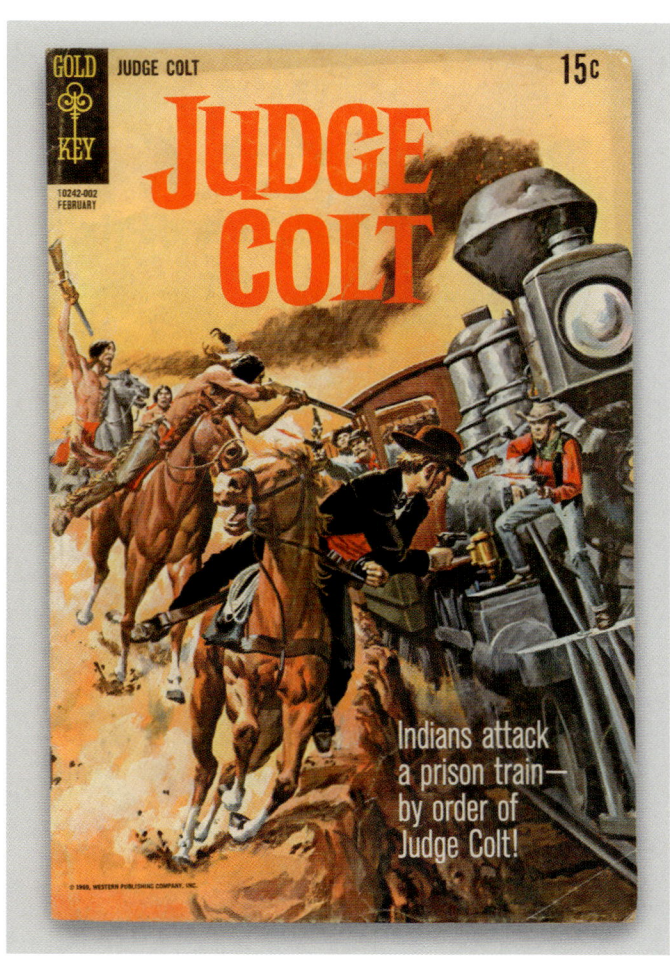

Colt comic books.   Karen Green Collection.

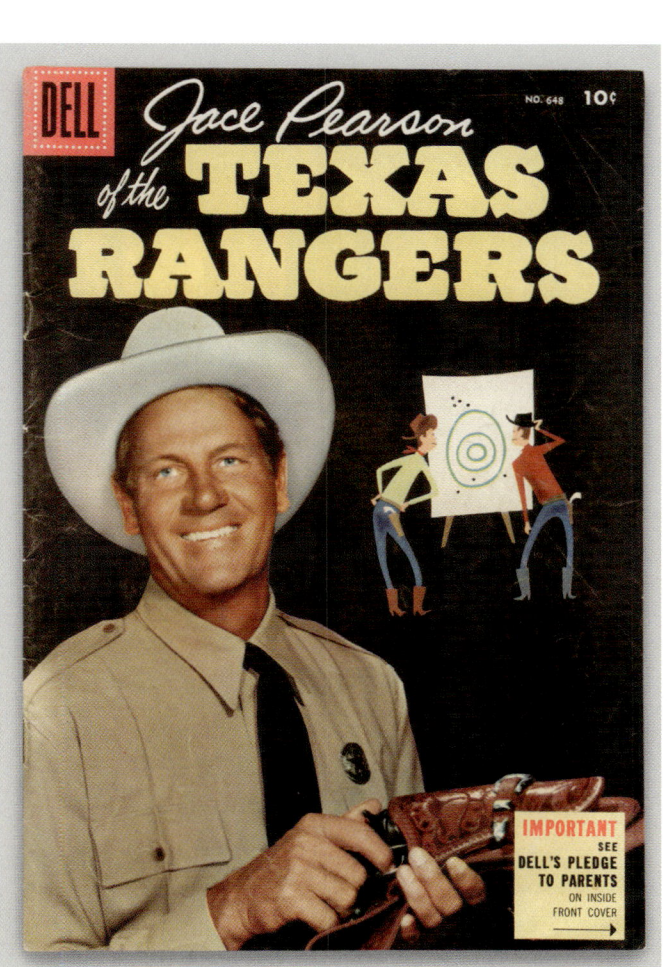

Colt comic books.   Ron Cantrell Collection.

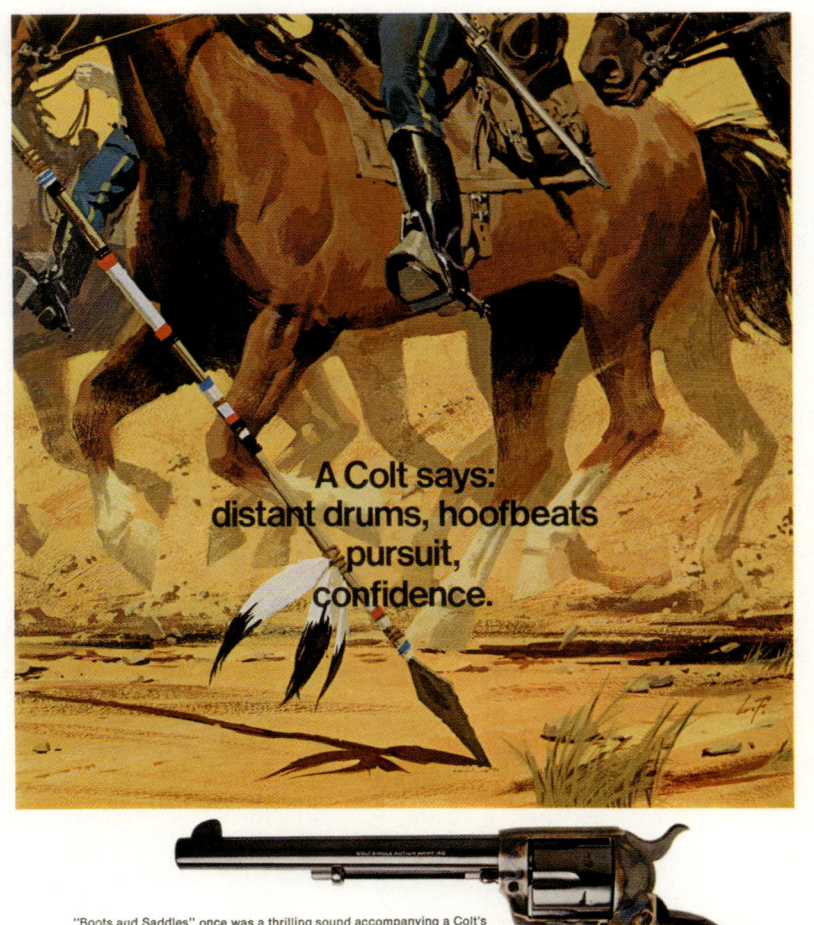

Advertising poster, 12 x 16.

Karen Green Collection.

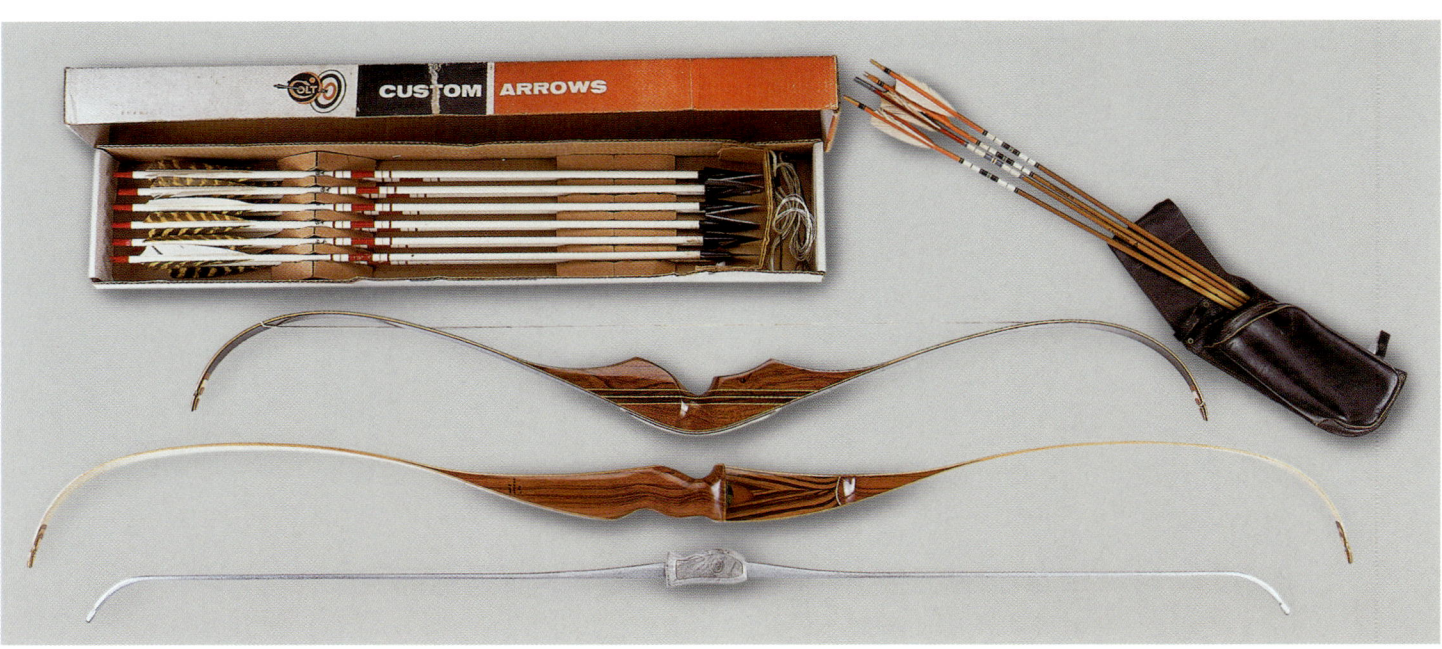

Colt bows, arrows and quiver.

Mike McHugh Collection.

Advertising Poster. Karen Green Collection.

*Colt Single Action Army ashtray.
Robert Hartman Collection.*

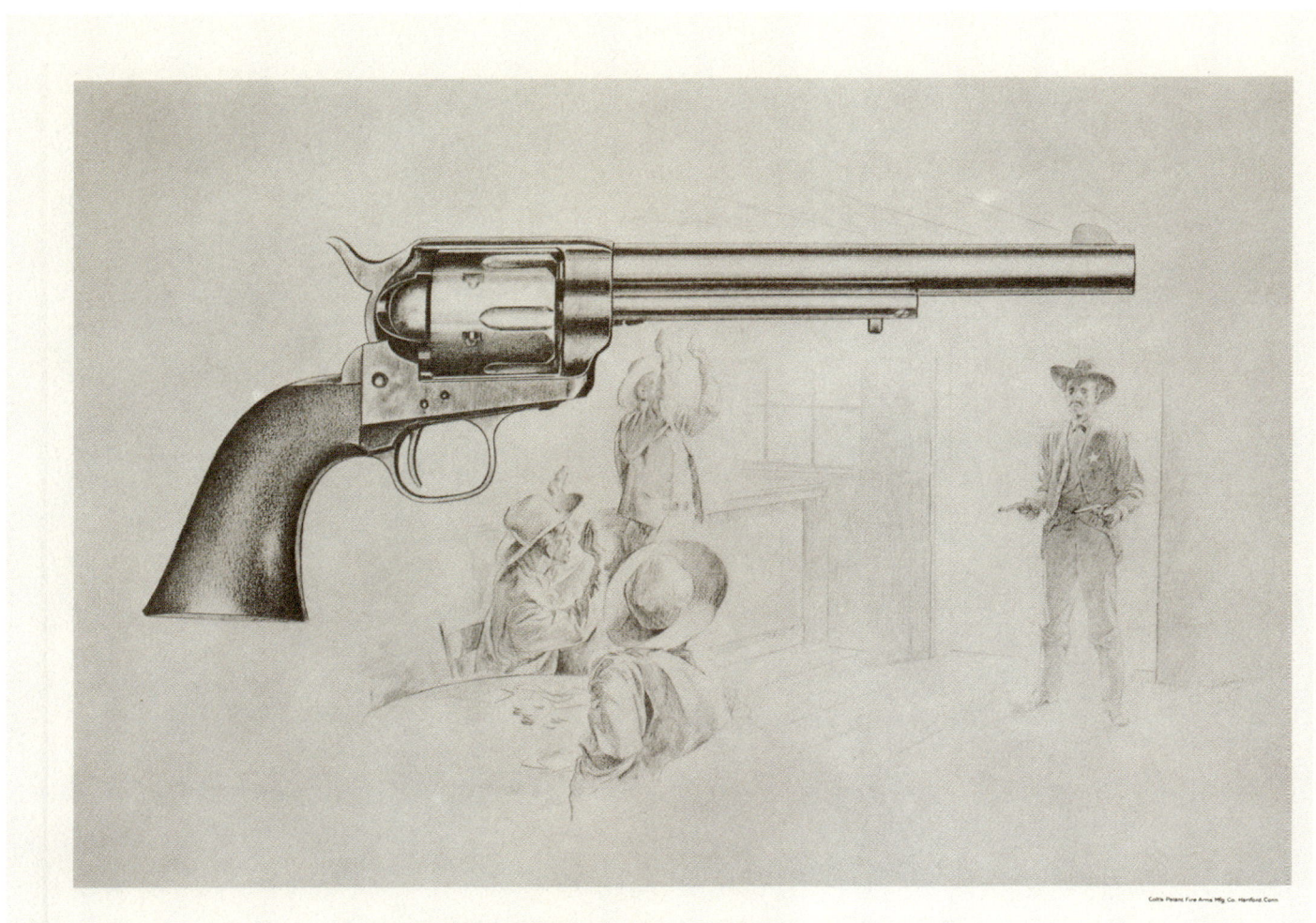

Colt Peacemaker .45 cal.-1873

In 1943 the Colt company issued a series of prints illustrating six of their more famous revolvers. This illustration presents the Colt Peacemaker.

Belle of the Ranch. Photogravure circa 1910. The 100,000-acre 101 Ranch in Oklahoma produced a traveling Wild West show. Working cowgirls performed trick shooting and riding. A Kansas photographer produced portraits of the women. This one is of interest because of the Colt Bisley in the cowgirl's holster.

Karen Green Collection.

Authenticated autographed photograph of the four stars of the 1985 film Silverado. From left to right: Kevin Costner, Scott Glenn, Kevin Kline, and Danny Glover.

Mike Holloway Collection.

A photograph of a scene from the film Rio Bravo with John Wayne and Ward Bond.

Colt's Manufacturing Company, Inc. Collection.

Bibliography

Adler, Dennis. *Blue Book of Modern Black Powder Values.* Minneapolis, MN: Blue Book Publications, Inc. 2002.

———*Colt Blackpowder Reproductions & Replicas.* Minneapolis, MN: Blue Book Publications, Inc. 1998.

Bailey, Thomas A. & David M. Kennedy. *The American Pageant: A History of the Republic.* Massachusetts & Toronto: D.C. Heath & Co. 1987.

Barnard, Henry. *Armsmear The Home, the Arm and the Armory.* Hartford, CT. Mrs. Samuel Colt. 1868.

Barnes, Will C. *Arizona Place Names.* Tucson: University of Arizona Press. 1988.

Beard, Charles A. & Mary R. Beard. *New Basic History of the United States.* Garden City, New York: Doubleday & Co., Inc. 1960.

Bellesiles, Michael. *Disarming America.* New York: Alfred Knopf. 2001.

Boddington, Craig, ed. *America: The Men and Their Guns That Made Her Great.* Los Angeles: Peterson Publishing Co. 1981.

Boorman, Dean K. *The History of Colt Firearms.* New York, NY: Lyons Press. 2001.

Breslin, John D., Pirie, William Q. and Price, David E. *Variations of Colt's New Model Police & Pocket Breech Loading Pistols.* Lincoln, RI: Andrew Mowbray Inc.-Publishers. 2003.

Brown, Richard Maxwell. *No Duty to Retreat: Violence and Values in American History and Society.* New York: Oxford University Press. 1991.

Brunner, John W. *The Colt Pocket Hammerless Automatic Pistols.* Williamstown, NJ: Phillips Publications. 1996.

Cary, Lucian. *The Colt Gun Book.* New York, NY: Arco Publishing Company, Inc. 1961.

Chin, Lt. Col. George M. (U.S.M.C.) *The Machine Gun* Washington, DC: U.S. Navy Bureau of Ordnance. 1951

Clawson, Charles W. *Colt .45 Service Pistols.* Fort Wayne, IN: C. W. Clawson. 1991.

Cochran, Keith. *Colt Peacemaker British Model.* Rapid City, SD: Cochran Publishing Co. 1989.

Cody, Louisa Frederici and Cooper, Courtney Riley. *Memories of Buffalo Bill.* New York: Appleton. 1919.

Crockett, David. *A Narrative of the Life of David Crockett of the State of Tennessee.* Knoxville: University of Tennessee Press. 1973.

Cummings, Neil and Lewandowska, Marysia. *The Value of Things.* Basel, Boston and Berlin: Birkhäuser. 2000.

Cunningham, Eugene. *Triggernometry: a Gallery of Gunfighters.* Norman, OK. 1996

Dwight, Timothy. *Travels in New England and New York*, 4 vols. New Haven. 1821-1822.

Dykstra, Robert R. *The Cattle Towns.* New York: Alfred Knopf. 1968.

Edwards, William B. *The Story of Colt's Revolver.* Harrisburg, Pennsylvania: Stackpole Company. 1953.

Ezell, Edward C. *The Great Rifle Controversy.* Harrisburg, PA: Stackpole Co. 1984.

Farish, Thomas Edwin. *History of Arizona,* Vol. I. Phoenix: State of Arizona, 1915.

Fees, Paul. "In Defense of Buffalo Bill: A Look at Cody in and of his Times," in Chris Bruce, ed., *The Myth of the West.* Seattle: University of Washington Press, 1990.

———"The Hunter Hero in America," in Paul A. Hutton, ed., *Sunrise in His Pocket: The Life, Legend, and Legacy of Davy Crockett.* Norman: University of Oklahoma Press. 2003.

Filson, John. *The Discovery, Settlement and Present State of Kentucke: ...To which is added, an Appendix, Containing I. The Adventures of Col. Daniel Boon, One of the First Settlers ...* Wilmington, DE: 1784.

Fischer, David Hackett. *Albion's Seed: Four British Folkways in America.* New York: Oxford University Press. 1989.

Fjestad, S.P. *Blue Book of Gun Values*, 23rd Edition. Minneapolis, MN: Blue Book Publications, Inc. 2002.

Goddard, William H. D. *The Government Models: The Development of the Colt Model of 1911.* Lincoln, RI: Andrew Mowbray Inc.-Publishers. 1988.

Goldsmith, Dolf L. *The Devil's Paintbrush: Sir Hiram Maxim's Gun.* Toronto, Ontario: Collector Grade Publications, Inc. 1989.

Graham, Ron; Kopec, John A. and Moore, C. Kenneth. *A Study of the Colt Single Action Army Revolver.* La Puente, CA: John A. Kopec. 1976.

Grant, Ellsworth S. *The Colt Armory: A History of Colt's Manufacturing Company, Inc.* Lincoln, RI: Andrew Mowbray Inc.-Publishers. 1995.

———*The Colt Legacy – The Colt Armory in Hartford, 1855-1980.* Providence, RI: Mowbray Company. 1982.

Greener, W. W. *The Gun and its Development.* London. 1910.

Haven, Charles T. and Frank Belden. *A History of the Colt Revolver.* Fairfax, VA: National Rifle Association. 1997.

Hill, Tracie L. *Thompson: the American Legend. The First Submachine Gun.* Cobourg, Ontario: Collector Grade Publications, Inc. 1996.

Hindle, Brooke, and Steven Lubar. *Engines of Change: The American Industrial Revolution, 1790-1830.* Washington, D.C.: Smithsonian Institution Press. 1986.

Hollon, W. Eugene *Frontier Violence: Another Look.* New York: Oxford University Press. 1974.

Horsman, Reginald. *The Frontier in the Formative Years. 1783-1815.* New York: Holt, Rinehart and Winston. 1970.

Hosley, William. *The Making of an American Legend* Amherst: University of Massachusetts Press. 1996.

Houze, Herbert G. *Colt Presentations From the Factory Ledgers 1856-1869.* Lincoln, RI: Andrew Mowbray Inc.-Publishers. 2003.

———*Colt Rifles & Muskets From 1847 to 1870.* Iola, WI: Krause Publications, Inc. 1996.

———"The 1861 Inventory of the Arms and Miscellaneous Material in the Office of Colonel Samuel Colt" ARMAX. Vol. 1, No. 1 (Spring/Summer 1987).

———"The 1861 Inventory of the Arms and Miscellaneous Material in the Museum Room of the Colt Factory" ARMAX. Vol. 1 No. 2 (Fall/Winter 1987).

———*Winchester Repeating Arms Company: Its History & Development from 1865 to 1981.* Iola, WI: Krause Publications Inc.; 1994

Howe, Henry. *Adventures and achievements of Americans: a series of narratives illustrating their heroism, self-reliance, genius and enterprise.* Illustrated by F. O. C. Darly and others. New York: G.F. Tuttle, 1859.

Kirkland, K.D. *America's Premier Gunmakers – Colt.* New York, NY: Exeter Books. 1988.

Kopec, John A. and Fenn, H. Sterling. *Colt Cavalry & Artillery Revolvers ... a Continuing Study.* Whitmore, CA: John A. Kopec. 1994.

Leckie, Shirley. *Elizabeth Bacon Custer and the Making of an American Myth.* Norman: University of Oklahoma Press, 1993.

Leonard, Elizabeth Jane and Goodman, Julia Cody. *Buffalo Bill: King of the Old West*, ed. James Williams Hoffman. New York: Library Publishers. 1955.

James Lindgren, James and Heather, Justin Lee. "Counting Guns in Early America." *William and Mary Law Quarterly* 43(5). 2002.

Lofaro, Michael. *The Life and Adventures of Daniel Boone.* Lexington, KY: University Press of Kentucky. 1986.

Longfield, G. Maxwell and Basnett, David T. *Observations on Colt's Second Contract* November 2, 1847. Bloomfield, Ontario: Museum Restoration Service (Historical Arms Series No. 37). 1998.

McCarty, Lea F. *The Gunfighters.* Oakland: CA. 1991

McDowell, R. Bruce. *A Study of Colt Conversions and Other Percussion Revolvers.* Iola, WI: Krause Publications Inc. 1997.

McGaw, Judith, ed. *Early American Technology.* Chapel Hill: University of North Carolina Press. 1994.

McGivern, Ed. *Fast and Fancy Revolver Shooting.* Chicago, 1975.

Marohn, Richard C., M.D. "The Colt Model 1877 Double Action Revolver: A Twenty-Year Review 1877 to 1897" Man at Arms, Vol. 19, No. 6. December, 1997.

Marohn, Richard C. *The Last Gunfighter.* College Station, Texas, 1995.

Maxwell, Samuel L., Sr. *The Colt-Burgess Magazine Rifle* (S. L. Maxwell, Sr. 1985.

Meadows, Edward Scott. *U.S. Military Automatic Pistols, Volume 1: 1894-1920.* Moline, IL: Richard Ellis Productions. 1993.

Millennium Year by Year. London, England: DK Publishing. 1999.

Mills, Fred P. L. *Colt's Double Rifles.* Greenfield, MS: F. P. L. Mills. 1953.

Mitchell, James L. *Colt – The Man, the Arms, the Company.* Harrisburg, PA: The Telegraph Press. 1959.

Moore, C. Kenneth. *Colt Single Action Army Revolvers and the London Agency.* Lincoln, RI: Andrew Mowbray Inc.-Publishers. 1990.

———*Colt Single Action Army Revolvers U.S. Alterations.* Lincoln, RI: Andrew Mowbray Inc.-Publishers. 1999.

Mowbray, Stuart C. *Civil War Arms Purchases and Deliveries* Lincoln, RI: Andrew Mowbray Inc.-Publishers. 2000.

Mowbray, Stuart C. and Heroux, Jennifer (editors) *Civil War Arms Makers and their Contracts. A facsimile reprint of the Report by the Commission on Ordnance and Ordnance Stores, 1862.* Lincoln, RI: Andrew Mowbray Inc.-Publishers. 1998.

Muensterberger, Werner. *Collecting: An Unruly Passion: Psychological Perspectives.* Princeton, NJ: Princeton University Press. 1994.

Noon, Fred. "Arivaca History," *Arivaca Visitors Guide.* Arivaca, AZ: *The Connection* Newspaper. 2002.

Nye, Russell Blaine. *The Cultural Life of the New Nation, 1776-1830.* (New York: Harper and Row. 1960.

Parsons, John E. *Sam Colt's Own Record 1847.* Hartford, CT: Connecticut Historical Society. 1949.

Pate, Charles W. *U.S. Handguns of World War II: The Secondary Pistols and Revolvers.* Lincoln, RI: Andrew Mowbray Inc.-Publishers. 1998.

Phillips, Catherine Coffin. *Jessie Benton Frémont: A Woman Who Made History.* San Francisco: J. H. Nash. 1935; Lincoln: University of Nebraska Press, Bison Books, 1995.

Potocki, John. *The Colt Model 1905 Automatic Pistol.* Lincoln, RI: Andrew Mowbray Inc.-Publishers. 1998.

Rapley, Robin J. *Colt Percussion Accoutrements 1834-1873.* Newport Beach, CA: Graphic Publishers. 1994.

Rohan, Jack. *Yankee Arms Maker: the Incredible Career of Samuel Colt.* New York: Harper & Brothers Publishers. 1935.

Rohan, Jack. *Yankee Arms Maker – The Story of Samuel Colt and his Six-shot Peacemaker*, revised edition. New York, NY: Harper & Brothers. 1948.

Roosevelt, Theodore. *Episodes from "The Winning of the West.* New York: G.P. Putnam's Sons. 1900.

Rosa, Joseph G., *Colonel Colt London – The History of Colt's London Firearms, 1851-1857.* Stoney Creek, Ontario: Fortress Publications, Inc. 1976.

Rosa, Joseph G. *The Taming of the West: Age of the Gunfighter*. New York and London: Smithmark Publishers. 1993.

Rosenberg, Bruce. *Code of the West*. Bloomington: Indiana University Press. 1982.

Russell, Don. *The Lives and Legends of Buffalo Bill*. Norman: University of Oklahoma Press. 1960.

Sheldon, Douglas, G. *Colt's Super .38: The Production History From 1929 Through 1971*. Willernie, MN: Quick Vend Inc. 1997.

Slotkin, Richard. *The Fatal Environment, The Myth of the Frontier in the Age of Industrialization, 1800-1890*. New York: Atheneum. 1985.

Slotkin, Richard. *Regeneration Through Violence: The Mythology of the American Frontier, 1600-1860*. Middletown, Conn.: Wesleyan University Press. 1973.

Sutherland, Robert Q. and Wilson, R. L. *The Book of Colt Firearms*. Kansas City, MO: R. Q. Sutherland. 1971.

Tivey, Ted. *The Colt Rifle 1884-1902*. Currumbin Waters, Queensland, Australia: T. Tivey. 1984.

Thomas, Chauncey. "Buffalo Bill's Last Interview," Outdoor Life 39(5), May, 1917.

Trebilcock, Clive. *The Vickers Brothers - Armament and Enterprise 1854-1914* (London: Europa Publications, Ltd. 1977.

Venturino, Mike. "How Far will a Sharps Shoot?" in Robert W. Hunnicut, ed., Shotgun News Treasury, 1997-2000. Peoria, IL. 2001.

Walter, John. *The Guns that Won the West*. London, England, and Mechanicsburg, Pennsylvania: Stackpole Books. 1999.

Wetmore, Helen Cody. *Last of the Great Scouts: The Life Story of Col. William F. Cody "Buffalo Bill"*. Duluth: Duluth Press Publishing Co., 1899. Reprint. Lincoln: University of Nebraska Press. 1965.

Wilkerson, Don. *Colt's Double Action Revolver Model of 1878*. Kansas City, MO: Don Wilkerson. 1998.

———*The Post-War Colt Single-Action Revolver, 1955-1975*. Kansas City, MO: Don Wilkerson. 1980)

———*The Post-War Colt Single-Action Revolver, 1976-1986*. Kansas City, MO: Don Wilkerson. 1980)

———*Colt Scouts Peacemakers and New Frontiers in .22 Caliber*. Kansas City, MO: Don Wilkerson. 1993)

———*Colt's Single Action Army Revolver Pre-War Post-War Model*. Kansas City, MO: Don Wilkerson. 1991)

Wilson, R. L. *The Book of Colt Engraving*. Los Angeles, CA: Beinfeld Publishing Co. 1974.

———*The Book of Colt Firearms*. 2nd edition. Minneapolis, MN: Blue Book Publications, Inc., 1993

———*Colt: An American Legend*. New York: Abbeville Press. 1985.

———*The Colt Engraving Book, Volumes One & Two*. New York: Bannerman's Publications Inc. 2001.

———*The Colt Heritage, the Official History of Colt Firearms from 1836 to the Present*. New York, New York: Simon & Schuster. 1989

———*Fine Colts: The Dr. Joseph A. Murphy Collection*. New Hope, PA: Republic Publishing Co. 1999.

———*The Rampant Colt – The Story of a Trademark*. Spencer, IN: Thomas Haas, 1969.

———*Samuel Colt Presents*. Hartford, CT: Wadsworth Athenaeum, 1962.

———*The Paterson Colt Book*. Palo Alto, CA: Strutz-LeVett Publishing Co. 2002.

———*The Peacemakers: Arms and Adventure in the American West*. New York, 1992

———*The World of Beretta – An International Legend*. New York, NY: Random House, Inc., 2000.

Wilson, R. L. and Hable, R. E. *Colt Pistols 1836-1976*. Dallas, TX: Jackson Arms. 1976.

Wilson, R. L. and Phillips, P. R. *Paterson Colt Pistol Variations*. Dallas, TX: Jackson Arms. 1979.

Wister, Owen. *The Virginian*. Cody, WY: Buffalo Bill Historical Center. 2002.

Yost, Nellis Snyder. *Buffalo Bill: His Family, Friends, Fame, Failures and Fortunes*. Chicago: Sage Books. 1979.

Index

Ace Model 197
Aircrewman Revolver Model of 1951 145
Alamo, The 17
Allen, Mary Jester 59-62
American Federation of Labor (A.F. of L.) 37
Amherst Academy 22
Anthony, Graham 40
Aravaca, Arizona 58
AR-15 Rifle 42, 45, 189, 265
AR-15 Sporter 188
Armsmear 27, 37, 50, 58
Authentic Blackpowder Series 43
Automatic Colt Pistol 196
Auto-Ordnance Company 36, 265

B.A.R. (Browning Automatic Rifle) 42, 46, 265
Baby Dragoon 26
Banker's Special 36, 145
Barnard, Henry 59
Benke, Paul 40
Berdan, Colonel Hiram 100, 178
Beretta, Dr. Ugo 43
Berkley, William R. 45
Billy the Kid 53, 129
Bisley Model Single Action Army Revolver 276
Bland, Chester 40
Blickhan, John 63-64
Blickhan, Kitten 63, 66
Bomford, Colonel George 25
Boone, Daniel 16-17, 19
Border Patrol Revolver Model of 1952 145
Brash, Fred 23
Brown, Moses 48
Browning Automatic Rifle. *See* B.A.R.
Browning, John M. 20, 33, 35, 196, 254-255, 265
Browning, Matt 33, 35
Buffalo Bill Historical Center xi, xiii
Buffalo Bill Museum 69-61
Buffalo Bill's Wild West 18-19, 56, 58, 62-63
Buntline Model 307
Buntline, Ned 53
Burgess, Andrew 32, 179

Caldwell, Major John 21, 60
California Gold Rush 26
Camp Perry target pistol 36
Cerro Colorado mine 58
Challenger Model 255
Champion, Nate 54
Charter Oak 29
  Hall 50, 60
Chase, Anson 23
Cherry, Kevin 65
Cherry, Robert E. 42

Cherry's Sporting Goods 42
Civil War, U.S. 15-16, 20, 178, 264
Clanton, Billy 53
Clanton, Ike 53
Cloverleaf (House Pistol) 101
Cobra Revolver 145
Cody Firearms Museum xiii, 46
Cody, Louisa 58-59
Cody, William F. "Buffalo Bill" 16-19, 53-54, 58-63, 129
Colt Blackpowder Arms Company 337
Colt Armory
  building of 27
  Civil war and 29
  end of production at 45
  fire and 30
  flood and 37
  Great Depression and 36-37
  rebuilding of 31
  sale of 34
  World War I and 35-36
  World War II and 39
Colt, Caldwell 21
Colt, Christopher J. 21
Colt Collectors Association xi-xii, 45, 63-64
Colt Custom Shop 43
Colt, Elisha 26
Colt, Elizabeth Hart Jarvis 20-21, 25-30, 32-33, 57, 60
Colt 57 Sporting Rifle 188
Colt Industries 42
Colt, James Benjamin 21
Colt, John Sr. 21
Colt Patent Fire-Arms Manufacturing Company 26
colt, rampant 20
Colt, Roswell 23
Colt, Samuel
  and Armsmear 27
  as a collector 63
  early life 22-23
  final days 29-30
  marriage of 28
Colt, Samuel Caldwell 26, 60
Colt, Sarah Ann 21
Colt, Sarah Caldwell 21
Colt-Sauer 189
Colteer 1-22 188
Coltiana 379
Coltsman 188
Coltsman Standard Pump Shotgun 188
Coltrock (Coltstone) 36, 50, 379
Colt's Arms Manufacturing Company 28
Colt's Historical Department 46
Colt's Manufacturing Company 28
Commander Series 368
commemoratives 41, 336

Connecticut Citizens Action Group 43
Connecticut River 27
Connecticut State Library 41, 64
Conner, B. Franklin 40
Corvo, The 22, 58
Coult, The Celebrated Doctor 22, 58
Courier 189
Crawford, Captain Jack 129
Crispin, Silas 100
Crockett, David 17, 19
Custer, Elizabeth Bacon 59
Custer, George A. 31, 59-61

Dalton, Emmett 54
Deere, John 48
Defender Series 368
Deringer
   First Model 101
   Second Model 101
   Third (Thuer/New Patent) Model 101
Detective Special Model 145
Dickens, Charles 29
Dickerson, Edward N. 27
Dixon, Billy 55-56
Double Action Revolver 45
Dragoons, United States 24
Dragoon, Baby 26

Earp, Morgan 53
Earp, Virgil 53
Earp, Wyatt 53
Eaton, David 40
Ehbets, Carl J. 179
Ehlers, John 70
Eickhoff, Theodore 265
Elliot, William H. 179
Equalizer, The 276
Evans, Oliver 48

Fabrique Nationale of Liege, Belgium (FN) 35, 188
Fairbanks-Morse Company 41
First Model Pocket Pistol commemorative 336
Fitch, Mary 21
Fitz-Gerald Special Revolver 145
Florida
   Camp Jupiter 24
   Everglades 24
   Saint Augustine 24
   Punta Gorda 33
Forgett, Val 337
Franchi, Luigi 188
Franklin, William B. 30
Franklin Magazine Rifle of 1887 and 1888 179
Frémont, Jessie Benton 59
Frémont, John Charles 59
French, Gary W. 40
Frontier Six-Shooter 276

Gamble, Richard F. 40
Garrett, Pat 54, 56, 129
Gatling gun 31, 264
Gatling, Richard 31, 264
Gold Cup Series 368
Goldbach, William 40
Grant, Ulysses S. 31, 336
Great Exhibition of 1851 28, 49
Green, Karen 65
Gremler, Volker 65
Grover, Lewis C. 34, 40

Hall, John 34, 38, 40
Hall, John H. 24
Hamilton, Alexander 48
Hardin, John Wesley 55-56, 129
Harney, William S. 24
Hawken Brothers 17
Hays, Colonel J.C. 26
Heckler & Koch 43
Heintzelman Mine 58
Henshaw, Carolyn 23, 25, 60
Hickok, James Butler "Wild Bill" 53-56
High Standard Manufacturing Company 39, 255
Holliday, John "Doc" 53
Hough, Emerson 53
House Pistol 101
Houston, Colonel Samuel 26
Hoyt, Kathleen 43
Huntsman Model 255

Imperato, Lou and Anthony 337
Independent Association for Colt Employees 37
Ingraham, Prentiss 53
Iver Johnson 337

Jackson, Andrew 17
James, Frank 53
James, Jesse 53-54, 56
Jarvis, Reverend William 28, 49
Jarvis, Richard 31, 40
Jastrem, John F. 40
Jefferson Manufacturing Company 188

Karstensen, Tor 64
Keys, LTGEN Wm. M. USMC (ret.) 40, 46
King, General Charles 61
Kittridge, Benjamin 128
Korean Conflict 40

labor problems 33-35, 37, 42
Laidley Breech-loading Rifle 179
Landa, Alfons 41
Lee, Robert E. 336
Leisester, Julia 25, 60
Lightning Magazine Rifle 179, 188
Lightning Model 128

Lincoln, Abraham 15-16, 61
Lindneux, Robert 60-61
London Armory 28-29
Lowe, Rowdy Joe 129
Lowell, Francis Cabot 48-49

M-2 .50 caliber machine gun 265
M-14 Rifle 368
M-16 Rifle 188, 265
Margolis, David 42
Marlin, John 20
Mason, William 29-30, 100-101, 128
Mauser 188
Maxim, Hiram S. 264
Maxim-Vickers Machine Gun 36
McCormick, Cyrus 48
McGivern, Ed 54
McLaury, Frank 54
Mechanics Institute of New York 23
memorabilia 378
Model 1851 Navy 80
Model 1855 Pocket Pistol 80
Model 1861 U.S. Rifle Musket 337
Model 1873 Single Action Army Revolver 306
Model 1877 Double Action Revolver 128-129
Model 1878 Double Action Revolver 128-129
Model 1902 Semiautomatic Pistol 196
   Sporting Model and Military Model 196
Model 1911 Military 197
Model 1911 Government Model 368
Moore, Daniel 101
Moore, Fred 33, 36
Morse, Samuel F.B. 21, 48

Nasmith, J. 51
National Match Model 197
New House Pistol 101
New Line Revolver 101
New Model Army Pistol 80
New Model Holster Pistol 336
New Model Navy Pistol 80, 336
New Model Pocket Pistol of Navy Caliber 336
New Model Police Pistol 80, 336-337
New Navy Double Action Revolver 144-145
New Police Revolver 101
New Service Model Revolver 145
New Service Target Pistol 145
Nicholas I, (czar of Russia) 21
Number 1 Pistol (Paterson) 70
Number 3 Belt Pistol (Paterson) 70
Number 5 Holster Pistol (Paterson) 70, 337
Nutting, Mighill 25

Oakley, Annie 18
Officers Model Revolver 145
Official Police Revolver 145
O.K. Corral 53

Old Model Navy Pistol 336
Omohundro, "Texas" Jack 18
"Open Top" Revolvers 101
Oracle, Arizona 58

Patent Arms Manufacturing Company 25, 70
Paterson, New Jersey 25, 70, 80
Pauli, Lowell 64-66
Pawnee Bill 129
Payne, Oscar 265
Peacemaker, The 276
Pearson, John 23
Penn-Texas 41
Philippine Model of 1902 Double Action Revolver 129
Pickering, Robert B. 65
Police Positive Revolver 145
Pomeroy, H.A.G. 50
Post, J.W. 23
potato digger. see Model 1895 Machine Gun 265
Potsdam Village 37, 51
Pratt & Whitney Aircraft 41
Python Revolver 145, 368

Rainmaker Model 128
Rampant Colt, The xi
Reinhard-Fajen 188
Remington, Eliphalet 20
Remington, Frederic 18, 54-55, 129
Richards, Charles B. 100-101
Ring-lever series 70
Robinson, Charles L.F. 35-36, 41
Roff, Fred A. Jr. 37, 40, 42
Root, Elisha King 22, 24, 27-30, 40
Russell, Charles 54

Sako 188
Sargent, Olivia 21, 57
Sauer 43, 189
Schuyler, Hartley & Graham 101
Scott, David C. 401
Second Model Navy Pistol commemorative 336
Second Model Holster Pistol (Second Model Dragoon) 336
Second Model Pocket Pistol 337
Selden, Dudley 23-25
Seminole War, The 24
Serrell, Lemuel W. 23
Service Model Ace Pistol 197
Seymour, Governor Thomas 20
Sharps-Borchardt Rifle 189
Sheridan, General Philip 31
Sheriff's Model Single Action Revolver 307
Sig-Sauer 43
Signature Series 337
Silberstein, Leopold D. 41
Single Action Army Revolver 31, 42, 46, 276
   Second Generation 307
      Third Generation 307

Sitting Bull 17-18
Skinner, William C. 34-36, 40
Slater, Samuel 48
Sliwa, Steven M. 40
Smith, William T. 20
Smith & Wesson 20, 31, 38, 43-44
Sneider, Charles E. 100
Snider breech-loading system 178
Sonora Exploring & Mining Company 58
Stagecoach Rifle 189
Stewart, Ronald L. 40
Stewart, Sidney 41
Stilwell, Ronald E. 40
Stone, Samuel 31, 36-37, 40
Stoner, Eugene 42, 265
Strichman, George 42
Sturm, Ruger & Company 44, 255

Targetsman Model 255
Taylor, General Zachary 26
Texas
   Navy 26, 70
   Paterson 26
Rangers 26
Third or Thuer Model Deringer 101
Third Model Holster Pistol commemorative 336
Thompson, John T. 265
Thompson Submachine Gun 36, 265
Thuer, F. Alexander 100
Thunderer (Model 1877 Double Action Revolver) 128
Tutt, Davis 53-54
Twain, Mark 31

Ultra Light Arms Company 189
United States Special Rifle Musket 81, 178
United Auto Workers (UAW) 44
United Electrical, Radio and Machine Workers
   of America 39

Vickers machine gun 264
Vietnam War 42-43
Villa, Pancho 15
Von Oppen, Baron Frederick 25, 32, 128

Wadsworth Atheneum 28-29, 63
Walker, Colonel Samuel Hamilton 26, 46, 80
Walker revolver 26, 40
Walther 44
Wappenhans, C.F. 51
War of 1812 21
Ware, Massachusetts 21-22
Warner, C. Edward 40
Washington, George 14-16, 18
Wesson, Daniel 20
Whitaker, Ronald C. 40, 45
White, Rollin 100
Whitney, Eli Jr. 26, 48-49

Whitneyville-Hartford Holster Pistol 337
Whitneyville-Walker Holster Pistol 336
Winchester, Oliver 20
Winchester Repeating Rifle Company 31-33, 34-35, 38,
   44, 179
Wister, Owen 18-19, 54
Wolf, E.N. 15
Wolf, George C. 15
Wolf, Paul D. 15
Woodsman 254
   Match Target Model 254
   Sport Model 254
   Target Model 254
World War I 35-36, 39, 42, 265
World War II 36, 39-40, 42, 44, 306

XSE Series 368

Yellow Hair 60-61
Young, Gustaf 21
Younger, Bob 54
Younger, Cole 54

Zilkha & Company 45